Population Change
and European Security

Also available from Brassey's

BOUTWELL
The German Nuclear Dilemma

CAMPBELL
Germany's Past and Europe's Future

GROVE
Global Security

HIGGINS
Plotting Peace

HOLDEN REID & DEWAR
Military Strategy in a Changing Europe

IISS
Strategic Survey 1990–91

LEECH
Halt! Who Goes Where? The Future of NATO in the New Europe

Population Change and European Security

Edited by

Lawrence Freedman & John Saunders

BRASSEY'S (UK)

(Member of the Maxwell Macmillan Group)

LONDON • WASHINGTON • NEW YORK

First English edition 1991

UK editorial offices: Brassey's, 50 Fetter Lane, London EC4A 1AA
orders: Brassey's, Headington Hill Hall, Oxford OX3 0BW

USA editorial offices: Brassey's, 8000 Westpark Drive, First Floor,
McLean, Virginia 22102
orders: Macmillan Publishing Company, Front and Brown Streets,
Riverside, NJ 08075

Distributed in North America to booksellers and wholesalers by the
Macmillan Publishing Company, N.Y., N.Y.

**Library of Congress Cataloging in Publication Data
available**

**British Library Cataloguing in Publication Data
available**

ISBN 0-08-040349-2

Printed in Great Britain by B.P.C.C. Wheatons Ltd., Exeter

Contents

Contents

Editors' Note

These chapters were originally presented at a conference on Demographic Change and Western Security organised jointly by the Center for International Security and Strategic Studies, Mississippi State University and the Department of War Studies, King's College, London in July 1988. Although the chapters were ready for publication by late 1989 it was decided to offer the authors an opportunity to revise them in the light of the retreat of communism in Eastern Europe. It was not possible to organise a complete revision – for example there are still separate figures for East and West Germany – but we are convinced that this collection now provides a unique and generally up to date analysis of this key aspect of contemporary affairs.

The Authors

Mikhail Bernstam is Senior Research Fellow at the Hoover Institution on War, Revolution and Peace, Stanford University

Brian Bond is Professor of Military History at King's College, London

Yves Boyer is Deputy Director of the Centre d'Etude des Relations entre Technologies et Strategies, Paris

Lawrence Freedman is Professor of War Studies at King's College, London

Ward Kingkade is a member of the Center for International Research, US Bureau of the Census

Admiral Pierre Lacoste is President, Fondation pour les Etudes de Défense National (FEDN), Paris

Everett Lee is Professor of Sociology and Demography, University of Georgia

Anne Lee is a Demographic Consultant

John Long is Branch Chief of the Population Division, US Bureau of the Census

Simon Lunn is Deputy Director of the North Atlantic Assembly

Teresa Rakowska-Harmstone is Professor of Political Science, Carleton University, Ottawa

John Saunders is Professor of Sociology at Mississippi State University

List of Tables and Figures

Tables

Chapter 1

Chapter 3

Chapter 4

Chapter 5

List of Tables and Figures

Chapter 6

Chapter 7

Chapter 10

FIGURES

Chapter 4

Chapter 5

Chapter 6

Chapter 7

1
Introduction:
Population and Security
John Saunders

The relevance of population size and characteristics to national security has often been acknowledged but rarely analysed. The importance of the size of armies was recognised by Clausewitz, who in his classic *On War* begins a chapter titled the Superiority of Numbers by writing:

> 'This [the superiority of numbers] is in tactics, as well as in strategy, the most general principle of victory.'

He extended his analysis to include the size of civilian populations that might provision armies:

> 'It is but natural that the subsistence [of armies] should be more easily carried out in rich and well-peopled countries than in the midst of a poor and scanty population . . . there is infinitely less difficulty in supporting an Army in Flanders than in Poland.' (1968: 103)

Pétain attributed France's defeat in 1940 to 'too few children, too few arms and too few allies.'

The number of inhabitants of a nation and their characteristics influence, directly and indirectly, its ability to survive. The potential size of armed forces is obviously related to the size of the population. But the ability of such forces to defend is also a product of the qualities of the civilian population, of the resources at their disposal, and of their unity of purpose. It is for these reasons that population trends merit attention where security is concerned.

European population growth rates differ within Europe and between Europe and other regions of the world. Within Europe, the East is an area of high fertility as compared to the West and, consequently, experiences relatively high population growth. Growth rates have declined in East and West but the difference has been maintained. With regard to numbers of persons this has meant that, between 1971 and 1990, the population of Western

1

Europe[1] increased by 24 million, from 354 to 377 million, or 6 per cent, while that of the East[2] grew by 58 million from 357 to 415 million or 16 per cent.

In addition to changes in the relative size of these two groups of nations, changes are occurring in the composition of European populations. Three influences are at work: immigration from Africa, the Far and Near East, changes in the size and proportion of the population that is in the productive years caused by declining birth rates and changing proportions in various ethnic groups occasioned by different rates of fertility.

Immigration to Western Europe is contributing to increased cultural heterogeneity and, possibly, to a reduced sense of a shared national purpose which could have negative consequences for national unity in a time of crisis. The guest worker programme in Germany, for instance, is having unanticipated consequences for the make-up of the population as guest workers become permanent and the fertility of the immigrant population exceeds that of the native born.

Declining fertility is producing a contraction of the population of working age and an expansion of the population that is past working age. More dependents will rely on fewer producers. Demands on the state by dependents, for income maintenance and the provision of health care, housing and other welfare benefits, will increase and consume ever larger fractions of national wealth, reducing the ability of the state to raise and maintain effective military forces.

Reduced proportions of the population in the 18–64 age group imply a diminished ability to raise armies given a smaller manpower pool of military age and a smaller labour force with which to provision and support them.

Also significant are the different population growth rates which characterise European and Asian sections of the Soviet Union. One consequence is that the relative importance of the European Soviet population is diminishing as compared to that of the Asian, with repercussions in the ethnic mix of the Soviet armed forces. Asian troops tend to be more costly to train because of an educational system that does not meet the standards of the European Soviet Union and because Russian is not their primary language.

Population projections indicate the probability that, while in 1990 the population of Western Europe stood at 377 million and that of Eastern Europe at 415 million, by the year 2020 the former will have increased by less than one per cent to 380 million while the latter will have increased by 18 per cent to 490 million.

The significance of low rates of reproduction to the international status of the European Community was recognised by the European Parliament which in resolution C127/78, 14.5.84 stated:

The European Parliament,
(A) aware that Europe's standing and influence in the world depend largely on the vitality of population and on the confidence placed by parents in the future

and well-being of their children and the prospect of giving them a proper up-bringing and education in a balanced family environment,
(B) seriously disturbed by the recent statistics showing a rapid decline in the total fertility rate in the EEC which fell from 2.79 in 1964 to 1.68 [well below replacement] in 1982,
(C) whereas, unless steps are taken to reverse this trend the population of the Europe of Ten will account for only 4.5 per cent of the total world population by the year 2000 and 2.3 per cent in 2025, as opposed to 8.8 per cent in 1950,
. . .
   1. Considers that population trends in Europe will have a decisive effect on the development of Europe and will determine the significance of the role which Europe will play in the world in future decades:
   2. Considers that measures to combat this market trend toward population decline, which is common to all the Member States, could usefully be taken at the Community level and would be of both political and social significance . . .

Differences in the rate of population growth of different world regions are also of importance for Western security. Beyond the scope of this volume, but of interest to Europe and referred to in passing elsewhere in these pages, is the population of Northern Africa. The tier of nations that stretches from Morocco to Egypt is much poorer than the developed nations of Europe. The latter have per capita incomes that dwarf those of the former, being eleven times greater, a discrepancy that will probably widen in future (Table 1.1). Of particular concern to France is the growing population of its former North African colonies, Morocco, Algeria and Tunisia.

While the developed European nations now have a virtually stationary population, the inhabitants of Northern Africa are increasing at a rate that will double their numbers in 25 years. In 1990, those countries were one-third as large as Developed Europe; in 2025 they will be three-fifths as large.

Such a gap in incomes between populations that will soon be of the same size, separated by a large lake, cannot but bring problems. Some can already be seen. The pressure to emigrate to Europe, illegally if necessary, will increase. Unemployed youth, their numbers multiplied by high birth rates, may well join radical and terrorist or guerilla groups as an alternative to poverty having nothing to lose and much to gain by doing so. Radical political movements rooted in misery, uncertainty about the future and, most of all, disillusionment will find favourable conditions for their development.

Similar trends may be discerned for the world at large. Income in high-income economies is now no less than 44 times greater than that in low-income economies, a discrepancy that is also likely to increase. The population of high-income economies will expand by 16 per cent between 1990 and 2025 while that of low-income economies will grow by 73 per cent. The share of the world population held by developed Europe and by high-income economies will be reduced by about a third. (Table 1.2) If poverty in general, and relative poverty in particular, contribute to instability we may expect

3

TABLE 1.1   Gross National Product Per Capita for Selected World Groupings, 1988

Region or group	Gross national product per capita $	Ratio of developed Europe to region or group
Developed Europe[a]	14.200	1.0
World	3,470	4.1
Northern Africa[b]	1,287	11.0
High income economies[c]	17,080	0.8
Low income economies[c]	320	44.4

[a]   Northern Europe, Western Europe, Spain and Italy.
[b]   Algeria, Egypt, Libya, Morocco and Tunisia.
[c]   As defined by the World Bank in *World Development Report, 1990*.

much of it in future. There will be increasing demands by low-income countries (the 'South') for a global redistribution of income.

Population trends do not themselves cause conflict or bring about events that affect national security. They may, however, contribute to the creation of conditions that affect it. Examples are not hard to find. The much faster rate of population growth of the Palestinian West Bank population than that of the Israeli population has created conditions that make resolution of the conflict between them more difficult and the situation potentially more dangerous for both. Although this imbalance is being righted by the current wave of immigration from the Soviet Union, this is but a temporary respite.

In 1969 El Salvador had a feudal landholding system, a population density of 435 persons per square mile, and a population whose growth rate implied a doubling every 21 years. The Salvadoran population had spilled over into neighbouring Honduras where 300,000 were living illegally, many squatting on land near the border between the two countries, the others working as agricultural labourers. On April 30, 1969, the Salvadorans were ordered off the land by the Honduran government and given 30 days in which to move. By the end of May, about 11,000 had returned to El Salvador with stories of beatings, murder and rape.

'With passions high on both sides of the border a riot in San Salvador centering on a World Cup elimination match between the teams of the two countries pushed tensions beyond the breaking point. On July 14, 1969, the army of El Salvador invaded and from 2,000 to 5,000 were killed (mostly Hondurans) and about 100,000 became refugees (mostly Salvadorans returning home).' (DeWitt, 1986:7). The sudden return of the refugees to a country where land was unavailable and unemployment very high in turn produced domestic tensions that contributed to the as yet unresolved civil war in El Salvador.

TABLE 1.2   Population Data for Selected World Regions and Groups, 1990 and 2025[a]

Region or group	Population 1990	Population 2025	Percentage change	Percentage of world 1990	Percentage of world 2025
Developed Europe	366.8	370.0	0.9	6.9	4.2
World	5,321.0	8,713.0	63.7	100.0	100.0
Northern Africa	118.2	213.1	80.3	2.2	2.4
High income economies	790.0	918.0	16.2	14.8	10.5
Low income economies	3,009.0	5,200.0	72.8	56.5	59.7

[a]   For notes see Table 1.1.

The role that immigration can play is illustrated by the demographic history of the United States. The population of the United States which numbered 11 million in 1824, was 114 million strong in 1924, an increase of 936 per cent in only a century. This extraordinary increase was mainly the consequence of unrestricted immigration. On the eve of the Second World War, in 1937, the U.S. population stood at just under 129 million. It exceeded the combined populations of Italy and Germany by 18.6 million and that of Japan by 59 million. In the absence of immigration the U.S. population would have been less than half as large in 1940, American national power significantly smaller and the outcome of the war possibly disastrous (Saunders, 1986:13).

Each situation is unique, the effect of population is indirect and population trends are of no importance in many circumstances. Consequently, statistical analyses that seek to find systematic relationships between such factors as population growth or population density and different kinds of conflict fail.

National security in Clausewitz' day and until recently, has been regarded as having to do with protection from attack by hostile nations. In a more complex and interdependent world it has also come to encompass defence against subversion whether instigated from abroad or from within, freedom from social turmoil, and the ability to compete politically and economically as well as militarily with other nations.

In the chapters that follow demographic trends are explored as they relate to past and future European fertility (Saunders), affect the future composition of the labour force in Europe (Lee and Lee), influence the composition of the population of the Soviet Union (Kingkade), and limit the viability of the Soviet economy with consequences for conflict dissipation (Bernstam).

Security issues are analyzed by Freedman who looks at the relationship between demographic changes and strategic calculations, and by Bond, who

5

John Saunders

discusses the link between military manpower policies and security. Lunn examines the relationship throughout European history of numbers to military outcomes arguing that demographic considerations continue to be significant in conventional warfare. Rakowska-Harmstone scrutinises demographic trends in the Soviet nationalities and ethnic groups as they affect the Soviet Armed Forces. Boyer considers some possible consequences of population trends in several world regions as they may affect security and Lacoste outlines three approaches to the analysis of the role of demographic factors in security. Finally, Freedman presents a summation.

Notes

1. Including former East Germany.
2. Excluding former East Germany.

References

Carl von Clausewitz, *On War*, Vol. II. (New York: Barnes and Noble, 1968).

John DeWitt, 'Population Growth, Population Pressure and Political Stability in Latin America,' Ch. 1 in John Saunders, ed., *Population Growth in Latin America and U.S. National Security*, (London: Allen and Unwin, 1986).

John Saunders, 'Population, National Power and Security: The United States and Latin America.' Ch. 2 in John Saunders, ed., *Population Growth in Latin America and U.S. National Security*. (London: Allen and Unwin, 1986).

2

Demographic Change and Strategic Studies

Lawrence Freedman

It is at the same time both extremely easy and extremely difficult to write on demographic change and strategic studies. It is easy because there is remarkably little recent literature on the subject. The great texts of contemporary strategic studies ignore demography completely. This of course explains the difficulty: there are few established concepts and propositions upon which to build.

My first task in this chapter is to describe briefly the field of strategic studies and suggest why it has thus far failed to take account of demography. I will argue that strategic studies has developed over the past few decades as a response to the intellectual challenge posed by nuclear weapons. One of the defining features of the nuclear age was seen to be the virtual irrelevance of population as a source of military power.

The nuclear bias in strategic studies has for some time been recognised as being too limiting. One of the central issues of security policy in the West is the growing role of conventional deterrence as confidence declines in nuclear deterrence. A revival of concern with issues of classical military strategy has encouraged a resurgence of interest in more traditional intellectual approaches to military affairs, drawing on history and geography, as much as the economics and engineering that have had so much influence on nuclear strategy. Although this tendency is now beginning to embrace demographic studies, there are a number of areas where such studies have clear relevance. In the later sections of this chapter I will sketch out a rudimentary framework for the analysis of manpower issues in stategic studies. I will also consider the impact of social divisions on the effectiveness of armed forces, and on the shaping of the conflicts in which these forces are used.

7

Lawrence Freedman

Strategic Studies

Defined most broadly, strategic studies are concerned with the means by which individuals and groups seek to obtain their political objectives, and the extent to which the means available and their capacity to exploit them influence the objectives themselves. More narrowly, strategic studies focus on the relationship between *military* means and political ends. However even with this more narrow focus, it is often necessary to compare military means with alternatives – for example, economic sanctions or diplomacy. Furthermore, the basic principles can have a wider application, from industrial relations to child rearing.

The fascination of strategy is that it is concerned with politics at its most pure and raw – the pursuit of interests even where they conflict with those of others, the problems of anticipating the decisions of competitors or rivals when taking one's own, the attempt to manipulate and shape the environment rather than simply become the victim of forces beyond control.

As such, strategy has long fascinated students of politics – Machiavelli is considered to be one of its founding fathers.[1] I believe that it should be acknowledged as one of the central branches of political theory. However, prior to the start of the nuclear age, no established framework existed for the academic study of military strategy. Diplomatic historians were aware of individual strategies; students of international relations understood why strategies were needed; military practitioners busied themselves with the design of strategies; political theorists and international lawyers sought to re-order the world so that strategy would be irrelevant. But the experience of the 1930's and 1940's knocked much of the idealism out of political and intellectual life. A world war followed so quickly by a cold war might have encouraged the study of strategy under any circumstances. The advent of nuclear weapons pushed questions of strategy right to the fore of political life, and once they were there it could not be long before the academic community would follow.

In fact it was not until the middle of the 1950's – 1954 to be precise – following the adoption of the doctrine of 'massive retaliation' by the Eisenhower Administration, that the boom in strategic studies took place. It appeared as if US security policy was going to depend on a threat to inflict terrible damage on the Soviet Union and its allies as punishment for even the smallest transgression. This was despite the declining credibility of such a threat as the Soviet capacity for counter-punishment grew.

It was initially the students of history and politics who worried most about the sense of all this. Those from that background tended to doubt whether nuclear strength could be turned into a decisive military asset when faced with an adversary of some – even if inferior – nuclear strength. But the two superpowers were acting and talking as if nuclear weapons had superseded all other types of weapon, and that commitments to allies had been made on

8

exactly this supposition. So the classical strategists found themselves presented with a conundrum for which their intellectual traditions had left them unprepared. Into the breach stepped a new breed of strategists, often from schools of economics and engineering rather than politics and history, who sought to demonstrate how a wholly novel situation might be mastered by exploiting novel methodologies.[2]

This new approach derived its significance largely from their concentration on those features of the nuclear age which distinguished it from the exercise of military power in prenuclear times. This inevitably led to the neglect of the traditional sources of military power. In addition, because so much of the intellectual attraction of the new methodologies derived from their abstract nature, they made no attempt to relate decision-making to any recognisable social and political context in the scenarios of future conflict that they explored. Almost by definition, should anything remotely resembling these scenarios ever come to pass, the political and social context would be utterly transformed. Indeed, to the extent that social forces and human passions must inevitably be in play, their role should be minimised, for there would be a premium on cool, rational decision-making if there was to be any satisfactory result to a nuclear confrontation. Managerial rationality, not mass emotion, must govern decisions. At most, the prospect of mass emotion might be used by the calculating manager to persuade his opponent that the time had come to strike a bargain.

So, in their attempt to control nuclear power, the new strategists sought to turn states into rational decision-makers, maximising utilities. Assigning values to these utilities was inevitably arbitrary. In consequence, it was not always evident that the fate of the world's great cities and densely populated societies were under discussion.

Those who had to turn this new thinking into policy, drew on the new strategy for key concepts and themes. In particular, they found the theories of deterrence and arms control useful and compatible with the circumstances of the Cold War. They tended to ignore the more exotic notions of nuclear war-fighting. The link between strategic study and practice was sufficiently close for it to become institutionalised.

However, while the particular features of the Cold War and arms race, circa 1960, helped to create modern strategic studies, the context has since changed. A sense of the flaws in the reasoning (if not the performance) of nuclear deterrence created pressures for intellectual innovation. In order to understand where this might lead, and the implications for demography, we need first to examine nuclear strategy.

Nuclear Strategy and Demography

So long as strategic studies were dominated by nuclear weapons then demography appeared virtually irrelevant. This irrelevance was in itself significant for it meant the eclipse of one of the traditional sources of military power. The very designation 'weapon of mass destruction' drove the point home. In the months following the first atomic explosion at Hiroshima and Nagasaki, it was assumed that the new weapons might 'equalise' international relations:

> The small country will again be more than a cipher or a pawn in power politics, provided it is big enough to produce atom bombs. The small country will still not have a defense against an aggressor great country, but even the strongest country will no longer have any reasonable prospects of costless victory over even the smallest country with a stock of atomic bombs.[3]

In practice, nuclear weapons did not turn out to be quite the great 'equalisers' expected. Only the major powers acquired them, thereby, if anything, raising them even higher above the other classes of international actors. Even among the nuclear powers themselves it took time before 'assured destruction' became accepted as a matter of fact.

Up to the late 1950's, Soviet leaders were suggesting that the sheer size of the Soviet Union and dispersal of its population gave it a strategic advantage *vis-a-vis* the United States. By this time, at least in private, they were already coming to terms with the vulnerability. A few years later, in reminding the Chinese that nuclear weapons do not 'obey the class principle', they castigated the recklessness of Chinese claims to be able to withstand nuclear attack. This is, of course, when Mao was said to have observed that even if 300,000 Chinese were killed, there would be another 300,000 ready to continue with the fight. In his memoirs, Khrushchev recalled a conversation with Mao by the side of a swimming pool which began with the Chinese leader describing the military might of the socialist world in terms of the number of potential divisions that all the member countries could raise:

> Comrade Mao Tse-tung, nowadays that sort of thinking is out of date. You can no longer count the alignment of forces on the basis of who has the most men. Back in the days when a dispute was settled with fists or bayonets, it made a difference who had the most men and the most bayonets on each side. Then, when the machine gun appeared, the side with more troops no longer necessarily had the advantages. And now, with the atomic bomb, the number of troops on each side makes practically no difference to the alignment of real power and to the outcome of a war. The more troops on a side, the more bomb fodder.[4]

Yet this view assumed that nuclear weapons could be readily incorporated into classical military strategy. It was one thing to accept them as terrible reminders of just how horrible a future war might be, and in this way to encourage statesmen to rule out total war as a plausible means of solving disputes (and few were prepared to quarrel with the thought that some of these weapons needed to be kept in reserve to deter the other side from using them first) but it was much more difficult to explain how they could be usefully employed once hostilities had begun in earnest.

There has been a continuing resistance to the idea of strategies of mass destruction, as an affront to Western values and the ethical tradition of the 'just war'. This resistance crystallised initially around the production of the hydrogen bomb at the start of the 1950's. But those of this persuasion found it difficult to identify an escape route from the dilemma of the nuclear age, and gradually they came to accept that the best hope was to make the destructive capacity so unambiguous that nuclear strategy could be seen to have no other logic and therefore, ultimately, no rationality other than deterrence. This was making a virtue of necessity. Hopes for complete nuclear disarmament had long been dismissed as Utopian, while schemes for the more limited use of nuclear weapons came up against the probability of retaliation and the consequent risk of escalation to mutual mass destruction.

Initial ideas on the use of nuclear weapons on the battlefield, dating from the 1950s, were based on gearing nuclear systems to attacking military 'mass' rather than civilian 'mass', with an appropriate reduction of 'yield' to the reduced size of the target. This was seen as a means of using improved firepower to compensate for Warsaw Pact manpower advantages. It was assumed that the concentration of forces necessary for an offensive would provide lucrative targets. Once Soviet forces could also use battlefield nuclear weapons, then there was a risk of retaliation. This would make NATO reluctant to strike early, which, in turn, meant that by the time that NATO was prepared to consider a strike, the enemy forces would be less concentrated and well into friendly territory – thereby rendering a nuclear strike even less rational than before.

The critique of mutual assured destruction that gathered pace during the 1970's saw as an alternative the possible use of nuclear weapons in small, accurately delivered packages to concentrate firepower in order to make out specific military targets with the minimum of collateral damage. In different ways, this philosophy influenced concepts for using nuclear weapons both on the battlefield and at the strategic nuclear level. This is not the place to assess this attempt to devise strategies based on selective and controlled strikes. All that is relevant for our purposes is to note that political support could be generated for the idea of developing a range of options to ensure that an appropriate response would always be available should the Soviet Union take the nuclear initiative; it was far more difficult to make the case for options that would allow the West to initiate nuclear war. The risk of escalation to mass destruction could not be removed, despite discomfort with 'genocidal strategies'. The French, who had never believed it could be otherwise, argued with conviction that the deterrent effect of nuclear weapons could be maximised through what they described, in a stunning euphemism, as 'demographic' targeting. Only the French seemed entirely comfortable with this notion, though Britain and the United States also continued in large measure to base their security upon the possibility.

The discomfort surrounding nuclear strategy, boosted by popular protest,

11

meant that it could not crowd out conventional strategy indefinitely. The relative lack of nuclear proliferation, compared to what had been expected, meant that wars in the Third World continued as if nuclear weapons did not exist and, to the extent that the nuclear powers began to get entangled in these wars, then they too had to fight on the same basis.

Even at the point of confrontation in Europe, the role of nuclear deterrence became subject to severe challenge, in spite of the absence of evidence of failure. There came to be a widely acknowledged need to shift the balance from nuclear to conventional strategy. To some this needed be no more than raising the nuclear threshold and moving away from dependence on 'early use' of nuclear weapons. Others went further, to formal declaration of no-first-use, and still others wanted complete abandonment of nuclear deterrence. This trend encouraged a move towards conventional strategy, although the end of the basic East-West antagonism has rendered many of these issues moot, at least in Europe.

The Rediscovery of the Operational Art

Many students have addressed conventional strategy with essentially the same conceptual framework with which they addressed nuclear strategy. But the former is, however, immensely more complicated than the latter. Furthermore, a return to conventional strategy allowed for a return to the excitement and drama of battle itself, with national decision-makers being replaced by generals and utility maximisation by bold manoeuvre.

This approach to conventional strategy manifested itself in the rediscovery of the operational art that had up to this point been lost somewhere between strategy and tactics. At its highest form the application of this art could produce the decisive campaigns, a series of imaginative operations, skillfully executed, that could by themselves determine the outcome of war.

From this perspective, the military establishment of the United States appeared not only uninspired but quite hopeless. The wars in which the United States has been involved since 1945 have been 'limited', in the sense that the security of US territory has not been at stake and the country's total resources have not been applied. From an operational perspective, US performance during these various conflicts was not impressive. The military was handicapped by inter-service rivalries, failures of command and a decline in the military art. The system was severely criticised for becoming geared to the procurement of highly complex, advanced weaponry and the management of a substantial budget. Old-fashioned generalship had been forgotten.[5]

The critics went on to warn that the Soviet Union had never allowed itself to forget the 'operational art' – the term itself was taken from the Soviet literature. Following further what was believed to be the Soviet example, it was argued that a revival of the operational art would require a move away from a simple reliance on attrition through concentrated firepower towards a greater awareness of the potential of manoeuvre.

This critique gathered added force from a sense that the capability of nuclear weapons to control conflict was in decline, especially for the West, largely because of American vulnerability to Soviet nuclear retaliation. The 'new' strategists toyed with the possible application of the operational art to the nuclear area. During the 1970s there was a persistent fascination with what was decried as 'nuclear war-fighting' based on the production of limited nuclear options. These reflected the technological development of precision guidance and small-yield warheads. However, at most these options rarely went beyond denying the other side any advantage for seizing the nuclear initiative rather than devising means to initiate nuclear war with the prospect of something that might usefully be called 'victory'. The risk of retaliation and escalation into all-out nuclear exchanges could never be removed. The failure of strategic imagination in the nuclear arena put even greater pressure for it to succeed in the conventional arena.

Certainly the intellectual difficulties in this area are far less fundamental, but they are still considerable. The real difficulty is that the analyses of conventional military operations are becoming almost as unreal as analyses of nuclear operations. They can be based on existing inventories, force structures and doctrines but there is often little sense of how all these elements would interact in practice. Despite the use of the term 'conventional' we have no known 'conventions' to guide us, for these conventional weapons are really far removed from those of the last world war, and their limited use in more modest conflicts, even in the Gulf, tells us little.

As with nuclear strategy, a lack of real experience encourages a rather formal and mechanical approach to conventional strategy. At the simplest level there is the 'bean count', through which two inventories are directly compared. This tells us precious little about future combat. (It would certainly have predicted little in the Arab-Israeli Wars or the Falklands). There are more complicated 'dynamic' models of the military balance which crank in considerations of geography alliance, mobilisation, training, doctrine and so on, as well as equipment and manpower. However, the variables are so many, and individually they can vary so much, that the conclusions from such analyses can never be treated with confidence.

The 'operational' school has tended to pay less attention to aggregate military balances and more to alternative strategies, with a particular focus on the consequences of efficient mobilisation by the Warsaw Pact. This would be intended to catch NATO relatively unprepared and then by using mannoeuvre groups, to disorient the West further, by moving to the rear. However, while these analyses introduced genuine operational considerations, they still often appear over-precise and systematic, given our fundamental lack of knowledge of the character of warfare in these circumstances. The technical revolutions in surveillance, guidance, communications, all-weather and all-day capabilities produce a mix for which it was almost impossible to plan sensibly against a comparably endowed opponent though they proved decisive in the Gulf against an inferior opponent.

Conventional Strategy and Demography

This focus encourages the tendency of those preoccupied with the operational art to ignore the logistical and political dimensions of strategy. The operational dimension is concerned with the actual encounter between the opposing forces. The logistical dimension refers to the generation of the resources necessary to sustain military operations and the means by which these resources get to the front. Through the political dimension, the objectives of strategy are discerned and domestic and alliance political structures make themselves felt. All these dimensions relate to each other – success in operations will influence popular willingness to bear the burdens of war, and so the readiness of people to continue to work at the war effort. The extent of this war effort, reflected through logistics, depends on the operations to be undertaken, and these, in turn, depend on the political ends being pursued.[6]

Demographic factors play on all these dimensions. Most fundamentally they play on the political dimension. However, this is so fundamental that this will be considered at length in the concluding section.

Conventional military operations present a variety of possible manpower implications. At one simple level, a lot of manpower is required: to cover ground or to provide reserves as attrition takes its toll. But quantity is not sufficient in itself – the recent failure of 'human wave' tactics by China (against Vietnam in 1979) and Iran (against Iraq) warns that raw manpower is not enough. In addition, at least these days, it may only be non-plural societies, encouraging the sense of an aggregated 'mass', which can even begin to think of 'human waves'.

Modern armies need troops capable of more than just rushing against the enemy: they must be able to operate sophisticated military equipment, carry out subtle tactics and implement complicated commands in a confined and fraught environment. The extent to which these qualities are required depends on the extent to which they are also displayed by enemy forces and the extent to which political and physical conditions give them scope. In low-intensity warfare, effective forces may need to be of unusually high quality, but not necessarily be very large. Thus Jeffrey Record has argued

> small wars waged in rugged natural environments against evasive opponents require a level of physical stamina, independent judgement, and initiative greater than that traditionally associated with mass combat between mechanically mobile forces.[7]

In higher-intensity conflicts, it may be more possible to compensate for individual weaknesses, but larger numbers and more powerful weapons are required.

14

Those concerned with meeting these manpower requirements often rightly charge that their tasks are greeted with indifference by military commanders and civilian strategists alike. One US military specialist has complained: 'strategists view manpower experts in the same way they view logisticians – with extreme distaste'.[8] Far more attention is given to new technologies and even new operational concepts than to the human resources necessary to make them work. The issues in manpower policy involve not only the business of getting the right numbers of people but also ensuring that they are of the necessary educational background and will stay in service long enough for their training to yield results. In addition, they must cohere together in combat. Here the manpower planners are dependent on the degree of coherence within the wider society from which these forces will be drawn.

Different societies will therefore, by necessity, produce different military manpower policies. These will not only reflect the needs of the military command, or attempts to adjust to the strengths and weaknesses of the educational system or the particular racial/ethnic mix, but also the cultural traditions affecting the relations between a society and its armed forces. Honouring those traditions may restrict military options. For example, a conscript rather than a volunteer army may reflect a democratic tradition. However, this may create inhibitions on using that army for purposes other than the defence of the homeland.

For all these reasons, demographic changes can have a critical impact on strategic calculations. If the racial/ethnic mix changes and produces societal tensions, then it will be difficult to shelter front-line forces from those tensions. If the number of young men of service age is declining (and this can happen through economic pressures as well as demography) then commanders may have to do with less men, or less-educated men, or more women to replace less men, or rely on governments to shift young men, through the use of economic incentives or some form of draft, into the military sector.

This set of options is very much on the current agenda for the main military powers, and they are coming up with different answers. It is perhaps notable that this issue, which has significant implications at a time of declining support for nuclear deterrence, has been inadequately addressed in the Western debate. In the United States, concern has been expressed that strategic potential has been driven far too much by what technology can offer rather than by what the available manpower makes possible. Michael Handel has commented sharply that:

> the United States, a modern and advanced industrial nation with armed forces possessing the most sophisticated weapons in existence, has gradually been reduced to recruiting soldiers on the level of an underdeveloped society.[9]

At the very least, in such circumstances, there is a need to relate weapons

15

procurement policies to manpower recruitment, so that new weapons systems are easier to operate and maintain and need fewer, rather than more, highly-trained men.[10]

The available pool of trainable young men, and to a lesser extent, young women in a given society is a function of the basic size of the population, demographic trends, social and cultural factors and economic performance. At times of high unemployment, the available pool may be higher; on the other hand, weak economic performance may affect government revenues so that potential recruits cannot be paid enough to attract them into service. The most obvious limit to the pool is the total size of the population. However, the capacity to mobilise human resources at times of national emergency can be remarkable. One can see a spectrum from small numbers of regular forces, through a conscript army, which can be extended through lengths of service or the age range, inclusion of women either directly or indirectly (through taking over other civilian jobs from men), on to expedients such as home guards and young children carrying arms.

Some small countries with a keen sense of threat have a constantly high rate of popular mobilisation. Israel is an obvious example. Others feel able to mobilise manpower at a time of crisis or even during the course of war. Such a policy relies, of course, on maintaining a reasonable reserve capacity and timely warning. It also creates a *strategic* problem in that mobilisation strategies are inherently much more sensitive to the accurate reading of a developing crisis, to those which are based on maintaining a constant level of sufficient front-line forces, presuming that they are truly sufficient. If the decision to mobilise has to be taken rather early on in the crisis, then it can be a cause of aggravation by provoking similar responses from the adversary. This, after all, is a popular interpretation of the outbreak of the First World War.

In extremis, the mobilisation capacity of a population may not be much less than its total size. However, states with security problems of some severity cannot tolerate total mobilisation for extended periods. Within the military sphere itself, there is no point in having large numbers of people in service if they cannot be properly equipped. That requires a functioning economy – either to generate the resources or justify the debt necessary to produce and to purchase.

The trade-offs facing governments go beyond 'equipment versus manpower' in the military sphere, or between the 'military and the civilian budgets'. There are social trades as well. One of the reasons why warfare is so often associated with social change is that, by necessity, it often draws into a national effort groups which are otherwise kept on the periphery or disadvantaged. This can go for ethnic minorities or even women (whose role during the First World War made universal suffrage inevitable).

War-time necessity may involve raising the profile and stations of certain groups, and so changing the character of society itself. For precisely this reason, governments reflecting the established order are reluctant to concede these changes before they are absolutely necessary. To the extent that they have no choice, there is then a risk of exacerbating social tensions, or introducing such tensions into the armed forces themselves.

The role of blacks in the United States is one obvious example of such a tension. Officers may find all sorts of rationales with regard to group cohesion to exclude blacks from particular units or senior command. Blacks are understandably resentful at being expected to sacrifice their lives, and often being prepared for use as little more than cannon-fodder, while being denied prospects of advancement.

Military proficiency cannot therefore be separated from questions of social cohesion. Cohesion in any society will be threatened by a war which is being prosecuted unsuccessfully, or incompetently for purposes which are either obscure or barely taken seriously by public opinion. This tends to mean that cohesion is more of a problem in relation to the more intensive limited wars fought overseas than with total wars in which there is no reason to doubt one's individual stake in the outcome. In recent decades, total war has been steadily ruled out among the industrial countries because of its nuclear implications.

Societies which are already divided are likely to suffer more in these circumstances than others, in that disadvantaged groups are more likely to be cynical about the overseas objectives of the advantaged. Thus the complaint during Vietnam – 'the black man is being forced to fight the yellow man to help the white man protect the land he took from the red man'.

These divisions will be even greater when there is reason for one of the disadvantaged groups to feel a degree of commonality with the adversary. This is a common problem, especially in Third World conflicts. Governments sometimes attempt to exploit such links. In Afghanistan, the Soviet Union hoped that the use of troops from the Muslim Asian regions of the USSR would help in winning over the Muslim Afghans. This hope did not last long and the real issue from Moscow was soon seen to be whether Islamic rebellion in Afghanistan might prove contagious with the Soviet Union. Iran and Iraq, when conducting their offensives in the early eighties, both appeared to hope that they would be welcomed by some elements on the other side of the border. Both were wrong, indicating that loyalties to ethnic groups or religious sect are by no means inevitably higher than loyalty to state. Nonetheless, the possibility of exploiting these tensions can offer an opportunity for an adversary. If Nazi disdain for Slavs had not been so high, the degree of disaffection among the Soviet population from the Soviet state could probably have been turned to substantial – and possibly even decisive – advantage.

A state which contains a substantial disaffected group which can call upon another state for aid may end up by proving non-viable. This may have been the fate of Pakistan in 1971.

Lawrence Freedman

Population and the Causes of War

This brings us on to the relevance of demographic trends to the sources of international conflict. In Quincy Wright's book, *The Study of War*, there is a section on 'Population Changes and War' which concludes with the observation that:

> Alarming statements regarding the relations of population conditions to international conflict have often been made as propaganda for policies of value to the few, rather than the many; consequently it is in the general interest that the indeterminateness of the actual relationship should be understood.[11]

Wright was referring mainly to assertions based on the impact of projected population growth to the incidence of war. He considered that unsound economic theories, based on population change, were likely to be more influential – in a negative sense – than population growth itself. Although, in earlier periods, population conditions would have been more determinate, the complexity of modern international relations meant that these conditions were no longer the critical independent variable in themselves but that their influence depended on so many other factors as to defeat attempts at prediction.

Nonetheless, based on his study of previous periods, he did offer a number of propositions. Differentials of population pressure in neighbouring areas, he suggested, might tend to lead to international violence if a number of other conditions were met: the differential must be known to the inhabitants of the overpopulated area and maintained by artificial barriers to trade and migration. These people must have energy and mobility, be accustomed to the use of violence as an instrument of policy, and 'dominated, as people in the mass usually are, by political rather than by economic objectives'.

Differential rates of population growth might also disturb the local balance of power to the extent that population itself is a key factor in military potenial. As, since the Second World War, it has been less significant, this factor has tended to diminish in importance. Distinguishing between imperial wars and balance of power wars, he suggests that the former may be initiated by countries with rising populations, which they wish to accommodate, while the latter are initiated by alliances with less rapidly rising populations – all other factors being equal.[12]

The analysis in the preceding sections supports the tentative view that population growth might become more important in balance of power terms, but only if one introduces questions of education and social cohesion into the equation. There is little doubt that a declining population base can induce a sense of insecurity. One example might be the Soviet concern about China in the late 1960's which was in part due to concerns that the Chinese birth rate would create pressures for territorial expansion. Countries such as France remain extremely sensitive to the potential implications of population size for ranking great powers.

However, it would seem that differential population growth has been less critical in the post-1945 era in terms of relations between states and more in terms of relations within states. The post-colonial era has brought into being a number of states which have involved awkward amalgamations of different groups.

The delicate balances between various groups who do not necessarily co-exist in harmony provides the central challenges for many states. A familiar cause of civil war is a fear that the domestic demographic balance is in danger of shifting away from one group to another. This, after all, has been Lebanon's fate – the constitution itself reflected a delicate understanding between Christians and Moslems. In Israel, the debate over the future of the occupied West Bank and Gaza strip has revolved around the higher birth rate of the Arab population as against the Jews, with the result that at some point early next century the Arabs in a greater Israel would outnumber the Jews, leading to a choice between abandoning democracy, if the intention is to create a Jewish state in greater Israel, or a deal which would see the bulk of the Palestinians in their own state. This debate was given a further twist in 1990 as large numbers of Soviet Jews made their way to Israel (many having been prevented from going to their preferred destination of the United States) and so promised an extension of the Jews' demographic advantage.

In international terms, critical political consequences are likely to result from a movement of population. Prolonged war can lead to people seeking to escape, thereby creating new problems wherever they camp down. Refugees from East Pakistan in 1970–71 helped to create the conditions in India which led Mrs Gandhi's government to launch the campaign which led to the creation of Bangladesh in December 1971. Khmer refugees in Thailand and Afghan refugees in Pakistan during the 1980s involved those countries in the wars taking place in neighbouring states. Attempts to escape from the civil wars in Sudan and Ethiopia were partly responsible for the terrible famines which afflicted those countries.

In Europe too, population movements have exercised a major influence on political life. The movement of East Germans to the West during 1989, helped by Hungary's open border with Austria, led to the breach of the Berlin Wall. The continued movement from the East to the West once the direct route was open, as much for economic as political reasons, led inexorably to German unification. Elsewhere in Europe there are worries with regard to the social consequences of an influx of refugees from North Africa and the potential of a massive movement of population out of the old communist countries, including the Soviet Union, if their attempts to democratise and modernise themselves result in chaos.

From all of this it is difficult to formulate general propositions, except to note the many ways in which strategic studies must take account of demographic factors. In the post Cold-War world, strategic studies are becoming less dominated by technical assessments of military balances and more sensitive to the fundamentals of political life, including the size, growth and composition of the populations of states.

Notes

1. He is the first to be considered in Edward Meade Earle's *Makers of Modern Strategy* (Princeton University Press: 1962).
2. This is discussed in my, *The Evolution of Nuclear Strategy* (London: Macmillan, 2nd ed. 1989), especially Section Five.
3. Jacob Viner, 'The implications of the atom bomb for international relations', *Proceedings of the American Philosophical Society* XC:1 (January 1946)., p. 55.
4. *Khrushchev Remembers*, Vol. 1 (London: Andre Deutsch, 1971), pp. 467–70.
5. See for example, Edward Luttwak, *The Pentagon and the Art of War* (New York, Simon and Schuster, 1984).
6. I have developed this framework further in Lawrence Freedman, *Strategic Defence in the Nuclear Age*, Adelphi Paper, (London: IISS, 1987)
7. Jeffrey Record, 'Implications of Future Conflict Environments' in Gregory D Foster, Alan Ned Sabrosky and William J Taylor (ed.), *The Strategic Dimension of Military Manpower* (Cambridge, Mass: Ballinger, 1987), p.153.
8. General (retired) Paul Gorman quoted in Gregory D Foster, Alan Ned Sabrosky and William J Taylor (ed.), *The Strategic Dimension of Military Manpower* (Cambridge, Mass: Ballinger, 1987), p.213.
9. Michael Handel, 'Numbers do Count: The Question of Quality versus Quantity',*The Journal of Strategic Studies 4:3* (September 1981), pp. 245–6.
10. Martin Binkin, *Military Technology and Defense Manpower* (Washington DC: The Brookings Institution, 1986).
11. Quincy Wright, *The Study of War* (University of Chicago Press, 1942). (Abridged version edited by Louise Leonard Wright, University of Chicago Press, 1964), p. 295.
12. *Ibid*, pp. 294–5.

3

Population Change in Europe: Past Experience and Future Prospects

John Saunders

Among demographic theories, that of the demographic transition proposed in 1945 by Frank W Notestein and Kingsley Davis in parallel articles, is the best known. It refers to the shift, which has occurred in all European populations, from low population growth rates as a consequence of high birth rates but also of high death rates to low population growth rates as a result of low birth and death rates.

The decline in mortality has been easily explained. Improved food supplies due to more efficient agricultural practices produced healthier populations that were more resistant to disease. Better distribution and marketing systems for food eliminated famines, once a common occurrence in Europe, as a cause of death. An understanding of the association of poor sanitation and deficient hygiene with the spread of infectious and contagious diseases lead to corrective measures which greatly lowered mortality from these causes. Modern medical technology such as antibiotics and vaccines which are of more recent origin contributed comparatively little to the reduction of deaths.[1]

Fertility began to drop in France in about 1770 and in other European populations after 1850 until by 1990 a sustained decline in fertility had begun almost everywhere in Europe (Coale, 1965:207). The decrease in fertility continued unabated with only slight variations until near the end of the Second World War. Fertility rose, following the War, during the late 1940s and the 1950s, but resumed its descent in the mid 1960s dropping to the historically low levels of the present.

Below Replacement Fertility

A total fertility rate, or the mean number of children borne by women during their lifetimes, of 2.1, is necessary for population replacement[2]. Today in

21

every nation of Northern and Western Europe with the sole exception of
Ireland, and in Greece, Italy, Portugal and Spain in Southern Europe, the
population is reproducing at a level insufficient for its replacement (Table
3.1). In Eastern Europe, Bulgaria, Czechoslovakia and Hungary are also
below replacement. A continuation of below replacement fertility rates will
soon lead to an excess of deaths over births in these nations.

In several countries, the numerical decline in population that this situation
portends has either begun or is on the verge of occurring. In 1990, in
Denmark and Germany, the annual number of births equalled that of deaths,
and in several other nations of Northern and Western Europe they are very
nearly matched.

Although the experience of Eastern and Southeastern Europe is essentially
similar to that of Northern and Western Europe, fertility rates in these
regions have not dropped as much. In several of the nations in this group
rates are still high in relation to the remainder of the continent. Albania,
Poland, Romania, and the Soviet Union all have total fertility rates at or
above replacement. However, in Hungary births are now exceeded by
deaths.

Projected population change for 1990–2020 and projected population size
for the year 2000 and 2020 are also presented in Table 3.1.

In Europe, the international competition for power and influence shifted,
after the Second World War, from one that pitted European nations against
each other to one of confrontation between NATO and the Warsaw Pact.
Although the intensity of the confrontation has been weakened by recent
events, it cannot be presumed that differences which have persisted so long in
economic organisation, political ideology and military alliance will entirely
disappear in the near future, leading to a politically and economically homogeneous Europe free of the old rivalries.

The commonality of interests among those nations that, have for the past
half century adopted a socialist approach to the ordering of economic life and
single party rule for the control of power, will not soon be erased. The
boundaries separating the old dichotomy have been blurred but have not, as
yet, disappeared. For these reasons, the data in Table 3.1 are grouped under
West and East.

The populations of the West have total fertility rates that, generally, are
well below replacement and well below those of Eastern populations. The
largest Eastern populations (Poland, Romania, Yugoslavia and the Soviet
Union), which in 1990 contained 91 per cent of the inhabitants of this group
of nations were reproducing at or above replacement.

Because of its large size, the Soviet Union will account for 64 million of the
increase of 76 million anticipated in Eastern Europe by the year 2020. With
the exception of Hungary, the populations in that region will gain between
1990 and 2020. In the West, declines will total 4.9 million and increases 8.2
million for a net gain of only 5.3 million or less than one per cent, while

Population Change in Europe

TABLE 3.1 Population of Western and Eastern Europe, 1990, 2000 and 2020, Percentage Change 1990–2020, and Total Fertility Rate, 1990

Region and nation	Population (millions)			Percentage change 1990–2020	Total fertility rate 1989[a]
	1990	2000	2020		
West	376.3	384.9	379.6	0.9	1.7[b]
Austria	7.6	7.7	7.6	–	1.4
Belgium	9.9	9.9	9.4	– 5.1	1.6
Denmark	5.1	5.2	4.9	– 3.9	1.6
Finland	5.0	5.0	4.9	– 2.0	1.7
France	56.4	57.9	58.7	4.1	1.8
Germany	79.5	81.2	77.3	– 2.8	1.5
Greece	10.1	10.2	9.9	– 2.0	1.5
Italy	57.7	58.6	56.1	– 2.8	1.3
Ireland	3.5	3.5	3.4	– 2.9	2.2
Netherlands	14.9	15.3	15.0	0.7	1.5
Norway	4.2	4.3	4.3	2.3	1.8
Portugal	10.4	10.7	10.7	2.9	1.6
United Kingdom	57.4	59.1	60.8	5.9	1.8
Spain	39.4	40.7	40.7	3.3	1.5
Sweden	8.5	8.8	9.0	5.9	2.0
Switzerland	6.7	6.8	6.9	3.0[b]	1.6
East	414.4	440.2	490.2	18.3	2.3[b]
Albania	3.3	3.8	4.7	42.4	3.2
Bulgaria	8.9	9.0	9.1	2.2	2.0
Czechoslovakia	15.7	16.3	17.0	8.2	2.1
Hungary	10.6	10.6	10.4	– 1.9	1.8
Poland	37.8	38.9	41.7	10.3	2.1
Romania	23.3	24.5	26.0	11.6	2.3
Yugoslavia	23.8	25.1	26.3	10.5	2.0
U.S.S.R.	291.0	312.0	355.0	22.0	2.5
All	790.7	825.1	869.8	10.0	1.9[b]

Source: Based on data in *World Population Data Sheet, 1990*. Washington, D.C.: Population Reference Bureau, 1990.[3]

[a] Population replacement corresponds to a total fertility rate of 2.1.
[b] Unweighted mean.

Eastern populations are anticipated to grow by 18 per cent.

This difference in growth rates will increase the disparity in population size between the two. Over the next 30 years, the size of Eastern populations will increase in relation to those of Western ones until by 2020 the latter will be only 77 per cent as large as the former, down from 91 per cent in 1990 (Table 3.2).

TABLE 3.2   Ratio of the Population[a] of Western to Eastern Europe, 1990, 2000 and 2020

Year	West (a)	East (b)	Ratio (a)/(b)
1990	376.3	414.4	0.91
2000	384.9	440.2	0.87
2020	379.6	490.2	0.77

Source: Table 3.1.

[a]   In millions.

From the standpoint of the effect that demographic imbalances may have on the relative sizes of the populations of Western and Eastern Europe, it is not the level of the rate of reproduction that matters so much as the relative population sizes that will result. From this perspective, declining fertility is not to be feared if it does not result in a population that loses out numerically to that of rivals.

The Modernisation Paradigm

The first set of explanations of reduced fertility relied on the concept of modernisation, the process by which traditional rural-agrarian societies are transformed into modern urban-industrial ones, an explanation suggested by Notestein in *'Population – The Long View'* (1945).

According to this scheme, urbanisation and industrialisation created conditions which were unfavourable for procreation. Among these were increased costs of children. The shift from the family as a production and consumption unit to one that only consumed and the change in place of work from homes to offices, factories and other businesses caused children to lose their economic value to parents, becoming instead a liability, there no longer being a family economic enterprise in which they could participate.

Status ascription by the family gave way to status achievement by the individual. As increased education and training became necessary for status achievement and to safeguard the child's position in society, the costs of children escalated. Parents, facing a conflict between their personal wants

24

and desires and the needs of children, chose fewer children rather than a lowered consumption of goods and services.

> In short, under the impact of urban life, the social aim of perpetuating the family gave way progressively to that of promoting the health, education, and material welfare of the individual child; family limitation became widespread; and the end of the period [of population growth] came in sight (Notestein, 1945:41).

More recently, to the catalogue of the effects of modernisation have been added secularisation, the growth of individualism, expanded participation of women in the labour force and increasing social equality between the sexes (cf Westoff, 1978:53, 1983).

In a perceptive analysis and elaboration of the value of children theme, using 'a competitive market approach to below-replacement fertility,' Bernstam (1987:112–117) argues that fertility levels are inversely related to the intensity of competition between parents for their children's future welfare. The future welfare of one's children may depend on the investment in the quantity and quality of training that they are given so as to compete with the children of other parents when they enter the labour market. The price of the upbringing required to accomplish this end, as perceived by parents, may be high.

> 'The eventual number of children will thus depend on the parents' expected lifetime income and their chosen anticipated expenditures per child. The latter . . . depend also on the parents' assessment of the intensity of competition with other children . . .' (p. 112).

Another economic explanation derived from the modernisation paradigm that focuses on the value of children is offered by Caldwell (1981, 1982). In what he calls 'the wealth flows theory' he proposes that the shift from high to low fertility occurred as a consequence of the reversal of the flow of wealth between generations within the family. As the familial mode of production was replaced by the labour market mode of production, children ceased to contribute to their family's welfare by doing productive labour as well as by rendering services to their elders both in childhood and in adulthood, thereby increasing the family's wealth. Instead, wealth began to flow from parents to children, transforming them from economic assets into economic liabilities.

The most difficult question that any theory which attempts to account for variations in fertility in the West must deal with is the cause of the unexpectedly long rise in fertility following the Second World War which dramatically interrupted a secular decline which had lasted about one hundred years in most of Europe and well over one hundred in France. In some European countries fertility began its ascent in the early 1940s, before the war had ended. An explanation of this phenomenon has been offered for the United States by Easterlin.

In *Birth and Fortune* (1987) he argues that fertility was high in the 1950s and 1960s because the parents of those years were part of a small cohort of births which occurred during the 1920s and the economic depression of the 1930s. Their numbers being small their economic opportunities were great, their incomes rose, their ability to pay for children was enhanced and was of less concern to them. This produced earlier marriages and more births. Thus, members of small cohorts have more economic opportunities and more offspring and vice-versa. This theory has the advantage of affording a prediction which is that fertility will rise again when the children of the small cohorts of the late 1960s, 1970s and 1980s, begin to form families starting in the 1990s.

While Easterlin regards individual prosperity as favouring fertility, Lesthaeghe (1983:430) believes that the effect is opposite:

> '. . . rapid increases in real income fuel individual aspirations and . . . the opening up of new employment opportunities creates an impression of lowered economic vulnerability. This, in turn, allows individuals to be more self-sufficient and more independent in the pursuit of their goals which ultimately stimulates self-orientation and greater aversion to long-term commitments'

which militate against marriage and reproduction.

One of the principal consequences of modernisation which has a negative impact on fertility is increased employment of women outside of the home. Numerous studies have revealed that such women are less fertile than those who do not have outside employment. Baldwin and Nord (1984) attribute delayed childbearing in the United States in part to economic difficulties created by scarce employment opportunities. Also responsible, in their view, is the increased educational achievement of women which leads to better jobs and a greater commitment to the labour force.

The Changing Structure of the Family

The rise throughout the West of the fraction of women who are engaged in gainful employment is interpreted by Davis (1984) in a thoughtful article as signalling the demise of the 'breadwinner' system. With the industrial revolution men and women no longer participated jointly in generating family income under the household production system. Instead, men left home to work, thus becoming the main economic support of the family. Under this system, the wife and children had no control over their destinies; the husband and impersonal forces beyond the family prevailed. Wives remained at home, deriving their status and their meaning from child-rearing and housekeeping.

The maintenance of this system required strong normative controls. The husband's duty to support his wife and children had to be enforced by law, divorce was made difficult and punished with opprobrium. Marriage was promoted by rewarding brides and mothers of many children with praise and

admiration, and by ridiculing spinsters. The expanding labour force participation of women which gave them greater economic independence eroded the
system. Young women increased their educational level and their labour
force participation at the same time and at the expense of marriage and
childbearing (Davis and van den Oever, 1981:7). Today large families are
looked at askance.

Divorce has been facilitated by the growing economic independence of
women. In the 1960s, children were removed as barriers to divorce and in
most cases family size no longer influences divorce and re-marriage (Festy,
1985:203–205) Child-rearing has become much less central to the role of
woman and wife. The spread of egalitarianism has been accompanied by
decreased fertility[4]. The ultimate goal of the feminist movement, which has
arisen out of dissatisfaction with the customary duties and responsibilities of
men and women in society, appears to be the complete elimination of all sex-
based divisions of labour (Davis and van den Oever, 1982:509). Such an
arrangement, by de-emphasising the woman's child-rearing role, can only
have a negative effect on fertility. In the past, the subordination of women
channelled their energies toward child-rearing, making high fertility possible. Low fertility is the natural outcome of gender equality (Keyfitz,
1987:148).

The most obvious and dramatic consequences of the movement towards an
egalitarian system fuelled by higher educational and occupational statuses of
women, has been the rise in cohabitation, 'dependent' marriages resulting
from pre-nuptial conceptions, illegitimate births, and divorces. Marriage is
failing in its procreative role, losing its monopoly over births and is being
ignored by many as the institutional and normative basis for the regulation of
sexual intercourse.

The postponement of marriage, reflected in increasing proportions of
single persons especially under age 30 (in Denmark about 80 per cent of
women 20–24 years old are single) has lead to an increase in informal or
'paperless' cohabitation and to a rise in illegitimacy. In Sweden, often at the
forefront of such changes, 44 per cent of women between the ages of 20 and
24 are cohabiting. These, in turn, amount to 75 per cent of all unions, formal
and informal, of persons of these ages (Westoff, 1987:156). Overall, in the
United States in 1983, an estimated two million couples were engaged in
'paperless' marriages (Glick, 1985:210 quoted in Westoff, 1987:157)[5].

Not unexpectedly, these trends have been accompanied by increases in
illegitimate fertility. In every nation of Northern and Western Europe the
proportion of live births which is illegitimate increased between the 1950s
and 1980s. In Sweden, Iceland, and Denmark it now falls between 38 and 44
per cent. In East Germany, it is 29 per cent (Bourgeois-Pichet, 1987:15).

Bourgeois-Pichat speaks of a category of marriages that he calls 'dependent'. These are marriages that followed conception and are presumed to
have occurred as a consequence of it. For those European nations for which

such data are available, the proportion of all marriages that are dependent has tended to increase (1987:17). In these instances, cohabitation and not marriage is regarded as promoting fertility, marriage being a consequence instead of a cause, thus reversing the historic relationship between these events.

The Transformation of Norms and Values

Such far-reaching and pervasive behavioural changes as those sketched above could not have occurred without corresponding changes in the values that underlie them and of the norms that define appropriate behaviour.

In the Netherlands, a remarkable change in attitudes regarding fertility-related behaviours has occurred since about 1965 (Table 3.3). The proportion of respondents to a national survey that agreed with statements reflecting greater liberality towards sexual intercourse rose significantly between the mid 1960s and the mid-1980s. Similarly, larger proportions agreed in the latter period than in the former with statements reflecting a devaluation of marriage. Only 21 per cent of the 1980s respondents considered the married to be happier than the single. Likewise, abortion and childlessness won high approval ratings. It is evident that in the Netherlands, at least, there has been a substantial liberalisation of norms concerning sexual intercourse, marriage, abortion and childlessness which clearly reflect a depreciation of marriage and parenthood.

A comparison of attitudes across generations was done in a study of 'materialist' and 'post-materialist' attitudes in six Western European nations. Progressive or post-materialist attitudes that reflect a disenchantment with the customary ordering of society were found to be increasingly prevalent the more recent the birth cohort (Inglehart, 1985 cited in Lesthaeghe and Meekers 1986:228). Although firm data are lacking there is no reason to doubt that these trends, with national variations, have been general throughout Europe, as has been the decline in fertility which occurred with remarkable simultaneity across the continent (Bourgeois-Pichat, 1981).

Changing Values

The principal social value that has been transformed has been that of the child. The decline of fertility that began in the late nineteenth century was a result of increasing concern with and focus on the welfare and future life chances of children. This concern caused parents to restrict fertility in order to be able to use their limited resources to better prepare their children for a future in an industrialised and technologically-oriented society. In these behaviours, the child was central. The reduction of fertility that followed the Second World War (referred to as the second demographic transition by van de Kaa, 1987) and that has taken fertility to below replacement levels, is a

TABLE 3.3   Survey of Attitudes Toward Sexual Intercourse, Marriage, Abortion and
Childlessness, the Netherlands, 1965 and 1985–86

	Percentage in Agreement	
Statement	**1965**	**1985–86**
Sexual Intercourse		
There is no objection to sexual relations for people intending to marry.	21	72 (1980)
A girl can have sexual relations with a boy if she likes him a lot.	19 (1970)	59 (1980)
In certain cases, a husband's infidelity is acceptable.	20	45 (1980)
Cohabitation with no intention of marrying is acceptable.	41 (1980)	56
Marriage		
Married people are generally happier than single people.	60	21
In a bad marriage it is better to divorce even if there are children living at home.	12	43
Labour force participation of married women with school-age children is acceptable.	17	69
Abortion and Childlessness		
A woman should be free to have an abortion if she wishes.	43 (1970)	49
Voluntary childlessness of a couple is acceptable.	22	86

Source: Adapted from Table 1 in van de Kaa, 1987.

consequence of increasing individualism, self-preoccupation and self-centredness, in a word, hedonism (cf Aries, 1981 and Preston, 1987).

The German Federal Institute for Population Research expressed concern in a report that babies were not as attractive as other goods (Keyfitz, 1987:145). Children have become a means by which to achieve personal fulfillment rather than ends in themselves or, perhaps, are often altogether unintended. The attitudes reflected in Table 3.3, are anti-natalist, and consistent with hedonism. Thus fertility is reduced at different times by the action of different values. The gradual loosening of social ties between individual, family and community in the post-war world has been accompanied by diminished social cohesion. This has contributed to rising illegiti-

29

macy as the young escaped from the control of family and community that once regulated their fertility. It has lead to lowered marital fertility as concern for self overcame the call of familial obligation.

Emergent Norms

Parents of one or two, who may themselves have cohabited and/or had illegitimate offspring, will find it difficult to demand (if they should so desire) a different standard of their own children. The behaviour tends to be perpetuated, and in time a new normative order may evolve.

Pronatalist Population Policy

Should there be a governmental response to low fertility? Do growing disparities in the size of the populations of rival nations or groups of nations threaten peace by contributing to power imbalances, and threaten prosperity by expanding the burden placed on the society by aged dependents?

The most consistent case for the importance of population to national security and power has been made by France. French preoccupation with *dénatalité* or low fertility has been the object of official concern. A cabinet level minister was appointed to deal with the problem of insufficient births.

Until 1800, France had one of the three largest populations in the West, matched only by those of the Austro-Hungarian Empire and Russia. Its military superiority made it the superpower of that day on the continent. Yet, between 1800 and the beginning of the Second World War, French power and influence gradually declined. This decline was matched by the loss of her demographic ascendancy. Between the conclusion of the disastrous Franco-Prussian War in 1870 and 1940, France's population remained constant at 40 million, while that of Germany increased from 40 to nearly 70 million.

The extraordinary mortality suffered by France in the First World War created a deficit of births during the inter-war years. Marshal Pétain attribu-ted France's defeat in 1940 to 'Too few children, too few arms and too few allies.' (Thomlinson, 1984:112–113). Yet, a consensus does not exist in France concerning the significance of low fertility nor of measures which might be adopted to correct it. McIntosh (1983:223–246) reported that there was no desire on the part of the political élites in France, Sweden and the Federal Republic of Germany to adopt policies to promote population growth. Rather, they were content with a level of reproduction that fluctuates around replacement.

Other governments have, at various times, desired to increase the birth rate of the population out of concern for national power and influence. The spectre of declining numbers (not faced in earlier times) and an ageing population led France, the German Democratic Republic and other Eastern European nations to adopt measures intended to correct this situation. In a review of the success of pronatalist policies in Eastern Europe, David (1982) reports that abortion was restricted and economic incentives adopted with the intention of raising fertility. Among the economic incentives were birth grants, paid maternity leave, child allowances and low interest loans to newly married couples. Initially, these policies produced the desired response but soon lost their effectiveness.

The limitation on legal abortions was countered by resorting to contraception and to illegal abortions. Cash incentives appear to have advanced the occurrence of first and second births without causing couples to have a third birth which would be needed to bring fertility above replacement. Bourgeois-Pichat argues that the recent fertility increases in Eastern Europe were due to rising illegitimate births. Marital fertility, the target of pronatalist policy, was unchanged[6].

Some incentives may work either way. Child care centres and facilities such as day nurseries can be pronatalist by easing problems of working mothers and anti-natalist by encouraging women to seek paid employment. A scrutiny of pronatalist policies by Sandre concluded that although fertility may rise after the institution of family allowances, there are no research findings that prove what effect family allowances have on fertility. Results, although inconclusive, suggest that there is a zero or even a negative correlation between family allowances and family size (1978:159). Similar conclusions with regard to pronatalist policies adopted in the Netherlands were arrived at by Leeuw (1986:325–326). A divergent view, however, is held by Ekert who argues that full reimbursement by the state of the cost of children would raise the total fertility rate by 0.5 (1986:348). Even should such a policy succeed, fertility would still be insufficient for growth (a total fertility rate of 2.2 or higher) in ten European nations (see Table 3.1).

For pronatalist policies to succeed, they will need to do more than simply offer marginal financial benefits. The opportunity costs of the mother's time, or the income she will forego in exchange for child-rearing, will need to be replaced for several years or the financial inducements will be regarded as being meaningless. Keyfitz reports knowing a Swedish mother who uses her children's allowances to provide pocket money for them (1987:153). Even full reimbursement by the state of opportunity costs (at a price to which the public is certain to object) will appeal only to a fraction of potential parents, those who would willingly forego the kind of life they can lead unencumbered by the three or more children that would be needed for significant population growth, in favour of the responsibilities of child-rearing. The data reported above suggest that this fraction may already be small and decreasing in size.

In order to induce these potential parents to raise children, sometime more than financial incentives will be needed. It has been suggested (Keyfitz, 1987:153) that parenthood should be 'professionalised' by providing services to parents such as child care centres, provision for caring for children while parents are on vacation and prompt and convenient medical services. Others come to mind: assistance with housekeeping chores, transportation for children, and expanded recreational services for children. A reversal of values is unlikely. For a pronatalist policy to succeed, it must, therefore, accommodate and account for the values that have resulted in low fertility. This means significant financial and lifestyle incentives.

Immigration is, apparently, never considered as a means to counter population decline, although its potential is great. The fear of cultural destabilisation probably lies behind this reluctance. Yet the experience of Australia, Argentina, Brazil, Canada, the United States and Venezuela does not support this concern.

Future Prospects

Below replacement fertility is an adjustment to new social and economic circumstances in which increasing levels of consumption of goods and services and altered individual aspirations have become incompatible with high fertility rates and prolonged population growth. The social changes which might reverse this condition and lead to rising fertility, such as a return to cottage industries, labour intensive agriculture, and household production systems that harbored social arrangements favouring high fertility, are unlikely in the absence of catastrophic events. The continuation of fertility levels close to replacement and, frequently below it, seems assured for the foreseeable future.

Within this context several possibilities exist.

Continued below replacement fertility compensated for in whole or in part by immigration;
Fluctuations in fertility around the replacement level resulting in equilibrium and stable numbers over the long run;
A combination of these two outcomes which would result in growth;
A long run decline in numbers uncompensated for by immigration, eventually producing new national alignments and entities.

It is well to be reminded, however, that demographic projections are never perfect. Notestein, in 1945, in the article referred to above projects a world population of 3.3 billion in the year 2000, a number that has already surpassed 5.1 billion and seems certain to reach 6 billion by the end of the millennium. His projection for the Americas in 2000 was 490 million, a number that now stands at 751. For Europe, however, west of the pre-war boundaries of the Soviet Union, for which much better demographic data were available in 1945, a year 2000 projection of 417 million was arrived at; not far short of the presently anticipated 502 million within current boundaries. Present day demographic techniques, data, and understanding of population dynamics lend greater confidence to our anticipations of the demographic future.

Notes

1. The germ theory of disease dates from 1865. The drop in death rates was more than fifty per cent complete by then and more than two-thirds complete later in the century when the fruits of Pasteur's discoveries began to be harvested.
2. A rate slightly larger than two is required because of the death of some females between birth and puberty (each female that is born must have one female child to replace her) and, principally, because more boys are born than girls, so that more than two births are needed to assure that the mother will be replaced by a female child.
3. The Population Reference Bureau, in turn, relies on data produced and published by the United Nations Statistical Office, the World Bank and the US Bureau of the Census.
4. An intriguing contrast is provided by Jordanian data (Cornelius, 1988). Jordanian women experience high total fertility rates even when age at marriage, educational attainment, place of residence (whether alone or with relatives) are controlled. However, few work and they are part of a patriarchal system in which subordination to men means economic dependence, preference for male children, dependence on them, and little or no access to a husband's resources.
5. For an interesting analysis of the characteristics of cohabiting couples in Hungary see Carlson and Klinger, 1987, in which they find this practice more common among divorced than single persons, among married than childless women and among the less educated.
6. Personal communication from M Bernstam.

References

Phillippe Aries, circa 1981, 'Two Successive Motivations for the Declining Birth Rate in the West.' In *Determinants of Fertility Trends: Theories Re-examined*, Charlotte Hohn and Rainer Mackensen, eds., (Liege: Ordina Editions, pp. 123–130).

Wendy K Baldwin and Christine Winquist Nord, 1984. Delayed Childbearing in the US: Facts and Fictions. *Population Bulletin* 39:4 (November). (Washington, D.C.: Population Reference Bureau).

Mikhail Bernstam, 1987. 'Competitive Human Markets, Inter-family Transfers, and Below-Replacement Fertility,' in *Below Replacement Fertility in Industrial Societies: Causes, Consequences, Policies*. Kingsley Davis, Mikhail S Bernstam and Rita Ricardo-Campbell, eds. (London: Cambridge University Press, pp. 111–136).

Jean Bourgeois-Pichat, 1981. 'Recent Demographic Changes in Western Europe: An Assessment.' *Population and Development Review*, 7:1, 19–42.

Jean Bourgeois-Pichat, 1987. 'The Unprecedented Shortage of Births in Europe.' In *Below Replacement Fertility in Industrial Societies: Causes, Consequences, Policies*. Kingsley Davis, Mikhail Bernstam and Rita Ricardo-Campbell, eds. (New York: Cambridge University Press, pp. 3–25).

John C Caldwell, circa 1981. 'The Wealth Flows Theory of Fertility Decline.' In *Determinants of Fertility Trends: Theories Re-examined*. Charlotte Hohn and Rainer Mackensen, eds. (Liege: Ordina Editions, pp. 169–171).

John C Caldwell, 1982. *A Theory of Fertility Decline*. (London: Academic Press).

Elwood Carlson and Andras Klinger, 1987. 'Partners in Life: Unmarried Couples in Hungary.' *European Journal of Population*, 3:85–89.

Ansley J Coale, 1965. 'Factors Associated with the Development of Low Fertility in Historic Summary.' In United Nations, *Proceedings of the World Population Conference Belgrade 1965*, Vol. 2, Selected Papers, pp. 205–209.

Diana L Cornelius, 1988. 'Rising Women's Status and Persistent High Fertility: The Case of Jordan.' Paper read at the annual meeting of the Population Association of America, 1988.

Henry P David, 1982 *Eastern Europe: Pronatalist Policies and Private Behavior.* Population Bulletin 36:6 (February). (Washington, D.C.: Population Reference Bureau).

Kingsley Davis, 1945. 'The World Demographic Transition.' *The Annals of the American Academy of Political and Social Science*, 237 (January), 1–11.

Kingsley-Davis, 1984. 'Wives and Work: The Sex Role Revolution and its Consequences.' *Population and Development Review*, 10:3 (September), 397–417.

Kingsley Davis and Pietronella van den Oever, 1981. 'Age Relations and Public Policy in Advanced Industrial Societies.' *Population and Development Review*, 7:1, 1–18.

Kingsley Davis and Pietronella van den Oever, 1982. 'Demographic Foundations of New Sex Roles.' *Population and Development Review*, 8:3 (September), 495–511.

Richard A Easterlin, 1987. *Birth and Fortune: The Impact of Numbers on Personal Welfare*, 2nd Ed. (First published 1980). (Chicago: University of Chicago Press).

Olivia Ekert, 1986, 'Effets et Limites des Aides Financieres aux Familles.' *Population*, 41:2, 327–348.

Patrick Festy, 1985. 'Evolution Contemporaine du Mode de Formation des Familles en Europe Occidentale.' *European Journal of Population*, 1, 179–205.

Paul C Glick, 1985. 'American Household Structure in Transition.' *Family Planning Perspectives*, 16:5 (September–October) 205–211.

R Inglehart, 1985. 'Aggregate Stability and Individual-Level Flux in Mass Belief Systems: The Level of Analysis Paradox.' *American Political Science Review*, 79, 97–116.

Dirk J van de Kaa, 1987. 'Europe's Second Demographic Transition.' *Population Bulletin*, 42:1 (March). Washington, D.C.: Population Reference Bureau.

Nathan Keyfitz, 1987. 'The Family That Does Not Reproduce Itself.' In *Below Replacement Fertility in Industrial Societies: Causes, Consequences, Policies.* Kingsley Davis, Mikhail Bernstam and Rita Ricardo-Campbell, eds. (New York: Cambridge University Press, 139–154).

Franz L Leeuw, 1986. 'On the Acceptability and Feasibility of Pronatalist Population Policy in the Netherlands: An Empirical Approach.' *European Journal of Population*, 3, 307–334.

Ron Lesthaeghe, 1983. 'A Century of Demographic and Cultural Change in Western Europe: An Exploration of Underlying Dimensions.' *Population and Development Review*, 9:3 (September), 411–435.

Ron Lesthaeghe and Dominique Meekers, 1986. 'Value Changes and the Dimensions of Familism in the European Community.' *European Journal of Population*, 2, 225–268.

Frank W Notestein, 1945. 'Population – The Long View.' In *Food for the World*, Theodore W Schultz, ed. (Chicago: University of Chicago Press, pp. 36–57).

Population Reference Bureau, 1990. *1990 World Population Data Sheet.* (Washington,D.C.).

Samuel H Preston, 1987. 'Changing Values and Falling Birth Rates.' In *Below Replacement Fertility: Causes, Consequences, Policies.* Mikhail S Bernstam, Kingsley Davis and Rita Ricardo-Campbell, eds. (New York: Cambridge University Press) 176–195.

Paolo De Sandre, 1978, 'The Influence of Governments.' *Population Decline in Europe: Implications of a Declining or Stationary Population,* Council of Europe. (New York: St. Martin's), pp. 145–170.

Richard Thomlinson, 1984, 'The French Population Debate.' *The Public Interest,* 76 (Summer), 111–120.

Charles F Westoff, 1978. 'Marriage and Fertility in Developed Countries.' *Scientific American,* 229:6 (December), 51–57.

Charles F Westoff, 1983. 'Fertility Decline in the West: Causes and Prospects.' *Population and Development Review,* 9:1 (March), pp. 99–104.

Charles F Westoff, 1987. 'Perspective on Marriage and Fertility.' In *Below Replacement Fertility in Industrial Societies: Causes, Consequences, Policies.* Kingsley Davis, Mikhail Bernstam and Rita Ricardo-Campbell, eds. (New York: Cambridge University Press, 155–169).

4

Population and Labour Force
in Western Europe

Everett S and Anne S Lee

Alarmed by rapid population growth in countries with limited resources, demographers and environmentalists have traditionally centred much of their attention upon the less developed countries. An opposite situation is now attracting attention and studies are focusing upon the more developed countries where population growth is near zero, where the aged form an ever larger share of the population, and where a shortage of young, well-qualified workers looms. Western Europe, the core area of western civilisation, is in such a state. We therefore consider here the present and projected population and labour force of its constituent nations.

In Western Europe there are already countries where deaths exceed births, and others seem fated to share that lot. Every year its population becomes a lesser part of the world's population, a lesser part of the population of the more developed regions, and a lesser part of the population of Europe. At present it has about 5 per cent of the world's population, 20 per cent of the population of the more developed regions, and 49 per cent of the population of Europe. By the year 2025 those proportions are projected to fall to 3, 17, and 45 per cent respectively. Currently, Europe's population is almost the same as that of the United States; by 2025 it will be smaller by 50 million. (See Table 4.1.)

The importance of demographic decline in this part of the world has far more than local significance. Western Europe is the geographic centre of the world's land masses and, since the time of Charlemagne, it has also been a centre for cultural, economic and technological progress. The Industrial Revolution first occurred there and was accompanied by improved living conditions and falling mortality. The resulting high rates of population increase, previously unknown for large nations, provided a base for economic growth and made possible the expansion of Western Europeans into the Americas and the Pacific into the 20th century.

TABLE 4.1   Population by Age, 1985–2050

	Thousands				Percentage Change				
	1985	2000	2025	2050	1985–2000	2000–2025	2025–2050	1985–2025	1985–2050
World									
Total	4840340	6175844	8187679	9523120	27.6	32.6	16.3	69.2	96.7
0–14	1631648	1919094	2011121	1992564	17.6	4.8	−0.9	23.3	22.1
15–64	2925192	3848866	5416091	6245095	31.6	40.7	15.3	85.2	113.5
65+	283500	407884	760467	1285461	43.9	86.4	69.0	168.2	353.4
20–29	826945	1024508	1287833	1335989	23.9	25.7	3.7	55.7	61.6
More Developed Countries									
Total	1177494	1262707	1337599	1333210	7.2	5.9	−0.3	13.6	13.2
0–14	260004	250718	252665	252913	−3.6	0.8	0.1	−2.8	−2.7
15–64	785515	843853	842455	820092	7.4	−0.2	−2.7	7.2	4.4
65+	131975	168136	242479	260205	27.4	44.2	7.3	83.7	97.2
20–29	192434	173162	166178	167585	−10.0	−4.0	0.8	−13.6	−12.9
Less Developed Countries									
Total	3662847	4913140	6850077	8189665	34.1	39.4	19.6	87.0	123.6
0–14	1371644	1668377	1758457	1739652	21.6	5.4	−1.1	28.2	26.8
15–64	2139674	3005015	4573632	5424785	40.4	52.2	18.6	113.8	153.5
65+	151529	239748	517988	1025228	58.2	116.1	97.9	241.8	576.6
20–29	634509	851345	1121657	1168269	34.2	31.8	4.2	76.8	84.1
United States									
Total	239282	262461	284657	280399	9.7	8.5	−1.5	19.0	17.2
0–14	51544	51916	52624	52403	0.7	1.4	−0.4	2.1	1.7
15–64	159605	178759	176198	170812	12.0	−1.4	−3.1	10.4	7.0
65+	28133	31786	55835	57184	13.0	75.7	2.4	98.5	103.3
20–29	42670	34071	33636	34612	−20.2	−1.3	2.9	−21.2	−18.9
Soviet Union									
Total	277424	307737	344184	362838	10.9	11.8	5.4	24.1	30.8
0–14	68891	70733	71800	72002	2.7	1.5	0.3	4.2	4.5
15–64	182894	201284	221760	230073	10.1	10.2	3.7	21.3	25.8
65+	25639	35720	50624	60763	39.3	41.7	20.0	97.4	137.0
20–29	48671	43550	46368	47186	−10.5	6.5	1.8	−4.7	−3.1
Europe									
Total	492172	509832	518914	504601	3.6	1.8	− 2.8	5.4	2.5
0–14	102247	94287	94293	94345	−7.8	0.0	0.1	−7.8	−7.7
15–64	328320	340052	326407	307158	3.6	−4.0	−5.9	−0.6	−6.4
65+	61605	75493	98214	103098	22.5	30.1	5.0	59.4	67.4
20–29	76354	69403	62794	62863	−9.1	−9.5	0.1	−17.8	−17.7
Western Europe									
Total	239117	239355	231279	214826	0.1	−3.4	−7.1	−3.3	−10.2
0–14	43591	39851	39350	39250	−8.6	−1.3	−0.3	−9.7	−10.0
15–64	161762	161018	143560	128748	−0.5	−10.8	−10.3	−11.3	−20.4
65+	33764	38486	48369	46828	14.0	25.7	− 3.2	43.3	38.7
20–29	37304	29915	26313	26347	−19.8	−12.0	0.1	−29.5	−29.4

TABLE 4.1   continued

	Thousands				Percentage Change				
	1985	2000	2025	2050	1985–2000	2000–2025	2025–2050	1985–2025	1985–2050
Austria									
Total	7546	7537	7357	6901	−0.1	−2.4	−6.2	−2.5	−8.5
0–14	1384	1306	1287	1276	−5.6	−1.5	−0.9	−7.0	−7.8
15–64	5092	5086	4623	4175	−0.1	−9.1	−9.7	−9.2	−18.0
65+	1070	1145	1447	1450	7.0	26.4	0.2	35.2	35.5
20–29	1229	928	836	852	−24.5	−9.9	1.9	−32.0	−30.7
Belgium									
Total	9854	9824	9523	8887	−0.3	−3.1	−6.7	−3.4	−9.8
0–14	1827	1663	1646	1638	−9.0	−1.0	−0.5	−9.9	−10.3
15–64	6681	6537	5870	5356	−2.2	−10.2	− 8.8	−12.1	−19.8
65+	1346	1624	2007	1893	20.7	23.6	−5.7	49.1	40.6
20–29	1575	1238	1076	1092	−21.4	−13.1	1.5	−31.7	−30.7
Denmark									
Total	5109	5034	4793	4359	−1.5	−4.8	−9.1	−6.2	−14.7
0–14	939	787	783	787	−16.2	−0.5	0.5	−16.1	−16.2
15–64	3414	3469	2950	2574	1.6	−15.0	−12.7	−13.6	−24.6
+65	756	778	1060	998	2.9	36.2	−5.8	40.2	32.0
20–29	766	675	536	528	−11.9	−20.6	− 1.5	−30.0	−31.1
Finland									
Total	4918	5121	5139	4872	4.1	0.4	−5.2	4.5	−0.9
0–14	947	910	911	905	−3.9	0.1	−0.7	−3.8	−4.4
15–64	3365	3472	3113	2947	3.2	−10.3	−5.3	−7.5	−12.4
65+	606	739	1115	1020	21.9	50.9	−8.5	84.0	68.3
20–29	773	625	581	598	−19.1	−7.0	2.9	−24.8	−22.6
France									
Total	55171	58770	61805	60837	6.5	5.2	−1.6	12.0	10.3
0–14	11763	11325	11320	11292	−3.7	0.0	−0.1	−3.8	−4.0
15–64	36499	38651	38437	36985	5.9	−0.6	−3.8	5.3	1.3
65+	6909	8794	12048	12560	27.3	37.0	4.2	74.4	81.8
20–29	8549	7857	7455	7523	−8.1	−5.1	0.9	−12.8	−12.0
Germany, Federal Republic									
Total	61013	58951	52821	45939	−3.4	−10.4	−13.0	−13.4	−24.7
0–14	9263	8459	8314	8255	−8.7	−1.7	−0.7	−10.2	−10.9
15–64	42906	40474	32220	27088	−5.7	−20.4	−15.9	−24.9	−36.9
65+	8844	10018	12287	10596	13.3	22.6	−13.8	38.9	19.8
20–29	9890	6334	5500	5551	−36.0	−13.2	0.9	−44.4	−43.9
Ireland									
Total	3560	4020	4741	5036	12.9	17.9	6.2	33.2	41.5
0–14	1019	959	961	963	− 5.9	0.2	0.2	− 5.7	− 5.5
15–64	2161	2654	3165	3132	22.8	19.3	− 1.0	46.5	44.9
65+	380	407	615	941	7.1	51.1	53.0	61.8	147.6
20–29	585	686	637	639	17.3	− 7.1	0.3	8.9	9.2

TABLE 4.1   continued

	Thousands				Percentage Change				
	1985	2000	2025	2050	1985–2000	2000–2025	2025–2050	1985–2025	1985–2050
Italy									
Total	57129	57693	56037	52218	1.0	− 2.9	− 6.8	− 1.9	− 8.6
0–14	11059	9349	9340	9414	−15.5	− 0.1	0.8	−15.5	−14.9
15–64	38544	38661	35012	30914	0.3	− 9.4	−11.7	− 9.2	−19.8
65+	7526	9683	11685	11890	28.7	20.7	1.8	55.3	58.0
20–29	8610	7889	6518	6350	− 8.4	−17.4	− 2.6	−24.3	−26.2
Netherlands									
Total	14488	15172	15187	13955	4.7	0.1	− 8.1	4.8	− 3.7
0–14	2792	2597	2539	2525	− 7.0	− 2.2	− 0.6	− 9.1	− 9.6
15–64	9982	10498	9339	8323	5.2	−11.0	−10.9	− 6.4	−16.6
65+	1714	2077	3309	3107	21.2	59.3	− 6.1	93.1	81.3
20–29	2482	1958	1698	1702	−21.1	−13.3	0.2	−31.6	−31.4
Norway									
Total	4147	4274	4356	4146	3.1	1.9	− 4.8	5.0	0.0
0–14	827	762	758	757	− 7.9	− 0.5	− 0.1	− 8.3	− 8.5
15–64	2677	2864	2714	2486	7.0	− 5.2	− 8.4	1.4	− 7.1
65+	643	648	884	903	0.8	36.4	2.1	37.5	40.4
20–29	628	584	510	508	− 7.0	−12.7	− 0.4	−18.8	−19.1
Sweden									
Total	8359	8309	8086	7596	− 0.6	− 2.7	− 6.1	− 3.3	− 9.1
0–14	1522	1396	1387	1387	− 8.3	− 0.6	0.0	− 8.9	− 8.9
15–64	5428	5511	4914	4557	1.5	−10.8	− 7.3	− 9.5	−16.0
65+	1409	1402	1785	1652	− 0.5	27.3	− 7.5	26.7	17.2
20–29	1134	1056	931	930	− 6.9	−11.8	− 0.1	−17.9	−18.0
Switzerland									
Total	6453	6537	6302	5787	1.3	− 3.6	− 8.2	− 2.3	−10.3
0–14	1131	1086	1062	1052	− 4.0	− 2.2	− 0.9	− 6.1	− 7.0
15–64	4425	4389	3812	3468	− 0.8	−13.1	− 9.0	−13.9	−21.6
65+	897	1062	1428	1267	18.4	34.5	−11.3	59.2	41.2
20–29	982	771	696	708	−21.5	− 9.7	1.7	−29.1	−27.9
United Kingdom									
Total	56541	56883	56937	55130	0.6	0.1	−3.2	0.7	−2.5
0–14	10881	10577	10362	10291	−2.8	−2.0	−0.7	−4.8	−5.4
15–64	37087	37403	35828	33728	0.9	−4.2	−5.9	−3.4	−9.1
65+	8573	8903	10747	11111	3.8	20.7	3.4	25.4	29.6
20–29	8650	7171	6794	6889	−17.1	− 5.3	1.4	−21.5	−20.4

Source: K C Zachariah and My T Vu *World Population Projections, 1987–88 Edition* (Published for the World Bank by the John Hopkins University Press Baltimore and London, 1988)

Much of the regions we now term 'more developed' were settled by Western Europeans. Spreading in nearly contiguous fashion across the Northern Hemisphere and with outliers in the South Pacific, the more developed countries contain about 40 per cent of the world's land area and a considerably larger share of its arable land and other natural resources. At the time of the First World War they also had about 40 per cent of the world's population.

That situation, however, has changed drastically. Once again, Western Europe is setting the demographic pace, this time in establishing reverse trends. Its low rates of population increase have spread to the rest of Europe, into North America, and into all those parts of the more developed countries where Western culture prevails. The more developed countries have maintained their hold on the world's lands but their populations have fallen far below those of the less developed countries. By the end of the Second World War, the more developed regions accounted for less than a third of the world's population. Currently that proportion is about 24 per cent; in 2025 it is projected to be 16 per cent and in another 25 years 14 per cent. The more developed countries still follow the lead of Western Europe.

Assuming that attitudes toward ages of beginning and retiring from work, toward women working, and toward immigration remain the same as now, similar statements can be made with equal emphasis for the labour force. A labour force that is declining, either absolutely or relatively, represents a greater loss of power and productivity than equal declines in the population of which it is part. Fortunately, changes in attitude and recognition of need can bring about fairly rapid changes in labour force participation and slow a loss of power and productivity that would otherwise occur.

Western Europe's current share of the population of working age (using here the conventional range of 15–64) is slightly larger than its share of total population. It now has 6 per cent of the world's working age population, 21 per cent of that in more developed regions, and 49 per cent of that in Europe as a whole. By 2025 those percentages will probably have shrunk to 3, 17, and 44. Today, the population of working age in Western Europe slightly exceeds that of the United States; by 2025 it will be smaller by more than 30 million.

Data and Coverage

The nations covered in this paper are the 13 included by the Economic Commission for Europe in its *Economic Survey of Europe in 1986–1987*. (United Nations, 1987). Included with France, Austria, Belgium, Switzerland, the Netherlands, and the Federal Republic of Germany are Scandinavia, the United Kingdom, Ireland, and Italy. For the sake of brevity we shall refer to these countries as Western Europe and simply note that no account is taken of Luxembourg and smaller though sovereign entities which are certainly Western European in geographic location and cultural orientation.

To make what in our minds are necessary comparisons, we include data in Table 4.1 for the Soviet Union, Europe outside the Soviet Union, and the United States. Broadening the scope somewhat further, we also give totals for the more developed and less developed regions. Data have been amassed up to the year 2050, a period almost as long as that which included the Franco-Prussian and two World Wars, all of which had enormous consequences. Not even Bismarck could have foreseen the changes which would take place within the lifetime of a child born in his day, nor could he have guessed the effects of technological change on population growth and distribution. Neither can we; all we can do is project current trends and assume that the world will not be shaken by catastrophic events. The longer the period, the less likely that will be, so for the most part we shall only consider changes until the year 2025, a period not much longer than a generation (taken by demographers as the age of the mother at the birth of the median child and estimated at about 28 years).

Estimates of the labour force are made from projections of population and participation rates by sex and age. By necessity, we use several sources for population projections and participation rates – in general, publications of the United Nations, the Economic Commission for Europe, the World Bank, and the Census Bureau of the United States. Made at different times by different people, using different assumptions, they do not agree exactly. We have relied most heavily upon the World Bank because theirs are the latest projections and therefore based upon the most recent data. However, the differences are such that no general conclusions would be affected if we had used United Nations' or other data. In all instances we have adopted the 'medium variant', in effect the one that is considered most likely. 'High variant' projections all depend upon increases in birth rates which do not now seem likely. Even 'medium variants' seem to yield projections that will be somewhat high for Western Europe and the other more developed countries.

Factors in the Growth of Population and Labour Force

Population growth results from the interaction of mortality, fertility, and migration. The high rates of population increase that preceded and accompanied the Industrial Revolution in Western Europe came when rates of mortality fell while rates of fertility remained relatively high or even increased. Over the years, rates of mortality have continued to fall, and the point has now been reached where only limited improvements can be made unless better ways are found to deal with accidents, violence, and the deterioration that accompanies aging. Later to decline, birth rates have recently fallen faster than death rates. Today natural increase, the balance of the two, is close to zero in industrialised countries and still falling.

41

Everett S and Anne S Lee

The remaining factor in population growth, and one of special importance for the labour force, is migration. From the 17th into the 20th century, Western Europe sent millions of migrants abroad, primarily to North America. Continuing into the 1970s, a movement of professionals and highly trained technicians from Western Europe spurred economic growth and scientific accomplishment in the United States. However, since the 1960s, Western Europe has attracted more migrants than it has lost.

In addition to overall population growth and changes in age composition, the labour force is also affected by changes in participation rates, the proportion that at each age is at work or looking for work. Participation rates differ by sex and, were it not for the sharp rise in female rates since the Second World War, the labour force of Western Europe would be much smaller than it now is. Here too, Western Europe has led the world, as it allowed its women to work outside the home and in non-domestic enterprises.

To understand better the ways in which demographic factors have interacted with other aspects of change in Western Europe, it is useful to consider mortality, fertility, and migration separately before analyzing the joint effects.

Mortality, morbidity and survival

In 1800 the expectation of life at birth in Western Europe was about 35 years and in 1900 it was still below 50. Today it is about 73 for males and 79 for females. Put another way, out of every 100 live births, 99 will survive to enter elementary school, 98 to the age of higher education or entry into the labour force, and 80 to age 65. After age 65 males can expect to live for another 16 years and females for another 20. About 85 per cent of those entering the labour force at age 20 will still be alive at age 65. On average, males should complete about 40 working years. For females, the average length of working life is shorter but is increasing.

The reduction of mortality implies a reduction of morbidity. Even when we take AIDS into account, we find a continuous reduction of illnesses and an increase in physical and mental fitness. Though we have offset much of the effects of infectious diseases, we are still far from overcoming or even understanding mental disorder. Increasingly, debility, personal inefficiency and death can be traced to mental disorders or to self-induced maladies like those attributable to smoking, alcohol or drugs. Still, the quality of the labour force is continually improving because of better health and more education.

- Here we should note that urbanisation and industrialisation have been accompanied by differential falls in mortality for males and females. In Western Europe, as in most of the more developed countries, females outlive males by 6 to 8 years. (See Table 4.2.) Obviously, the lower mortality of

42

females is a factor in their increasing proportion in the labour force, but a minor one in relation to the growing economic and cultural freedom of women.

Fertility Changes

Given the relatively low impact of mortality and assuming zero net migration, it is clear that the number of persons reaching working age 18 or 20 years from now will differ little from the numbers born in the last couple of years. The great majority of males and an increasing proportion of females will stay in the labour force until retirement. Until 2005 or so, persons who will become of working age have already been born and therefore pose little problem in estimation. Estimates of labour force entrants in later years will be affected by assumptions as to birth rates. However, the consensus is that birth rates by age of mother will remain constant or fall even further. Because of the steadily decreasing numbers of births after the early 1970s, there will be a decreasing pool of potential mothers at a time when there will be more and more incentives for women to be in the labour force. We have not yet reached the low point in either births or birth rates.

This causes us to consider both the positive and negative implications of low birth rates. When birth rates are low, women are freer to enter and remain in the labour force. In fact, most of the increase that has taken place in the labour force of Western Europe over the last few decades has been due to increases in the proportion of women in it. (See Table 4.3.) Participation rates have increased for married women with children as well as for single and childless women. The proportion of women in the labour force will doubtless increase even further as the shortage of new workers becomes more apparent and as women who have opted to remain childless, or have few children, replace the older generations who were less likely to do paid labour and more likely to reproduce themselves. Negative factors often associated with low birth rates are higher proportions of births outside marriage and increases in the number of female-headed households. The greatest problem, however, is that births are not sufficient to replace the population.

Migration

The remaining factor in population change is migration. Until the early 1970s, several Western European countries encouraged the immigration of workers on a temporary basis. By 1974, the unemployment of natives and difficulties in assimilation had led to increased restrictions on immigrant workers. Even so, millions have become permanent residents and their numbers still swell as family members join them.

There are advantages and disadvantages in attracting migrants, and these depend in part upon the kinds of migrants who arrive. A major advantage is that migrants tend to be young adults ready for immediate service in the work

TABLE 4.2   Social and Demographic Indicators

	Expectation of life at birth		Total fertility ratio 1987	Percentage enrolled in tertiary education Ages 20–24 1986	Percentage of population foreign born
	Male	Female			
Austria	69.5	76.6	1.5	28	3.9
Belgium	70.1	77.0	1.6	32	8.9
Denmark	71.5	77.5	1.5	29	3.1
Finland	70.4	78.8	1.6	35	0.8
France	71.2	79.3	1.8	30	11.1
Germany, F.R.	70.5	77.1	1.4	30	7.4
Ireland	70.1	75.8	2.3	22	2.6
Italy	71.0	77.7	1.3	25	1.7
Netherlands	73.0	79.7	1.6	32	3.8
Norway	72.9	79.2	1.8	28	2.0
Sweden	73.8	78.8	1.9	37	5.1
Switzerland	73.0	79.6	1.6	23	16.7
United Kingdom	71.6	76.9	1.8	22	6.3

Sources: Expectation of Life: World Development Report, 1989
Total Fertility Ratios: World Development Report, 1989
Percent Enrolled in Tertiary Education: World Development Report 1989
Percent Foreign Born: UN 1987 World Monitoring Report

place. Many are willing to take the low-paying jobs that require minimal skills and are no longer attractive to native workers. Whenever industry expands to near maximum capacity such workers add considerably to productivity. However, they may come from a radically different culture and resist integration into the native society. They also bring along family members and their children may not assimilate readily into the educational system. Turks in Germany and Caribbeans in Britain illustrate the difficulties that can arise when migrants are drawn from highly different cultures.

At the other end of the scale are the migrants who are drawn to the larger, freer, and economically more advanced countries because they will have more of a chance to make optimal use of their skills and energy. The United States has long depended upon such migrants for improvements in its cultural and economic development. Above all others, that nation has been fortunate in attracting large numbers of scientists, artists, and developers; for example, the Hungarian, Danish, and Italian scientists who played so large a role in the development of atomic energy, and the Asian-Americans who are disproportionately represented among more recent innovators in physics and chemistry. Western European countries have also benefitted considerably from the

Population and Labour in Western Europe

TABLE 4.3 Labour Force Participation

| | Labour force participation rates | | | | | | Females as percentage of labour force | | Percentage of males in labour force at ages** | | |
| | —1970— | | | —1987— | | | | | | | |
	Total	Male	Female	Total	Male	Female	1970	1987	15–19	55–59	60–64
Austria	67.3	85.2	50.9	66.9	80.1	54.4	39.6	41.6	56.3	68.8	15.9
Belgium	62.8	85.7	40.1	67.8	81.4	54.3	32.1	40.1	–	70.7	32.3
Denmark	74.9	91.8	58.0	82.5	87.6	77.4	38.6	46.3	70.3	81.8	46.8
Finland	74.2	85.3	63.5	77.2	81.4	73.0	43.8	47.1	41.6	63.6	35.5
France	67.7	87.0	48.3	65.7	76.0	55.4	35.6	42.2	17.8	69.9	26.2
Germany, F.	68.9	91.5	47.9	71.7	88.3	55.5	35.9	39.0	47.9	79.1	33.0
Ireland	65.8	96.4	34.3	59.1	81.9	35.5	25.8	29.6	39.5	83.4	66.8
Italy	60.1	87.0	34.1	62.1	80.6	43.4	28.8	34.8	27.6	69.8	37.6
Netherlands	59.7	87.1	31.9	59.2	75.2	42.8	26.6	35.6	22.1	61.5	17.8
Norway	64.1	89.0	38.9	79.9	86.9	72.5	30.1	44.3	45.3	86.0	71.3
Sweden	74.3	88.8	59.4	82.0	85.0	78.9	39.5	47.5	44.1	86.5	65.0
Switzerland	78.4	104.5*	52.7	73.7	92.8	54.5	33.9	37.0	–	–	–
United Kingdom	72.3	94.3	50.7	74.4	87.3	61.4	35.3	41.2	51.5	91.6	75.0
Western Europe	67.5	89.9	45.6	68.6	82.9	54.6	34.2	39.7	–	–	–

Notes * Exceeds 100 because total workers including those under 15 and 65 and over were related to population aged 15–64
** For Sweden and Norway rate is for ages 16–19 instead of 15–19. Year of reference is either 1985 or 1986

Sources: ILO: Yearbook of Labour Statistics, 1987
Economic Commission for Europe: Economic Survey of Europe in 1987–1988
Economic Commission for Europe: Economic Survey of Europe in 1986–1987.

immigration of talented people, even while others were leaving for the United States. Given changing economic conditions and rising investments in research, it seems likely that Western Europe will increasingly compete with the United States for ambitious and innovative migrants from less developed countries.

Growth and Changes in Age Structure

Growth

We may now put the demographic factors together to consider the growth and composition of population and labour force in more detail. First we consider overall growth. From now to the year 2000 the population of Western Europe will be approximately stable at 239 million. By 2025 it is projected to fall to 231 million and by 2050 to 215 million. Of the 13 countries considered here, seven are expected to have registered outright losses by 2025 and only France and Ireland will have gained as many as a million people. By the year 2050 all of the Western European countries except Ireland will have moved into the losing column.

Of the two largest countries of Western Europe, one is projected to be the greatest gainer and the other the greatest loser. France, with an increase of 7 million by 2025, will gain the most, and the Federal Republic of Germany, whose population will fall by 8 million, will lose the most. With about 60 million people, the Federal Republic is now the largest country of Europe, but by 2025 it will have only 53 million people. By 2050 it will have shrunk to 46 million. Soon after the year 2000 it will have fewer people than France and by 2015 it will also have fallen below Italy and the United Kingdom. (See Fig. 4.1.)

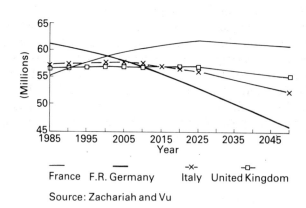

Source: Zachariah and Vu

FIGURE 4.1   Population of Largest European Countries, 1985–2000

Loss of rank among the countries of the world will be more dramatic. At the beginning of the Second World War, Germany was fifth largest among the independent nations of the world and one of its segments, the former Federal Republic, is now the 14th largest. Close behind are Italy, the United Kingdom, and France, ranked 15th, 16th, and 17th. However, by the year 2025 only France will be among the top 25 nations in population, and among these it will rank last (United Nations, 1988). In 1939 United Germany was half again as large as France and over half as large as the United States. In 2025 the former Federal Republic will be less than a fifth the size of the United States and a reunited Germany will be less than a fourth as large. So goes the balance of power.

Losses in population and in world rank have occurred because of declining fertility. Births have fallen so much that in Denmark and the Federal Republic of Germany deaths exceeded births in 1987 (United Nations, 1989). Only in Ireland did the total fertility rate (the expected number of live births per woman) reach the 2.1 level necessary to reproduce the population. In other Western European countries the range was from 1.3 in Italy to 1.9 in Sweden. (See Table 4.2.) In the Federal Republic the total fertility rate, 1.4, was about two thirds of the number necessary for reproduction and in France it fell short by 14 per cent.

Given such low fertility and the consequent shortage of young workers, it is not surprising that workers have been imported. While no other nation had the 14 million foreign born counted in the US Census of 1980, a greater number are found in the combined nations of Western Europe, an area with about the same total population as the United States. Of course, some countries have attracted many international migrants and others relatively few. As compared with the 40 thousand in Finland, there were 6 million in France, 5 million in the Federal Republic of Germany, and 3 million in the United Kingdom. Even tiny Switzerland was home to over a million foreign born in 1980 (United Nations, 1988, pp. 228–229).

Indeed, it could be argued that parts of Western Europe have become more of a melting pot than the United States, the nation that was created by migrants. Whereas the proportion of foreign-born in the United States at the last count was 6.2 per cent, it was 7.4 per cent in the Federal Republic, 8.9 per cent in Belgium, 11.1 per cent in France, and 16.7 per cent in Switzerland. Just as the United States depended upon migrants for its economic growth and political survival in the early years, Western Europe is now subject to a similar dependence.

Age structure

Changes in population such as those portrayed above imply a drastic reshaping of age structures. The loss of 8 million people in Western Europe between 1985 and 2025 will be arrived at through a decrease of 4 million in the

47

number of children under 15, a decline of 18 million in the number aged 15–64, and an increase of 15 million in the number of retirement age. Much of the fall in the number of working age will be due to the decline in the number 20–29, the new workers upon which so much depends. Thus a decline of only 3 per cent in total population will be accompanied by a 10 per cent decrease in the number of children, an 11 per cent decrease in the number of working age, a 30 per cent decrease in the number of new workers, and a 43 per cent increase in the number aged 65 and over. Over this forty-year period the only age groups to increase in number will be those 50 and over.

Only in France, Ireland and Norway is an increase in the number of working age projected. The greatest loser in this respect will be the Federal Republic of Germany where the number aged 15–64 will fall by almost 11 million. Again this illustrates the shift in power between the two largest nations. In 1985 the 36 million persons of working age in France compared with 43 million in the Federal Republic. By 2025, however, the positions will have been reversed. France will have increased the number aged 15–64 to 38 million while in the Federal Republic the number will have fallen to 32 million. The 25 per cent decrease in the Federal Republic in this forty-year period will be the greatest in Western Europe.

Again we emphasise the decrease in the number of young workers. Relatively, this will be much greater than the change in the total number of working age. The heaviest decline of persons aged 20–29 will be 44 per cent for the Federal Republic of Germany, and the least (Ireland excepted) will be 13 per cent for France, another indication of the differing demographic development of these two countries.

A decrease in the number of young workers also means a decrease in the number of potential parents. It is no surprise, therefore, to find that in every country of Western Europe the number of children will fall, the losses between 1985 and 2025 ranging from 4 per cent in France and Finland to 17 per cent in Denmark. Even in Ireland, where birth control is still resisted, thre will be a decrease of 6 per cent in the number aged 0–14, and in Italy the decline of 16 per cent will almost equal that of Denmark.

Offsetting the projected losses in the number of children will be huge increases in the elderly population. These range from about 25 per cent in Sweden and the United Kingdom to 93 per cent in the Netherlands. In the Federal Republic of Germany an increase of 39 per cent compares with one of 74 per cent in France. Such extreme differences can only be partly understood by reference to patterns of past birth rates. War losses, migration, and other factors also play a part.

Increasing the difficulties posed by the growing number of elderly persons is the rising percentage of the 'oldest old', those aged 75 and over. At present this group constitutes 6 per cent of the total population of Western Europe. That proportion will rise to 9 per cent in 2025. Among those who are 65 years old and over, about 43 per cent are aged 75 and more and this proportion is not expected to change greatly before 2025. By 2050, however, the 'oldest old' could constitute more than half of the population who are aged 65 and over. (Zachariah and Vu, 1989)

Older women form a larger proportion of the oldest old than men. Whereas males of 75 and over now constitute only 4 per cent of the total number of males and 39 per cent of those 65 and over in Western Europe, the corresponding percentages for females are 8 and 46. Furthermore, though women live longer than men, they are nevertheless more likely to require medical care and hospitalisation as they pass through the older ages.

Dependency Ratios

The net result of contrasting changes in the youngest and oldest segments of the population will be a remarkable uniformity in the proportion of working age from country to country in Western Europe. Roughly two thirds of the population of Western Europe were 15–64 years old in 1985. Only in the Federal Republic of Germany did the proportion reach 70 per cent and, except for Ireland, the lowest proportion was 65 per cent for Norway and Sweden. By the year 2025 the various countries are expected to be even more alike in this respect, though the percentage of the population of working age in Western Europe will have fallen from 67 to 62 per cent. Again disregarding Ireland, the variations from the 62 per cent level are small, ranging from a low of 60.5 in Switzerland to a high of 62.8 per cent in Austria.

The usual way of assessing potential relationships between workers and non-workers is to divide the populations aged 0–14 and 65 and over by that of 15–64. Expressed in terms of dependents per 100 persons of working age, these afford some measure of the burden imposed upon workers by children and the old, and the sum of the two is termed the total dependency ratio. Of course, dependency ratios derived in this fashion only generally indicate relationships to the actual labour force. The size of the labour force is determined not only by age structure but by participation rates which vary in Western Europe more from country to country than do percentages of working age. Dependency ratios do, however, roughly assess the burdens placed by the young and the old upon those in the ages of greatest productivity, a category that includes mothers who do not work outside the home.

In 1985 the total dependency ratio for Western Europe was slightly lower than 50, indicating that there was nearly one person of dependent age for each two of working age. Among the nations the range was not very great – Ireland excepted. In 1985 the lowest in Europe was 42 for the Federal Republic of Germany. The major reason why the total dependency ratio for the Federal Republic was so low was that there were few children. Its youth dependency ratio of 22 per hundred persons aged 15–64 compares with corresponding figures of 47 for Ireland and 27 for Western Europe as a whole. At the same time, elderly dependency in the Federal Republic was about average for Western Europe. At 21 it was not strikingly higher than for Ireland where it was 18 per 100 persons aged 15–64.

The Federal Republic, however, is the prime example of how drastically dependency ratios can change in a relatively short time. In only 40 years, the Federal Republic will move from the lowest total dependency ratio in Western Europe to the highest, estimated at 64 in the year 2025. That is a 50 per cent increase. Again, a comparison with France is instructive. In France the total dependency ratio in 1985 was 51, 20 per cent higher than in the Federal Republic, but in 2025 it will be 61, about 5 per cent lower. That is another instance of the changing balance of power between the two nations.

Generally speaking, youth dependency ratios will not change greatly in Western Europe over the next forty years, the major exception being the sharp decrease to be experienced in Ireland. It is increases in the elderly dependency ratio that will raise the total burden of dependents upon potential workers. As elderly dependency increases by an average 13 points, it will drive up the total dependency ratio by about the same amount.

Labour Force Participation

An increase of 13 persons of dependent age upon each 100 of working age is in itself an horrendous figure, but it becomes more so when we consider that only about two thirds of the persons aged 15–64 are currently in the labour force. This and the coming shortage of new workers should lead to an immediate consideration of ways of increasing labour force participation rates or of encouraging immigration. We are assuming, of course, that the nations of Western Europe will not take gladly to a rapidly lessening role in continental and world affairs.

A quick look at participation rates given in Table 4.3 for the population aged 15–64 in 1987 shows surprising variation from country to country. Also, patterns of change since 1970 differ considerably. Currently the highest participation rates for ages 15–64, both sexes taken together, are for the Scandinavian countries. Their 77 to 83 per cent participation at these ages contrasts sharply with the 59 per cent for the Netherlands. In Switzerland the participation rate fell from 78 in 1970 to 74 in 1987 but in Denmark it increased from 75 to 83 per cent. In Norway the increase was even greater, from 64 to 80 per cent. As shown in Table 4.3 the relative change for most other Western European countries was not great.

However, it would have been startling had not so many more women than men entered the labour force during these years. In the 16-year period, 1970–1976, the male labour force of Western Europe grew by little more than a million while the female labour force increased by nearly 12 million. In other words, 90 per cent of the increase was female. Actually, in four countries – Belgium, the Federal Republic of Germany, Sweden, and Switzerland – the number of males in the labour force decreased so all of the increase was attributable to females. Except for Ireland and Austria, where the share of the increase attributable to females was only 55 or 60 per cent, females accounted for 73 per cent or more of the total growth in the labour force (Economic Commission for Europe, 1987)

In every country of Western Europe participation rates for males fell from 1970 to 1987 – in France, Ireland, and the Netherlands by 10 percentage points or more. For Western Europe as a whole there was a 7 percentage point fall in the participation rate for males. Females, on the other hand, registered a 9 percentage point gain in participation rates for the entire region. That, however, was a minor increase as compared with the 34 point gain in Norway and the 19 point gains in Sweden and Denmark. In Denmark and Sweden higher percentages of females were in the labour force than was true of males in France, 77 and 79 per cent as against 76.

Increases in the labour force will continue to be dominated by females because the rates for males are currently much higher. In Western Europe over 80 per cent of males 15–64 are now in the labour force as compared with 55 per cent of females. For both sexes, the possibilities can be better judged if we look at participation rates for specific age groups.

For males between the ages of 25 and 55 labour force participation is well over 90 per cent in nearly all countries of Western Europe. At ages 20–24 participation varies by country from 70 to 90 per cent, reflecting in part differences in educational enrollment. Even in the 15–19 group, participation may reach 70 per cent, suggesting low proportions in secondary or higher education. In a number of countries participation of men falls off sharply after age 60, possibly because early retirement is permitted or even encouraged. At any rate major increases in the labour force participation of males will have to occur at the older ages.

For females the situation is quite different. At the younger ages there is little difference in male and female participation rates. This is generally true at ages 15–19 and in several countries at ages 20–24 as well. At older ages participation rates for males are generally well above those of females. Though participation rates for females do not peak in some countries until ages 40 to 50, they tend to decline thereafter even more sharply than do those for males. Bringing female participation rates closer to male levels in countries where female rates are low could add 10 or more points to the total participation rate.

Differences between countries in male and female participation rates by age are illustrated in Fig. 4.2 where rates for Sweden and the Federal Republic are compared. In Sweden and in Germany the participation rates for males and females are nearly the same for ages 15–19 through 20–24. However, in Sweden the rate for females remains high, 85 per cent to age 55 and almost 50 per cent at ages 60–64. In the Federal Republic, however, the rate for females declines from 74 per cent at ages 15–19 to 50 per cent at 50–54 and 11 per cent at 60–64.

At first thought, one might suspect that the German women have left the labour force in order to bear more children while Swedish women have forgone child bearing in an overpowering desire to match male representation in the labour force. Note, however, that the total fertility rate of 1.4 for the Federal Republic in 1987 was one of the lowest in the world while that of Sweden was 1.9.

Women would make greater contributions to the labour force if they were as likely as men to work full time. Incomplete figures for Western Europe show that 70 to 90 per cent of the part-time workers are women. In France in 1986, 23 per cent of employed females worked part time, as did 90 per cent of those in the Federal Republic in 1984. In countries like Denmark and Sweden, where unemployment rates have been low and participation rates high, the percentage of women employees on part time has fallen. This probably presages a trend for the whole of Western Europe. (United Nations, 1988)

Concluding Remarks

In summary, we repeat that the countries of Western Europe are in a state of demographic decline. Population growth is already slow and will soon turn negative in most countries. The number of persons of labour force age will fall even faster. The number of young, new entrants to the labour force is already in sharp decline, forcing up the median age of working persons. The decrease in the number of young persons is crucial for the military, but it is also of major importance to industry. It is such persons who man new industries, who have recently been taught the latest technology, and are likely to be the most innovative.

Some answers to the emerging manpower problems of Western Europe are evident. One involves the increasing use of females across the age span, and their involvement in full-time jobs. Many who are listed as working are in fact employed only part time and in jobs that could easily be automated. Thousands of such jobs exist only because they can be 'womaned' cheaply. We must not forget, however, that security in the next generation depends upon the children of this generation. If women are to work at about the same rate as men, it will be necessary to encourage, not just allow, pregnancy leaves. Adequate child care must be reckoned one of the costs of security. To be economically realistic we must include reproductivity as a factor to be reckoned with in assessing long-term productivity.

Another answer lies in the immigration of younger workers. The United States still benefits enormously from such immigrants, in particular the mathematically, scientifically, and technically inclined Asians. In Africa, Asia, and in Southern and Eastern Europe there are many such young people

Federal Republic of Germany, 1985

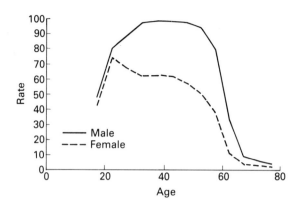

Sweden, 1986

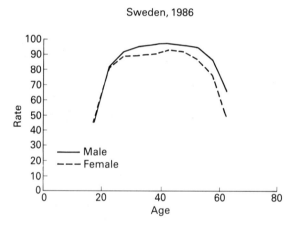

FIGURE 4.2   Labour Force Participation Rates

who would be delighted to work in Western Europe. The Federal Republic of Germany has gained as it became possible for East Germans and ethnic Germans in other countries to emigrate more freely. Also, as the European Economic Community removes its restrictions on the movement of workers from one country to another, many will migrate from the less industrialised to the more industrialised countries, thus increasing their contributions to the wider economy.

In Western Europe, as in the United States, steps should be taken to increase the span of working years. At the younger levels, schooling can begin earlier and proceed faster, if necessary by increasing the length of the school year. Years saved in this way would either permit more years in the labour force to gain time for intense technological and professional training. At the other end of the scale, retirement comes much too early. We are approaching the point where for each two years of service in the labour force a year of retirement benefits must be provided.

Budgetary gains made by lessening the number of non-productive years could be enormous. At the lower level, years saved by faster progress through elementary and secondary school could increase the number of years in the labour force or permit earlier entry into tertiary education. Even more years can be saved by postponing the age of retirement for those whose physical health and mental competence permits. The increasing strain on national budgets through pensions and the rising cost of health care will demand this treatment of the elderly, but we should not overlook the possibilities afforded by the accelerated maturation of children. Neither the young nor the old are physically or mentally the same as they were in Bismarck's day, as the spate of ten-year old mothers and septuagenarian or octogenarian world leaders might suggest.

In addition to increasing the proportion of workers, it is important to improve their quality. The rules of the game, military and economic, have changed. For an increasing number of tasks a high degree of literacy and mathematical sophistication is necessary. Also, as the size of the market is increased by free movement of goods and people within the European Economic Community, and as international enterprises multiply, the demand for highly trained specialists will increase even further. Western Europe has maintained its place in the World more by maintaining higher levels of education than by increasing population. The future will be no different.

One final note. For centuries individual nations of Western Europe have shaped or shaken the political and economic state of the world. No one of them is now large enough to play such a role and none will have as much as one per cent of the world's population in 2025. The economic union foreseen in the European Economic Community and the defensive union represented by NATO would seem to be beginnings rather than ends in the creation of units large enough to be influential in world affairs.

References

Economic Commission for Europe. *Economic Survey of Europe in 1986–1987*. (New York: United Nations, 1987)

Economic Commission for Europe. *Economic Survey of Europe in 1987–1988*. (New York: United Nations, 1988)

United Nations. *Population and Vital Statistics Report, Series A, Vol. XLI, No. 1.* (New York, United Nations, 1989)

United Nations. *World Population Trends and Policies: 1987 Monitoring Report*. (New York, United Nations, 1988)

World Bank. *World Development Report 1989*. (Oxford, Oxford University Press, 1989.) (Published for the World Bank)

Zachariah, K C and My T Vu. *World Population Projections, 1987–1988 Edition*. Baltimore, The John Hopkins University Press, 1988 (Published for the World Bank)

5

The Future Population of the Soviet Union

Ward Kingkade

During the 1980s the Soviet Union entered a period of sharply diminished growth in population and labour resources. The increases in the total and able-bodied populations projected for the remainder of this century are minimal in comparison with those experienced in the postwar period up to 1980. Economic growth must therefore be attained through increases in labour productivity instead of by the traditional means of expanded employment. Faced with the increasing need to husband human resources, the Soviet government has responded with initiatives aimed at stimulating fertility and improving the health of the Soviet population. Yet to a great extent the population's current structure determines its future growth, particularly over the remainder of this century. The evolution of the Soviet population is explored through comparison of alternative population projections in the analysis below.

Perhaps the most essential feature of Soviet society is its ethnic diversity, which is embodied in the constitution of the Soviet state. The Soviet Union is not a nation state in the Western sense, but an amalgamation of national governments corresponding to specific ethnic groups. Such deeply rooted cultural, social, and economic divisions are encompassed in this structure that it can be difficult to decide whether to consider the Soviet Union as a single country or an assortment of several nations. Although Soviet political theory stresses the international character of the society, ethnic cleavages remain pronounced. Linguistic variety reflects this panorama. Upwards of 100 languages are said to be in use among the Soviet population [Isayev, 1970, p. 6], of which 78 have written literatures and 67 are broadcast by radio [Guboglo, 1984, p. 5].

Imbalances in growth among subpopulations are a crucial feature of the Soviet Union's current demographic situation. While the European nationalities comprise the majority of the Soviet population, their share has been

56

declining due to the more rapid growth of the non-European nationalities, particularly Central Asians [Feshbach, 1982]. Among most European Soviet nationalities fertility has been near or below the level that would achieve long-run zero population growth, whereas the high fertility of the Central Asian nationalities is generating rapid population growth. As a result, increases in labour supply are not forthcoming from the indigenous populations of the European republics where most Soviet industry is concentrated. The Central Asian nationalities are an unpromising source of additional industrial labour, being among the least mobile, least urbanised, and least proficient in Russian, segments of the Soviet population [Di Maio, 1981, p. 20; and Feshbach, 1982, p. 28].

The military significance of the trend in ethnic composition, which implies that approximately one-third of the draft-age population in the year 2000 will come from non-European nationalities, has been discussed by a number of Western analysts [Feshbach, 1982, p. 29; Meyer, 1978, pp. 157–158; Crisostomo, 1983, p. 2; and Di Maio, 1981, p. 20]. Most concur that poor command of Russian and inadequate technical education have limited the utility of Central Asian recruits to the armed forces. Central Asians have, in the past, been employed primarily in construction battalions and support units requiring minimal technical and communication skills. Although the Soviet Union has made remarkable progress in equalising national educational levels among the younger generations [Jones, 1985, pp. 189–190; and Lewis et al., 1976, pp. 359–361], the explosive growth of the Central Asian population entails rapidly mounting numbers of school-age children. If the educational levels of Central Asians are not to fall behind, this calls for substantial further investment in educational facilities in an era of diminishing resources.

Various opinions have been ventured about the political implications of the ethnic shift in the Soviet Union. The Soviet Union is the only major power whose dominant nationality barely comprises a majority. According to one viewpoint, growth in the Central Asian share of the population may increase the influence and political assertiveness of these nationalities, promoting political-administrative decentralisation in the long run [Di Maio, 1981, p. 37; and Heer, 1981b]. Another possibility is that intensified competition for resources between nationalities may lead to greater Russian chauvinism [Pipes, 1975, p. 5].

Soviet concern about these issues during the 1970's led to increased efforts to promote literacy in Russian among non-Russian nationalities [Solchanyk, 1982; Shamsutdinova, 1981; and *Narodnoye obrazovaniye*, 1981] as well as to a wide-ranging population policy debate [Weber and Goodman, 1981; and Di Maio, 1981]. In 1981, the 26th Communist Party Congress adopted a pronatalist fertility policy centring on paid annual maternity leave for working women [Postanovleniye, 1981], who are found more commonly among European than non-European nationalities [Heer, 1981a, p. 84]. Since 1982,

57

fertility has risen in every European union republic while declines continue to be registered in those Central Asian republics and Azerbaydzhan, whose indigenous (historically Muslim) nationalities predominate.

Little has been added to this picture from the 27th Communist Party Congress in 1986. The period of paid maternity leave has been extended to 1.5 years [*Osnovnyye*, 1986, p. 64]. The new edition of the Communist Party Programme contains the cryptic pronouncement: 'The nationality problem of the past has been successfully resolved in the Soviet Union' [*Kommunist*, 1986, p. 127]. While reiterating the traditional rhetoric about the rights of all Soviet nationalities to their own languages, knowledge of Russian as a second language is advocated as a means of access to the achievements of modern technology as well as Soviet culture (*otechestvennaya kul'tura*).

Total Population

Given the Soviet Union's vast geographic endowment, which includes an extensive land border, the traditionally favourable attitude of the Soviet government towards population growth is understandable. Soviet economic planning has relied on increases in labour supply as a principal means of attaining increases in output. Throughout the twentieth century, the fertility of the Soviet Union's population has been sufficient to ensure continued growth. However, the transition to small family size norms which has characterised so many of the world's industrial societies has also embraced the Soviet population, especially its European segments [Coale et al., 1979; Vishnevskiy and Volkov, 1983, pp. 127–240]. During the postwar period, Soviet fertility has fallen into the vicinity of the two-child family, implying negligible growth in the long run. Table 5.1 illustrates the resulting trends in the total and working age populations of the Soviet Union. The rate of population growth has fallen from a high of 1.7 to 1.8 per cent in the 1950s to roughly half that value at present. (For all Tables and Figures refer to pages 79 to 127).

During the 1980s, growth in the working age population of the Soviet Union has been sharply reduced in comparison to the preceding decade. The projected growth of the working age population from 1970 to 2000 is less than that for the 1970s alone. Moreover, the apparent recovery around 1995 is mainly the result of a temporary decline in the number of those leaving the working ages through retirement, rather than an upswing in young entrants to the working ages. The constraint that these trends impose on the compara- tively labour-intensive economy of the Soviet Union is well appreciated by Soviet policymakers, and has figured as a major influence on Gorbachev's drive for increased efficiency.

Mortality

After a decade's lapse, the Soviet Union has resumed publication of the standard demographic measures which describe the mortality condition of the population. The official life expectancies at birth register a decline during the 1970s, particularly among males (Table 5.2). Soviet accounts explain this deterioration in terms of increases in mortality from accidents and degenerative diseases associated with a complex of lifestyle factors in which alcoholism figures prominently [Andreyev, 1979, p. 28; Fedorenko, 1976, p. 55; Polyakov et al., 1984, pp. 18–19]. This factor is also cited in explanations of the sex differential [Bednyy, 1979, pp. 145–151; Ryabushkin and Galetskaya, 1983, pp. 186–187; Steshenko et al., 1977, pp. 147–148], which is extreme by world standards.

Soon after Gorbachev became General Secretary, a major campaign against alcoholism was initiated. The Supreme Soviet and the Council of Ministers adopted resolutions which limit the distribution and consumption of alcoholic beverages and impose penalties for appearing inebriated in public or for permitting drunkenness in the workplace [postanovleniye, 1985; ukaz, 1985]. Especially strict regulations apply to workers in vehicular transport ['Zakon', 1985]. Penalties for private production of alcoholic beverages (*samogon*) are included in the legislation, and state sales have been sharply reduced.

Although official statements attributing the recent decline in mortality to the anti-alcoholism campaign should be interpreted cautiously, it is likely that the campaign has had a beneficial effect. Penalties for public drunkenness and drinking on the job would be consistent with reported declines in accident mortality and, less immediately, mortality from cardiovascular conditions. Soviet analyses finding that as much as 70 per cent of all accident deaths involve inebriated individuals [Kopyt, 1985, p. 5; Polyakov et al., 1984, p. 18] indicate that further reductions in alcohol-related mortality are eminently possible.

Additional influences on the decline in mortality in the recent past should not be overlooked. An ambitious programme to expand the coverage of the clinical health service in an effort to combat degenerative disease has been underway in various parts of the Soviet Union in the 1980s [Demchenkova et al., 1985, 8–9; Novgorodtsev et al., 1984]. Its expansion is included among the elements of the 'Basic Guidelines for Economic and Social Progress for the Years 1986–1990 and the Period to 2000' [*Osnovnyye*, 1986, p. 306] as well as the guidelines for restructuring the health system [*Osnovnyye*, 1987]. The latter include much needed increases in expenditures on medical facilities and supplies.

Mortality varies significantly among Soviet sub-populations. Infectious and respiratory diseases play a greater role among the Asian and 'Southern Tier' nationalities, while degenerative disease is more dominant among the European strata [Bednyy, 1979, pp. 130–131; Vishnevskiy and Volkov, 1983, pp. 102–113; Tadzhiev and Avazov, 1985, p. 68; Gamzayan, 1979, pp. 79–80]. This difference in cause structure is associated with characteristic differentials in levels and age-patterns of mortality, which is higher on

59

average for southern tier nationalities, but particularly so in infancy [Vishnevskiy and Volkov, 1983, pp. 105–113, 120–122]. Table 5.3 presents estimates of life expectancy for five major nationalities which comprise roughly three quarters of the Soviet population. According to this sensitive indicator of the quantity and quality of life, the three Slavic nationalities fare better than the average for the population of the Soviet Union, with Belorussians appreciably better off than Russians and Ukrainians. The differences between the life expectancies for the Kirgiz, a Central Asian nationality, and Russians are comparable to the Black-White differential in the United States, although the American levels are higher. The lower standard of living in rural areas may account for the similarity between the Kirgiz life expectancy and that of the predominantly rural Moldavians.

Fertility

Fertility levels differ widely among Soviet nationalities, spanning most of the range of variation observed around the world. Soviet demographers typically regard the European nationalities of the Soviet Union as having completed the 'demographic transition' from natural to controlled reproduction, Central Asians as being in the initial stages, and Transcaucasians (usually grouped with Moldavians) as transitional. Table 5.4 presents estimates of the fertility levels of the 20 major nationalities at three benchmark dates in the recent past. The total fertility rate (TFR), representing the number of children a woman would bear in her reproductive life if it were spent entirely under the given fertility schedule, reflects variations in the intensity of fertility independently of differences in age composition between nationalities.[1] Although most of the estimates are based on data for union republics, which are geographic entities, in several instances the estimates have been refined by considering the republic's ethnic composition or the geographic distribution of the nationality. In addition, direct data on the fertility of four Central Asian nationalities were available [Karakhanov, 1983, p. 139].

As Table 5.4 indicates, by 1978–79 the TFRs of European nationalities had fallen to near, or below, the replacement value of 2.11 which corresponds to zero population growth in the long run. At the opposite extreme, the Central Asian nationalities register fertility levels that equal or exceed the average for Third World countries. The obvious implication of this differential fertility is a decline in the European share of the Soviet population. This is particularly true for Russians given the low fertility level of the RSFSR relative to other European republics. The Russians, who comprised a majority of every age group in 1959, had become a minority of children by 1970. During the 1970s the survivors of these children entered the working-age population, impinging on the civilian labour force and the military. By 1979, Russians are estimated to have become a minority of the population aged 15–19, which includes the draft-age population together with new entrants to the labour force.

Faced with the prospect of a stationary or declining labour supply in the European areas of the Soviet Union, where most industry is concentrated, the 26th Communist Party Congress, in 1981, adopted the pronatalist policy (discussed below) that has remained in effect with minor modifications to this day. Since 1981, fertility has risen in every European republic.[2] This striking reversal of the trend of declining fertility in the European republics is illustrated in Figure 5.1, where Moldavia has been excluded because of the significantly higher level of Moldavian fertility. Intriguingly, the European fertility levels in Figure 5.1 have converged to approximate replacement fertility. (For all Tables and Figures refer to pages 79 to 127).

Until recently, there has been little evidence of fertility decline among the indigenous nationalities of Central Asia. Fertility schedules have been reported specifically for four Central Asian nationalities (Kirgiz, Tadzhiks, Turkmen, and Uzbeks) from the mid-1960's to the mid-1970's, with no apparent decline in overall fertility levels [Karakhanov, 1983, p. 139]. However, there is reason to believe that the fertility of these nationalities declined afterwards. Figure 5.2 displays the trends in reported fertility for the three Central Asian union republics whose indigenous nationalities predominate, revealing clear declines in each, beginning in 1976. Given that the indigenous nationality's share of the population rose in each of these republics between the 1970 and 1979 censuses while the Russian shares declined [Kozlov, 1982, pp. 117–122], it appears likely that the republic trends reflect actual declines in the fertility of Central Asian nationalities. In addition, Soviet presentations of nationally representative sample survey results reveal pronounced declines in family size expectations among women of Central Asian nationalities born at successive dates in the postwar period [Belova, 1983; Bondarskaya, 1985, p. 29; Vishnevskiy and Volkov, 1983, pp. 235–241]. Although to some extent these findings may reflect the fact that women born earlier had longer time to experience unwanted pregnancies, this would still indicate a reserve of unwanted fertility among native Central Asians which could potentially be reduced with increasing involvement of women in the labour force, expansion of education, and urbanisation.

In each of the three republics in Figure 5.2 fertility appears to have risen somewhat in recent years. This short-term movement has not progressed far enough to constitute more than a temporary pause in the secular trend of declining Central Asian fertility levels. It is by no means certain that the recent upturn in Central Asian fertility indices reflects actual increases in the lifetime fertility levels of Central Asian women; this could easily be due to more compressed spacing of children among the younger cohorts of Central Asian women of childbearing age.

Fertility trends in the Caucasian union republics are exhibited in Figure 5.3, where the impressive decline in Azerbaydzhan dominates. An appreciable decline is registered in Armenia, while the Georgian trend is more modest. However, in the latest year, fertility rose in Armenia and Georgia while the decline in Azerbaydzhan visibly slackened. These results may reflect the influence of the fertility programme, whose implementation was slated to commence in non-European areas of the Soviet Union in 1983 [Ryabushkin and Galetskaya, 1983, pp. 209–210].

Maternity Incentives

The precipitous drop in Soviet fertility in the 1950s and 1960s brought much of the European population below the replacement level, with unattractive implications in terms of future labour resources. In apparent response, the government enacted legislation intended to stimulate fertility in the early 1970s. The more significant of these measures included extension of fully paid maternity leave for 56 days before and after birth to all working women regardless of length of employment, along with child support payments for low-income families [Ryabushkin and Galetskaya, 1983, pp. 204–209]. These incentives had little effect on the trends in fertility. The shortlived upswing in the early 1970s had come to a halt prior to the adoption of the measures. During the remainder of the decade European fertility continued to decline.

Against the background of Brezhnev's appeal for an 'effective demographic policy' at the 25th Communist Party Congress in 1976, Soviet intellectuals debated alternative strategies for influencing fertility [Weber and Goodman, 1981, pp. 279–295; Di Maio, 1981, pp. 16–43]. A number of European demographers, noting that high fertility was occurring in areas far removed from the industrial centres where growth was needed, advocated a regionally differentiated approach that would stimulate the fertility of low-fertility populations while lowering the fertility of high-fertility populations in the direction of the 3–4 child family [Litvinova, 1978, p. 136; Urlanis, 1980, p. 46; Kvasha, 1978]. Others, including the Kazakh demographer Tatimov [1978, p. 74], argued that any such approach would amount to discrimination. At the 26th Communist Party Congress in 1981, the former school of thought prevailed.

The 'Measures to Strengthen Governmental Assistance to Families with Children' adopted by the 26th Party Congress [postanovleniye, 1981a] represented a major expansion of legal incentives to encourage fertility. A central element of this package is the right to partially paid maternity leave for a year after birth for all women employed at their current jobs for a year or more, with the option for an additional half year of unpaid leave without loss of seniority. Lump sum payments of 50 rubles upon birth of the first child and 100 rubles for second and third births were added to the existing structure of payments to working mothers, producing a schedule which rewards fourth and fifth births at lower rates than third births. In addition, the measures call for the provision of housing (in the form of individual rooms) to recently married couples as well as housing improvement loans and priority for admission to housing cooperatives. The measures were scheduled to go into effect first in the 'hardship' areas of the RSFSR (Far East, Siberia, Far North, Non Black Earth Zone) in 1981, other European areas in 1982, and the remainder of the Soviet Union in 1983 [postanovleniye, 1981, p. 631]. Although the phraseology of the legislation avoids any suggestion of differential treatment of European and non-European nationalities, the emphasis on working women implies a much greater impact among the Europeans, whose rates of female employment are substantially higher than those of non-Europeans.

Little has been added to this picture from the 27th Party Congress in 1986. Partially paid maternity leave has been extended to 1.5 years while retaining the additional half year of optional leave (*Oznovnyye*, 1986, p. 64]. The 'Basic Guidelines for Economic and Social Progress' for the 12th Five Year Plan include provision of free pharmaceuticals for children under 3 years of age [ibid., p. 67]. More liberal provision of temporary leave to working mothers when a child is ill has been introduced recently.

Although the pronatalist measures have probably been instrumental in bringing about the rise in Soviet fertility in the 1980s, the prospects for further gains are less certain. The measures partially alleviate some of the most adverse consequences of childbearing, such as loss of income and strain on dwelling space, which inhibit couples from having the number of children they desire. A permanent increase in family size norms among the urban European population is another matter. The proportion of births comprised by third children has risen only slightly, from 22 per cent in 1980 to 26 per cent in 1986 [Nar Khoz, 1987, p. 404]. East European experience suggests that gains in fertility due to material incentives tend to be shortlived [David, 1982].

PROJECTION SCENARIOS

In view of this background, an assessment of the effect of fertility conditions on the future ethnic composition of the Soviet population seems called for. Moreover, from a practical standpoint, it can be demonstrated that fertility variations play a far more important role in determining future population composition than do plausible variations in mortality. To investigate fertility's effect, the future course of fertility is varied over several alternative scenarios. Three ('principal') scenarios represent high, median, and low courses of fertility developed on substantive grounds from global as well as historical Soviet experience. Because fertility trends in the very recent past have, in many instances, run counter to the long-run secular decline, separate assumptions regarding the short-run and long-run courses of fertility are distinguished. Nationalities are grouped into three regional clusters of nationalities having common trajectories of fertility: 1) Europeans, including

Tatars and Chuvash; 2) Transcaucasians, treating Azeris somewhat differently from Armenians and Georgians because of the higher level of Azeri fertility; and 3) Central Asians, including Kazakhs. Within each cluster, individual nationalities are allowed separate fertility levels. In addition, each nationality's fertility has been inflated by 3.5 per cent to adjust for under-registration of births, as indicated in a previous evaluation of completeness of Soviet birth registration [Kingkade, 1985, pp. 24–29].

The median scenario, representing the most reasonable prognosis, has been guided by the experience of East European countries which experimented with pronatalist fertility policies during the 1960's and 1970's [David, 1982; and David and McIntyre, 1981]. Only Romania achieved a lasting rise in fertility, due largely to a sweeping ban on abortions.[3] Because Soviet experience with similar bans met with much less success, while engendering higher maternal mortality from illegal abortions [David, 1970, pp. 9–62], it is unlikely that the Soviets will introduce a wholesale ban at the present time. In the East European countries whose pronatalist programs emphasized material incentives, fertility rose for only a few years before falling again despite expansion and improvement of the benefits.

The median scenario for Armenians and Georgians (together with the European nationalities) assumes a symmetric increase and decline in fertility over an 8-year period. For Europeans the period is centred at 1986, reflecting the extension of paid maternity leave by the 27th Communist Party Congress. Because the maternity benefit scheme was introduced in European areas a year earlier than in the remainder of the country, the period of increased fertility is centred a year later for Armenians and Georgians. Fertility decline among Central Asians and Azeris is assumed to reflect fundamental socio-structural changes associated with urbanisation and education that are beyond the reach of the current fertility policy. Nevertheless, even among the southern tier nationalities there is an educated and/or urban stratum likely to contain some couples whose fertility could potentially be accelerated by the maternity incentives. For this reason, the median scenario assumes that Central Asian and Azeri fertility continues to decline, but with a slackened pace through 1987.[4]

In the median scenario, the fertility levels of each nationality are assumed to converge ultimately to a TFR of 1.81 in the distant future. The convergence assumption is based on the hypothesis that the current gap between the fertility levels of Central Asians and the remaining nationalities is largely the result of differences in the timing of the onset of fertility decline. That the fertility decline has begun among Central Asian nationalities is borne out by the data in Figure 5.2 as well as in Soviet accounts of fertility trends [Belova et al., 1983; Vishnevskiy and Volkov, 1983, pp. 235–241; Bondarskaya, 1985, p. 29]. The fertility levels of those countries that have completed the fertility transition have clustered in the vicinity of somewhat below replacement level [Monnier, 1985, p. 757]. It would be reasonable to expect subpopulations within a country – at least one which remained intact – to follow a similar tendency. At the same time, it appears worthwhile to allow for the possibility that fertility decline will not entirely eliminate the differentials between nationalities. For this reason, the national fertility levels have been assumed to converge asymptotically (approaching, but never attaining, the same value). Figure 5.4 illustrates the median fertility assumptions for selected nationalities representing the extremes of variation among Europeans, Transcaucasians, and Central Asians, respectively. Differences among and between Europeans and Transcaucasians are dwarfed by the gulf separating these nationalities from Central Asians. The short-run rise and fall of the European/Transcaucasian fertility is minor in comparison to the Central Asian fertility decline. The convergence of national fertility levels does not become salient until well after the turn of the century.

The high variant represents a permanent rise in the fertility of European nationalities following the Romanian model. For all nationalities, fertility rises by the unusually high factor of 5 per cent in 1985. Thereafter, the fertility levels of European and Transcaucasian nationalities rise until 1990 at the rapid pace exhibited in the last two years of reported data, while fertility declines at a reduced pace among Central Asian nationalities. After 1990, the TFRs of all nationalities tend gradually to a common asymptote of 2.6, substantially higher than the fertility of most of the developed countries today.

Fertility declines throughout the low variant, representing a pessimistic fertility scenario. In this variant, fertility falls among all nationalities by a factor of 5 per cent in 1985. Thereafter, the national TFRs converge to a value of 1.55, on a par with the current levels of some of the lower-fertility countries in Western Europe as well as East Germany [Monnier, 1985, p. 757].

In addition to the principal projection scenarios, several ('analytical') scenarios have been included to examine possibilities inherent in the current situation that are judged to be unlikely on substantive grounds and to ascertain the limits bounding the future evolution of the Soviet population by exploring extreme cases. The first of these scenarios involves the eminently conceivable example in which the fertility levels of all nationalities remain constant at their 1984 levels. This serves to illustrate the implications, however unlikely, of the status quo. A second analytical scenario investigates the momentum of population growth inherited from the past. In this scenario the fertility of each nationality is kept constant at the replacement level throughout the projection, representing the demographic equivalent of slamming the brakes on the growth of the respective national populations. The resulting population trajectories indicate the inertia present in the current population, which constitutes the foundation over which population policies are superimposed.

Two further fertility scenarios are synthesized from the former analytical

65

scenarios. These additional scenarios embody the polar combinations of high fertility among European nationalities with replacement fertility for non-Europeans, on one hand, and low European fertility combined with constant non-European fertility on the other. The two synthetic scenarios indicate the respective upper and lower extremes of variation in the European population share.

In the projections, the short-term rise in mortality has been assumed not to continue. Mortality has been held constant from 1979 to 1984. Thereafter mortality for each nationality has been assumed to decline, converging in 2015 to a level and pattern representative of present-day low-mortality countries.[5] In essence, Soviet mortality has been assumed to lag more than a generation behind the most advanced industrialised countries. For the Soviet Union as a whole, this implies a slight improvement in female mortality and a modest improvement in male mortality, both of which are within Soviet and world experience [Vishnevskiy and Volkov, 1983, pp. 297–299; United Nations, 1982, pp. 438–465; and United Nations, 1961, pp. 622–641]. The more significant improvement assumed for Central Asians remains well within historical experience of the Soviet Union, and reflects the observation that, as a result of technology transfer, mortality decline in third world countries has occurred much more rapidly than it did in those countries which were first to industrialise [Merrick, 1986, p. 11; and United Nations, 1973, pp. 110–115]. Presumably the Central Asian republics can borrow analogously from the example of the European Soviet republics. After 2015 mortality has been assumed to remain constant.[6]

Those nationalities for which separate mortality estimates could not be identified have been assigned the mortality of the nationality in Table 5.3 believed to bear the closest resemblance in terms of demographic characteristics. The Kirgiz mortality pattern is assumed for the other Central Asian nationalities including Kazakhs, while the Baltic nationalities, together with Germans and Jews, receive the Belorussian mortality schedule. All remaining nationalities are given the mortality pattern of the Soviet Union as a whole.

International migration has been taken into account for the three nationalities which have emigrated in substantial numbers during the recent past: Jews, Germans, and Armenians. The emigration streams for each of these nationalities peaked during the late 1970's to early 1980's, followed by marked declines to the mid-1980s [Goodman, 1984; Heitman, 1986; Kingkade, 1988, p. 29]. Emigration is assumed to remain at its 1985 level over the projection period.[7]

PROSPECTIVE POPULATION TRENDS

Total Population

Table 5.5 contains the projected total populations for broad nationality groupings under the various projection scenarios. In most scenarios, the fertility of at least one sub-population remains above replacement, so that the total population of the Soviet Union grows over the projection period. The maximum projection for the near future is obtained under the high scenario, which assumes the recent rise in the period fertility levels of European nationalities represents a lasting increase in completed fertility. As fertility evens off among the European nationalities while declining among others to the European level, total population growth for the Soviet Union settles down to an even pace of roughly 10 per thousand annually. Intriguingly, the maximum population in the long-run occurs under the constant scenario, reflecting the explosive multiplication implicit in current Central Asian fertility levels. In the constant fertility scenario, the total population of the Soviet Union grows at an accelerating pace, as Central Asians comprise an ever increasing share of the Soviet population, eventually outstripping the projected population of the high-fertility scenario. The two synthetic scenarios which combine the highest fertility assumptions for Europeans with the lowest for non-Europeans and vice versa are dominated by the expanding population segments, following trajectories similar to the high and constant scenarios, respectively (see Figure 5.5).

Two of the projection scenarios imply eventual decline in the Soviet population. The low-fertility variant assumes immediate disappearance of the recent rises in the fertility of European nationalities followed by further substantial decline, coupled together with rapid sustained declines in the fertility of other Soviet nationalities. In this case the European nationalities begin to register population declines shortly after the end of the century, while the total population of the Soviet Union begins to shrink in 2030. Only Central Asians continue to experience growth at the end of the projection period.

A more plausible prognosis is provided by the median scenario, in which European fertility gains dissipate according to the East European model while Central Asian fertility proceeds more gradually than in the low variant. This postpones the onset of population among European nationalities to 2020, so that decline in the total population of the Soviet Union does not begin until the end of the projection period. Even so, the trend in the Soviet Union's total population in the median scenario is dominated by the Central Asian population, which experiences nearly a fourfold increase from 1979 to 2050. The Central Asians, who at present comprise roughly 12 per cent of the Soviet population, will account for 46 per cent of total population growth in the Soviet Union to the year 2000 and 69 per cent of all growth over the projection period.

In the median and low scenarios, the Central Asian population continues to grow through the year 2050, after fertility has dropped to the replacement level, while the same is true of European nationalities during the early portions of the projection period. The phenomenon in which a population with a history of growth continues to grow at rates higher than implied by its

Ward Kingkade

current fertility was first designated by the term 'population momentum' by Keyfitz [1971], who analysed the case of a growing population whose fertility drops suddenly to replacement. A population with a heritage of high fertility will possess an age distribution which ensures increases in the population in the reproductive ages for a considerable period of time, and will continue to grow for at least a generation after fertility has fallen to replacement. To assess the effect of population momentum on the future ethnic composition of the Soviet population is the motivation behind the replacement scenario, under which the fertility levels of all nationalities are held constant at replacement from 1985 onwards. Under this scenario growth continues throughout the projection period, albeit at declining rates, in every nationality category. As expected, the greatest momentum is exhibited by Central Asians, whose population would double even in this incredible scenario. For European nationalities the replacement scenario is less far-fetched; what is surprising is the magnitude of the gains accruing to these nationalities. Even Russians, whose fertility has been below replacement for over 20 years, would multiply by a factor of 22 per cent. Clearly, in both the European and non-European segments of the Soviet population, momentum inherited from the past acts to deter population decline and provides a favorable setting for policies intended to stimulate population growth.

Draftage Population

The ethnic composition of the draftage population is of particular interest. One begins to appreciate its significance in the Soviet context by noting that the (Russian) language of the armed forces is the native tongue to only a minority of current recruits. While Russians comprised a majority of draftage cohorts in the 1970 census, they are estimated to have become a minority by 1979. Brezhnev's appeal to the 25th Party Congress and the ensuing population policy debate were more than casually related to this trend.

Table 5.6 presents projected numbers of draftage males under alternative fertility scenarios. This cohort, whose size is estimated to have declined by 20 per cent from 1979 to 1985, is projected to recover over the remainder of the century. By 2000, according to the projections, the number of 18 year-old males will have returned to roughly its 1979 level. What happens thereafter is highly dependent on the course of fertility in the near future. Under constant or high fertility and in the related synthetic scenarios, substantial growth would occur. In the low-fertility scenario, on the other hand, the draftage population shrinks by one third over the rest of the projection period. The median scenario features sizeable fluctuations, with a modest overall decline as of 2050.

The evolving ethnic make-up of the draftage population reflects the complex interplay of fertility differentials and trends as well as the initial population composition. Figure 5.6 illustrates the range of possibilities for the

68

numbers of Russian and Central Asian draftage males. With constant fertility (of the order of 3 children per parent) Central Asians would eventually overwhelm Russians even if the fertility of the latter were significantly higher than its present level. Under the median scenario, the relative sizes of the Russian and Central Asian draftage cohorts converge from the 1979 origin, in which 18 year-old Russian males outnumber their Central Asian counterparts by 3 to 1, to arrive at a ratio of 1.26 to 1 in 2050. The size of the absolute difference shrinks from three quarters of a million 18 year old males in 1979 to 200 thousand in 2050. The momentum of the Central Asian population can be inferred from the replacement scenario. Although this scenario represents a higher fertility trajectory for Europeans than the median scenario, the gap between the Russian and Central Asian draftage cohorts in 2050 remains about the same as in 1979.

According to our projections, the ethnic breakdown of draftage males will evolve gradually from its present condition, in which two thirds are European with half of the remainder Central Asian, to a situation in 2010 where 40 per cent of 18 year-old males are non-European and one in four are Central Asian. By the end of the projection period, Europeans in the median scenario account for slightly more than half the number of draftage males, 30 per cent of whom are Central Asian, at which time the Russian plurality begins to be jeopardized. This implies a country very different from the Soviet Union we know today.

In order to halt the decline in the European share of the draftage population, it would be necessary to increase the fertility of Europeans substantially while reducing fertility in other nationalities. Under the extreme scenario of high European fertility combined with replacement fertility for other nationalities, the European and Russian numerical predominance in the draftage population is reasserted. Nevertheless, the small magnitude and slow rate of growth in the corresponding proportions indicate the limits to even the most radical differentiated population policy.

Working Age Population

Future trends in the working age population, consisting of men ages 16–59 and women ages 16–54 according to long-standing Soviet legislation, are examined in Table 5.7. Persons born during the projection period do not begin to enter the working ages until 2000, so that the scenarios do not differ before that date. Because the size of the Soviet labour force depends on the working age population, short term trends in this population segment have obvious impacts on the Soviet economy. The fact that non-European nationalities account for the current growth in the working age population of the Soviet Union, whose European working age population is currently declining, deserves special emphasis. Concern about this has undoubtedly been one source of impetus for the development of the system of fertility incentives.

Ward Kingkade

The projected recovery around 1995 is more apparent than real, resulting in the main from a temporary decline in numbers leaving the working ages, as the small cohorts born during the Second World War and the immediate postwar years reach retirement age. The rise in fertility in the 1980s exercises a more modest effect.

Differences between fertility scenarios begin to impact the working age population after the close of this century. Under the median fertility assumptions, the working age population of European nationalities is projected to decline from the year 2005 onwards, totalling about 8 million less in 2050 than in 1979. The Central Asian working age population, in contrast, grows by 44 million, which represents almost a fivefold increase. A permanent rise in European fertility above the replacement level would reverse the decline in the able bodied population of European nationalities, as the high scenario demonstrates. Decline in the European share of the working age population seems inescapable, however. Even if the fertility of all non-European nationalities were suddenly brought to replacement, the fertility of European nationalities would have to rise to levels above the high scenario to avert a decline in the European share of the working age population.

Age Composition

An important set of consequences of variations in fertility with implications for economic growth pertains to their effect on the population's age composition. Fertility at Third World levels generates a burden of young dependents who must be supported by the productivity of the adult population. At the opposite extreme, the below-replacement fertility experience of many Western countries today raises the disturbing prospect of an excess of elderly. Both cases are represented among Soviet nationalities.

Changes in the age distributions of various nationalities are examined in terms of these broad categories in Table 5.8. In each scenario, the working age share of the population declines in the Soviet Union as a whole and among Europeans in particular. The pension age share of the European population increases in every scenario, registering the unavoidable outcome of the decline of fertility to the replacement level prior to the beginning of the projection period. As the high scenario reveals, a rise in fertility would lessen the aging of the European population largely at the cost of greater young age dependency.

The working age share of the Central Asian population increases in every scenario in which Central Asian fertility falls. Under constant fertility the working age fraction of Central Asians would decline. In the median scenario, the age distributions of Europeans and Central Asians converge remarkably from quite dissimilar starting points. Whereas in 1979 more than 18 per cent of Central Asians would have to be redistributed into other age groups in order to reproduce the European distribution, by 2050 this share would have fallen to 5.5 per cent.

The Labour Force

The economic impact of population trends is closely related to the size and composition of the labour force. Projecting the economically active population is simply a matter of applying one or more schedules of labour force participation rates to a projected base population. The rates employed in the present analysis are shown in Table 5.9. In many adult ages, the rates were close to 100 per cent as of 1979, reflecting the Soviet régime's commitment to full employment as well as its generous definition of economic activity. Central Asians exhibit lower activity rates than do others in most age categories. The higher Central Asian rates for 16–19 year-olds are consistent with the lower than average educational levels of Central Asians, which imply earlier entry into the labour force on the part of Central Asians in comparison to other Soviet nationalities. Among older males, the predominantly rural Central Asians are less susceptible to mandatory retirement regulations and more apt to engage in private agriculture (a traditional element of the Soviet economy) than their counterparts in the European nationalities of the Soviet Union. Over the projection period, modest increases in economic activity levels have been assumed for all nationalities.

Table 5.10 presents the projected economically active populations for the various nationality groups at four points spanning the projection period. In each fertility scenario the economically active population of every group is greater in 2050 than in 1979. Prospects for the near future appear significantly brighter than what was suggested by trends in able-bodied populations. Under median fertility the economically active population of European nationalities is projected to increase between 1979 and the year 2000 by 13 million persons, or 22 per cent of its 1979 size, despite the negligible growth of the European working age population over this time. The projected increase among Central Asians is almost as large, practically doubling their labour force by 2000.

In the long-run, fertility trends exercise their inevitable effects on the trajectory of the economically active population. After 2025 the European labour force declines in the median- and low-fertility scenarios. Central Asian population growth ultimately acquires a dominant role. Even when projected with fertility constant at the replacement level, the Central Asian labour force would triple in size from 1979 to 2050. Under median fertility, a sixfold increase in the Central Asian economically active population, from 11 to 67 million, is projected. According to this scenario, the Central Asian fraction of the Soviet labour force would rise from its 1979 level of 7 per cent to 27 per cent in 2050, at which date the combined European share would comprise only 41 per cent of the USSR's labour force. A sustained rise in European fertility, combined with replacement fertility among other nationalities, would eventually reverse the convergence in economically active populations. In this case, the Russian share would still be lower and the Central Asian share higher in 2050 than in 1979.

From an economic standpoint, it is appropriate to compare the contribution of a group to the national economy with the resources its members consume. A rough indication of these relations in the Soviet case can be obtained from the total labour force participation rates in Table 5.10, which relate the sizes of the economically active populations of the various nationalities to their total populations. Because the economically active population contains some members in the pension ages but excludes children under 16, the total labour force participation rate is inversely related to the level of fertility. The lower rates for Central Asians relative to other nationality groups in Table 5.10 reflect the smaller weight of the working ages in the Central Asian population as much as differences in labour force participation. With declining fertility, the economically active share of the total population rises among all nationalities. Under most scenarios the Central Asian and European ratios converge to similar values by 2050. The exceptions are the scenarios involving constant Central Asian fertility, in which case the mounting dependency burden offsets the effect of increases in economic activity rates among these nationalities. Ultimately this would bring about a deterioration in the all-Union index, as Figures 5.7 and 5.8 illustrate.

CONCLUSION

The Soviet economy is being confronted with a reduction in the growth of its manpower resources that will persist for the near future. Economic growth in this situation requires more efficient utilisation of available labour. The current demographic circumstances are exacerbated by the fact that a substantial share of foreseeable increases in labour resources will be contributed by the non-European Soviet nationalities. While the European nationalities of the Soviet Union have had fertility levels at or below replacement for some time, the reproduction rates of Soviet Central Asians are high by Third World standards. As a result of this heritage, the non-European population of the Soviet Union will continue to grow well into the 21st century. Without a major rise in fertility among European Soviet nationalities, permanent decline in their fraction of the population is inevitable. The loss of the Russian majority appears unavoidable without appreciable assimilation of non-Russians.

Although fertility has risen in the European parts of the Soviet Union under the pro-natalist fertility policy adopted in 1981, a much greater increase would have to occur in order to achieve a lasting effect on the national composition of the population. Population momentum has forced

China to adopt its one-child family policy to curb population growth. Equally radical measures, such as a ban on abortions in European areas, coupled with comprehensive dissemination of fertility control in Central Asia, would be necessary to maintain the European share of the Soviet population. It is doubtful that anything of this kind would be politically or economically tenable.

The eventual rise in the Central Asian share of the Soviet population and labour force means that an increasing proportion of the Soviet Union's manpower will be drawn from areas which at present are poorly equipped to efficiently employ the potential of their human resources. Soviet discussions often refer to the 'excess' of underutilised Central Asian labour reserves. To convert this predominantly rural stratum of the population, illiterate in Russian as its members are, into an industrial labour force will require significant investments in educational facilities.

Thus far, efforts to encourage out-migration of natives from Central Asia have had little success. The alternative, redirecting investment into the region, is likely to incur resentment on the part of the European population. The current emphasis on subordination of local interests to the priorities of the national economy is being asserted at a time when non-European native elites are sensing the potential impact inherent in their increasing numbers. Thanks to *glasnost'*, we are now receiving more concrete accounts of the friction these forces engender.

Notes

1. The TFR represents the sum of the age-specific fertility rates over all ages of the childbearing period, and is therefore a standardised (age-adjusted) rate where the standard is a uniform distribution [Shryock et al., 1975, p. 484].
2. It should be kept in mind that the official fertility series are reported for union republics. The trends in the official data examined in the present discussion should be indicative of trends in fertility for nationalities.
3. Romania's TFR in 1965 was 1.9 [David, 1982, p. 15]. Soon after abortion restrictions were introduced in 1966, fertility rose spectacularly, attaining a TFR of 3.7 in 1967. This was followed by a precipitous decline until the early 1970's, after which the TFR stabilised in the 2.4–2.7 range. After 1980, Romanian fertility began to decline significantly, dropping below replacement levels in 1983 [Monnier, 1985, p. 757]. However, fertility has risen subsequently to a TFR of 2.3 (unpublished CIR estimate) in 1985 in conjunction with a governmental campaign to stiffen enforcement of the abortion legislation initiated in 1984 [*Radio Free Europe*, 1984, pp. 33–35]. Additional measures were introduced in 1986 [*Radio Free Europe*, 1986, pp. 19–22], with the potential to further increase fertility.
4. The projections were conducted in 1986, at which time the most current Soviet fertility schedules referred to the 1983–84 period. Data received subsequently indicate a slight upturn in the period fertility levels of the three Central Asian republics where the indigenous nationalities predominate starting in 1984–85

(see Figure 5.2). The magnitude and duration of this increase thus far do not warrant revision of the projections at the present time.

5. This has been guided by the notion that it is preferable to interpolate within the range of known experience than to extrapolate. In terms of mortality, the Soviet Union lags sufficiently behind the most progressive countries to permit this approach. The mortality schedule reported for Japan in 1981 [United Nations, 1982, pp. 400–401], with life expectancies at birth of 73.91 for males and 79.16 for females, has been chosen to represent target mortality for 2015.

6. Convergence was set for the year 2015 in order to conform to assumptions made in the Center for International Research (CIR)'s projections of the population of the Soviet Union as a whole [Kingkade, 1987, pp. 12–13].

7. The dramatic upsurge of emigration from the Soviet Union in the late 1980s can potentially have a significant impact on the populations of Soviet Jews and Germans, particularly if they are assumed to predominate in the emigration stream. For the larger aggregates distinguished in the present report, however, this effect is much less important.

Bibliography

Anderson, B and B Silver, 1984. 'Permanent and Present Populations in Soviet Statistics.' *Brown University Population Studies and Training Center Working Paper No. WP-84-06.*

Andreyev, Ye M, 1979. 'Prodolzhitel'nost' zhizni v SSSR: Differentsial'nyy analiz,' in Ye M Andreyev, and A G Vishnevskiy (Eds.), *Prodolzhitel'nost' zhizni: Analiz i modelirovaniye.* (Moscow: Statistika), pp. 7–30.

Andreyev, Ye M and V M Dobrovol'skaya, 1979. 'Ob odnom metode izucheniya krivykh dozhitiy,' in Ye M Andreyev, and A G Vishnevskiy (Eds), *Prodolzhitel'nost' zhizni: Analiz i modelirovaniye.* (Moscow: Statistika, pp. 80–103.)

Bakuskiy, S V, 1984. *Sotsial'no-ekonomicheskiye problemy demograficheskogo razvitiya Moldavskoy SSR.* (Kishinev, Shtiintsa).

Baldwin, G S, 1979. *Population Projections by Age and Sex: For the Republics and Major Economic Regions of the USSR 1970 to 2000.* U S Bureau of the Census, International Population Reports, Series P-91, No. 26. (Washington, D.C.: U S Government Printing Office).

——, 1973. *Estimates and Projections of the Population of the USSR by Age and Sex: 1950-2000.* U S Bureau of the Census, International Population Reports, Series P-91, No. 23. (Washington, D.C.: U S Government Printing Office).

Bednyy, M S, 1979. *Mediko-demograficheskoye izucheniye narodonaseleniya.* (Moscow: Statistika).

Belitsr, V N, N I Vorob'yev, and L N Terent'yev et al., 1964. *Narody yevropeyskoy chasti SSR. Tom II.* (Moscow: Nauka).

Belova, V, G Bondarskaya, and L Darskiy, 1983: 'Dinamika i differentsiatsiya rozhdayemosti,' *Vestnik statistiki,* No. 12, December, pp. 14–24.

Bennett, N and L Garson, 1983. 'The Centenerian Question and Old Age Mortality in the Soviet Union,' *Demography,* Vol. 20, No. 4, pp. 587–606.

Bondarskaya, G A, 1985. 'Rozhdayemost' u narodov SSSR,' in E K Vasiliyeva (Ed.), *Sto natsii i narodnostey.* (Moscow: Mysl'), pp. 19–30.

——, 1977. *Rozhdayemost' v SSSR.* (Moscow: Statistika).

The Future Population of the Soviet Union

Brackett, J, 1964. *Projections of the Population of the USSR by Age and Sex: 1964–1985.* International Population Report, Series P-91, No. 13. (Washington, D.C.: US Government Printing Office).

Bromley, Yu V, I S Gurvich, and V I Kozlov et al., 1977. *Sovremenyye etnicheskiye protsessy v SSSR.* (Moscow: Nauka).

Brunner, E, 1981. *Soviet Demographic Trends and the Ethnic Composition of Draft Age Males, 1980–1995.* (Santa Monica: The Rand Corporation).

Burmin, L. S, N I Kim, and V I Kirchenko, 1981. 'Dolgoletiye i prodolzhitel'nost' zhizni naseleniya Kirgizskoy SSR,' *Zdravookhraneniye Kirgizii,* No. 2, pp. 7–12.

Coale, A J, B A Anderson, and E Harm, 1979. *Human Fertility in Russia Since the Nineteenth Century.* Princeton, N.J.: Princeton University Press.

Crisostomo, Rosemarie, 1983. *The Demographic Dilemma of the Soviet Union.* International Research Document No. 10. (Washington, D.C.: U S Bureau of the Census, Center for International Research).

David, H P, 1982. 'Eastern Europe: Pronatalist Policies and Private Behavior,' *Population Bulletin,* 36(6).

——, 1970. *Family Planning and Abortion in the Socialist Countries of Central and Eastern Europe.* (New York: The Population Council).

David, H P, and R J McIntyre, 1981. *Reproductive Behavior: Central and Eastern European Experience.* (New York: Springer).

Di Maio, A J, 1981. 'Contemporary Soviet Population Problems' in H Desfosses (Ed.), *Soviet Population Policy.* (New York: Pergammon Press, pp. 16–43).

Ekonomicheskaya gazeta, No. 43, 1986. 'Naseleniye SSSR,' pp. 6–7.

Feshbach, Murray, 1985. 'The Age Structure of the Soviet Population: Preliminary Analysis of Unpublished Data,' *Soviet Economy,* No. 2, pp. 177–193.

——, 1982. 'The Soviet Union: Population Trends and Dilemmas,' *Population Bulletin,* Vol. 37, No. 3.

Freedman, R O, 1984. *Soviet Jewry in the Decisive Decade, 1971–1980.* (Durham, NC: Duke University Press).

Gamzayan, G S, 1979. 'O sovremennykh tendentsiyakh smertnosti i sredney prodolzhitel'nosti zhizni v Azerbaydzhanskoy SSR,' *Izvestia Akademii nauk Azerbaydzhanskoy SSR, seriya ekonomika,* No. 1, pp. 74–80.

Goskomstat SSSR (Gosudarstvennyy komitet SSSR po statistike). 1988a. *Narodnoye khozyaystvo SSSR v 1987 g.: Statisticheskiy yezhegodnik.* (Moscow: Finansy i statistika).

——, 1988b. *Naseleniye SSSR 1987.* (Moscow: Finansy i statistika).

Guboglo, M N 1984. *Sovremennyye etnoyazykovyye protsessy v SSSR.* (Moscow: Nauka).

Heer, D, 1981a. 'Fertility and Female Work Status in the USSR,' in Helen Desfosses (Ed.), *Soviet Population Policy.* New York: Pergamon Press, pp. 62–94.

——, 1981b. 'Soviet Population Policy: Four Model Futures,' in H Desfosses (Ed.), *Soviet Population Policy.* (New York: Pergamon Press), pp. 124–154.

Isayev, M I, 1970. *Sto tridtsat' ravnopravnykh.* (Moscow: Nauka).

Izvestiya, May 23, 1985. 'Zakon protiv p'yanstva,' p. 3.

Jones, E, 1985. *Red Army and Society.* (Boston: Allen and Unwin).

Karakhanov, M K, 1983. *Nekapitalisticheskiy put' razvitiya i problemy narodonaseleniya.* (Tashkent: FAN).

Keyfitz, N, 1971. 'On the Momentum of Population Growth,' *Demography,* Vol. 8, No. 1, pp. 71–80.

Ward Kingkade

Keyfitz, N and W Flieger, 1971. *Population: The Facts and Methods of Demography.* (San Francisco: W H Freeman & Sons).

Kingkade, W Ward, 1987. *Estimates and Projections of the Population of the USSR: 1979 to 2025.* CIR Staff Paper No. 33. (Washington, D C: U S Bureau of the Census, Center for International Research).

——, 1985. *Evaluation of Selected Soviet Population Statistics.* CIR Staff Paper No. 9. (Washington, D C: U S Bureau of the Census, Center for International Research).

Kirdyakin, V D and G G Fayzulin, 1974. *Rost narodonaseleniya i formirovaniye trudovykh resursov Moldavskoy SSR.* (Kishinev: Karta molodovenyaske).

Kommunist, No. 4, 1986. 'Programma Kommunisticheskoy Partii Sovetskogo Soyuza,' pp. 99–152.

Kozlov, V I, 1982. *Natsional'nosti SSSR: Etnodemograficheskiy obzor.* Second edition. (Moscow: Finansy i statistika).

Kvasha, A Ya, 1978. 'Demograficheskaya situatsiya i demograficheskaya politika,' *Ekonomicheskiye nauki*, No. 2, pp. 47–54.

——, 1970. 'Ob optimal'nom tipe vosproizvodstva naseleniya SSSR,' in A G Volkov, L Ye Darskiy, and A Ya Kvasha (Eds.), *Voprosy demografii.* (Moscow: Statistika), pp. 33–47.

Land, K C, 1986. 'Methods for National Population Forecasts: A Review,' *Journal of the American Statistical Association*, 81(386), December, pp. 888–901.

Lewis, R S, R H Rowland, and R S Clem, 1976. *Nationality and Population Change in Russia and the USSR.* (New York: Praeger).

Litvinova, G I, 1978. 'Vozdeystviye gosudarstva i prava na demograficheskiye protsessy,' *Sovetskoye gosudarstvo i pravo*, No. 1, pp. 132–136.

Merrick, Thomas W, 1986. 'World Population in Transition,' *Population Bulletin*, Vol. 41, No. 2.

Meyer, H E, 1978. 'The Coming Soviet Ethnic Crisis,' *Fortune*, August 14, pp. 156–166.

Monnier, A, 1985. 'La conjoncture demographique: l'Europe et les pays sous-developpes d'outre-mer,' *Population* 40(4–5), pp. 749–763.

Mullyadzhanov, I R, 1983. *Demograficheskoye razvitiye Uzbekskoy SSR.* (Tashkent: Izdatel'stvo Uzbekistan).

Myers, R J, 1964. 'Analysis of Mortality in the Soviet Union According to 1958–59 Life Tables,' *Transactions of the Society of Actuaries*, Vol. 16, pp. 309–317.

Narkhoz 85. Tsentral'noye statisticheskoye upravleniye (TsSU) pri Sovete Ministrov SSSR. *Narodnoye khozyaystvo SSSR v 1985 godu: statisticheskiy yezhegodnik.* (Moscow: Finansy i statistika, 1986).

Narodnoye obrazovaniye, No. 1, 1981. 'O vypolnenii rekomendatsiy Tashkentskoy nauchno-teoreticheskoy konferentsii po russkomu yazyku,' p. 96.

Osnovnyye napravleniya, ekonomicheskogo i sotsial'nogo razvitiya SSSR na 1986–1990 godov i na period do 2000 goda, 1986. (Moscow: Politizdat).

Pipes, R, 1975. 'Introduction: The Nationality Problem,' in Z Katz, R Rogers, and F Harned (Eds.), *Handbook of Major Soviet Nationalities.* (New York: The Free Press), pp. 1–5.

Polyakov, I V et al., 1984. 'Nekotoryye osobennosti smertnosti naseleniya krupnogo goroda,' *Zdravookhraneniye Rossiskoy federatsii*, No. 4, pp. 16–19.

Ponomarev, B I, 1982. *Konstitutsiya SSSR: Politiko-pravovy kommentariy.* (Moscow: Politizdat).

The Future Population of the Soviet Union

Postanovleniye Soveta Ministrov SSSR, 1985. 'O merakh po preodoleniyu piyanstva i alkogolizma iskoreniyu samogonovareniya,' 7 May.

Postanovleniye Ts K KPSS i Soveta Ministrov SSSR, 1981. 'O merakh po usileniyu gosudarstvennoy pomoshchi semyam imeyushchim detey,' in *KPSS v resolyutsiyakh i resheniyakh syezdov, konferentsy i plenumov Tsk, 14, 1980–81*, pp. 125–132.

Preston, S H, N Keyfitz, and R Schoen, 1972. *Causes of Death.* (New York: Seminar Press).

Radio Free Europe Research, February 14, 1986. 'New Moves to Boost the Birthrate,' pp. 19–22.

——, April 19, 1984. 'A Bleak Demographic Picture,' pp. 33–35.

Ryabushkin, T V and R A Galetskaya, 1983. *Naseleniye i Sotsialisticheskoye Obshchestvo.* (Moscow: Finansy i statistika).

Ryzhkov, N I, 1986. Ob osnovnykh napravleniyakh ekonomicheskogo i sotsial'nogo razvitiya SSSR na 1986–1990 gody i na period do 2000 goda: Doklad XXVII s"yezdu KPSS, 3 marta 1986 g. (Moscow: Politizdat).

Serenko, A F, and V V Yermakov, 1984. *Sotsial'naya gigiyena i organizatsiya zdravookhraneniya.* Second edition. (Moscow: Meditsina).

Shakhot'ko, L P, 1985. *Vosproizvodstvo naseleniya Belorusskoy SSR.* (Minsk: Nauka i tekhnika).

Shamsutdinova, S, 1981. 'Yazyk druzhby i sotrudnichestva narodov SSSR,' *Narodnoye obrazovaniye*, No. 1, pp. 48–50.

Shryock, H S, J S Siegel, and Associates, 1975. *The Methods and Materials of Demography.* U S Bureau of the Census, third printing (revised). (Washington, D.C.: U S Government Printing Office).

Sidorov, K, 1975. 'Dinamika rozhdayemosti i plodovitosti v Chuvashskoy ASSR,' *Vestnik statistiki*, No. 1, January, pp. 34–39.

Solchanyk, R, 1982. 'Soviet Language Policy: Two Steps Forward, One Step Back,' *Radio Liberty Research*, RL 47/82, January 28.

Spencer, G, 1984. *Projections of the Population of the United States by Age, Sex, and Race: 1983 to 2080.* U S Bureau of the Census, Current Population Reports, Series P-25, No. 952. (Washington, D C: U S Government Printing Office).

Stetsenko, S G and I V Kozachenko, 1984. *Demograficheskaya statistika*, (Kiev: Vishchashkola).

Stetshenko, V S, L V Chuyko, and A F Zagrobskaya et al., 1977. *Demograficheskoye razvitiye Ukrainskoy SSR.* (Kiev: Naukova Dumka).

Tadzhiyev, Ya T and M A Avazor, 1985. 'Tendentsii v sostoyanii zdoroviya naseleniya Tadzhikskoy SSR,' *Zdravookhraneniya Tadzhikistana*, No. 6, pp. 63–70.

Tatimov, M B, 1978. *Razvitiye narodonaseleniya i demograficheskaya politika.* (Alma-Ata: Izdatel'stvo 'Nauka' Kazakhskoy SSR).

TsSU SSSR (Tsentral'noye statisticheskoye upravleniye pri Sovete Ministrov SSSR), 1984. *Chislennost i sostav naseleniya SSSR po dannym Vsesoyuznoy perepisi naseleniya 1979 goda.* (Moscow: Finansy i statistika).

——, 1975. *Naseleniye SSSR 1973.* (Moscow: Statistika).

——, 1973. *Itogi Vsesoyuznoy perepisi naseleniya 1970 goda. Tom IV.* (Moscow: Statistika).

——, 1963. *Itogi Vsesoyuznoy perepisi naseleniya 1959 goda. RSFSR.* (Moscow: Gosstatizdat).

Ward Kingkade

——, 1962. *Itogi Vsesoyuznoy perepisi naseleniya 1959 goda. SSSR.* (Moscow: Gosstatizdat).

Ukaz Preziduma Verkhovnogo Soveta SSSR, 1985. 'Ob usilenii bor'by s p'yanstvom,' *Vedomosti Verkhovnogo soveta SSSR*, No. 21, pp. 320–323.

United Nations, Department of Economic and Social Affairs, 1982. *Demographic Yearbook 1982.* (New York: United Nations).

——, 1973. *The Determinants and Consequences of Population Trends*, Vol. I. (New York: United Nations).

——, 1961. *Demographic Yearbook 1961.* (New York: United Nations).

United Nations, Population Division, 1986. *Population Newsletter*, July.

Urlanis, B Ts, 1980. 'Demograficheskaya nauka i demograficheskaya politika,' *Vestnik Akademii nauk SSSR*, No. 1, pp. 41–49.

——, 1978. *Narodonaseleniya stran mira: Spravochnik.* Second edition. (Moscow: Statistika).

Urlanis, B Ts and V A Borisov, 1984. *Narodonaseleniye stran mira: Spravochnik.* Third edition. (Moscow: Finansy i statistika).

——, 1983. *Narodonaseleniya stran mira.* (Moscow: Finansy i statistika).

U S Bureau of the Census. Unpublished component projections.

U S Bureau of the Census, Center for International Research. Unpublished data.

U S Department of State. Unpublished data.

Vestnik statistiki, No. 11, 1985. 'Yestestvennoye dvizheniye naseleniya v SSSR,' November, pp. 77–80.

——, No. 11, 1984. 'Yestestvennoye dvizheniye naseleniya v SSSR,' November, pp. 75–79.

——, No. 12, 1983. 'Yestestvennoye dvizheniye naseleniya v SSSR,' December, pp. 51–55.

Virganskaya, I M, 1984. 'K voprosu o predstoyashchey prodolzhitel'nosti zhizni v trudosposobnom vozraste,' *Zdravookhraneniye Rossiskoy federatsii*, No. 7, pp. 24–27.

Vishnevskiy, A G and A G Volkov, 1983. *Vosproizvodstvo naseleniya SSSR.* (Moscow: Finansy i statistika).

Yakimov, V I, 1972. *Rayonnyye osobennosti vosproizvodstva naseleniya SSSR: Materialy Vsesoyuznogo mezhvuzskogo nauchnogo simposiuma.* (Cheboksary).

Weber, C and A Goodman, 1981. 'The Demographic Policy Debate in the USSR,' *Population and Development Review*, Vol. 7, No. 2, pp. 279–295.

The Future Population of the Soviet Union

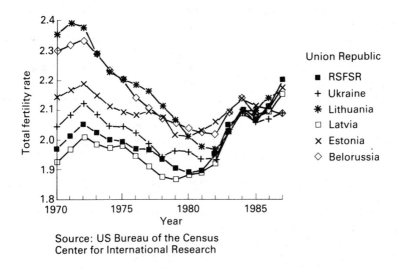

Source: US Bureau of the Census
Center for International Research

FIGURE 5.1   Fertility Levels of Union Republics: European Union Republics

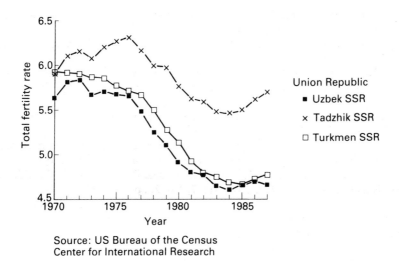

Source: US Bureau of the Census
Center for International Research

FIGURE 5.2   Fertility Levels of Union Republics: Central Asian Union Republics

79

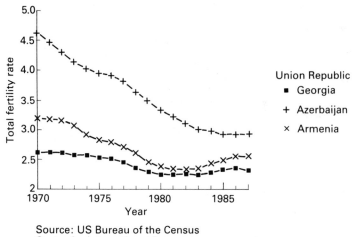

Source: US Bureau of the Census
Center for International Research

FIGURE 5.3   Fertility Levels of Union Republics: Transcaucasian Union Republics

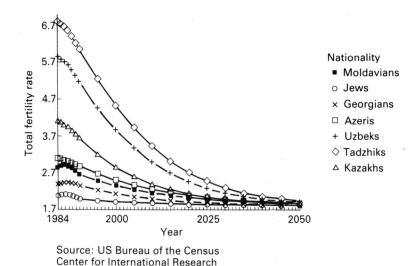

Source: US Bureau of the Census
Center for International Research

FIGURE 5.4   Projected Fertility Levels of Soviet Nationalities: Median Series, 1984–2050

80

The Future Population of the Soviet Union

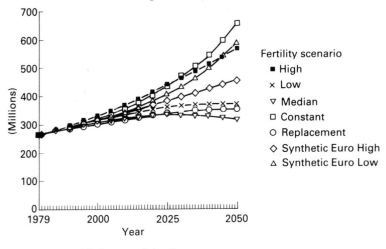

Fertility scenario
- ■ High
- × Low
- ▽ Median
- □ Constant
- ○ Replacement
- ◇ Synthetic Euro High
- △ Synthetic Euro Low

Source: US Bureau of the Census
Center for International Research

FIGURE 5.5   USSR: Projected Total Population

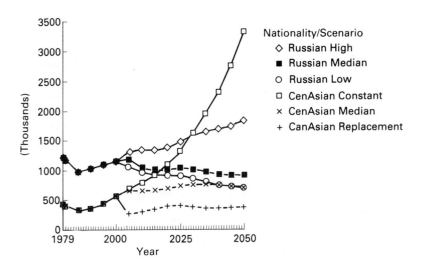

Nationality/Scenario
- ◇ Russian High
- ■ Russian Median
- ○ Russian Low
- □ CenAsian Constant
- × CenAsian Median
- + CanAsian Replacement

FIGURE 5.6   USSR: Draft Age Males by Nationality

81

Ward Kingkade

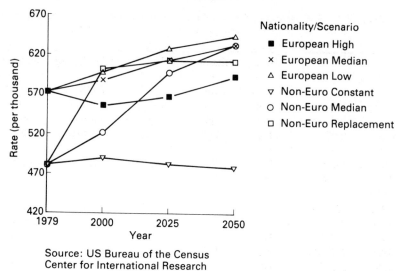

Source: US Bureau of the Census
Center for International Research

FIGURE 5.7   Economically Active Population Per Thousand Total Population

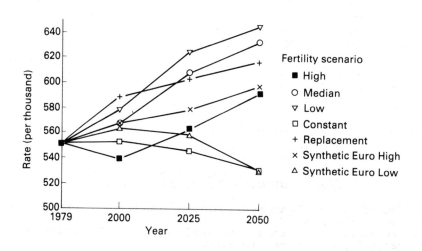

FIGURE 5.8   Economically Active Population Per Thousand Total Population

82

TABLE 5.1   Estimated and Projected Population Growth, USSR 1950–2020
Median Fertility

Year	Total population			Working age population		
	Midyear population (000s)	Average annual increment (000s)	Growth rate (per 000)	Midyear population (000s)	Average annual increment (000s)	Growth rate (per 000)
1950	180,526	3,225	17.10	103,345	2,263	20.76
1955	196,650	3,643	17.71	114,658	960	8.20
1960	214,865	3,330	14.92	119,459	937	7.69
1965	231,514	2,252	9.50	124,142	1,726	13.44
1970	242,774	2,397	9.63	132,774	2,252	16.27
1975	254,756	2,346	9.00	144,035	2,090	14.00
1980	266,488	2,662	9.75	154,484	594	3.81
1985	279,797	2,596	9.07	157,454	607	3.82
1990	292,775	2,170	7.28	160,491	738	4.54
1995	303,626	2,016	6.53	164,180	1,735	10.29
2000	313,705	1,928	6.05	172,853	2,273	12.73
2005	323,347	2,018	6.15	184,220	1,082	5.79
2010	333,438	1,977	5.84	189,629	410	2.15
2015	343,323	1,765	5.08	191,678	346	1.80
2020	352,147	1,510	4.24	193,407	819	4.19
2025	359,695	1,055	2.91	197,500	926	4.63
2030	364,971	656	1.79	202,130	452	2.22
2035	368,250	319	.86	204,389	− 155	− .76
2040	369,844	136	.37	203,615	− 562	− 2.78
2045	370,522			200,804		

Note: Sources for Figures 5.1 to 5.3

The TFRs were calculated as five times the sums of the age-specific fertility rates for republics and dates in the sources listed below.
The data are reported as 2-year averages centered on January 1. The TFRs derived from these data are plotted against the midpoint dates in the figures.

Sources:
1970–75: B Ts Urlanis, *Narodonaseleniye stran mira: Spravochnik.* Second edition. (Moscow: Statistika, 1978), pp. 75–78.
1976–81: B Ts Urlanis and V A Borisov. *Narodonaseleniye stran mira: Spravochnik.* Third edition. (Moscow: Finansy i statistika, 1984), pp. 41–44.
1982: 'Yestestvennoye dvizheniye naseleniya v SSSR,' *Vestnik statistiki,* No. 12, 1983, p. 52.
1983: 'Yestestvennoye dvizheniye naseleniya v SSSR,' *Vestnik statistiki,* No. 11, 1984, p. 76.
1984: 'Yestestvennoye dvizheniye naseleniya v SSSR,' *Vestnik statistiki,* No. 11, 1985, p. 78.
1985–87: Goskomstat SSSR, 1988b. *Naseleniye SSSR 1987,* pp. 211–214.

Ward Kingkade

TABLE 5.2   Official Life Expectancies at Birth for the USSR: 1968–86

Date	Both Sexes	Male	Female
1968–71	69.5	64.6	73.5
1971–72	69.5	64.5	73.6
1978–79	67.9	62.5	72.6
1983–84	67.9	62.6	72.8
1984–85	68.1	63.3	72.7
1985–86	69.0	64.2	73.3
1986–87	69.8	65.0	73.8

Source: Goskomstat SSSR (Gosudarstvennyy komitet SSSR po statistike), *Narodnoye khozyaystvo SSSR v 1987 godu: statisticheskiy yezhegodnik (The National Economy of the USSR in 1987: Statistical Yearbook).* (Moscow: Finansy i statistika, 1988a), p. 357; 'Smertnost' i srednyaya prodolzhitel'nost' zhizni naseleniya SSSR (1968–1971 gg.) (Mortality and Life Expectancy of the Population of the USSR [1968–1971]),' *Vestnik statistiki,* 2:94–95, February 1974.

TABLE 5.3   Soviet Life Expectancies at Birth, by Nationality and Sex: 1979

Nationality	Male	Female
USSR	62.45	72.77
Russians	62.96	73.12
Ukrainians	64.14	74.07
Belorussians	67.22	76.83
Moldavians	59.31	68.65
Kirgiz	56.47	66.12

Source and methodology:
The mortality schedule for the Soviet Union as a whole in 1979 has been estimated from registered deaths together with the age-sex distribution reported by Feshbach [1985, p. 179] using the procedure described in CIR Staff Paper No. 33 [Kingkade, 1987, pp. 25–32]. For Russians and Ukrainians, estimates of mortality derived from survival over the intercensal period 1959 to 1970 have been projected to 1979 with the age-sex-specific trends estimated for the Soviet Union. The mortality schedule for Belorussians has been constructed by subdividing Shakhot'ko's [1985, p. 76] republic mortality schedule by sex according to the sex ratios of the estimated USSR life table death rates.

Union republic data for Moldavia have been accepted as representing the mortality of the Moldavian nationality. Bakurskiy [1984, p. 33] reports indices of deaths by age for Moldavia which measure changes in age-specific mortality over the 1970's. These indices have been used to inflate the 1969–70 republic mortality schedule reported in Kirdyakin and Fayzulin [1974, p. 34]. The resulting mortality schedule has been smoothed and then subdivided by sex following the procedure employed for Belorussians.

Kirgiz comprise a minority of the population of the Kirgiz SSR, which includes sizeable subpopulations of European nationalities. The Kirgiz national mortality schedule has therefore been estimated on the assumption that the republic mortality profile represents a mixture of European and Central Asian mortality patterns. A mortality schedule for the Kirgiz SSR has been derived from age-sex-specific life expectancies excerpted by Burmin et al. [1981, p. 8] from their 1978–79 republic life table. The sex detail of these data indicates higher mortality among females than among males at ages 5–9. Such a pattern is seldom (if ever) seen where data are of good quality, but has been known to occur in data from Third World countries affected by reporting errors. For this reason the mortality schedule for the Kirgiz SSR has been estimated accepting the age pattern of the reported data while adopting the procedure used for Moldavians and Belorussians to provide sex detail. Given this republic mortality schedule, the Kirgiz national schedule has been estimated as a residual assuming that the republic schedule is an average, weighted by population shares, of the mortality schedules of the following nationalities: 1) Russians, 2) Ukrainians, 3) Belorussians, 4) Germans (given Belorussian mortality), and 5) Kirgiz. The resulting mortality schedule resembles the Moldavian schedule at younger ages but is appreciably lower at older ages, particularly ages over 60. This could be produced by a variety of causes other than actual mortality differentials, including variations in national composition between age groups as well as such errors as age misreporting and underregistration. Previous analyses have concluded that errors of the type described are present in official Soviet data [Bennett and Garson, 1983; Brackett, 1964; and Myers, 1964]. On this basis the Moldavian mortality pattern has been employed to extend the Kirgiz life table beyond age 60.

TABLE 5.4 Total Fertility Rates, by Nationality: 1969–84

Nationality	1969–70	1978–79	1983–84
USSR	2.389	2.285	2.412
Urban	1.941	1.877	1.996
Rural	3.182	3.240	3.515
Russians	1.971	1.902	2.083
Ukrainians	2.044	1.962	2.100
Lithuanians	2.354	2.067	2.091
Latvians	1.926	1.865	2.100
Estonians	2.143	2.014	2.134
Belorussians	2.298	2.058	2.141
Germans	2.298	2.058	2.141
Jews	1.877	1.877	1.996
Moldavians	2.755	2.551	2.712
Tatars	2.397	2.274	2.433
Chuvash	3.118	2.474	2.523
Georgians	2.493	2.294	2.282
Azeris	4.633	3.484	2.982
Armenians	3.195	2,460	2.422
Uzbeks	7.255	6.369	5.670
Kirgiz	6.669	6.394	5.829
Tadzhiks	7.285	7.286	6.604
Turkmen	7.507	6.937	6.093
Kazakhs	5.186	4.397	3.969

The Future Population of the Soviet Union

Note:

Total fertility rates in this table represent the number of children a woman would bear over her reproductive lifetime under the fertility schedule for the given year and nationality.

Source and methodology:

The Slavic and Baltic nationalities together with Armenians and Azeris have been assigned the fertility reported for their respective union republics [Urlanis and Borisov, 1983, pp. 41–44; *Vestnik statistiki*, 1983, p. 52; 1984, p. 76; and 1985, p. 78].

The fertility levels of Kirgiz, Tadzhiks, Turkmen, and Uzbeks have been derived from the fertility schedules reported by Karakhanov [1983, p. 139] for these nationalities as of 1970 and 1975. The 1975 fertility levels were projected to subsequent dates using the average trend for Uzbek, Tadzhik, and Turkmen SSRs.

Tatar fertility has been estimated as a weighted average of four geographic subpopulations residing in 1) the Tatar ASSR (TASSR), 2) elsewhere in the RSFSR, 3) Central Asia, and 4) elsewhere in USSR. The fertility level of Tatars residing in the TASSR in 1970 has been derived from the reported TASSR crude birth rate assuming that the non-Tatar population of the TASSR (51 per cent) had th average fertility reported for the RSFSR. Tatars living elsewhere in the RSFSR have been given the RSFSR fertility level, while Central Asians Tatars have been assigned the fertility level for urban areas of Uzbekistan – the only Central Asian republic for which urban-rural fertility detail is available in a form that eliminates the confounding effect of age structure [Mullyadzhanov, 1983, p. 239]. Tatars residing in the rest of the Soviet Union are predominantly urban, and have been assumed to experience the average fertility of the urban population of the USSR. The estimated Tatar fertility level for 1979 has been obtained by a parallel procedure. The fertility level for Tatars in the TASSR has been projected using the RSFSR trend. From 1979 onward the fertility level of Tatars has been projected employing the average trend for European Union republics.

Chuvash fertility in 1970 has been assumed to equal the fertility level reported for the Chuvash ASSR (CASSR) [Sidorov, 1975, p. 37]. The 1979 value has been obtained by extrapolating the 1959–70 trend for the CASSR. From 1979 onwards the methodology used for the Tatars has been employed.

For Jews, the fertility level of urban areas of the USSR in 1979 (which is approximately equal to that for urban areas of Ukraine in 1970) [Stetshenko et al., 1977, p. 129] has been adopted for the period through 1979. From 1979 onwards the fertility levels reported annually for urban areas of the USSR have been employed [Urlanis and Borisov, 1983, p. 40; *Vestnik statistiki*, 1983, p. 52; 1984, p. 76; and 1985, p. 78].

Germans have been assigned the fertility of Belorussians partly because of the similarity in levels or urbanization of these two nationalities in the two most recent censuses [Kozlov, 1982, p. 100], and partly on the empirical ground that this minimizes the discrepancies between the reported number of Germans in the 1979 Census and the number projected forward from the 1970 census (taking account of emigration).

The 1970 and 1979 fertility levels of Georgians, Kazakhz, and Moldavians have been derived as residuals from the reported union republic fertility levels, assuming the latter are weighted averages of national components and assigning to republic sub-populations the fertility level estimates for the corresponding nationalities whenever appropriate.

From 1979 onwards, fertility has been projected using the trends observed for republics in three regions: 1) Europe including the RSFSR; 2) Transcaucasia; and 3) the Central Asian republics whose indigenous nationalities predominate (Tadzhik SSR, Turkmen SSR, and Uzbek SSR).

TABLE 5.5 Projected Total Population in Major Nationality Groups, Various Fertility Scenarios (absolute figures in thousands)

	1980	1990	2000	2010
HIGH FERTILITY				
TOTAL	266,488	296,711	330,383	367,186
European	203,551	217,402	232,835	249,083
Slavic	191,463	204,510	218,888	233,994
Russian	139,124	149,117	159,844	171,227
Other Slavic	52,339	55,393	59,044	62,766
Other European	12,088	12,891	13,947	15,089
Central Asian	27,183	38,172	50,492	64,806
Other	35,753	41,138	47,056	53,297
Percentage of Population				
TOTAL	100.00	100.00	100.00	100.00
European	76.38	73.27	70.47	67.84
Slavic	71.85	68.93	66.25	63.73
Russian	52.21	50.26	48.38	46.63
Other Slavic	19.64	18.67	17.87	17.09
Other European	4.54	4.34	4.22	4.11
Central Asian	10.20	12.86	15.28	17.65
Other	13.42	13.86	14.24	14.51
MEDIAN FERTILITY				
TOTAL	266,488	292,775	313,705	333,438
European	203,551	214,592	220,421	224,613
Slavic	191,463	201,880	207,269	211,076
Russian	139,124	147,188	151,350	154,450
Other Slavic	52,339	54,693	55,919	56,626
Other European	12,088	12,711	13,152	13,536
Central Asian	27,183	37,802	49,071	61,050
Other	35,753	40,381	44,213	47,775
Percentage of Population				
TOTAL	100.00	100.00	100.00	100.00
European	76.38	73.30	70.26	67.36
Slavic	71.85	68.95	66.07	63.30
Russian	52.21	50.27	48.25	46.32
Other Slavic	19.64	18.68	17.83	16.98
Other European	4.54	4.34	4.19	4.06
Central Asian	10.20	12.91	15.64	18.31
Other	13.42	13.79	14.09	14.33

TABLE 5.5 – continued

	2020	2030	2040	2050
HIGH FERTILITY				
TOTAL	413,191	461,008	510,232	564,764
European	270,487	293,244	317,502	346,141
Slavic	253,848	274,948	297,438	324,062
Russian	186,027	201,513	217,839	237,254
Other Slavic	67,821	73,436	79,599	86,808
Other European	16,639	18,296	20,064	22,079
Central Asian	81,644	98,792	115,809	132,965
Other	61,059	68,972	76,921	85,658
Percentage of Population				
TOTAL	100.00	100.00	100.00	100.00
European	65.46	63.61	62.23	61.29
Slavic	61.44	59.64	58.29	57.38
Russian	45.02	43.71	42.69	42.01
Other Slavic	16.41	15.93	15.60	15.37
Other European	4.03	3.97	3.93	3.91
Central Asian	19.76	21.43	22.70	23.54
Other	14.78	14.96	15.08	15.17
MEDIAN FERTILITY				
TOTAL	352,147	364,971	369,844	370,192
European	227,353	226,766	222,077	215,926
Slavic	213,467	212,724	208,123	202,205
Russian	156,509	156,028	152,567	148,233
Other Slavic	56,958	56,696	55,556	53,972
Other European	13,886	14,042	13,954	13,722
Central Asian	73,641	84,649	93,233	99,589
Other	51,153	53,556	54,534	54,678
Percentage of Population				
TOTAL	100.00	100.00	100.00	100.00
European	64.56	62.13	60.05	58.33
Slavic	60.62	58.29	56.27	54.62
Russian	44.44	42.75	41.25	40.04
Other Slavic	16.17	15.53	15.02	14.58
Other European	3.94	3.85	3.77	3.71
Central Asian	20.91	23.19	25.21	26.90
Other	14.53	14.67	14.75	14.77

TABLE 5.5 – continued
(absolute figures in thousands)

	1980	1990	2000	2010
LOW FERTILITY				
TOTAL	266,488	290,380	307,720	321,793
European	203,551	212,843	216,581	217,459
Slavic	191,463	200,246	203,690	204,401
Russian	139,124	145,989	148,736	149,570
Other Slavic	52,339	54,257	54,954	54,831
Other European	12,088	12,597	1,891	13,058
Central Asian	27,183	37,310	47,488	57,911
Other	35,753	40,227	43,651	46,423
Percentage of Population				
TOTAL	100.00	100.00	100.00	100.00
European	76.38	73.30	70.38	67.58
Slavic	71.85	68.96	66.19	63.52
Russian	52.21	50.28	48.33	46.48
Other Slavic	19.64	18.68	17.86	17.04
Other European	4.54	4.34	4.19	4.06
Central Asian	10.20	12.85	15.43	18.00
Other	13.42	13.85	14.19	14.43
CONSTANT FERTILITY				
TOTAL	266,488	293,374	321,976	357,520
European	203,551	214,453	222,659	230,312
Slavic	191,463	201,754	209,345	216,317
Russian	139,124	147,119	152,913	158,351
Other Slavic	52,339	54,635	56,432	57,966
Other European	12,088	12,699	13,314	13,995
Central Asian	27,183	38,381	54,040	76,832
Other	35,753	40,540	45,277	50,376
Percentage of Population				
TOTAL	100.00	100.00	100.00	100.00
European	76.38	73.10	69.15	64.42
Slavic	71.85	68.77	65.02	60.50
Russian	52.21	50.15	47.49	44.29
Other Slavic	19.64	18.62	17.53	16.21
Other European	4.54	4.33	4.14	3.91
Central Asian	10.20	13.08	16.78	21.49
Other	13.42	13.82	14.06	14.09

TABLE 5.5 – continued

	2020	2030	2040	2050
LOW FERTILITY				
TOTAL	322,265	335,385	328,859	316,861
European	215,588	209,777	198,912	186,172
Slavic	202,494	196,875	186,507	174,439
Russian	148,490	144,445	136,769	127,939
Other Slavic	54,004	52,430	49,738	46,499
Other European	13,094	12,903	12,405	11,734
Central Asian	68,136	76,316	81,634	84,372
Other	48,542	49,292	48,313	46,317
Percentage of Population				
TOTAL	100.00	100.00	100.00	100.00
European	64.88	62.55	60.49	58.76
Slavic	60.94	58.70	56.71	55.05
Russian	44.69	43.07	41.59	40.38
Other Slavic	16.25	15.63	15.12	14.68
Other European	3.94	3.85	3.77	3.70
Central Asian	20.51	22.75	24.82	26.63
Other	14.61	14.70	14.69	14.62
CONSTANT FERTILITY				
TOTAL	405,673	466,461	545,504	656,560
European	238,229	244,695	248,680	252,881
Slavic	223,418	229,056	232,248	235,584
Russian	163,867	168,051	170,284	172,688
Other Slavic	59,551	61,004	61,963	62,896
Other European	14,811	15,640	16,432	17,297
Central Asian	111,138	159,471	228,769	329,334
Other	56,306	62,295	68,055	74,345
Percentage of Population				
TOTAL	100.00	100.00	100.00	100.00
European	58.72	52.46	45.59	38.52
Slavic	55.07	49.10	42.57	35.88
Russian	40.39	36.03	31.22	26.30
Other Slavic	14.68	13.08	11.36	9.58
Other European	3.65	3.35	3.01	2.63
Central Asian	27.40	34.19	41.94	50.16
Other	13.88	13.35	12.48	11.32

TABLE 5.5 – continued
(absolute figures in thousands)

	1980	1990	2000	2010
REPLACEMENT FERTILITY				
TOTAL	266,488	286,342	301,932	317,743
European	203,551	214,020	221,591	228,399
Slavic	191,463	201,454	208,607	215,006
Russian	139,124	146,919	152,424	157,481
Other Slavic	52,339	54,535	56,184	57,525
Other European	12,088	12,567	12,984	13,393
Central Asian	27,183	32,764	37,559	43,437
Other	35,753	39,557	42,781	45,906
Percentage of Population				
TOTAL	100.00	100.00	100.00	100.00
European	76.38	74.74	73.39	71.88
Slavic	71.85	70.35	69.09	67.67
Russian	52.21	51.31	50.48	49.56
Other Slavic	19.64	19.05	16.81	18.10
Other European	4.54	4.39	4.30	4.22
Central Asian	10.20	11.44	12.44	13.67
Other	13.42	13.81	14.17	14.45
SYNTHETIC: EUROPEANS HIGH FERTILITY, OTHERS REPLACEMENT				
TOTAL	266,488	289,723	313,176	338,426
European	203,551	217,402	232,835	249,083
Slavic	191,463	204,510	218,888	233,994
Russian	139,124	149,117	159,844	171,227
Other Slavic	52,339	55,393	59,044	62,766
Other European	12,088	12,891	13,947	15,089
Central Asian	27,183	32,764	37,559	43,437
Other	35,753	39,557	42,781	45,906
Percentage of Population				
TOTAL	100.00	100.00	100.00	100.00
European	76.38	75.04	74.35	73.60
Slavic	71.85	70.59	69.89	69.14
Russian	52.21	51.47	51.04	50.60
Other Slavic	19.64	19.12	18.85	18.55
Other European	4.54	4.45	4.45	4.46
Central Asian	10.20	11.31	11.99	12.84
Other	13.42	13.65	13.66	13.56

TABLE 5.5 – continued

	2020	2030	2040	2050
REPLACEMENT FERTILITY				
TOTAL	332,275	343,664	349,465	353,236
European	235,079	240,104	242,303	244,442
Slavic	221,282	225,973	228,014	230,046
Russian	162,451	166,008	167,480	169,023
Other Slavic	58,831	59,964	60,534	61,023
Other European	13,797	14,131	14,289	14,396
Central Asian	48,432	52,493	54,987	56,000
Other	48,764	51,067	52,175	52,795
Percentage of Population				
TOTAL	100.00	100.00	100.00	100.00
European	70.75	69.87	69.34	69.20
Slavic	66.60	65.75	65.25	65.13
Russian	48.89	48.31	47.92	47.85
Other Slavic	17.71	17.45	17.32	17.28
Other European	4.15	4.11	4.09	4.08
Central Asian	14.58	15.27	15.73	15.85
Other	14.68	14.86	14.93	14.95
SYNTHETIC: EUROPEANS HIGH FERTILITY, OTHERS REPLACEMENT				
TOTAL	367,683	396,804	424,664	454,935
European	270,487	293,244	317,502	346,141
Slavic	253,848	274,948	297,438	324,062
Russian	186,027	201,513	217,839	237,254
Other Slavic	67,821	73,436	79,599	86,808
Other European	16,639	18,296	20,064	22,079
Central Asian	48,432	52,493	54,987	56,000
Other	48,764	51,067	52,175	52,795
Percentage of Population				
TOTAL	100.00	100.00	100.00	100.00
European	73.57	73.90	74.77	76.09
Slavic	69.04	69.29	70.04	71.23
Russian	50.59	50.78	51.30	52.15
Other Slavic	18.45	18.51	18.74	19.08
Other European	4.53	4.61	4.72	4.85
Central Asian	13.17	13.23	12.95	12.31
Other	13.26	12.87	12.29	11.60

Ward Kingkade

TABLE 5.5 – continued
(absolute figures in thousands)

	1980	1990	2000	2010
SYNTHETIC: EUROPEANS LOW FERTILITY, OTHERS CONSTANT				
TOTAL	266,488	291,764	315,898	344,667
European	203,551	212,843	216,581	217,459
Slavic	191,463	200,246	203,690	204,401
Russian	139,124	145,989	148,736	149,570
Other Slavic	52,339	54.257	54,954	54,831
Other European	12,088	12,597	12,891	13,058
Central Asian	27,183	38,381	54,040	76,832
Other	35.753	40,540	45,277	50,376
Percentage of Population				
TOTAL	100.00	100.00	100.00	100.00
European	76.38	72.95	68.56	63.09
Slavic	71.85	68.63	64.48	59.30
Russian	52.21	50.04	47.08	43.40
Other Slavic	19.64	18.60	17.40	15.91
Other European	4.45	4.32	4.08	3.79
Central Asian	10.20	13.15	17.11	22.29
Other	13.42	13.89	14.53	14.62

TABLE 5.5 – continued

	2020	2030	2040	2050
SYNTHETIC: EUROPEANS LOW FERTILITY, OTHERS CONSTANT				
TOTAL	383,032	431,544	495,736	589,852
European	215,588	209,777	198,912	186,172
Slavic	202,494	196,875	186,507	174,439
Russian	148,490	144,445	136,769	127,939
Other Slavic	54,004	52,430	49,738	46,499
Other European	13,094	12,903	12,405	11,734
Central Asian	111,138	159,471	228,769	329,334
Other	56,306	62,295	68,055	74,345
Percentage of Population				
TOTAL	100.00	100.00	100.00	100.00
European	56.28	48.61	40.12	31.56
Slavic	52.87	45.62	37.62	29.57
Russian	38.77	33.47	27.59	21.69
Other Slavic	14.10	12.15	10.03	7.88
Other European	3.42	2.99	2.50	1.99
Central Asian	29.02	36.95	46.15	55.83
Other	14.70	14.44	13.73	12.60

TABLE 5.6   Projected 18 Year Old-Males in Major Nationality Groups, Various Fertility Scenarios (absolute figures in thousands)

	1980	1990	2000	2010
HIGH FERTILITY				
TOTAL	2,545	2,196	2,591	3,137
European	1,739	1,522	1,648	1,963
Slavic	1,632	1,430	1,549	1,837
Russian	1,188	1,034	1,147	1,341
Other Slavic	444	396	402	496
Other European	107	92	99	126
Central Asian	404	359	557	694
Other	402	315	385	480
Percentage of Population				
TOTAL	100.00	100.00	100.00	100.00
European	68.33	69.28	63.62	62.58
Slavic	64.12	65.09	59.78	58.55
Russian	46.67	47.07	44.28	42.75
Other Slavic	17.45	18.02	15.50	15.81
Other European	4.21	4.20	3.84	4.02
Central Asian	15.88	16.36	21.51	22.12
Other	15.78	14.36	14.87	15.30
MEDIAN FERTILITY				
TOTAL	2,545	2,196	2,591	2,542
European	1,739	1,522	1,648	1,507
Slavic	1,632	1,430	1,549	1,410
Russian	1,188	1,034	1,147	1,030
Other Slavic	444	396	402	381
Other European	107	92	99	97
Central Asian	404	359	557	656
Other	402	315	385	378
Percentage of Population				
TOTAL	100.00	100.00	100.00	100.00
European	68.33	69.28	63.62	59.30
Slavic	64.12	65.09	59.78	55.49
Russian	46.67	47.07	44.28	40.51
Other Slavic	17.45	18.02	15.50	14.98
Other European	4.21	4.20	3.84	3.81
Central Asian	15.88	16.36	21.51	25.81
Other	15.78	14.36	14.87	14.89

TABLE 5.6 – continued

	2020	2030	2040	2050
HIGH FERTILITY				
TOTAL	3,244	3,832	4,112	4,470
European	1,998	2,313	2,470	2,686
Slavic	1,872	2,164	2,310	2,513
Russian	1,372	1,585	1,688	1,840
Other Slavic	499	579	621	673
Other European	126	149	160	173
Central Asian	766	939	1,017	1,103
Other	480	580	625	681
Percentage of Population				
TOTAL	100.00	100.00	100.00	100.00
European	61.57	60.36	60.07	60.10
Slavic	57.68	56.46	56.16	56.22
Russian	42.29	41.36	41.05	41.16
Other Slavic	15.39	15.10	15.11	15.06
Other European	3.89	3.89	3.90	3.87
Central Asian	23.62	24.50	24.73	24.67
Other	14.80	15.15	15.21	15.24
MEDIAN FERTILITY				
TOTAL	2,505	2,614	2,447	2,381
European	1,461	1,472	1,347	1,313
Slavic	1,369	1,377	1,259	1,227
Russian	1,004	1,010	921	900
Other Slavic	365	367	338	328
Other European	92	96	88	85
Central Asian	679	756	739	714
Other	364	385	361	354
Percentage of Population				
TOTAL	100.00	100.00	100.00	100.00
European	58.34	56.34	55.06	55.13
Slavic	54.65	52.67	51.47	51.55
Russian	40.07	38.65	37.66	37.78
Other Slavic	14.58	14.03	13.81	13.76
Other European	3.69	3.66	3.59	3.58
Central Asian	27.11	28.93	30.20	29.99
Other	14.55	14.73	14.74	14.88

Ward Kingkade

Table 5.6 – continued
(absolute figures in thousands)

	1980	1990	2000	2010
LOW FERTILITY				
TOTAL	2,545	2,196	2,591	2,374
European	1,739	1,522	1,648	1,406
Slavic	1,632	1,430	1,549	1,317
Russian	1,188	1,034	1,147	962
Other Slavic	444	396	402	355
Other European	107	92	99	90
Central Asian	404	359	557	605
Other	402	315	385	362
Percentage of Population				
TOTAL	100.00	100.00	100.00	100.00
European	68.33	69.28	63.62	59.24
Slavic	64.12	65.09	59.78	55.47
Russian	46.67	47.07	44.28	40.51
Other Slavic	17.45	18.02	15.50	14.96
Other European	4.21	4.20	3.84	3.77
Central Asian	15.88	16.36	21.51	25.50
Other	15.78	14.36	14.87	15.26
CONSTANT FERTILITY				
TOTAL	2,545	2,196	2,591	2,802
European	1,739	1,522	1,648	1,598
Slavic	1,632	1,430	1,549	1,496
Russian	1,188	1,034	1,147	1,093
Other Slavic	444	396	402	402
Other European	107	92	99	103
Central Asian	404	359	557	790
Other	402	315	385	413
Percentage of Population				
TOTAL	100.00	100.00	100.00	100.00
European	68.33	69.28	63.62	57.05
Slavic	64.12	65.09	59.78	53.38
Russian	46.67	47.07	44.28	39.03
Other Slavic	17.45	18.02	15.50	14.35
Other European	4.21	4.20	3.84	3.67
Central Asian	15.88	16.36	21.51	28.20
Other	15.78	14.36	14.87	14.75

TABLE 5.6 – continued

	2020	2030	2040	2050
LOW FERTILITY				
TOTAL	2,272	2,221	1,978	1,819
European	1,326	1,247	1,094	1,007
Slavic	1,243	1,166	1,023	942
Russian	911	856	749	691
Other Slavic	331	310	274	251
Other European	84	80	71	65
Central Asian	613	647	601	554
Other	333	328	283	258
Percentage of Population				
TOTAL	100.00	100.00	100.00	100.00
European	58.37	56.12	55.32	55.36
Slavic	54.69	52.50	51.73	51.78
Russian	40.11	38.55	37.87	37.98
Other Slavic	14.59	13.95	13.86	13.80
Other European	3.68	3.62	3.58	3.59
Central Asian	26.98	29.13	30.37	30.44
Other	14.65	14.75	14.32	14.20
CONSTANT FERTILITY				
TOTAL	3,132	3,825	4,523	5,628
European	1,620	1,699	1,678	1,728
Slavic	1,515	1,583	1,560	1,601
Russian	1,111	1,162	1,141	1,173
Other Slavic	403	421	419	428
Other European	105	116	119	127
Central Asian	1,083	1,631	2,318	3,324
Other	429	495	526	576
Percentage of Population				
TOTAL	100.00	100.00	100.00	100.00
European	51.72	44.41	37.11	30.71
Slavic	48.36	41.38	34.49	28.46
Russian	35.47	30.38	25.23	20.85
Other Slavic	12.88	11.00	9.26	7.61
Other European	3.36	3.03	2.62	2.25
Central Asian	34.58	42.65	51.26	59.07
Other	13.70	12.95	11.63	10.23

TABLE 5.6 – continued
(absolute figures in thousands)

	1980	1990	2000	2010
REPLACEMENT FERTILITY				
TOTAL	2,324	2,369	2,314	2,378
European	1,585	1,640	1,609	1,642
Slavic	1,490	1,543	1,514	1,546
Russian	1,095	1,136	1,111	1,136
Other Slavic	395	408	403	409
Other European	94	96	95	97
Central Asian	392	376	357	380
Other	347	353	348	356
Percentage of Population				
TOTAL	100.00	100.00	100.00	100.00
European	68.19	69.23	69.53	69.06
Slavic	64.14	65.16	65.42	65.00
Russian	47.12	47.96	48.00	47.79
Other Slavic	17.02	17.20	17.42	17.21
Other European	4.06	4.07	4.11	4.06
Central Asian	16.89	15.86	15.44	15.97
Other	14.92	14.91	15.03	14.97

SYNTHETIC: EUROPEANS HIGH FERTILITY, OTHERS REPLACEMENT

	1980	1990	2000	2010
TOTAL	2,737	3,042	3,175	3,422
European	1,998	2,313	2,470	2,686
Slavic	1,872	2,164	2,310	2,513
Russian	1,372	1,585	1,688	1,840
Other Slavic	499	579	621	673
Other European	126	149	160	173
Central Asian	392	376	357	380
Other	347	353	348	356
Percentage of Population				
TOTAL	100.00	100.00	100.00	100.00
European	73.00	76.04	77.79	78.50
Slavic	68.38	71.14	72.74	73.44
Russian	50.14	52.11	53.17	53.77
Other Slavic	18.25	19.03	19.57	19.68
Other European	4.61	4.90	5.05	5.06
Central Asian	14.34	12.35	11.25	11.10
Other	12.67	11.61	10.96	10.40

TABLE 5.6 – continued

	2020	2030	2040	2050
REPLACEMENT FERTILITY				
TOTAL	2,545	2,196	2,591	2,200
European	1,739	1,522	1,648	1,566
Slavic	1,632	1,430	1,549	1,473
Russian	1,188	1,034	1,147	1,079
Other Slavic	444	396	402	395
Other European	107	92	99	93
Central Asian	404	359	557	297
Other	402	315	385	336
Percentage of Population				
TOTAL	100.00	100.00	100.00	100.00
European	68.33	69.28	63.62	71.19
Slavic	64.12	65.09	59.78	66.97
Russian	46.67	47.07	44.28	49.03
Other Slavic	17.45	18.02	15.50	17.94
Other European	4.21	4.20	3.84	4.22
Central Asian	15.88	16.36	21.51	13.52
Other	15.78	14.36	14.87	15.29
SYNTHETIC: EUROPEANS HIGH FERTILITY, OTHERS REPLACEMENT				
TOTAL	2,545	2,196	2,591	2,597
European	1,739	1,522	1,648	1,963
Slavic	1,632	1,430	1,549	1,837
Russian	1,188	1,034	1,147	1,341
Other Slavic	444	396	402	496
Other European	107	92	99	126
Central Asian	404	359	557	297
Other	402	315	385	336
Percentage of Population				
TOTAL	100.00	100.00	100.00	100.00
European	68.33	69.28	63.62	75.59
Slavic	64.12	65.09	59.78	70.74
Russian	46.67	47.07	44.28	51.64
Other Slavic	17.45	18.02	15.50	19.09
Other European	4.21	4.20	3.84	4.86
Central Asian	15.88	16.36	21.51	11.45
Other	15.78	14.36	14.87	12.95

TABLE 5.6 – continued
(absolute figures in thousands)

	1980	1990	2000	2010
SYNTHETIC: EUROPEANS LOW FERTILITY, OTHERS CONSTANT				
TOTAL	2,545	2,196	2,591	2,610
European	1,739	1,522	1,648	1,406
Slavic	1,632	1,430	1,549	1,317
Russian	1,188	1,034	1,147	962
Other Slavic	444	396	402	355
Other European	107	92	99	90
Central Asian	404	359	557	790
Other	402	315	385	413
Percentage of Population				
TOTAL	100.00	100.00	100.00	100.00
European	68.33	69.28	63.62	53.89
Slavic	64.12	65.09	59.78	50.46
Russian	46.67	47.07	44.28	36.85
Other Slavic	17.45	18.02	15.50	13.61
Other European	4.21	4.20	3.84	3.43
Central Asian	15.88	16.36	21.51	30.27
Other	15.78	14.36	14.87	15.84

TABLE 5.6 – continued

	2020	2030	2040	2050
SYNTHETIC: EUROPEANS LOW FERTILITY, OTHERS CONSTANT				
TOTAL	2,838	3,373	3,938	4,906
European	1,326	1,247	1,094	1,007
Slavic	1,243	1,166	1,023	942
Russian	911	856	749	691
Other Slavic	331	310	274	251
Other European	84	80	71	65
Central Asian	1,083	1,631	2,318	3,324
Other	429	495	526	576
Percentage of Population				
TOTAL	100.00	100.00	100.00	100.00
European	46.73	36.96	27.78	20.52
Slavic	43.79	34.57	25.98	19.19
Russian	32.11	25.38	19.02	14.08
Other Slavic	11.68	9.19	6.96	5.11
Other European	2.94	2.38	1.80	1.33
Central Asian	38.15	48.36	58.87	67.75
Other	15.12	14.68	13.35	11.73

Ward Kingkade

TABLE 5.7 Projected Working Age Population in Major Nationality Groups, Various Fertility Scenarios (absolute figures in thousands)

	1980	1990	2000	2010
HIGH FERTILITY				
TOTAL	154,484	160,491	172,923	198,251
European	120,458	119,884	122,396	132,523
Slavic	113,650	112,979	115,238	124,499
Russian	83,188	82,690	84,837	91,467
Other Slavic	30,462	30,289	30,401	33,032
Other European	6,808	6,905	7,158	8,025
Central Asian	13,261	18,011	25,464	36,004
Other	20,764	22,596	25,063	29,724
Percentage of Population				
TOTAL	100.00	100.00	100.00	100.00
European	77.79	74.70	70.78	66.85
Slavic	73.57	70.40	66.64	62.80
Russian	53.85	51.52	49.06	46.14
Other Slavic	19.72	18.87	17.58	16.66
Other European	4.41	4.30	4.14	4.05
Central Asian	8.58	11.22	14.73	18.16
Other	13.44	14.08	14.49	14.99
MEDIAN FERTILITY				
TOTAL	154,484	160,491	172,853	189,629
European	120,458	119,884	122,368	126,127
Slavic	113,650	112,979	115,212	118,514
Russian	83,188	82,690	84,818	87,090
Other Slavic	30,462	30,289	30,394	31,425
Other European	6,808	6,905	7,156	7,613
Central Asian	13,261	18,011	25,444	35,326
Other	20,764	22,596	25,041	28,176
Percentage of Population				
TOTAL	100.00	100.00	100.00	100.00
European	77.97	74.70	70.79	66.51
Slavic	73.57	70.40	66.65	62.50
Russian	53.85	51.52	49.07	45.93
Other Slavic	19.71	18.87	17.58	16.57
Other European	4.41	4.30	4.14	4.01
Central Asian	8.58	11.22	14.72	18.63
Other	13.44	14.08	14.49	14.86

TABLE 5.7 – continued

	2020	2030	2040	2050
HIGH FERTILITY				
TOTAL	215,815	245,261	276,816	302,820
European	138,587	153,047	169,358	183,520
Slavic	129,981	143,436	158,538	171,737
Russian	95,167	105,194	116,089	125,693
Other Slavic	34,815	38,242	42,449	46,044
Other European	8,606	9,611	10,820	11,783
Central Asian	44,886	55,542	65,703	73,555
Other	32,341	36,672	41,755	45,745
Percentage of Population				
TOTAL	100.00	100.00	100.00	100.00
European	64.22	62.40	61.18	60.60
Slavic	60.23	58.48	57.27	56.71
Russian	44.10	42.89	41.94	41.51
Other Slavic	16.13	15.59	15.33	15.21
Other European	3.99	3.92	3.91	3.89
Central Asian	20.80	22.65	23.74	24.29
Other	14.99	14.95	15.08	15.11
MEDIAN FERTILITY				
TOTAL	193,407	202,130	203,615	198,483
European	122,035	122,128	118,051	112,203
Slavic	114,485	114,481	110,513	104,981
Russian	83,830	84,008	80,990	76,898
Other Slavic	30,655	30,473	29,523	28,083
Other European	7,550	7,647	7,538	7,222
Central Asian	42,767	50,356	55,622	57,075
Other	28,606	29,646	29,941	29,204
Percentage of Population				
TOTAL	100.00	100.00	100.00	100.00
European	63.10	60.42	57.98	56.53
Slavic	59.19	56.64	54.28	52.89
Russian	43.34	41.56	39.78	38.74
Other Slavic	15.85	15.08	14.50	14.15
Other European	3.90	3.78	3.70	3.64
Central Asian	22.11	24.91	27.32	28.76
Other	14.79	14.67	14.70	14.71

TABLE 5.7 – continued
(absolute figures in thousands)

	1980	1990	2000	2010
LOW FERTILITY				
TOTAL	154,484	160,491	172,792	185,939
European	120,458	119,884	122,310	123,609
Slavic	113,650	112,979	115,158	116,166
Russian	83,188	82,690	84,778	85,372
Other Slavic	30,462	30,289	30,380	30,793
Other European	6,808	6,905	7,153	7,443
Central Asian	13,261	18,011	25,433	34,439
Other	20,764	22,596	25,049	27,891
Percentage of Population				
TOTAL	100.00	100.00	100.00	100.00
European	77.97	74.70	70.78	66.48
Slavic	73.57	70.40	66.64	62.48
Russian	53.85	51.52	49.06	45.91
Other Slavic	19.72	18.87	17.58	16.56
Other European	4.41	4.30	4.14	4.00
Central Asian	8.58	11.22	14.72	18.52
Other	13.44	14.08	14.50	15.00
CONSTANT FERTILITY				
TOTAL	154,484	160,491	172,838	192,406
European	120,458	119,884	122,336	126,745
Slavic	113,650	112,979	115,182	119,093
Russian	83,188	82,690	84,798	87,547
Other Slavic	30,462	30,289	30,384	31,546
Other European	6,808	6,905	7,154	7,652
Central Asian	13,261	18,011	25,452	37,043
Other	20,764	22,596	25,050	28,619
Percentage of Population				
TOTAL	100.00	100.00	100.00	100.00
European	77.97	74.70	70.78	65.87
Slavic	73.57	70.40	66.64	61.90
Russian	53.85	51.52	49.06	45.50
Other Slavic	19.72	18.87	17.58	16.40
Other European	4.41	4.30	4.14	3.98
Central Asian	8.58	11.22	14.73	19.25
Other	13.44	14.08	14.49	14.87

TABLE 5.7 – continued

	2020	2030	2040	2050
LOW FERTILITY				
TOTAL	185,623	187,515	180,503	168,047
European	117,154	113,281	104,622	95,237
Slavic	109,934	106,227	97,989	89,150
Russian	80,504	77,974	71,839	65,330
Other Slavic	29,429	28,252	26,150	23,820
Other European	7,221	7,054	6,633	6,087
Central Asian	40,674	46,383	49,136	48,332
Other	27,794	27,851	26,744	24,477
Percentage of Population				
TOTAL	100.00	100.00	100.00	100.00
European	63.11	60.41	57.96	56.67
Slavic	59.22	56.65	54.29	53.05
Russian	43.37	41.58	39.80	38.88
Other Slavic	15.85	15.07	14.49	14.17
Other European	3.89	3.76	3.67	3.62
Central Asian	21.91	24.74	27.22	28.76
Other	14.97	14.85	14.82	14.57
CONSTANT FERTILITY				
TOTAL	206,697	235,782	273,207	322,554
European	125,519	129,587	131,487	132,768
Slavic	117,704	121,324	122,785	123,667
Russian	86,235	89,089	90,040	90,613
Other Slavic	31,468	32,236	32,745	33,054
Other European	7,815	8,263	8,702	9,101
Central Asian	50,998	73,089	105,389	150,554
Other	30,180	33,107	36,331	39,232
Percentage of Population				
TOTAL	100.00	100.00	100.00	100.00
European	60.73	54.96	48.13	41.16
Slavic	56.95	51.46	44.94	38.34
Russian	41.72	37.78	32.96	28.09
Other Slavic	15.22	13.67	11.99	10.25
Other European	3.78	3.50	3.19	2.82
Central Asian	24.67	31.00	38.57	46.68
Other	14.60	14.04	13.30	12.16

Ward Kingkade

TABLE 5.7 – continued
(absolute figures in thousands)

	1980	1990	2000	2010
REPLACEMENT FERTILITY				
TOTAL	154,484	160,491	172,343	180,698
European	120,458	119,884	122,302	126,065
Slavic	113,650	112,979	115,158	118,621
Russian	83,188	82,690	84,782	87,234
Other Slavic	30,462	30,289	30,377	31,388
Other European	6,808	6,905	7,144	7,444
Central Asian	13,261	18,011	25,064	27,587
Other	20,764	22,596	24,977	27,045
Percentage of Population				
TOTAL	100.00	100.00	100.00	100.00
European	77.97	74.70	70.96	69.77
Slavic	73.57	70.40	66.82	65.65
Russian	53.85	51.52	49.19	48.28
Other Slavic	19.72	18.87	17.63	17.37
Other European	4.41	4.30	4.15	4.12
Central Asian	8.58	11.22	14.54	15.27
Other	13.44	14.08	14.49	14.97

SYNTHETIC: EUROPEANS HIGH FERTILITY, OTHERS REPLACEMENT

	1980	1990	2000	2010
TOTAL	154,484	160,491	172,437	187,156
European	120,458	119,884	122,396	132,523
Slavic	113,650	112,979	115,238	124,499
Russian	83,188	82,690	84,837	91,467
Other Slavic	30,462	30,289	30,401	33,032
Other European	6,808	6,905	7,158	8,025
Central Asian	13,261	18,011	25,064	27,587
Other	20,764	22,596	24,977	27,045
Percentage of Population				
TOTAL	100.00	100.00	100.00	100.00
European	77.97	74.70	70.98	70.81
Slavic	73.57	70.40	66.83	66.52
Russian	53.85	51.52	49.20	48.87
Other Slavic	19.72	18.87	17.63	17.65
Other European	4.41	4.30	4.15	4.29
Central Asian	8.58	11.22	14.54	14.74
Other	13.44	14.08	14.48	14.45

TABLE 5.7 – continued

	2020	2030	2040	2050
REPLACEMENT FERTILITY				
TOTAL	180,392	184,770	184,014	185,300
European	124,182	127,230	127,889	128,141
Slavic	116,782	119,716	120,356	120,588
Russian	85,624	88,022	88,431	88,574
Other Slavic	31,158	31,694	31,925	32,014
Other European	7,400	7,514	7,533	7,553
Central Asian	29,156	29,981	28,510	29,405
Other	27,055	27,558	27,615	27,753
Percentage of Population				
TOTAL	100.00	100.00	100.00	100.00
European	68.84	68.86	69.50	69.15
Slavic	64.74	64.79	65.41	65.08
Russian	47.47	47.64	48.06	47.80
Other Slavic	17.27	17.15	17.35	17.28
Other European	4.10	4.07	4.09	4.08
Central Asian	16.16	16.23	15.49	15.87
Other	15.00	14.91	15.01	14.98
SYNTHETIC: EUROPEANS HIGH FERTILITY, OTHERS REPLACEMENT				
TOTAL	194,798	210,587	225,483	240,679
European	138,587	153,047	169,358	183,520
Slavic	129,981	143,436	158,538	171,737
Russian	95,167	105,194	116,089	125,693
Other Slavic	34,815	38,242	42,449	46,044
Other European	8,606	9,611	10,820	11,783
Central Asian	29,156	29,981	28,510	29,405
Other	27,055	27,558	27,615	27,753
Percentage of Population				
TOTAL	100.00	100.00	100.00	100.00
European	71.14	72.68	75.11	76.25
Slavic	66.73	68.11	70.31	71.36
Russian	48.85	49.95	51.48	52.22
Other Slavic	17.87	18.16	18.83	19.13
Other European	4.42	4.56	4.80	4.90
Central Asian	14.97	14.24	12.64	12.22
Other	13.89	13.09	12.25	11.53

TABLE 5.7 – continued
(absolute figures in thousands)

	1980	1990	2000	2010
SYNTHETIC: EUROPEANS LOW FERTILITY, OTHERS CONSTANT				
TOTAL	154,484	160,491	172,813	189,271
European	120,458	119,884	122,310	123,609
Slavic	113,650	112,979	115,158	116,166
Russian	83,188	82,690	84,778	85,372
Other Slavic	30,462	30,289	30,380	30,793
Other European	6,808	6,905	7,153	7,443
Central Asian	13,261	18,011	25,452	37,043
Other	20,764	22,596	25,050	28,619
Percentage of Population				
TOTAL	100.00	100.00	100.00	100.00
European	77.97	74.70	70.78	65.31
Slavic	73.57	70.40	66.64	61.38
Russian	53.85	51.52	49.06	45.11
Other Slavic	19.72	18.87	17.58	16.27
Other European	4.41	4.30	4.14	3.93
Central Asian	8.58	11.22	14.73	19.57
Other	13.44	14.08	14.50	15.12

TABLE 5.7 – continued

	2020	2030	2040	2050
SYNTHETIC: EUROPEANS LOW FERTILITY, OTHERS CONSTANT				
TOTAL	198,332	219,476	246,343	285,023
European	117,154	113,281	104,622	95,237
Slavic	109,934	106,227	97,989	89,150
Russian	80,504	77,974	71,839	65,330
Other Slavic	29,429	28,252	26,150	23,820
Other European	7,221	7,054	6,633	6,087
Central Asian	50,998	73,089	105,389	150,554
Other	30,180	33,107	36,331	39,232
Percentage of Population				
TOTAL	100.00	100.00	100.00	100.00
European	59.07	51.61	42.47	33.41
Slavic	55.43	48.40	39.78	31.28
Russian	40.59	35.53	29.16	22.92
Other Slavic	14.84	12.87	10.62	8.36
Other European	3.64	3.21	2.69	2.14
Central Asian	25.71	33.30	42.78	52.82
Other	15.22	15.08	14.75	13.76

TABLE 5.8 Distribution of the Population in Broad Age Groups by Major Nationality Categories, Various Fertility Scenarios (in per cent)

	1979	1990	2000	2050
HIGH FERTILITY				
ALL NATIONALITIES				
Total	100.00	100.00	100.00	100.00
Children	26.64	28.77	29.74	27.54
Able-bodied	57.94	54.09	52.34	53.62
Pension	15.42	17.14	17.92	18.85
EUROPEAN				
Total	100.00	100.00	100.00	100.00
Children	23.67	25.12	26.30	26.94
Able-bodied	59.24	55.14	52.57	53.02
Pension	17.09	19.74	21.14	20.04
SLAVIC				
Total	100.00	100.00	100.00	100.00
Children	23.64	25.06	26.19	26.91
Able-bodied	59.44	55.24	52.65	52.99
Pension	16.92	19.70	21.16	20.10
RUSSIAN				
Total	100.00	100.00	100.00	100.00
Children	23.79	25.33	26.24	26.87
Able-bodied	59.89	55.45	53.07	52.98
Pension	16.32	19.22	20.68	20.15
OTHER SLAVIC				
Total	100.00	100.00	100.00	100.00
Children	23.24	24.34	26.04	27.02
Able-bodied	58.24	54.68	51.49	53.04
Pension	18.52	20.98	22.47	19.94
OTHER EUROPEAN				
Total	100.00	100.00	100.00	100.00
Children	24.06	25.97	27.96	27.45
Able-bodied	56.22	53.57	51.32	53.37
Pension	19.72	20.46	20.71	19.18
CENTRAL ASIAN				
Total	100.00	100.00	100.00	100.00
Children	45.35	47.29	43.97	28.74
Able-bodied	48.17	47.19	50.43	55.32
Pension	6.48	5.52	5.60	15.94
OTHER				
Total	100.00	100.00	100.00	100.00
Children	29.72	30.93	31.54	28.05
Able-bodied	57.78	54.93	53.26	53.40
Pension	12.50	14.15	15.20	18.55

TABLE 5.8 – continued

	1979	1990	2000	2050
MEDIAN FERTILITY				
ALL NATIONALITIES				
Total	100.00	100.00	100.00	100.00
Children	26.64	27.82	26.03	19.31
Able-bodied	57.94	54.82	55.10	53.62
Pension	15.42	17.37	18.87	27.08
EUROPEAN				
Total	100.00	100.00	100.00	100.00
Children	23.67	24.13	22.16	18.04
Able-bodied	59.24	55.87	55.52	51.96
Pension	17.09	20.00	22.33	30.00
SLAVIC				
Total	100.00	100.00	100.00	100.00
Children	23.64	24.09	22.06	18.00
Able-bodied	59.44	55.96	55.59	51.92
Pension	16.92	19.95	22.35	30.08
RUSSIAN				
Total	100.00	100.00	100.00	100.00
Children	23.79	24.35	22.12	17.99
Able-bodied	59.89	56.18	56.04	51.88
Pension	16.32	19.47	21.84	30.14
OTHER SLAVIC				
Total	100.00	100.00	100.00	100.00
Children	23.24	23.37	21.92	18.02
Able-bodied	58.24	55.38	54.35	52.03
Pension	18.52	21.25	23.72	29.94
OTHER EUROPEAN				
Total	100.00	100.00	100.00	100.00
Children	24.06	24.92	23.62	18.66
Able-bodied	56.22	54.32	54.41	52.63
Pension	19.72	20.75	21.97	28.71
CENTRAL ASIAN				
Total	100.00	100.00	100.00	100.00
Children	45.35	46.78	42.39	21.92
Able-bodied	48.17	47.65	51.85	57.31
Pension	6.48	5.58	5.76	20.77
OTHER				
Total	100.00	100.00	100.00	100.00
Children	29.72	29.63	27.19	19.60
Able-bodied	57.78	55.96	56.64	53.41
Pension	12.50	14.41	16.17	26.99

TABLE 5.8 – continued
(absolute figures in thousands)

	1979	1990	2000	2010
LOW FERTILITY				
ALL NATIONALITIES				
Total	100.00	100.00	100.00	100.00
Children	26.64	27.22	24.61	16.24
Able-bodied	57.94	55.27	56.15	53.03
Pension	15.42	17.51	19.24	30.73
EUROPEAN				
Total	100.00	100.00	100.00	100.00
Children	23.67	23.51	20.80	15.11
Able-bodied	59.24	56.33	56.47	51.16
Pension	17.09	20.16	22.72	33.73
SLAVIC				
Total	100.00	100.00	100.00	100.00
Children	23.64	23.47	20.72	15.07
Able-bodied	59.44	56.42	56.54	51.11
Pension	16.92	20.11	22.74	33.82
RUSSIAN				
Total	100.00	100.00	100.00	100.00
Children	23.79	23.73	20.77	15.07
Able-bodied	59.89	56.64	57.00	51.06
Pension	16.32	19.63	22.23	33.86
OTHER SLAVIC				
Total	100.00	100.00	100.00	100.00
Children	23.24	22.75	20.58	15.08
Able-bodied	58.24	55.83	55.28	51.23
Pension	18.52	21.42	24.14	33.69
OTHER EUROPEAN				
Total	100.00	100.00	100.00	100.00
Children	24.06	24.24	22.10	15.68
Able-bodied	56.22	54.82	55.49	51.87
Pension	19.72	20.94	22.41	32.45
CENTRAL ASIAN				
Total	100.00	100.00	100.00	100.00
Children	45.35	46.07	40.49	18.99
Able-bodied	48.17	48.28	53.56	57.28
Pension	6.48	5.65	5.95	23.73
OTHER				
Total	100.00	100.00	100.00	100.00
Children	29.72	29.36	26.23	15.75
Able-bodied	57.78	56.17	57.39	52.85
Pension	12.50	14 47	16.38	31.40

TABLE 5.8 – continued

	1979	1990	2000	2050
CONSTANT FERTILITY				
ALL NATIONALITIES				
Total	100.00	100.00	100.00	100.00
Children	26.64	27.96	27.94	35.32
Able-bodied	57.94	54.71	53.68	49.13
Pension	15.42	17.33	18.38	15.55
EUROPEAN				
Total	100.00	100.00	100.00	100.00
Children	23.67	24.09	22.95	21.75
Able-bodied	59.24	55.90	54.94	52.50
Pension	17.09	20.01	22.10	25.75
SLAVIC				
Total	100.00	100.00	100.00	100.00
Children	23.64	24.04	22.85	21.55
Able-bodied	59.44	56.00	55.02	52.49
Pension	16.92	19.96	22.13	25.96
RUSSIAN				
Total	100.00	100.00	100.00	100.00
Children	23.79	24.32	22.93	21.51
Able-bodied	59.89	56.21	55.45	52.47
Pension	16.32	19.48	21.62	26.02
OTHER SLAVIC				
Total	100.00	100.00	100.00	100.00
Children	23.24	23.29	22.65	21.65
Able-bodied	58.24	55.44	53.84	52.55
Pension	18.52	21.27	23.51	25.79
OTHER EUROPEAN				
Total	100.00	100.00	100.00	100.00
Children	24.06	24.85	24.57	24.49
Able-bodied	56.22	54.38	53.73	52.61
Pension	19.72	20.77	21.70	22.90
CENTRAL ASIAN				
Total	100.00	100.00	100.00	100.00
Children	45.35	47.58	47.67	47.63
Able-bodied	48.17	46.93	47.10	45.71
Pension	6.48	5.49	5.23	6.65
OTHER				
Total	100.00	100.00	100.00	100.00
Children	29.72	29.91	28.88	26.96
Able-bodied	57.78	55.74	55.33	52.77
Pension	12.50	14.35	15.79	20.27

TABLE 5.8 – continued
(absolute figures in thousands)

	19790	1990	2000	2010
REPLACEMENT FERTILITY				
ALL NATIONALITIES				
Total	100.00	100.00	100.00	100.00
Children	26.64	26.19	23.32	21.15
Able-bodied	57.94	56.05	57.08	52.46
Pension	15.42	17.76	19.60	26.39
EUROPEAN				
Total	100.00	100.00	100.00	100.00
Children	23.67	23.93	22.60	21.15
Able-bodied	59.24	56.02	55.19	52.42
Pension	17.09	20.05	22.21	26.43
SLAVIC				
Total	100.00	100.00	100.00	100.00
Children	23.64	23.92	22.59	21.15
Able-bodied	59.44	56.08	55.20	52.42
Pension	16.92	19.99	22.21	26.43
RUSSIAN				
Total	100.00	100.00	100.00	100.00
Children	23.79	24.21	22.69	21.15
Able-bodied	59.89	56.28	55.62	52.40
Pension	16.32	19.50	21.69	26.44
OTHER SLAVIC				
Total	100.00	100.00	100.00	100.00
Children	23.24	23.15	22.32	21.15
Able-bodied	58.24	55.54	54.07	52.46
Pension	18.52	21.31	23.61	26.39
OTHER EUROPEAN				
Total	100.00	100.00	100.00	100.00
Children	24.06	24.06	22.73	21.12
Able-bodied	56.22	54.95	55.02	52.47
Pension	19.72	20.99	22.25	26.41
CENTRAL ASIAN				
Total	100.00	100.00	100.00	100.00
Children	45.35	38.59	25.74	21.15
Able-bodied	48.17	54.97	66.73	52.51
Pension	6.48	6.43	7.53	26.34
OTHER				
Total	100.00	100.00	100.00	100.00
Children	29.72	28.17	24.90	21.15
Able-bodied	57.78	57.12	58.38	52.57
Pension	12.50	14.71	16.71	26.28

TABLE 5.8 – continued

	1979	1990	2000	2050
EXTREME SCENARIO:				
EUROPEANS HIGH FERTILITY, OTHERS REPLACEMENT				
ALL NATIONALITIES				
Total	100.00	100.00	100.00	100.00
Children	26.64	27.06	26.04	25.56
Able-bodied	57.94	55.39	55.06	52.90
Pension	15.42	17.55	18.90	21.54
EUROPEAN				
Total	100.00	100.00	100.00	100.00
Children	23.67	25.12	26.30	26.94
Able-bodied	59.24	55.14	52.57	53.02
Pension	17.09	19.74	21.14	20.04
SLAVIC				
Total	100.00	100.00	100.00	100.00
Children	23.64	25.06	26.19	26.91
Able-bodied	59.44	55.24	52.65	52.99
Pension	16.92	19.70	21.16	20.10
RUSSIAN				
Total	100.00	100.00	100.00	100.00
Children	23.79	25.33	26.24	26.87
Able-bodied	59.89	55.45	53.07	52.98
Pension	16.32	19.22	20.68	20.15
OTHER SLAVIC				
Total	100.00	100.00	100.00	100.00
Children	23.24	24.34	26.04	27.02
Able-bodied	58.24	54.68	51.49	53.04
Pension	18.52	20.98	22.47	19.94
OTHER EUROPEAN				
Total	100.00	100.00	100.00	100.00
Children	24.06	25.97	27.96	27.45
Able-bodied	56.22	53.57	51.32	53.37
Pension	19.72	20.46	20.71	19.18
CENTRAL ASIAN				
Total	100.00	100.00	100.00	100.00
Children	45.35	38.59	25.74	21.15
Able-bodied	48.17	54.97	66.73	52.51
Pension	6.48	6.43	7.53	26.34
OTHER				
Total	100.00	100.00	100.00	100.00
Children	29.72	28.17	24.90	21.15
Able-bodied	57.78	57.12	58.38	52.57
Pension	12.50	14.71	16.71	26.28

TABLE 5.8 – continued
(absolute figures in thousands)

	1980	1990	2000	2010
EXTREME SCENARIO:				
EUROPEANS LOW FERTILITY, OTHERS CONSTANT				
ALL NATIONALITIES				
Total	100.00	100.00	100.00	100.00
Children	26.64	27.57	26.56	34.76
Able-bodied	57.94	55.01	54.71	48.32
Pension	15.42	17.43	18.74	16.92
EUROPEAN				
Total	100.00	100.00	100.00	100.00
Children	23.67	23.51	20.80	15.11
Able-bodied	59.24	56.33	56.47	51.16
Pension	17.09	20.16	22.72	33.73
SLAVIC				
Total	100.00	100.00	100.00	100.00
Children	23.64	23.47	20.72	15.07
Able-bodied	59.44	56.42	56.54	51.11
Pension	16.92	20.11	22.74	33.82
RUSSIAN				
Total	100.00	100.00	100.00	100.00
Children	23.79	23.73	20.77	15.07
Able-bodied	59.89	56.64	57.00	51.06
Pension	16.32	19.63	22.23	33.86
OTHER SLAVIC				
Total	100.00	100.00	100.00	100.00
Children	23.24	22.75	20.58	15.08
Able-bodied	58.24	55.83	55.28	51.23
Pension	18.52	21.42	24.14	33.69
OTHER EUROPEAN				
Total	100.00	100.00	100.00	100.00
Children	24.06	24.24	22.10	15.68
Able-bodied	56.22	54.82	55.49	51.87
Pension	19.72	20.94	22.41	32.45
CENTRAL ASIAN				
Total	100.00	100.00	100.00	100.00
Children	45.35	47.58	47.67	47.63
Able-bodied	48.17	46.93	47.10	45.71
Pension	6.48	5.49	5.23	6.65
OTHER				
Total	100.00	100.00	100.00	100.00
Children	29.72	29.91	28.88	26.96
Able-bodied	57.78	55.74	55.33	52.77
Pension	12.50	14.35	15.79	20.27

TABLE 5.9   Estimated and Projected Economic Activity Rates, including Private Subsidiary Employment (per thousand)

	1959	1970	1979	2000	2025	2050
CENTRAL ASIANS						
Male						
16–20	466.64	561.42	577.67	614.88	657.45	697.63
20–29	901.15	856.01	878.80	920.16	952.40	972.02
30–39	960.39	948.52	968.23	989.96	997.50	999.38
40–49	938.23	891.60	916.75	956.05	979.97	990.99
50–54	901.31	855.72	879.60	922.38	954.97	974.26
55–59	862.54	818.65	841.10	884.71	922.73	948.93
60 and over	463.29	422.11	434.00	462.01	495.65	529.34
Female						
16–20	481.87	467.95	526.83	565.14	609.72	652.54
20–29	723.16	764.49	851.05	900.81	940.36	964.76
30–39	683.41	878.43	949.82	983.94	995.98	999.00
40–49	594.19	825.97	900.10	946.80	975.63	989.01
50–54	422.80	695.81	784.34	855.40	913.47	949.60
55–59	269.03	377.77	398.99	490.44	599.64	699.76
60 and over	79.94	173.86	170.97	187.63	209.06	232.24
OTHER NATIONALITIES						
Male						
16–20	554.63	530.52	489.72	528.35	573.86	618.15
20–29	912.67	900.23	898.83	933.87	960.81	977.05
30–39	950.86	977.91	976.59	992.65	998.17	999.55
40–49	931.42	963.60	962.00	980.39	991.19	996.06
50–54	874.47	902.71	901.29	936.92	963.64	979.30
55–59	795.08	797.88	796.36	850.07	898.19	932.11
60 and over	416.29	495.86	472.79	501.08	534.75	568.10
Female						
16–20	514.51	478.87	439.65	478.03	524.02	569.61
20–29	757.86	870.97	893.37	930.15	958.54	975.69
30–39	723.09	930.45	969.82	990.48	997.63	999.41
40–49	664.08	910.65	948.96	973.49	988.04	994.64
50–54	532.40	777.37	841.93	896.52	939.25	965.02
55–59	299.03	447.39	439.29	531.80	638.66	733.36
60 and over	107.65	254.24	244.43	265.96	293.11	321.81

Ward Kingkade

TABLE 5.10   Projected Economically Active Population by Major Nationality Group,
Various Fertility Scenarios
(absolute figures in thousands, activity rates per thousand total population)

	1979			2000		
	Total Population	Active Population	Activity Rate	Total Population	Active Population	Activity Rate
HIGH FERTILITY						
TOTAL	264,129	145,658	551.46	330,383	178,027	538.85
European	202,434	116,027	573.16	232,835	129,395	555.74
Slavic	190,362	109,330	574.33	218,888	121,828	556.58
Russian	138,267	79,638	575.97	159,844	89,282	558.56
Other Slavic	52,095	29,692	569.95	59,044	32,546	551.22
Other European	12,073	6,697	554.75	13,947	7,567	542.53
Central Asian	26,360	10,736	407.28	50,492	23,316	461.78
Other	35,335	18,895	534.73	47,056	25,316	537.99
Percentage of Total						
TOTAL	100.00	100.00		100.00	100.00	
European	76.64	79.66		70.47	72.68	
Slavic	72.07	75.06		66.25	68.43	
Russian	52.35	54.67		48.38	50.15	
Other Slavic	19.72	20.38		17.87	18.28	
Other European	4.57	4.60		4.22	4.25	
Central Asian	9.98	7.37		15.28	13.10	
Other	13.38	12.97		14.24	14.22	
MEDIAN FERTILITY						
TOTAL	264,129	145,658	551.46	313,705	177,990	567.38
European	202,434	116,027	573.16	220,421	129,381	586.97
Slavic	190,362	109,330	574.33	207,269	121,815	587.71
Russian	138,267	79,638	575.97	151,350	89,272	589.84
Other Slavic	52,095	29,692	569.95	55,919	32,543	581.96
Other European	12,073	6,697	554.75	13,152	7,566	575.27
Central Asian	26,360	10,736	407.28	49,071	23,305	474.91
Other	35,335	18,895	534.73	44,213	25,305	572.34
Percentage of Total						
TOTAL	100.00	100.00		100.00	100.00	
European	76.64	79.66		70.26	72.69	
Slavic	72.07	75.06		66.07	68.44	
Russian	52.35	54.67		48.25	50.16	
Other Slavic	19.72	20.38		17.83	18.28	
Other European	4.57	4.60		4.19	4.25	
Central Asian	9.98	7.37		15.64	13.09	
Other	13.38	12.97		14.09	14.22	

TABLE 5.10 – continued

| | 2050 | | |
	Total Population	Active Population	Activity Rate
HIGH FERTILITY			
TOTAL	564,764	333,996	591.39
European	346,141	205,130	592.62
Slavic	324,062	192,053	592.64
Russian	237,254	140,619	592.69
Other Slavic	86,808	51,434	592.50
Other European	22,079	13,076	592.24
Central Asian	132,965	78,376	589.45
Other	85,658	50,590	589.44
Percentage of Total			
TOTAL	100.00	100.00	
European	61.29	61.42	
Slavic	57.38	57.50	
Russian	42.01	42.10	
Other Slavic	15.37	15.40	
Other European	3.91	3.92	
Central Asian	23.54	23.47	
Other	15.17	15.12	
MEDIAN FERTILITY			
TOTAL	370,192	233,943	631.95
European	215,926	136,474	632.04
Slavic	202,205	127,790	631.98
Russian	148,233	93,646	631.75
Other Slavic	53,972	34,144	632.63
Other European	13,722	8,684	632.89
Central Asian	99,589	62,897	631.57
Other	54,678	34,572	632.28
Percentage of Total			
TOTAL	100.00	100.00	
European	58.33	58.34	
Slavic	54.62	54.62	
Russian	40.04	40.03	
Other Slavic	14.58	14.60	
Other European	3.71	3.71	
Central Asian	26.90	26.89	
Other	14.77	14.78	

TABLE 5.10 – continued
(absolute figures in thousands, activity rates per thousand total population)

	1979			2000		
	Total Population	Active Population	Activity Rate	Total Population	Active Population	Activity Rate
LOW FERTILITY						
TOTAL	264,129	145,658	551.46	307,720	177,959	578.31
European	202,434	116,027	573.16	216,581	129,352	597.25
Slavic	190,362	109,330	574.33	203,690	121,788	597.91
Russian	138,267	79,638	575.97	148,736	89,252	600.07
Other Slavic	52,095	29,692	569.95	54,954	32,535	592.05
Other European	12,073	6,697	554.75	12,891	7,564	586.79
Central Asian	26,360	10,736	407.28	47,488	23,298	490.60
Other	35,335	18,895	534.73	43,651	25,309	579.80
Percentage of Total						
TOTAL	100.00	100.00		100.00	100.00	
European	76.64	79.66		70.38	72.69	
Slavic	72.07	75.06		66.19	68.44	
Russian	52.35	54.67		48.33	50.15	
Other Slavic	19.72	20.38		17.86	18.28	
Other European	4.57	4.60		4.19	4.25	
Central Asian	9.98	7.37		15.43	13.09	
Other	13.38	12.97		14.19	14.22	
CONSTANT FERTILITY						
TOTAL	264,129	145,658	551.46	321,976	177,983	552.78
European	202,434	116,027	573.16	222,659	129,365	581.00
Slavic	190,362	109,330	574.33	209,345	121,800	581.82
Russian	138,267	79,638	575.97	152,913	89,262	583.75
Other Slavic	52,095	29,692	569.95	56,432	32,538	576.58
Other European	12,073	6,697	554.75	13,314	7,565	568.19
Central Asian	26,360	10,736	407.28	54,040	23,309	431.33
Other	35,335	18,895	534.73	45,277	25,309	558.99
Percentage of Total						
TOTAL	100.00	100.00		100.00	100.00	
European	76.64	79.66		69.15	72.68	
Slavic	72.07	75.06		65.02	68.43	
Russian	52.35	54.67		47.49	50.15	
Other Slavic	19.72	20.38		17.53	18.28	
Other European	4.57	4.60		4.14	4.25	
Central Asian	9.98	7.37		16.78	13.10	
Other	13.38	12.97		14.06	14.2	

TABLE 5.10 – continued

| | 2050 | | |
	Total Population	Active Population	Activity Rate
LOW FERTILITY			
TOTAL	316,861	204,151	644.29
European	186,172	119,684	642.86
Slavic	174,439	112,125	642.77
Russian	127,939	82,198	642.48
Other Slavic	46,499	29,926	643.58
Other European	11,734	7,559	644.22
Central Asian	84,372	54,377	644.49
Other	46,317	30,090	649.66
Percentage of Total			
TOTAL	100.00	100.00	
European	58.76	58.63	
Slavic	55.05	54.92	
Russian	40.38	40.26	
Other Slavic	14.68	14.66	
Other European	3.70	3.70	
Central Asian	26.63	26.64	
Other	14.62	14.74	
CONSTANT FERTILITY			
TOTAL	656,560	348,541	530.86
European	252,881	155,744	615.88
Slavic	235,584	145,317	616.84
Russian	172,688	106,526	616.87
Other Slavic	62,896	38,791	616.75
Other European	17,297	10,427	602.78
Central Asian	329,334	148,841	451.94
Other	74,345	43,957	591.26
Percentage of Total			
TOTAL	100.00	100.00	
European	38.52	44.68	
Slavic	35.88	41.69	
Russian	26.30	30.56	
Other Slavic	9.58	11.13	
Other European	2.63	2.99	
Central Asian	50.16	42.70	
Other	11.32	12.61	

TABLE 5.10 – continued
(absolute figures in thousands, activity rates per thousand total population)

	1979			2000		
	Total Population	Active Population	Activity Rate	Total Population	Active Population	Activity Rate
REPLACEMENT FERTILITY						
TOTAL	264,129	145,658	551.46	301,932	177,700	588.54
European	202,434	116,027	573.16	221,591	129,348	583.72
Slavic	190,362	109,330	574.33	208,607	121,788	583.82
Russian	138,267	79,638	575.97	152,424	89,254	585.57
Other Slavic	52,095	29,692	569.95	56,184	32,534	579.06
Other European	12,073	6,697	554.75	12,984	7,560	582.23
Central Asian	26,360	10,736	407.28	37,559	23,080	614.49
Other	35,335	18,895	534.73	42,781	25,272	590.73
Percentage of Total						
TOTAL	100.00	100.00		100.00	100.00	
European	76.64	79.66		73.39	72.79	
Slavic	72.07	75.06		69.09	68.54	
Russian	52.35	54.67		50.48	50.23	
Other Slavic	19.72	20.38		18.61	18.31	
Other European	4.57	4.60		4.30	4.25	
Central Asian	9.98	7.37		12.44	12.99	
Other	13.38	12.97		14.17	14.22	
SYNTHETIC: EUROPEANS HIGH FERTILITY, OTHERS REPLACEMENT						
TOTAL	264,129	145,658	551.46	313,176	177,747	567.56
European	202,434	116,027	573.16	232,835	129,395	555.74
Slavic	190,362	109,330	574.33	218,888	121,828	556.58
Russian	138,267	79,638	575.97	159,844	89,282	558.56
Other Slavic	52,095	29,692	569.95	59,044	32,546	551.22
Other European	12,073	6,697	554.75	13,947	7,567	542.53
Central Asian	26,360	10,736	407.28	37,559	23,080	614.49
Other	35,335	18,895	534.73	42,781	25,272	590.73
Percentage of Total						
TOTAL	100.00	100.00		100.00	100.00	
European	76.64	79.66		74.35	72.80	
Slavic	72.07	75.06		69.89	68.54	
Russian	52.35	54.67		51.04	50.23	
Other Slavic	19.72	20.38		18.85	18.31	
Other European	4.57	4.60		4.45	4.26	
Central Asian	9.98	7.37		11.99	12.98	
Other	13.38	12.97		13.66	14.22	

TABLE 5.10 – continued

	2050		
	Total Population	Active Population	Activity Rate

REPLACEMENT FERTILITY

TOTAL	353,236	217,675	616.23
European	244,442	151,177	618.46
Slavic	230,046	142,267	618.43
Russian	169,023	104,505	618.29
Other Slavic	61,023	37,761	618.80
Other European	14,396	8,911	618.97
Central Asian	56,000	33,802	603.61
Other	52,795	32,696	619.31

Percentage of Total

TOTAL	100.00	100.00	
European	69.20	69.45	
Slavic	65.13	65.36	
Russian	47.85	48.01	
Other Slavic	17.28	17.35	
Other European	4.08	4.09	
Central Asian	15.85	15.53	
Other	14.95	15.02	

SYNTHETIC: EUROPEANS HIGH FERTILITY, OTHERS REPLACEMENT

TOTAL	454,935	271,628	597,07
European	346,141	205,130	592.62
Slavic	324,062	192,053	592.64
Russian	237,254	140,619	592.69
Other Slavic	86,808	51,434	592.50
Other European	22,079	13,076	592.24
Central Asian	56,000	33,802	603.61
Other	52,795	32,696	619.31

Percentage of Total

TOTAL	100.00	100.00	
European	76.09	75.52	
Slavic	71.23	70.70	
Russian	52.15	51.77	
Other Slavic	19.08	18.94	
Other European	4.85	4.81	
Central Asian	12.31	12.44	
Other	11.60	12.04	

TABLE 5.10 – continued
(absolute figures in thousands, activity rates per thousand total population)

	1979			2000		
	Total Population	Active Population	Activity Rate	Total Population	Active Population	Activity Rate
SYNTHETIC: EUROPEANS LOW FERTILITY, OTHERS CONSTANT						
TOTAL	264,129	145,658	551.46	315,898	177,970	563.38
European	202,434	116,027	573.16	216,581	129,352	597.25
Slavic	190,362	109,330	574.33	203,690	121,788	597.91
Russian	138,267	79,638	575.97	148,736	89,252	600.07
Other Slavic	52,095	29,692	569.95	54,954	32,535	592.05
Other European	12,073	6,697	554.75	12,891	7,564	586.79
Central Asian	26,360	10,736	407.28	54,040	23,309	431.33
Other	35,335	18,895	534.73	45,277	25,309	558.99

TABLE 5.10 – continued

	2050		
	Total Population	Active Population	Activity Rate
SYNTHETIC: EUROPEANS LOW FERTILITY, OTHERS CONSTANT			
TOTAL	589,852	312,481	529,76
European	186,172	119,684	642.86
Slavic	174,439	112,125	642.77
Russian	127,939	82,198	642.48
Other Slavic	46,499	29,926	643.58
Other European	11,734	7,559	644.22
Central Asian	329,334	148,841	451.94
Other	74,345	43,957	591.26

6

Future Military Manpower Resources in East and West

John F Long

The future military manpower resources of East and West are likely to be quite different from past patterns. Recent declines in fertility in both East and West, combined with continued high fertility in the rest of the world, may well lead to significant shifts in world manpower resources. Both Eastern and Western countries may have slow or declining rates of growth in military manpower. Current indications are that for most of the next 40 years the military manpower resources of the West would grow less than those of the East. This effect will be accompanied by a marked increase in the percentage of the world's population (and military manpower resources) that is not located in either block. Future growth in the third world countries will far exceed that of the developed world.

This chapter examines this phenomenon by projecting Eastern and Western changes in military manpower resources. We define our populations of interest, review the causes for changing manpower size, determine the current and projected relative changes in Eastern and Western military manpower resources, examine uncertainty in the projected changes, and look to the projected manpower balance and its implications.

Definitions

Two critical definitions have to be established before we can quantify the differences in manpower resources between East and West. The first of these concerns the term 'military manpower resources.' This analysis uses a demographic definition of the term i.e.; 'the male population between the ages of 17 and 29 years.' These values were chosen to represent the wider ranges in age that might be available in war rather than the age structure of the armed formes of a typical European country in peace. Although the age-group selected is arbitrary (the overall trend of change being similar for any

128

reasonable age-group) the years 17–29 keep the emphasis upon the younger men traditionally serving in their country's armed forces. A wider age-bracket would moderate the likely demographic changes whilst a narrower one would exacerbate them.

Similarly, the restriction of the definition to males makes little difference in practice. Although females now play an important and substantial role in the armed forces of many countries, the great majority of all military manpower is male. This restriction by sex makes little difference either when we come to make comparisons between countries or groups of countries since the sex ratio of the young adult population varies very little across the area of study. What may vary (especially in the future) is the extent in which national policies encourage female participation in the armed forces.

A more important restriction implicit in this formulation is that military manpower resources are purely dependent on demographic considerations. It does not take into account any particular circumstances of individual countries' labour force or social conditions that might differentially reduce the availability of a sub-population for military service.

The second definition is that of the terms 'East' and 'West.' In this analysis, emphasis has been placed on comparing the populations of the two formally recognized mutual defence organisations, the North Atlantic Treaty Organization (NATO) and the former Warsaw Pact. Such an arrangement recognises formal commitments and balances the large population of the Soviet Union with the population of the United States and Canada. Other definitions have only European (or partially European nations such as the Soviet Union) and divided them into market and non-market economies (Saunders, 1988). In the detailed tables presented with this text several different national groupings are shown (NATO)[1] versus the former Warsaw Pact,[2] European Market Economies [3] versus Non-market Economies,[4] European NATO Countries [5] versus Non-market Economies (excluding the Soviet Union), and a broad definition of West [6] versus a broad definition of East.[7]

Method for Population Projections

The population projections used in this paper are from the US Bureau of the Census International data base (US Bureau of the Census, 1988). They are produced by the standard cohort-component method of population projection (Shryock and Siegel, 1976). This method uses an initial census or estimated population of the country by age, race, and sex and applies age-specific rates of fertility, mortality, and immigration to get the projected population.

Mortality and immigration are not important components for the age groups and countries of interest here. For the next 15 to 20 years, the current age structure of children in the initial population is far more significant. For

TABLE 6.1 Projected Total Population Changes of East and West Between 1986 – 2025 by Percentage

Country	1986–90	1990–95	1995–2000	2000–05	2005–10	2010–15	2015–20	2020–25	1986–2025
Austria	0.43%	0.55%	0.33%	0.00%	-0.52%	-0.59%	-0.72%	-1.21%	-1.88%
Belgium	0.30%	0.30%	0.07%	-0.42%	-0.83%	-1.02%	-1.12%	-1.37%	-4.04%
Canada	3.53%	3.57%	2.77%	2.27%	1.91%	1.60%	1.14%	0.47%	18.55%
Denmark	0.31%	0.38%	0.22%	-0.15%	-0.68%	-0.98%	-1.13%	-1.42%	-3.42%
Finland	1.17%	0.96%	0.50%	0.20%	-0.04%	-0.29%	-0.68%	-1.23%	0.56%
France	1.44%	1.51%	1.14%	0.60%	0.18%	-0.06%	-0.27%	-0.59%	3.99%
Germany, Fed. Rep.	-0.05%	-0.06%	-0.41%	-1.23%	-1.91%	-2.13%	-2.24%	-2.37%	-9.97%
Greece	1.07%	1.12%	0.91%	0.55%	-0.10%	-0.70%	-1.01%	-1.12%	0.69%
Iceland	3.08%	3.74%	3.13%	2.69%	2.30%	1.79%	1.25%	0.66%	20.20%
Ireland	5.14%	6.25%	5.80%	5.19%	4.73%	4.31%	3.89%	3.28%	45.72%
Italy	0.72%	0.76%	0.69%	0.07%	-0.72%	-1.11%	-1.22%	-1.33%	-2.14%
Luxembourg	0.10%	-0.01%	-0.32%	-0.83%	-1.30%	-1.56%	-1.72%	-2.00%	-7.42%
Netherlands	2.04%	2.27%	1.69%	0.87%	0.21%	-0.12%	-0.33%	-0.75%	5.97%
Norway	1.15%	1.11%	0.07%	0.28%	0.01%	-0.08%	-0.21%	-0.62%	2.35%
Portugal	2.83%	2.77%	1.95%	1.39%	0.91%	0.58%	0.35%	0.06%	11.33%
Spain	2.14%	2.48%	2.10%	1.50%	0.74%	0.17%	-0.08%	-0.23%	9.13%
Sweden	0.44%	0.07%	-0.37%	-0.71%	-0.89%	-0.99%	-1.18%	-1.62%	-5.15%
Switzerland	1.17%	0.89%	0.19%	-0.55%	-1.12%	-1.45%	-1.73%	-2.17%	-4.72%
Turkey	9.13%	10.64%	9.59%	8.71%	7.98%	7.34%	6.72%	6.07%	88.71%
United Kingdom	0.64%	0.69%	0.24%	-0.22%	-0.30%	-0.23%	-0.34%	-0.74%	-0.29%
United States	3.63%	3.84%	3.07%	2.68%	2.50%	2.29%	1.90%	1.34%	23.31%

TABLE 6.1 – continued

Country	1986-90	1990-95	1995-2000	2000-05	2005-10	2010-15	2015-20	2020-25	1986-2025
Albania	8.05%	8.58%	6.87%	5.82%	5.39%	4.91%	4.22%	3.34%	58.00%
Bulgaria	0.28%	0.35%	0.40%	-0.00%	-0.41%	-0.52%	-0.48%	-0.52%	-0.91%
Czechoslovakia	0.99%	1.37%	1.85%	1.54%	1.00%	0.67%	0.54%	0.31%	8.56%
German Dem. Rep.	-0.30%	-0.22%	-0.02%	0.16%	-0.04%	-0.50%	-1.03%	-1.17%	-3.08%
Hungary	-0.79%	-0.68%	0.03%	-0.11%	-0.56%	-0.72%	-0.61%	-0.57%	-3.94%
Poland	2.37%	2.15%	1.89%	1.84%	1.79%	1.40%	0.91%	0.50%	13.59%
Romania	1.90%	2.52%	2.20%	1.51%	0.98%	0.84%	0.76%	0.60%	11.87%
Soviet Union	3.37%	3.52%	3.47%	3.47%	3.58%	3.33%	2.89%	2.56%	29.39%
Yugoslavia	2.52%	2.65%	2.21%	1.61%	1.04%	0.58%	0.28%	0.05%	11.45%
World	7.10%	8.55%	8.08%	7.51%	7.20%	6.89%	6.47%	6.00%	74.68%
West	2.67%	2.96%	2.45%	1.97%	1.62%	1.40%	1.16%	0.78%	16 %
East	2.78%	2.94%	2.89%	2.80%	2.78%	2.52%	2.14%	1.85%	22.69%
NATO	2.77%	3.08%	2.56%	2.08%	1.73%	1.51%	1.25%	0.87%	16.97%
Warsaw Pact	2.76%	2.92%	2.90%	2.85%	2.86%	2.61%	2.23%	1.94%	23.08%
European NATO	1.00%	1.09%	0.75%	0.15%	-0.38%	-0.64%	-0.80%	-1.03%	0.11%
Warsaw Pact (excl USSR)	1.22%	1.36%	1.39%	1.17%	0.88%	0.59%	0.32%	0.10%	7.25%
Eur. Market Economies	1.00%	1.08%	0.74%	0.16%	-0.35%	-0.61%	-0.77%	-1.02%	0.21%
Non-market Economies	2.78%	2.94%	2.89%	2.80%	2.78%	2.52%	2.14%	1.85%	22.69%

Source: US Bureau of the Census International Data Base (1988)

TABLE 6.2   Projected Total Population of East and West: 1986–2025 (numbers in thousands)

Country	1986	1988	1990	1995	2000	2005	2010	2015	2020	2025
Austria	7,563	7,577	7,595	7,637	7,662	7,650	7,610	7,566	7,511	7,420
Belgium	9,866	9,881	9,895	9,925	9,932	9,891	9,808	9,708	9,599	9,467
Canada	5,623	6,088	6,527	7,473	8,233	8,873	9,423	9,893	30,232	30,375
Denmark	5,118	5,126	5,134	5,153	5,165	5,157	5,122	5,072	5,014	4,943
Finland	4,919	4,950	4,977	5,024	5,049	5,059	5,057	5,043	5,008	4,947
France	55,387	55,798	56,184	57,032	57,684	58,028	58,131	58,099	57,944	57,600
Germany, Fed. Rep.	61,007	60,980	60,977	60,938	60,688	59,943	58,799	57,547	56,261	54,927
Greece	9,960	10,015	10,066	10,179	10,271	10,328	10,317	10,245	10,142	10,029
Iceland	243	247	250	260	268	275	282	287	290	292
Ireland	3,655	3,749	3,843	4,083	4,320	4,544	4,759	4,964	5,157	5,326
Italy	57,245	57,455	57,657	58,097	58,499	58,543	58,124	57,476	56,775	56,019
Luxembourg	366	366	366	366	365	362	357	352	346	339
Netherlands	14,567	14,716	14,864	15,201	15,458	15,591	15,624	15,606	15,554	15,436
Norway	4,166	4,191	4,214	4,261	4,291	4,303	4,303	4,299	4,290	4,264
Portugal	10,239	10,388	10,528	10,820	11,031	11,184	11,286	11,351	11,392	11,399
Spain	38,792	39,210	39,625	40,608	41,460	42,081	42,394	42,466	42,433	42,335
Sweden	8,371	8,393	8,407	8,413	8,382	8,322	8,248	8,167	8,071	7,940
Turkey	51,818	54,168	56,549	62,564	68,565	74,535	80,481	86,386	92,188	97,788
United Kingdom	56,757	56,936	57,121	57,513	57,649	57,521	57,349	57,215	57,019	56,595
United States	241,596	246,043	250,372	259,944	267,987	275,167	282,037	288,488	293,488	297,915

Source: US Bureau of the Census International Data Base (1988)

TABLE 6.2 – continued

Country	1986	1988	1990	1995	2000	2005	2010	2015	2020	2025
Albania	3,024	3,147	3,268	3,548	3,792	4,013	4,299	4,229	4,624	4,778
Bulgaria	8,953	8,967	8,978	9,009	9,046	9,045	9,008	8,961	8,919	8,872
Czechoslovakia	15,541	15,621	15,695	15,910	16,204	16,454	16,619	16,730	16,820	16,872
German Dem. Rep.	16,628	16,597	16,578	16,542	16,539	16,565	16,656	16,476	16,306	16,115
Hungary	10,630	10,588	10,546	10,474	10,477	10,466	10,408	10,333	10,270	10,211
Poland	37,473	37,958	38,363	39,187	39,926	40,663	41,392	41,973	42,355	42,567
Romania	2,835	3,041	3,269	3,855	4,381	4,748	4,992	5,203	5,394	5,546
Soviet Union	281,462	286,435	290,939	301,184	311,637	322,463	334,004	345,121	355,093	364,182
Yugoslavia	3,278	3,580	3,864	4,498	5,040	5,433	5,707	5,857	5,930	5,943
World	4,965,301	5,141,299	5,318,035	5,772,511	6,238,924	6,707,456	7,190,263	7,685,391	8,182,705	8,673,323
West	673,808	682,868	691,778	712,227	729,659	744,018	756,101	766,722	775,584	781,598
East	419,824	425,934	431,500	444,207	457,042	469,861	482,918	495,091	505,710	515,087
Ratio	1.60	1.60	1.60	1.60	1.60	1.58	1.57	1.55	1.53	1.52
NATO	632,883	641,726	650,433	670,458	687,613	701,890	714,030	724,782	733,857	740,256
Warsaw Pact	393,522	399,207	404,368	416,161	428,210	440,405	452,982	464,797	475,157	484,365
Ratio	1.61	1.61	1.61	1.61	1.61	1.59	1.58	1.56	1.54	1.53
European NATO	313,846	315,428	316,985	320,428	322,829	323,315	322,088	320,015	317,459	314,178
Warsaw Pact (excl. USSR)	112,060	112,772	113,429	114,977	116,573	117,942	118,979	119,676	120,064	120,183
Ratio	2.80	2.80	2.79	2.79	2.77	2.74	2.71	2.67	2.64	2.61
Eur. Market Econ.	354,162	355,957	357,713	361,570	364,241	364,807	363,520	361,317	358,550	354,889
Non-market Econ	419,824	425,934	431,500	444,207	457,042	469,861	482,918	495,091	505,710	515,087
Ratio	0.84	0.84	0.83	0.81	0.80	0.78	0.75	0.73	0.71	0.69

TABLE 6.3 Projected National and Regional Populations as a Percentage of the World Population, 1986–2025

Country	1986	1988	1990	1995	2000	2005	2010	2015	2020	2025
Austria	0.17	0.16	0.15	0.12	0.10	0.09	0.08	0.08	0.07	0.06
Belgium	0.21	0.20	0.18	0.15	0.13	0.12	0.11	0.10	0.09	0.08
Canada	0.60	0.56	0.53	0.44	0.40	0.37	0.35	0.32	0.29	0.26
Denmark	0.10	0.10	0.10	0.08	0.07	0.06	0.05	0.05	0.05	0.04
Finland	0.10	0.09	0.09	0.07	0.07	0.06	0.06	0.05	0.05	0.04
France	1.13	1.10	1.06	0.94	0.83	0.74	0.69	0.63	0.56	0.51
West Germany	1.33	1.27	1.18	0.89	0.66	0.60	0.58	0.57	0.53	0.46
Greece	0.20	0.19	0.19	0.17	0.15	0.13	0.11	0.10	0.10	0.09
Iceland	0.01	0.01	0.01	0.00	0.00	0.00	0.00	0.00	0.00	0.00
Ireland	0.08	0.08	0.08	0.07	0.07	0.07	0.07	0.06	0.06	0.05
Italy	1.19	1.17	1.14	0.98	0.80	0.65	0.58	0.57	0.54	0.49
Luxembourg	0.01	0.01	0.01	0.01	0.00	0.00	0.00	0.00	0.00	0.00
Netherlands	0.33	0.32	0.30	0.25	0.20	0.18	0.17	0.16	0.15	0.13
Norway	0.09	0.08	0.08	0.07	0.06	0.05	0.05	0.05	0.04	0.04
Portugal	0.22	0.22	0.21	0.19	0.17	0.15	0.14	0.13	0.12	0.11
Spain	0.84	0.83	0.82	0.75	0.65	0.55	0.47	0.45	0.43	0.39
Sweden	0.15	0.15	0.14	0.13	0.11	0.10	0.09	0.08	0.08	0.07
Switzerland	0.13	0.13	0.12	0.10	0.08	0.07	0.07	0.06	0.06	0.05
Turkey	1.30	1.33	1.34	1.34	1.33	1.32	1.31	1.28	1.22	1.17
UK	1.20	1.17	1.12	0.93	0.77	0.70	0.68	0.63	0.56	0.49
USA	5.49	5.17	4.87	4.21	3.85	3.70	3.56	3.30	2.99	2.76

Source: US Bureau of the Census International Data Base (1988)

TABLE 6.3 – continued

Country	1986	1988	1990	1995	2000	2005	2010	2015	2020	2025
Albania	0.08	0.08	0.08	0.07	0.07	0.07	0.07	0.06	0.05	0.05
Bulgaria	0.17	0.16	0.16	0.15	0.14	0.12	0.11	0.10	0.09	0.09
Czechoslovakia	0.29	0.28	0.28	0.28	0.27	0.24	0.20	0.19	0.18	0.17
East Germany	0.35	0.33	0.31	0.25	0.22	0.22	0.20	0.18	0.16	0.15
Hungary	0.19	0.18	0.18	0.18	0.16	0.14	0.12	0.11	0.11	0.10
Poland	0.76	0.70	0.66	0.64	0.66	0.64	0.58	0.50	0.45	0.42
Romania	0.44	0.43	0.43	0.44	0.40	0.36	0.32	0.31	0.28	0.26
USSR	6.09	5.76	5.42	4.91	4.91	4.89	4.70	4.31	3.97	3.84
USSR	6.09	5.76	5.42	4.91	4.91	4.89	4.70	4.31	3.97	3.84
Yugoslavia	0.49	0.47	0.46	0.42	0.39	0.36	0.33	0.30	0.27	0.25
West	14.87	14.33	13.71	11.91	10.50	9.71	9.24	8.67	7.98	7.30
East	8.86	8.41	7.97	7.33	7.21	7.04	6.62	6.05	5.58	5.34
Total	23.73	22.74	21.68	19.24	17.71	16.75	15,86	14.72	13.56	12.64
NATO	14.03	13.53	12.95	11.27	9.95	9.21	8.77	8.23	7.58	6.94
Warsaw Pact	8.29	7.85	7.44	6.84	6.75	6.61	6.22	5.69	5.25	5.04
Total	22.32	21.38	20.39	18.11	16.70	15.82	14.99	13.92	12.83	11.98
European NATO	6.64	6.47	6.21	5.28	4.38	3.81	3.54	3.34	3.08	2.75
Warsaw Pact (excl USSR)	2.20	2.09	2.02	1.93	1.85	1.71	1.53	1.38	1.28	1.20
Total	8.84	8.56	8.23	7.21	6.23	5.52	5.07	4.72	4.36	3.95
Eur. Market Economies	7.46	7.26	6.96	5.92	4.92	4.30	4.00	3.77	3.47	3.10
Non-market Economies	8.86	8.41	7.79	7.33	7.21	7.04	6.62	6.05	5.58	5.34
Total	16.32	15.67	14.93	13.25	12.13	11.34	10.62	9.82	9.05	8.44

TABLE 6.4 Projected Change in Population of Males Aged 17–29 in East and West: 1987–2025

Country	1986–90	1990–95	1995–2000	2000–05	2005–10	2010–15	2015–20	2020–25	1986–2025
Austria	-2.67%	-12.63%	-12.92%	-4.07%	2.04%	-0.87%	-2.87%	-5.79%	-34.25%
Belgium	-4.42%	-8.63%	-7.46%	-4.52%	-1.04%	-1.47%	-3.33%	-4.93%	-30.85%
Canada	-5.82%	-9.82%	-2.28%	1.71%	1.18%	-2.70%	-5.15%	-3.98%	-24.31%
Denmark	0.61%	-6.41%	-11.79%	-10.65%	-3.14%	4.28%	0.48%	-4.68%	-28.20%
Finland	-5.35%	-7.20%	-3.11%	1.57%	-2.77%	-4.94%	-4.59%	-3.60%	-26.51%
France	0.61%	-3.70%	-4.97%	-4.66%	0.68%	-2.99%	-4.40%	-4.85%	-22.01%
Germany, Fed. Rep.	-5.45%	-17.93%	-19.54%	-3.37%	5.28%	4.06%	-1.45%	-8.26%	-40.24%
Greece	2.81%	-1.83%	-4.99%	-4.73%	-6.80%	-4.47%	-0.44%	-2.53%	-21.07%
Iceland	-1.31%	-1.65%	0.63%	-2.39%	-3.89%	-6.14%	-2.87%	-2.63%	-18.67%
Ireland	8.46%	3.77%	1.84%	3.06%	6.12%	3.16%	-0.35%	-1.77%	26.57%
Italy	2.68%	-6.58%	-12.38%	-12.45%	-3.81%	4.09%	2.28%	-4.08%	-27.72%
Luxembourg	-6.19%	-9.83%	-8.28%	-2.63%	0.18%	-1.69%	-3.53%	-5.39%	-32.09%
Netherlands	-2.45%	-9.99%	-12.55%	-6.28%	2.07%	2.65%	-1.87%	-6.56%	-30.87%
Norway	0.92%	-4.12%	-9.63%	-7.37%	-0.01%	0.79%	-2.00%	-5.06%	-24.05%
Portugal	3.95%	-1.33%	-4.84%	-6.09%	-3.12%	0.88%	-1.88%	-4.60%	-16.15%
Spain	4.40%	0.13%	-6.35%	-9.79%	-7.61%	2.01%	1.33%	-2.81%	-18.02%
Sweden	0.55%	-5.03%	-7.29%	-5.27%	0.05%	-0.18%	-3.45%	-4.98%	-23.14%
Switzerland	-3.84%	-11.63%	-10.50%	-2.89%	1.87%	-0.60%	-3.68%	-6.51%	-32.66%
Turkey	10.44%	8.54%	6.70%	7.39%	6.18%	3.89%	2.10%	1.63%	57.20%
United Kingdom	-0.17%	-9.88%	-9.98%	-2.17%	4.10%	-1.23%	-5.79%	-7.12%	-28.71%
United States	-5.05%	-6.13%	-1.10%	3.39%	3.09%	-1.01%	-3.44%	-2.07%	-12.04%

Table 6.4 – continued

Country	1986–90	1990–95	1995–2000	2000–05	2005–10	2010–15	2015–20	2020–25	1986–2025
Albania	5.07%	3.27%	3.55%	4.06%	3.66%	-1.19%	-5.14%	-3.62%	9.49%
Bulgaria	0.98%	2.60%	0.30%	-4.43%	-5.60%	-0.66%	0.81%	-1.53%	-7.55%
Czechoslovakia	2.39%	7.77%	5.08%	-5.03%	-8.20%	-0.30%	2.01%	0.01%	2.82%
German Dem. Rep.	-6.80%	-12.40%	-3.70%	5.57%	-0.63%	-5.86%	-4.15%	0.22%	-25.42%
Hungary	1.04%	9.44%	0.59%	-7.82%	-10.76%	1.79%	3.72%	-0.05%	-3.45%
Poland	-6.49%	4.22%	11.28%	4.70%	-3.36%	-7.80%	-4.49%	0.87%	-2.54%
Romania	4.84%	11.43%	-3.54%	-3.18%	-3.61%	2.14%	-1.08%	-3.88%	2.14%
Soviet Union	-4.62%	-1.74%	8.05%	7.24%	2.85%	-1.91%	-1.84%	2.54%	10.27%
Yugoslavia	-0.89%	0.03%	0.58%	-0.72%	-2.79%	-2.63%	-2.33%	-1.68%	-9.99%
World	7.32%	5.56%	3.10%	4.70%	6.74%	5.42%	3.73%	3.46%	47.66%
West	-1.24%	-5.66%	-4.73%	-0.60%	1.98%	0.35%	-2.04%	-3.00%	-14.19%
East	-3.65%	-0.12%	6.31%	4.90%	0.78%	-2.24%	-1.87%	1.54%	5.34%
NATO	-1.20%	-5.54%	-4.58%	-0.48%	2.04%	0.42%	-1.98%	-2.91%	-13.57%
Warsaw Pact	-3.90%	-0.17%	6.69%	5.23%	0.94%	-2.23%	-1.81%	1.76%	6.21%
European NATO	0.12%	-7.75%	-10.41%	-6.47%	-0.35%	0.87%	-1.80%	-5.42%	-27.75%
Warsaw Pact (excl USSR)	-1.89%	4.05%	3.24%	-0.11%	-4.51%	-3.21%	-1.75%	-0.65%	-5.02%
Eur. Market Economies	-0.11%	-7.76%	-10.09%	-6.05%	-0.21%	0.69%	-1.94%	-5.34%	-27.41%
Non-market Economies	-3.65%	-0.12%	6.31%	4.90%	0.78%	-2.24%	-1.87%	1.54%	5.34%

Source: US Bureau of the Census International Data Base (1988)

137

TABLE 6.5. Projected Population of Males 17–29 for East and West: 1986–2025 (numbers in thousands)

Country	1986	1988	1990	1995	2000	2005	2010	2015	2020	2025
Austria	819	816	797	697	607	582	594	589	572	539
Belgium	1,022	1,005	977	892	826	788	780	769	743	707
Canada	2,973	2,895	2,800	2,525	2,468	2,510	2,539	2,471	2,344	2,250
Denmark	517	521	520	487	429	384	372	388	389	371
Finland	491	478	465	432	418	425	413	393	375	361
France	5,623	5,661	5,657	5,448	5,177	4,936	4,969	4,821	4,609	4,385
Germany, Fed. Rep.	6,619	6,518	6,258	5,136	4,132	3,993	4,204	4,375	4,311	3,955
Greece	970	994	997	979	930	886	826	789	785	765
Iceland	28	28	28	28	28	27	26	24	24	23
Ireland	377	392	408	424	432	445	472	487	485	477
Italy	5,917	6,016	6,076	5,676	4,975	4,354	4,188	4,359	4,459	4,277
Luxembourg	36	35	34	31	28	27	27	27	26	25
Netherlands	1,648	1,639	1,608	1,447	1,265	1,186	1,210	1,243	1,219	1,139
Norway	426	430	430	412	373	345	345	348	341	324
Portugal	1,094	1,121	1,137	1,122	1,067	1,002	971	980	961	917
Spain	4,169	4,283	4,352	4,358	4,081	3,682	3,401	3,470	3,516	3,417
Sweden	765	769	770	731	678	642	642	641	619	588
Switzerland	662	653	637	563	504	489	498	495	477	446
Turkey	6,470	6,827	7,145	7,755	8,275	8,886	9,435	9,802	10,008	10,171
United Kingdom	5,943	6,004	5,933	5,347	4,813	4,709	4,902	4,842	4,561	4,237
United States	27,249	26,588	25,874	24,288	24,020	24,836	25,604	25,345	24,473	23,967

TABLE 6.5 – continued

Country	1986	1988	1990	1995	2000	2005	2010	2015	2020	2025
Albania	395	408	415	428	443	461	478	473	448	432
Bulgaria	822	818	830	851	854	816	770	765	771	760
Czechoslovakia	1,452	1,446	1,487	1,603	1,684	1,599	1,468	1,464	1,493	1,493
German Dem. Rep.	1,755	1,714	1,636	1,433	1,380	1,457	1,448	1,363	1,306	1,309
Hungary	925	912	935	1,023	1,029	948	846	861	893	893
Poland	3,775	3,618	3,530	3,679	4,093	4,286	4,142	3,819	3,647	3,679
Romania	2,193	2,224	2,299	2,562	2,471	2,392	2,306	2,356	2,330	2,240
Soviet Union	30,232	29,634	28,834	28,333	30,614	32,830	33,765	33,121	32,513	33,338
Yugoslavia	2,449	2,439	2,427	2,428	2,442	2,424	2,357	2,295	2,242	2,204
World	599,268	619,535	643,148	678,888	699,900	732,795	782,174	824,545	855,330	884,883
West	73,819	73,674	72,903	68,776	65,524	65,133	66,420	66,656	65,298	63,341
East	43,998	43,213	42,392	42,339	45,011	47,215	47,581	46,516	45,645	46,348
Ratio	1.68	1.70	1.72	1.62	1.46	1.38	1.40	1.43	1.43	1.37
NATO	69,683	69,561	68,849	65,038	62,060	61,762	63,020	63,282	62,027	60,224
Warsaw Pact	41,155	40,366	39,551	39,483	42,125	44,329	44,746	43,749	42,955	43,712
Ratio	1.69	1.72	1.74	1.65	1.47	1.39	1.41	1.45	1.44	1.38
Warsaw Pact (excl USSR)	10,922	10,732	10,716	11,150	11,511	11,499	10,981	10,628	10,442	10,374
Ratio	3.02	3.10	3.08	2.73	2.37	2.22	2.32	2.41	2.41	2.30
Non-market Economies	43,998	43,213	42,392	42,339	45,011	47,215	47,581	46,516	45,645	46,348
Ratio	0.84	0.86	0.87	0.81	0.68	0.61	0.61	0.62	0.62	0.58

Source: US Bureau of the Census International Data Base (1988)

TABLE 6.6 Projected Population of Males 17–29 as a Percentage of the Total Population: 1986–2025

Country	1986	1988	1990	1995	2000	2005	2010	2015	2020	2025
Austria	10.83%	10.76%	10.50%	9.12%	7.92%	7.61%	7.80%	7.78%	7.61%	7.26%
Belgium	10.36%	10.17%	9.87%	8.99%	8.31%	7.97%	7.95%	7.92%	7.74%	7.46%
Canada	11.60%	11.10%	10.56%	9.19%	8.74%	8.69%	8.63%	8.27%	7.75%	7.41%
Denmark	10.10%	10.17%	10.13%	9.45%	8.31%	7.44%	7.26%	7.64%	7.77%	7.51%
Finland	9.99%	9.65%	9.34%	8.59%	8.28%	8.39%	8.17%	7.78%	7.48%	7.30%
France	10.15%	10.14%	10.07%	9.55%	8.97%	8.51%	8.55%	8.30%	7.95%	7.61%
West Germany	10.85%	10.69%	10.26%	8.43%	6.81%	6.66%	7.15%	7.60%	7.66%	7.20%
Greece	9.74%	9.92%	9.90%	9.62%	9.05%	8.58%	8.00%	7.70%	7.74%	7.63%
Iceland	11.67%	11.51%	11.17%	10.59%	10.34%	9.82%	9.23%	8.51%	8.16%	7.90%
Ireland	10.30%	10.47%	10.63%	10.38%	9.99%	9.79%	9.92%	9.81%	9.41%	8.95%
Italy	10.34%	10.47%	10.54%	9.77%	8.50%	7.44%	7.21%	7.58%	7.85%	7.63%
Luxembourg	9.92%	9.65%	9.29%	8.38%	7.71%	7.57%	7.69%	7.68%	7.53%	7.27%
Netherlands	11.31%	11.14%	10.82%	9.52%	8.19%	7.61%	7.75%	7.96%	7.84%	7.38%
Norway	10.23%	10.25%	10.21%	9.68%	8.68%	8.02%	8.02%	8.09%	7.95%	7.59%
Portugal	10.68%	10.79%	10.80%	10.37%	9.68%	8.96%	8.60%	8.63%	8.44%	8.04%
Spain	10.75%	10.92%	10.98%	10.73%	9.84%	8.75%	8.02%	8.17%	8.29%	8.07%
Sweden	9.14%	9.16%	9.15%	8.69%	8.08%	7.71%	7.79%	7.85%	7.67%	7.41%
Switzerland	10.11%	9.90%	9.61%	8.42%	7.52%	7.34%	7.56%	7.63%	7.48%	7.15%
Turkey	12.49%	12.60%	12.64%	12.40%	12.07%	11.92%	11.72%	11.35%	10.86%	10.40%
UK	10.47%	10.55%	10.39%	9.30%	8.35%	8.19%	8.55%	8.46%	8.00%	7.49%
USA	11.28%	10.81%	10.33%	9.34%	8.96%	9.03%	9.08%	8.79%	8.32%	8.04%

TABLE 6.6 – continued

Country	1986	1988	1990	1995	2000	2005	2010	2015	2020	2025
Albania	13.05%	12.96%	12.69%	12.07%	11.70%	11.50%	11.31%	10.65%	9.70%	9.04%
Bulgaria	9.18%	9.13%	9.24%	9.45%	9.44%	9.02%	8.55%	8.54%	8.65%	8.56%
Czechoslovakia	9.35%	9.26%	9.48%	10.07%	10.39%	9.72%	8.84%	8.75%	8.88%	8.85%
East Germany	10.56%	10.32%	9.87%	8.66%	8.34%	8.80%	8.74%	8.27%	8.01%	8.12%
Hungary	8.70%	8.61%	8.86%	9.77%	9.82%	9.06%	8.13%	8.34%	8.70%	8.75%
Poland	10.07%	9.53%	9.20%	9.39%	10.25%	10.54%	10.01%	9.10%	8.61%	8.64%
Romania	9.60%	9.65%	9.88%	10.74%	10.14%	9.67%	9.23%	9.35%	9.18%	8.77%
USSR	10.74%	10.35%	9.91%	9.41%	9.82%	10.18%	10.11%	9.60%	9.16%	9.15%
Yugoslavia	10.52%	10.35%	10.17%	9.91%	9.75%	9.53%	9.17%	8.88%	8.64%	8.50%
West	10.96%	10.79%	10.54%	9.66%	8.98%	8.75%	8.78%	8.69%	8.42%	8.10%
East	10.48%	10.15%	9.82%	9.53%	9.85%	10.05%	9.85%	9.40%	9.03%	9.00%
NATO	11.01%	10.84%	10.59%	9.70%	9.03%	8.80%	8.83%	8.73%	8.73%	8.14%
Warsaw Pact	10.46%	10.11%	9.78%	9.49%	9.84%	10.07%	9.88%	9.41%	9.04%	9.02%
European NATO	10.51%	10.54%	10.42%	9.51%	8.46%	7.90%	7.90%	8.02%	7.94%	7.59%
Warsaw Pact (excl USSR)	9.75%	9.52%	9.45%	9.70%	9.87%	9.75%	9.23%	8.88%	8.70%	8.63%
Eur. Market Economies	10.46%	10.48%	10.35%	9.44%	8.43%	7.91%	7.92%	8.02%	7.93%	7.58%
Non-market Economies	10.48%	10.15%	9.82%	9.53%	9.85%	10.05%	9.85%	9.40%	9.03%	9.00%

Source: US Bureau of the Census International Data Base (1988)

141

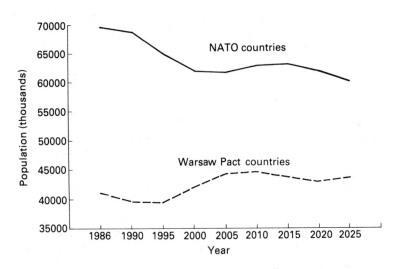

Source: Table 6.2

FIGURE 6.1   Projected Population of Males Aged 17–29 Years: NATO and Former
Warsaw Pact Countries

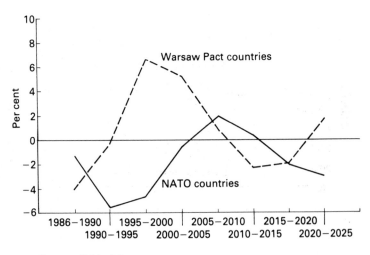

Source: Table 6.6

FIGURE 6.2   Projected Change in Population of Males Aged 17–29 Years: NATO and
Former Warsaw Pact Countries

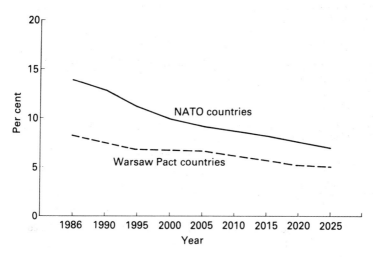

Source: Table 6.4.

FIGURE 6.3   Projected Population of NATO and Former Warsaw Pact Countries: As a Percentage of the World Population, 1986–2025

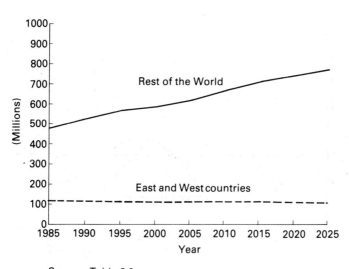

Source: Table 6.2.

FIGURE 6.4   Projected Population of Males Aged 17–29 Years: East and West Countries and the Rest of the World

143

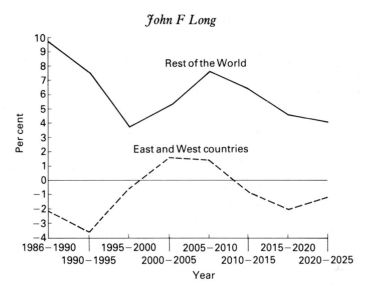

John F Long

Source: Table 6.2.

FIGURE 6.5　Projected Change in Population of Males Aged 17–29 Years: East and West Countries and the Rest of the World

population projections of available military manpower into the next century, the course of birth rates over the next 20 years is of great importance.

Projections of the Total Population of East and West

For many countries in both the East and West, the next 40 years will represent a time of population stability if not population decline. These declines result from the assumption of only moderate improvements in the already low rates of fertility and the larger numbers of deaths consistent with the relatively old populations of these countries.

Between the years 1988 and 2025, while the population of the world is increasing by 75 per cent, that of the countries in NATO will increase by only 17 per cent while those in the former Warsaw Pact will increase by 23 per cent. (Table 6.1) As Table 6.2 shows, this will lead to a declining ratio of the population of NATO countries to former Warsaw Pact countries from 1.61 to 1.53. The decline is more precipitous if we look at the ratio of European market economies to nonmarket economies sinking from 0.84 in 1986 to 0.69 in 2025.

Perhaps equally important in strategic terms, the populations of both NATO and former Warsaw Pact countries will become an ever smaller percentage of total world population. While the combined population of the

144

NATO and former Warsaw Pact countries represented 22 per cent of the world's population in 1986, they will decline to less than 12 per cent in 2025 (see Table 6.3). Confining our attention to European countries alone, the total falls from over 16 per cent in 1986 to below 9 per cent by 2025.

Population Projections in Relation to Military Manpower Resources

The relative growth differentials become much more marked when we confine our attention to what we earlier defined as the 'military manpower resources' within a population and selected the age-group 17–29 years, recognising that studies based upon other age-groups would give broadly similar results.

Since the fertility rates of developed countries have reached their lowest ebb in recent years, the differences between our chosen age-group in the developed countries and the rest of the world have become exaggerated. We find that whilst the world population within that age-group will increase by no less than 48 per cent between the years 1986 and 2025, the corresponding figures for the former Warsaw Pact is only 6 per cent growth and that among NATO countries a decline of no less than 14 per cent will occur (see Figure 6.1). Similarly, the differences between the populations of the European market and non-market economies (see Table 6.4) are even larger, with a 27 per cent decline for the former and a 5 per cent increase for the latter in the number of men in the prime military age group.

In consequence of these large growth differentials, the ratio of potential military manpower resources between West and East will suffer a major decline over the next four decades. The ratio of military manpower between NATO and the countries forming the erstwhile Warsaw Pact will decline from 1.69 in 1986 to 1.38 by 2025. The ratio of European market to non-market economies will decline from .84 in 1986 to only .58 in 2025 (see Table 6.5). The East will experience a major decline during the next four decades. The ratio of military manpower between NATO and the former Warsaw Pact will decline from 1.69 in 1986 to 1.38 by 2025. The ratio of European market to non-market economies will decline from .84 in 1986 to only .58 in 2025 (Table 6.5).

As Figure 6.2 shows, this process will not be smooth. Until 1990, the elements of the populations of both NATO and the former Warsaw Pact which are of military age will decline. Between 1990 and 2005, the NATO countries will show significant declines whilst those of the former Warsaw Pact will reflect increases. From 2005 to 2015, the military manpower resources of the NATO countries will increase slightly but not enough to overcome the relative advantages built-up within the former Warsaw Pact during the preceding 15 years. After the year 2015, the growth advantage will shift again to the former Warsaw Pact countries.

John F Long

Changing Percentage of the Population of Military Ages

One of the less well-known aspects of these demographic shifts is the change in the structure of the respective national populations. As the fertility rates decreased, the proportion of population in the younger years declined leaving a much older population and a heavy old-age dependency ratio. As Table 6.6 shows, the proportion of the population of NATO countries of prime military age and sex was over 11 per cent in number in 1986 but will decline to little over 8 per cent by 2025. The corresponding proportion in former Warsaw Pact countries will be much more stable, declining from slightly over 10 per cent today to around 9 per cent by 2025. In both groups of countries however, the social demands on national budgets of an historically large retirement-aged population, in relation to the population of working age, could divert substantial monetary resources that might otherwise be spent on defence.

Importance and Uncertainty of Future Fertility Levels

Changes in the population in the prime military ages for the next few years can be assessed fairly accurately since that population has already been born. However, projections of the population for future years depends on the course of future fertility. Fertility levels are notoriously hard to project and reasonable men can disagree. The projections used in this analysis are slightly optimistic, assuming as they do a gradual rise in fertility rates in the lowest-fertility countries.

John Saunders has commented in Chapter 3 on some of the causes for past fertility declines and on the prospects for future fertility growth. His discussion of policy initiatives to change fertility levels is quite comprehensive. Here is one additional factor that could change future manpower levels – immigration. While some immigration occurs at ages too old to influence the size of the militarily eligible population, over half of all immigration is made before the age of 30. Whether these immigrants are eligible for military service is not a demographic question but one that requires considerable discussion. An even more important question arises over the fertility levels of future immigrants. Were immigration levels from high-fertility countries to rise substantially in future years, the number of births to immigrants could substantially change the demographic outlook for the young adult population in the countries of their adoption.

There is one further (although unlikely) caveat. These projections assume the continued very low mortality of the young male population. Were some catastrophic increase in mortality to be observed in these age groups (as with some of the more drastic forecasts of deaths due to AIDS), these projections would have to be substantially revised. One would expect (and certainly hope) that such dramatic increases in mortality would not be forthcoming.

146

Conclusions

It is clear that the predictable demographic trends for the next forty years throughout the world, and particularly the trends within those areas we have defined in this analysis as East and West, are going to have considerable significance for European security.

First and foremost, as Table 6.2 and Figures 6.3, 6.4 and 6.5 show, not only will the total population for East and West contract in relation to that of the rest of the world but contraction reflects a dramatic decline in their available military manpower resources (in the age-group 17–29). Within the broad terms of that decline, the total number of persons within the prime military age group will rise only slightly in the East and decline sharply in the West so that there will be a consequential decline in the ratio of military manpower resources between the two.

A profound social, and hence budgetary, problem will arise from the proportion of persons reaching retirement age within both blocks, but particularly in the West, thereby creating competition for scarce financial resources between the demands of society and defense.

Finally, the fertility rate will continue to fall below the replacement level throughout most of the West and in parts of the East with consequences already discussed in earlier chapters of this book.

These trends portend major shifts in manpower and economic resources with consequences for security concerns.

Notes

1. NATO countries include Canada, Denmark, France, the Federal Republic of Germany, Greece, Iceland, Italy, Luxembourg, the Netherlands, Norway, Portugal, Spain, Turkey, the United Kingdom, and the United States.
2. In this analysis the term Warsaw Pact includes Bulgaria, Czechoslovakia, the German Democratic Republic, Hungary, Poland, Romania, and the Soviet Union.
3. The European Market Economies, as defined by Saunders, include Austria, Belgium, Denmark, Finland, France, Federal Republic of Germany, Greece, Ireland, Italy, Luxembourg, the Netherlands, Norway, Portugal, Spain, Sweden, Switzerland, and the United Kingdom.
4. The Non-market Economies, as defined by Saunders, include Albania, Bulgaria, Czechoslovakia, the German Democratic Republic, Hungary, Poland, Romania, Yugoslavia, and the Soviet Union.
5. The European NATO countries exclude Canada, Turkey, and the United States.
6. The West includes all countries in NATO and all other countries listed as European Market economies above.
7. The East includes all the Non-market Economies listed above.

Bibliography

Austria Central Statistical Office. 1987. *Bevolkerungsvorausschatzung für Osterreich: 1987–2015.*

John F Long

Statistics Canada. 1985. *Population Projections for Canada, Provinces, and Territories.*

Czechoslovak Federal Statistical Office. 1987. *Projection of Czechoslovak Population until 2012.*

Federal Republic of Germany, Federal Statistical Office. 1987. *Modelrechnungen zur Bevolkerungsentwicklung in der Bundesrepublik Deutsch.*

Finland Central Statistical Office. 1987. *Population Projections for Finland: 1981–2020.*

France. INSEE. 1985. *Projection de Population Totale pour la France: 1985–2040.*

Ireland. Central Statistics Office. 1988. *Population Projections: 1991–2021.*

Netherlands Central Bureau of Statistics. 1987. *Population Forecasts for the Netherlands: 1987–2035.*

Saunders, John. 1988. 'Population Change in Europe: Past Experience and Future Prospects,' Paper presented at the international conference on Demographic Change and Western Security. London, July 21–22 1988.

Shryock, Henry S and Jacob S Siegel (eds.) *The Methods and Materials of Demography* (New York: Academic Press. 1976).

Statistic Sweden. 1986. *The Future Population: Projections for the Years 1986–2035.*

United Kingdom. Government Actuary's Department. 1986. *Population Projection: 1985–2035.*

United States Bureau of the Census. Center for International Research. 1988. *International Demographic Data Base.*

7

Economic Systems, Demographic Change and Global Conflict

Mikhail S Bernstam

The central idea of this chapter is that competitive markets dissipate inter-national conflicts. A collateral idea is that long-term demographic trends contribute to this outcome both directly and indirectly, in paradoxical ways. I will discuss the nature of conflicts, why they dissipate, and the crucial role played by economic systems and demographic changes.

Among the questions that I will answer are the following: if two countries, A and B (the United States and the Soviet Union, for example), are in a state of conflict, does it matter that one of them has a socialist economy? How is the socialist economic system related to global conflict? Can global conflict dissipate when a socialist economy breaks down and undergoes a reform? What domestic demographic changes influence these outcomes?

The literature is mostly mute on these questions. It assumes that conflicts are motivated by geopolitical factors and the expansion of power. Hence, although specific conflicts differ, conflict is taken to be a constant, not a variable. The absence of conflict is treated as a temporary condition, not as a different régime. From this perspective, there is no need to attribute conflicts to the impacts of different economic systems.

Demographic change is seldom integrated into the study of conflicts (Simon, 1989 is an important exception). The major reason is that a corre-lation between demographic pressures and conflicts seems to be absent (Keyfitz, 1980).

After a brief section on definitions and framework, this chapter is divided into two parts. The first, *Population, Markets and International Conflicts*, discusses the relationship between secular demographic change, open com-petitive markets, economic development, and international conflicts. The second, *Socialism, Demographic Change and Global Conflict*, deals with socia-lism, demographic change, and global conflict in the twentieth century. The Soviet Union serves as a case study.

149

Mikhail S Bernstam

Definitions and Framework

International conflicts can be defined as one nation's continuous claims, through the use of force or the threat of force, on the assets and on the freedom of action, of other nations. On the other hand, continuous market transactions betwen nations develop a vested interest in mutual well-being. Gains from trade replace gains from the absorption of assets or from the conquest and destruction of other nations. National property rights and national sovereignty are implicitly recognised and need no physical enforcement. An individualistic economic environment, a system of open competitive markets, superimposes the interests of private transactors on the expansionist interests of governments and political groups. In a market setting, this leads unintentionally to the dissipation of conflicts. I call this The Law of the International Invisible Hand.

This approach helps explain why many international conflicts dissipate when the economies of the antagonists develop markets while the global conflict between socialist and market countries does not. Economic statism under socialism leads to the maximisation of the input of resources, capital, and labour and thus to continuous expansion. In addition, the domestic enforcement of state power in socialist countries requires the elimination of alternative economic systems. Claims on the assets and on the independence of other nations supersede the need for trade. Global conflict becomes the default mode of international relations for socialist economies. Signs of its dissipation in the late-1980s and the 1990s have accompanied the dismantling of the socialist economic system itself. The more it is dismantled, the more will conflict with the West dissipate: consider for example, East Germany and Cuba in 1990.

In this context, demographic changes produce direct and indirect effects. In the absence of markets, population pressures contribute to international claims and wars. The current evidence from tribal warfare in Africa and in Soviet Central Asia expands a millennarian record.

When markets prevail, economic development and the demographic transition increase income from trade, reduce the value of land and resources, increase the value of human capital and of investment in it. They also promote immigration and the exchange of the fruits of human capital via international trade, and increase the value of human life. These trends help to dissipate conflicts. One of the most important contemporary demographic impacts, overlooked in the literature, is the dependence of economic growth under socialism on the growth of the urban industrial labour force. When the industrial labour force of socialist economies ceases to grow, an economic crisis is produced that leads to the dismantling of the system and to a potential dissipation of global conflict.

150

PART I. POPULATION, MARKETS, AND INTERNATIONAL CONFLICTS

Do Demographic Pressures Affect International Conflict?

Population size, density and growth are related to international conflicts in two ways. One is the ability to engage in conflict and transform it into war or a credible threat of war. Such a capacity obviously depends on manpower, but the commitment and facility with which manpower can be mobilised depends, in turn, on the intensity of the motivation for conflict and on other political and economic factors. Manpower was crucial during the Second World War, but, curiously, neither Nazi Germany nor the Soviet Union conscripted women. Apparently, long-term demographic considerations prevailed in both countries whose governments then promoted pronatalist policies. Manpower is an important complement to modern military technology even in the 1990s, judging from the emphasis on human numbers in contemporary arms control negotiations. Generally, however, the role of manpower has diminished over time, especially in the decades after the Second World War due to the substitution of modern technology for infantrymen. The conflict between Israel and the Arab nations is the most conspicuous example of this trend.

The second possible relationship between population parameters and international conflict concerns the origins of conflicts. Thomas Robert Malthus was probably the first to suggest that population pressures on resources breed wars. But Malthus also pioneered the view that the spread of competitive markets reduces population pressures via fertility control (Petersen, 1979, pp. 155, 184–192, 214–217) and, by implication, dissipates conflicts.

Modern literature shows that the pressure of population on resources creates many responses other than war. Among them are the control of reproduction, immigration (Davis, 1963), technological innovation (Boserup, 1981), the creation of market institutions and the spread of entrepreneurship (Brenner, 1983). Other responses are economic development and the discovery of new resources (Simon, 1981, 1986), the monetisation of the economy and the Industrial Revolution due to the match of abundant capital and cheap labour (Schofield and Wrigley, 1986; Bernstam, 1987a). Davis (1990) advances this line of thinking by noting that population pressure is a relative concept. Population pressures are relative to resources, but resources are variable. Resources may be found within as well as without national borders. Markets and international trade make resources mobile, eliminate the role of national boundaries in the availability of resources, and alleviate population pressures on the supply side.

Keyfitz (1980) investigated an extensive historical record looking for a relationship between population growth and wars and found none. Often, wars coincided with either high or low population density and growth. In many other instances, high population density and growth did not lead to

151

conflicts. Although population pressures may contribute to the intensity of conflicts in the presence of more fundamental causes, these pressures do not constitute either a necessary or a sufficient condition for conflict.

The evidence is varied. Many wars (e.g., the conquest of the Roman Empire by nomadic tribes, the Arab conquests, the Mongol victories in much of Eurasia, and the rise of the Ottoman Empire) can be related to the high population growth and the high demand for land by the nomads. As nomads they were unaffected by the seasons or the periodic failure of crops and thus had better nutrition than people who depended on sedentary agriculture. In conjunction with polygamy, this may explain why the fertility of nomadic tribes in Central Asia was apparently higher than that of sedentary groups (Jones and Grupp, 1987, pp. 94–104). Also, the fact that the nomads could mobilise more manpower and horses gave them greater mobility.

Numerous wars in ancient and feudal Europe occurred at times of low population growth. Ancient wars involved the conquest of slaves which implies population shortages rather than pressures. Feudal wars expanded the tax base for great landlords. It was a tax-and-protection racket in the absence of legal contracts between the citizenry and the state. This was not much different from the warfare in modern cities between gangs engaged in protection rackets or dealing in illegal goods (alcohol during the Prohibition, and narcotics today). Peasants and gentry participated in feudal wars for reasons which involved both demographic and economic considerations such as the lack of inheritance for sons of high birth order, loot, and an alternative gainful occupation for individuals who were not averse to risks. The Napoleonic wars are instructive in the sense that France, of all European countries, had very low population growth and had already started the demographic transition to low fertility (Bourgeois-Pichat, 1965; van de Walle, 1974). Perhaps, these wars were typical of newly-emerged nation-states at a time of transition between feudalism and developed international markets.

The rise of European colonial empires can also be understood from this perspective. Both France, with virtually zero population growth and low population density, and other European powers which then had high population growth and differing densities created colonial empires. Interestingly, European countries undertook decolonisation in the 1960s, the time of the baby boom, high population growth, and rising population density. Moreover, in the 1970s they sought immigrant labour from former colonies and elsewhere.

Furthermore, the European conquests of the Americas and other continents since the sixteenth century can be viewed in the context of emigration as a response to population pressures. This approach applies to many other conquests. Conquest is often a form of emigration. Emigration and conquests are inseparable in many instances.

The conflicts of the nineteenth and the twentieth centuries show no

Economic Systems

TABLE 7.1   Political Demography of Selected Countries in the 1930s

Nation	Population density per sq. km., 1937	Population growth % per year, per year 1930–40	Net reproduction rate, 1935
Aggressors			
Japan	183.9	1.05	n.a.
Germany[a]	144.2	0.81	0.906
Italy	139.5	0.84	1.131
Hungary	97.8	0.64	0.951[b]
Soviet Union	7.4	1.06[c]	1.438[b]
Objects of Aggression			
China	46.5	0.43	n.a.
Korea	103.7	1.44	n.a.
Spain	49.8	0.94	1.030[d]
Austria	80.6	0.07	n.a.
Czechoslovakia	112.9	0.50	0.755[d]
Poland	88.4	1.20	1.114[e]
Belgium	275.1	0.35	0.859[b]
France	74.8	−0.01	0.870
United Kingdom[f]	193.8	0.50	n.a.
England and Wales	271.5	0.52	0.764
Finland	9.5	0.69	1.040
Netherlands	264.0	1.12	1.145
Denmark	87.3	0.78	0.922
Norway	9.0	0.55	0.746
United States	16.5	0.70	0.975
Canada	1.2	1.03	1.173
India	89.8	1.40	n.a.
Neutral Countries			
Switzerland	101.2	0.43	0.790[g]
Sweden	14.0	0.37	0.739
Ireland	41.9	0.04	1.217

n.a. = not available
a: Area as of 1937; b: 1939; c: 1927–37; d: 1937; e: 1934; f: England and Wales, Scotland, and Northern Ireland; g: 1936.

Sources: United Nations, *Demographic Yearbook 1949–50* (New York: United Nations, 1950), pp. 83–103, 366–369; territory of China: United Nations, *Demographic Yearbook 1951* (New York: United Nations, 1951), p. 97; Soviet Union: USSR Central Statistical Administration, *Naselenie USSR*, 1973. *Statisticheskii Sbornik* (Moscow: Finansy i Statistika, 1975), pp. 7, 138.

153

Mikhail S Bernstam

relationship to population parameters. Following Keyfitz (1980) and employing data rather than anecdotes, one can consider the situation on the eve of the Second World War. After 1933, the national-socialist government of Germany justified its claims on other countries by alleging insufficient 'living space.' In fact, as Table 7.1 shows, population density in 1937 was almost twice as high in England (272 persons per square kilometer), the Netherlands (264 per sq. km.) and Belgium (275 per sq. km.) as in Germany (144 per sq. km.). German population growth was low, and its fertility was the lowest in the industrial world. The net reproduction rate fell to 0.698 in 1933 (United Nations, 1950, p. 367). Germany made explicit claims on the world, but demographically determined they were not. Nor did Germany have a population advantage when it attacked the Anglo-French alliance and later the Soviet Union. Japan, too, did not have a manpower advantage vis-a-vis the United States or China during the Second World War. Table 7.1 also shows that Japan's population density in the 1930s was not very high by the standards of the then developed countries. The other two aggressors of the Second World War, Italy and Hungary, had population density and growth either equal to, or lower than, many of the objects of their aggression. The Soviet Union, which effectively entered that war on the German side, had an extremely low population density and certainly experienced no pressure of population on resources.

For the sake of intellectual exercise, Table 7.1 divides the major countries on the eve of the Second World War into three categories: aggressors, objects of aggression, and neutral countries. There seem to be no observable differences between these three groups in terms of population density, population growth, and the net reproduction rate. If and when population pressures contribute to the intensity of conflicts, this contribution should be analysed in the context of fundamental causes.

Negative population pressures, or population shortages relative to resources, can also lead to conflicts. The extensive use of penal labour in the Soviet Union in the 1930s–1950s can be regarded as forced migration to sparsely populated areas rich in gold, timber, coal, and other resources. The demand for this labour produced waves of domestic civil wars and absorbed civilian prisoners and prisoners of war from the newly acquired territories. Slavery throughout history provides another illustration. Many wars in the ancient, medieval, and modern world were for the acquisition of slaves, especially to be used in agriculture. Slavery, exactly like penal labour, is a form of forced migration. It clearly implies shortages of labour relative to resources rather than a high pressure of population on resources.

Exchange Transactions and Claims On Assets

International conflicts were defined earlier as one nation's continuous claims through force or the use of force on the assets and freedom of action of other

154

nations. In order to examine the fundamental causes of international conflicts, one can briefly consider the juxtaposition of exchange transactions, or trade, and claims on assets. The juxtaposition can explain, for example, why the same demographic cause, rising population density relative to resources, may lead either to the conquest of another nation's land, to voluntary population transfers (migration), or to a transition from agriculture or mining to other industries and to trade.

Exchange transactions and claims on assets are basic alternative responses to the finite state of the world: scarcity. Claims are older than exchanges, they precede man. From this perspective, the drive for land belonging to others is independent of population pressures. Claims are the natural response to scarcity, whether by man or beast. They redistribute and perpetuate it. Exchange transactions are an inventive human escape from permanent scarcity. They create prosperity because they generate a supply of goods. Claims are merely a demand for the resources of others and do not stimulate the production of new goods.

In keeping with Samuelson (1958), one can say that exchange transactions that occur beyond immediate families are social contrivances. Exchange transactions were probably invented by hunters and gatherers in order to extend the utility of perishable food by trading surplus food for other objects, which could be used later. Two other social contrivances were necessary for the implementation of exchange transactions: recognisable property rights and a medium of exchange or money (see Kyotaki and Wright, 1989).

These two necessary complements made exchange transactions a practical alternative to claims on assets. Recognisable property rights made the objects of exchange transferable and tradeable (Buchanan, 1975, p. 17) and made the appropriation of the assets of others unlawful. Mediums of exchange placed specific values on assets and thus made exchange transactions possible. The relationship between the two activities, exchange transactions and claims on assets, became a matter of choice, subject to relative gains and costs. This applied to inter-personal and inter-group relations and later to international relations as I will discuss in the following sections.

The crucial aspect of the relationship between exchange transactions and claims on assets is that the former ultimately came to yield more than the latter. It only takes historical time, that is, economic development, to validate this rule, as I will show. Figure 7.1 reveals why exchange transactions become more advantageous than claims on assets. Resources that are claimed are not voluntarily supplied. They are simply demanded by claimants. This is why the claims curve on the figure is represented by the demand curve. The involuntary supply in response to claims along this curve has a negative elasticity; those who are subjected to claims pay their own price in the form of resistance in order to preserve their assets and to minimise what is yielded to claimants.

The amount of resources that can be obtained via claims is relatively small.

Mikhail S Bernstam

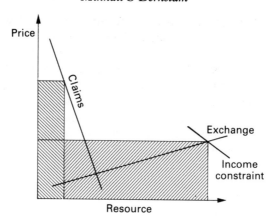

FIGURE 7.1   Exchange Transactions and Claims on Assets

It is limited by the current wealth of those upon whom claims are being made. Once absorbed, the resources are not readily replaced. The enforcement of a continuous flow of resources toward claimants is costly and not always feasible. Given the one-time nature and the discontinuity of claimed assets, the amount that can be claimed is limited. The price of claimed resources is very high in terms of risks, military effort, and losses of life sustained by the claimants. The curve is thus highly inelastic because claimants obtain but a small amount of resources and pay a high price.

Claims on richer countries or on larger amounts of assets make the inelastic slope of the curve less steep. Small quantities gained at a high price are the rule. Greater efforts to enforce claims will move the demand curve outward, but another inelastic curve yields only a few additional resources. The implication is that if all parties are engaged in making claims and resisting claims, as has been the rule through most of history, the volume of resources changing hands will be small. No new supplies emerge, and both sides remain poor.

Exchange transactions, on the other hand, create a continuous flow of resources in response to prices, and subject to income constraints. Continuous and voluntary supply and production provide more resources at any given price than do claims. In a competitive setting, the supply curve is highly elastic and resource prices are lower than when resources are secured through claims. Consequently, more resources are gained at lower prices from exchange transactions than from claims. As market exchanges increase wealth over the course of economic development, the income constraint moves outward, and resources increase rapidly. Exchange transactions become a more gainful mode of behaviour than claims on assets for most people and for entire nations, whereupon many international conflicts dissipate.

156

Demographic Transition, Economic Development and Conflict Dissipation

In the absence of widespread exchange transactions, conflict is a natural state of relations between individuals, groups, and nations. Secular demographic and economic change altered this natural state of mankind. The industrial revolution, the secular increase in incomes, economic and social modernisation, and the demographic transition to low fertility and mortality contributed to the dissipation of many international conflicts. Six major development factors and one paradox can be listed in this context.

First, secular growth of incomes makes gains from repeated exchange transactions exceed by far any possible gains from claims on assets. A series of one-time acquisitions of wealth (followed by destructions and slow recovery) is no match for a continuous flow of wealth in a high-income environment which any nation, however poor, can join. Under universal poverty, continuous short-term yields from exchanges were negligible for most nations. Conquests could only produce windfalls of wealth that were soon exhausted. Rising national incomes reversed this relationship.

One has to grasp the magnitude of the increase of global income since the Industrial Revolution. World population increased about 5.8 times from 1786 to 1986, from 845 million to 4,917 million (Lee, 1990). The average GNP (gross national product) *per capita* probably increased 19 times. In arriving at this conclusion I generously assumed the average GNP *per capita* in 1786 to be $150, on a par with today's Bangladesh, Mozambique, Nepal, and Zaire. In 1986 GNP *per capita* in developing countries was $610, in oil exporting countries it was $6,740, and in industrial countries $12,960 (The World Bank, 1988, pp. 222–223), and I generously assume the GNP *per capita* of developed socialist countries to be 40 per cent of that of market economies (see Illarionov, 1990, pp. 6–7). This makes the average global GNP *per capita* in 1986 equal to $2,850 and the global GNP equal to $14 trillion. The global GNP in 1786 can be estimated from the above numbers to have been $127 billion.

The growth of the world economy from 1786 to 1986 was thus 110 fold. The average annual growth rate is not remarkable: it is less than 2.4 per cent. The total magnitude of increase, the number of participants (five billion), and the continuous yields of income ($2,850 per capita per annum) are truly remarkable. To be sure, many countries are still poor, although few are as poor as the world was two centuries ago. Now it is even more advantageous to engage in international exchange transactions rather than lay claim to the assets of other nations.

A second, parallel development is the growth and spread of markets themselves, including international trade. A world economy has emerged. The resources and the fruits of the labour of one nation can readily be acquired by the inhabitants of another. Income from trade constitutes a growing proportion of national incomes.

The third major development is the extent of the international division of labour via trade and migration. Claims on the labour of foreign nationals are no longer necessary. The supply of voluntary immigrants to virtually any country with high-level, middle-level or even low-level incomes from poorer countries greatly exceeds the demand for them or the willingness to accept them. For the labour-receiving nations, immigration and the wealth arising from it substitute for conquests.

A fourth factor is the declining relative value of land, resources and physical assets, about which Schultz (1951) wrote almost forty years ago. Simon (1989) summarises evidence from the past of the conflicts arising from claims on agricultural land and natural resources. This includes not only backward countries and the European colonial powers, but also United States wars against American Indians, and Mexico. Then he calculates that only 3.1 per cent of United States GNP is now derived from agriculture. The total value of United States agricultural land is about 11 per cent of one year's GNP – this is the amount spent in two years for recreation plus the amount spent in one year on tobacco, without even including expenditures for liquor.

More relevantly, the total worth of US agricultural land is equal to one year's expenditure on health. The declining prices of natural resources and their substitution by newly invented materials leads to the depreciation of the relative value of land that contains resources.

Fifth, the absolute and relative value of human capital as a component of national wealth has risen dramatically and exceeds the value of monetary and physical assets. Becker (1988, p. 6) estimates that the value of human capital comprises from 50 per cent to 90 per cent of the total capital stock of the United States. In the case of open market economies, exchange transactions are based on the international division of this highly skilled, highly educated, highly productive labour. These transactions of inexpensive, high-quality goods such as advanced technology and other fruits of human capital, yield continuous gains for all participating nations. These gains, especially the long-term gains, are much higher than any hypothetical forceful appropriation of this human capital stock would yield. Exchange transactions based on a high level of labour productivity also yield higher gains than an appropriation of physical assets. One illustration to that effect is the different behaviour of the victors toward Germany after the two World Wars. Compare Keynes' (1919) description of the appropriation of German resources and the imposition of reparations in 1918 (which led to a resumption of conflict), with the Marshall Plan.

The sixth major change is the rise in the value of human life in conjunction with rising incomes and the increased value of human capital. This is reflected in endogenous mortality declines, rising life expectancy, rising health expenditures, and high insurance settlements (Jones-Lee, 1976; Linnerooth, 1979; Arthur, 1981; Williamson, 1984; Marshall, 1984; Rosen,

1988). The rising value of human life may be the best consequence of the nature and process of the demographic transition, the transition from high fertility and high mortality to low fertility and low mortality. It is also the transition from a small investment in a pattern of large families to a large investment in smaller ones. Pertinent to our analysis is that the high value of human life reduces the intensity of conflicts, given their potential for losses of life.

The economic and demographic components of these secular changes are inseparable. All the changes are interdependent. They ultimately derive from the spread of open competitive markets and rising incomes generated by market transactions. The latter two factors both depend on, and influence, population pressures in a complex way briefly described in the first section of this part of the chapter.

However, one obvious paradox follows from the secular rise of wealth. Although, for entire nations, exchange transactions become more and more gainful than claims on assets, international claims become potentially very profitable for concerted groups of claimants. These are political groups that specialise in claims and are not successful in exchange transactions. They have both absolute and comparative advantages in making claims on other people's wealth, inside their nations and on the international scene.

These groups are composed of revolutionaries, radical politicians, radical intellectuals, terrorists, and other marginal national and international elements. Once they engage in seeking power, the rising incomes of many nations increase the stake to be won in the game of claiming assets. When these groups assume power in one or another nation, they turn their countries into international claimants. The picture is familiar and does not require further elaboration. The point to underscore here is that rising incomes can cut both ways.

Figure 7.2 summarises the ideas of this and the two previous sections in a schematic form. To recapitulate, population pressures combined with open competitive markets contribute to the secular rise of incomes. In turn, rising incomes combined with competitive market institutions trigger the demographic transition and reduce population pressures (Bernstam, 1987b; Davis, 1990). In the absence of markets, however, population pressures translate into higher claims on assets. Rising market incomes lead to higher potential gains from claims on the part of professional claimants and this encourages large scale claimant activities. This is a major reason why new international conflicts emerge. Other impacts of rising market incomes lead to the dissipation of conflicts via such developments as the increased value of life, changes in the relative values of assets, and especially in the growth of gains from exchange transactions relative to gains from claims.

The net effect, shown in Figure 7.2, is complex. International conflicts dissipate between open competitive market economies and in the developing economies attached to the world market. At the same time, new revolution-

Mikhail S Bernstam

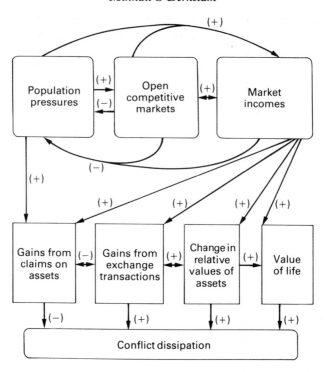

Figure 7.2 The Effects of Secular Economic and Demographic Changes on International Conflicts

ary claimants emerge. The world is no longer a place of the war of all against all as it was for millennia. There are sizeable peaceful, prosperous, and rapidly developing enclaves. There are also areas in conflict. On top of this, global conflict between socialist and market economies emerged at a time of secular dissipation of many past conflicts. Section 6 will show that the net effect of these secular developments ultimately depends on prevailing economic systems.

The Law of the International Invisible Hand and the Dissipation of Conflicts

The dissipation of international conflicts among market countries over the course of economic development was unintended. It was an unanticipated outcome of the replacement of international claims with exchange transactions extending to relations between nations. The spread of competitive markets and their development into an economic system provides an explanation.

160

Economic Systems

The underlying motive of exchange transactions is individual self-interest or profit-seeking. As Buchanan (1980, p. 4) summarised, 'since Adam Smith, we have known that the profit-seeking activity of the butcher and baker ensures results beneficial to all members of the community. . . . Profit-seeking as an activity produces consequences neither predicted nor understood by any single participant, but good . . .' for other people.

No benevolent intent is needed to conduct a mutually advantageous exchange and 'no particular interest in his [another agent's] well-being' (Buchanan, 1975, p. 17). Yet, the mutually beneficial results of exchange transactions occur as if such an interest existed. This effect is magnified when exchange transactions are repeated and occur continuously. International exchanges between firms simulate international relations. They are functionally equivalent to the presence of an interest in mutual well-being. International hatred, which may be intrinsic to human tribes, becomes economically costly in the same manner as racial discrimination is costly in open competitive markets (see Becker, 1971).

When, in the modern economic world, very sizeable proportions of national populations become engaged in international transactions as either producers or consumers or both, the aggregation of their individual self-interests leads to the simulation of an interest in mutual well-being. Pursuing their own economic interests, individuals and nations behave as if they had an interest in the well-being of other nations. This can be called the Law of the International Invisible Hand.

This simulation of interest in the well-being of other nations is best illustrated by the treatment of such volatile problems as sovereignty, national borders, and, generally, the property of nations and their inhabitants. National property rights are not readily enforceable by any international institution. In this context, international law seems to be an oxymoron. National property rights are enforceable only by physical force (national defence), which is costly. Among the reasons that international conflicts are so common is the fact that national property rights are not easily recognisable and are subject to the relative power of claimants and protectors. International treaties provide little help in this context. International treaties are meaningless if, in the absence of implicitly recognisable national property rights, their enforcement is impossible. If compliance must be exacted by force, they are superfluous.

An unintended miracle of international exchange transactions between individuals was that they stimulated recognition and enforcement of national property rights. They did so by dissipating claims on assets which become a less advantageous mode of operation. Through international exchange transactions, more resources became available at lower prices, and more resources were exchanged in trade and thus were recognised as property not subject to claims. Countries engaged in these market activities gradually dissipated their conflicts. The experience of former Second World War enemies, the

Mikhail S Bernstam

United States, England, and France versus Germany, Italy, and Japan, illustrates this point. International trade and the change in the relative value of assets made national property rights recognisable and respected simply because it was not profitable to violate them. The role of national defence in enforcing national property rights diminished. Competition for markets substituted competition for assets belonging to others; the developed open market world released its colonies.

The twentieth century, however, saw two major developments which countered the secular spread of open competitive markets and the concomitant dissipation of many international conflicts. These were the rise of the world socialist system and the subsequent emergence of global conflict between market and socialist countries. It seems that economic development moved in one direction but the development of economic systems pursued, at least for a number of decades, a different path.

Economic System, National Interests and International Conflicts

An implied necessary precondition for the dissipation of international conflicts is the coincidence of the interests of individuals and nations. Thus far I have discussed the relationship between international conflicts and amorphous groups of individuals engaged in either exchange transactions or claims on assets. However, individuals integrate into nations, the world consists of nations, and nations consist of diverse groups of individuals with various, often opposing special interests. In addition, there are governments and related groups that seek to maximise their power. For people involved in exchanges, exchange transactions are sufficient for conflict dissipation. Entire nations need markets to deliver the fruits of exchange.

The precondition of individual market interests coinciding with national interests is met when open competitive markets function as an economic system. There is a fundamental difference between exchange transactions as a series of occurrences and as an economic system of open competitive markets.

If only some enclaves of nations are interested in international exchange while other groups are either indifferent or interested in claims, this may lead to a partial and temporary dissipation of conflicts, not to general long-term dissipation. This is why international trade was never a guarantee for peace. Trade has existed in all societies and so have wars. The history preceding the two World Wars and the history of Soviet relations with the West are the two most recent examples. Trade and markets are simply not identical.

The constitutional rule of open competitive markets as an economic system has never been papered down. It can be defined as the separation between the state and productive activities. This means independence of the individual from the state and the integration of individual economic interests with the national interest via markets. To be sure, government regulations exist in

162

virtually all market economies. However, their purpose is to facilitate income transfers between groups. Regulations are thus equivalent to taxes and subsidies that redistribute the fruits of production but do not directly determine it.

Under the rule of separation between the productive economy and the state, interests involved in individual exchange transactions and the national interest coincide. Even if international trade involves only a small fraction of the population and is a small fraction of national income, the rest of the population and the economy become beneficiaries. This effect is produced by the production cycle of the economy which is separated from the state and dependent on competitive markets. The production cycle links inputs and outputs. Over the production cycle, the demand for inputs (including human consumption) generates the demand for outputs, while markets make the demand generate the supply. Once these links permeate the economy, everyone's well-being is enhanced by the most efficient market solutions arrived at by each economic participant. Thus international exchange transactions, in which only a fraction of the markets is involved, positively affects all other people. Every individual has his or her share of economic interest in international exchange. Through the market's integration of individual economic interests, the dissipation of conflicts becomes a national interest.

In a system of open competitive markets, individuals who are independent from the state expect their income and well-being to come from the markets. In a variety of statist economic systems individuals expect their income and satisfaction of needs to come from the state. The government co-ordinates or influences production activities and the entire production cycle. Even if a sizeable proportion of national income depends on international trade, the state, not the market, distributes the benefits of the exchange. Only a small minority of individuals is directly involved in transactions. Individual economic interests are thus integrated into the national interest by, and reside in, the government and the special interest groups of politicians and domestic monopolistic producers.

In some instances, these vested interests have a stake in international exchange transactions and conflict dissipation, usually for a limited period of time. But in many countries of Latin America, Africa, and in parts of Asia, state-subsidised private monopolies do not want competition from foreign imports. At the same time, these monopolies cannot be successful exporters because they cannot compete in price and quality on world markets. Imports undermine their monopolistic rents and government subsidies. The need for exports forces them to change their practices and perhaps lose their monopolistic position to new domestic producers. Monopolistic producers thus prefer a hostile international environment in which exchanges are curtailed.

In most instances,the economic interests of domestic monopolies and the political interests of anti-market leaders engage their countries in international conflicts. Generally, when economic relations are controlled by the state, individual economic interests are subordinated to the interests of the government. This explains why inter-state trade (or trade between the government of one nation and the private entrepreneurs of another) does not contribute to long-term conflict dissipation. Trade that is pursued by governments for the political goal of alleviating domestic economic problems can be easily subordinated to other political goals that serve the preservation and expansion of power. Only international exchanges between profit-seeking individuals and private firms is relevant, but even this is not sufficient. Neither trade expansion nor the mushrooming series of treaties between the Soviet Union and the West in the 1960s and the 1970s dissipated global conflict. Actually, global conflict was exacerbated during this period. It reached a stage at which the Soviet Union contemplated a winnable nuclear war against the West (Zagladin, 1988, p. 1). Another example is the behaviour of such Western trading partners as Libya, Iran, and Iraq.

Many situations may arise in which gains from claims on assets promise to exceed gains from exchange transactions for those groups that pretend to consolidate the national interest in statist economies. The Argentinean war against Great Britain over the Falkland Islands is a recent example. The war between Iraq and Iran in the 1980s is another. People participate in these ventures for many reasons. The one to underscore here is that individual economic interests are intertwined with those of the government.

When people expect their gains to come from the state and compete in making their claims on the state, while the state derives its gains from international claims on assets, the government is capable of integrating the national interest with that of international claimants. This is why nationalism is aggressive. Economic statism creates a collective stake in claims on the assets of other nations while reducing opportunities for individuals to gain from exchange whether domestically or internationally. Thus entire nations become involved either in the market production cycle of mutually beneficial exchanges or in the cycle of mutual claims of the claimants on the state. Differently integrated national interests mean that people are, in effect, shareholders either in international market operations or in international cycles of seizing each other's assets.

In addition, since an implicit interest in the well-being of other nations does not develop in the statist setting, perennial racial and ethnic animosities endure. The extent of tribal warfare in post-colonial Africa and South East Asia, the wars between Argentina and Chile, and numerous wars in the Middle East can probably be better understood from this perspective than from others. Ethnic hatred is natural, but it is a variable, not a constant. Statism keeps it inflamed.

In the modern world of expanding markets, rising incomes, but also of only partial participation of many countries in the global economy, international conflicts fluctuate. The co-existence of competitive market and statist economies is, in my view, the root cause of these trends. Most of these conflicts are regional and short-term or medium-term in duration. I will now turn to the extreme form of economic statism, the socialist economic system, and will discuss its impact on long-term global conflict.

PART II. SOCIALISM, DEMOGRAPHIC CHANGE, AND GLOBAL CONFLICT

Unlike other international conflicts, global conflict between the socialist system and Western market countries has never dissipated. What began to dissipate in the second half of the 1980s was the socialist economic system itself, and hence global conflict. These facts provide an empirical indication that the very nature and the very survival of the socialist economic system are embedded in claims on the rest of the world, especially in conflicts with the market world.

Input Maximisation Under the Socialist System of Regulated State Monopolies

The most conspicuous feature of socialist economies is their high and ever-increasing resource intensity and high and growing absorption of inputs of labour and capital. This creates their disadvantage for engaging in long-term international trade and generates incentives for claims on assets.

Table 7.2 and Figure 7.3 compare the trends in resource use in market and socialist economies. A special emphasis on energy is instructive because in industrial societies energy conversion constitutes about 50 per cent of total resource use (Haveman, 1974, p. 103). The data here show that resource use has been declining in market economies both *per capita* and per $1 of GNP, reflecting the growing efficiency of their national production. Resource use, on the other hand, has been increasing in most socialist countries.

At each level of economic development (approximated as GNP per capita) resource use *per capita* and per unit of GNP is significantly higher under socialism. Resource use *per capita* is either roughly the same with regard to energy or higher in socialist countries as concerns steel and other materials, although, as I mentioned above, socialism GNP *per capita* constitutes at most 40 per cent of that in the West. In terms of both energy and steel, the ratio of inputs per $1000 GNP in socialist and market economies increased from about 1.5:1 in the second half of the 1970s to about 3.5:1 in the mid-1980s. The gap is wider between the Soviet Union and the United States. Interestingly, Table 7.2 allows a comparison of East Germany with West Germany (before verification) and of North Korea with South Korea. In both cases, the trends and ratios are either the same or even more pronounced than between the two groups of countries on average. The general rule is that resource use per unit of GNP in socialist countries is about three times higher than in more developed market economies.

165

TABLE 7.2   Consumption of Energy and Steel Per Capita and Per $1000 of GNP, Selected Countries, 1965, 1980, and 1985–86

| | Energy (in kilograms of coal equivalent) | | | | Steel (in metric tons) | | | |
| | Per capita | | Per $1000 of GNP* | | Per capita | | Per $1000 of GNP* | |
Group Nation	1980	1986	1980	1986	1975	1985	1975	1985
Market Economies								
U.S.	10386	9489	690	590	541	448	40	28
Canada	10547	9694	840	740	581	471	51	35
Japan	3726	3625	410	330	580	553	78	51
United Kingdom	4850	5363	670	680	376	254	56	32
West Germany	5829	5672	600	550	489	481	60	47
France	4409	3881	500	430	365	258	48	29
Belgium	5997	5577	780	710	314	275	48	36
Switzerland	3636	3990	250	260	n.a.	n.a.	n.a.	n.a.
Austria	4058	4024	500	460	284	235	44	27
Denmark	5254	5331	340	290	n.a.	n.a.	n.a.	n.a.
Sweden	5376	4893	500	430	773	384	75	34
South Korea	1373	1625	870	790	52	198**	42	93**
Unweighted average	5450	5260	580	520	436	356	54	41
Socialist Economies								
Soviet Union	5549	6389	1130	1250	554	557	124	121
Bulgaria	5254	5780	1310	1590	252	336	64	80
Czechoslovakia	6364	6258	1160	1100	731	709	144	124
East Germany	7276	7944	1150	1920	566	574	101	82
Hungary	3787	3735	800	760	n.a.	n.a.	n.a.	n.a.
Poland	4935	4700	1150	1100	524	409	120	95
Romania	4505	4483	1340	1260	463	480	159	133
North Korea	2713	2771	2490	2450	186	413	177	356
Unweighted average	5048	5260	1320	1430	468	497	127	142

* In constant 1984 dollars. Estimates per $1000 GNP in socialist countries are corrected assuming the average GNP per capita in these countries equal to 40% of that in Western market economies (for recent semi-official Soviet estimates see A. Illarionov, 'Paradoksy Statistiki,' *Argumenty i Fakty*, no. 3 [1990], pp. 6–7). No corrections were made for North Korea due to lack of data. ** 1984.   n.a.: not available.

Source: US Bureau of the Census, *Statistical Abstract of the United States, 1989* (Washington, DC: USGPO, 1989), pp. 822, 832–834.

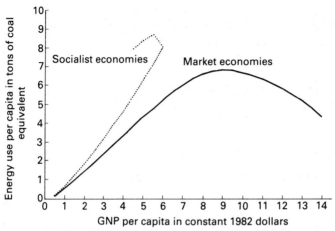

Sources: Derived from Jan Winiecki, *Economic Prospects – East and West* (London: The Centre for Research into Communist Economies, 1987), p. 25; Margaret E Slade, "Natural Resources, Population Growth, and Economic Well-Being," in D Gale Johnson and Ronald D Lee, eds., *Population Growth and Economic Development: Issues and Evidence* (Madison, WI: University of Wisconsin Press, 1987), p. 355; and from Table 7.2.

FIGURE 7.3   Relationship between Energy Use Per Capita and GNP Per Capita under Different Economic Systems

Figure 7.3 shows the split in the trends in resource use during the course of economic growth between market and socialist economies. In competitive market countries, the relationship between GNP *per capita* and resource use is initially positive. Resource use increases at a decreasing rate in response to economic growth, until the level of development achieved some time in the 1970s reverses the relationship. In socialist countries, resource use *per capita* grows continuously over the course of economic growth and even after the economies begin to decline. Eventually, in accordance with Figure 7.6 below, resource use may decline as the economies decline further. The curve thus becomes backward bending.

One can make a general comparison of the production cycle in the United States and in the Soviet Union. In the second half of the 1980s, while consuming about 1.6 times as much steel as the United States, the Soviet Union produced about 0.75–0.80 as much in physical volume of metal-originated machinery and other producer goods (Kheinman, 1989, p. 67). with this 75–80 per cent of producer goods, the Soviet Union made less than 33 per cent of final consumer goods relative to the United States (estimated from a Soviet GNP equal to 40 per cent that of the United States, consumption accounting for about 50 per cent of the Soviet GNP and 77 per cent of the United States GNP, and a Soviet population that is 18 per cent larger than that of the United States; see Appendix 1 for details). The socialist economy

167

Mikhail S Bernstam

can be thought of as a bottom-heavy pyramid, with spreading slopes of resources, a gigantic corpus of producer goods and a thin cap of final consumer goods. An overall ratio, roughly estimated, of resource inputs to final outputs (1.6:0.33) is about 4.8 times higher in the Soviet Union than in the United States.

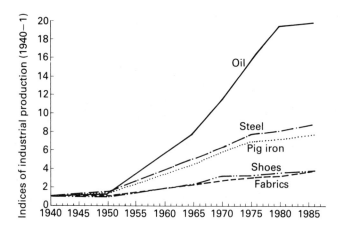

Source: USSR State Committee on Statistics, 'Razvitie Promyshlennosti SSSR', *Vestnik Statistiki*, No. 5 (1987), pp. 63–64.

FIGURE 7.4   Indices of Industrial Production: Resources and Final Goods, USSR, 1940–86

Figures 7.4 and 7.5 present evidence for the two largest socialist economies, the Soviet Union and the People's Republic of China since 1940 and 1950, respectively. In both countries the gap widened between the production of energy (oil), primary and fabricated metals (pig iron and steel) and final household goods made with the use of resources and producer goods (fabrics and shoes). The trends in production indices are remarkably similar although the Chinese economy has been fully independent of the Soviet economy since the late 1950s at the latest. This similarity in the lavish consumption of resources and intermediate inputs over the production cycle is a systemic feature of the two economies. The widening, during decades, of the gap between the amount of resource inputs and final household outputs, cannot simply be attributed to low technological levels. Technology improves over the course of economic development, but it was overpowered by systemic factors to which I now turn.

To emphasize the growth of producer goods relative to household goods, consider some general trends. The share that final consumer goods constitute of total Soviet industrial production declined from 60.5 per cent in 1928 to

168

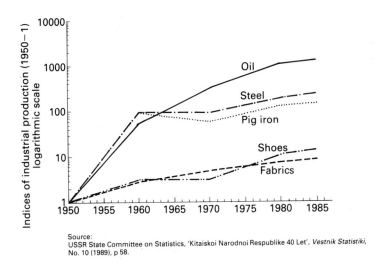

Source:
USSR State Committee on Statistics, 'Kitaiskoi Narodnoi Respublike 40 Let', *Vestnik Statistiki*,
No. 10 (1989), p 58.

FIGURE 7.5   Indices of Industrial Production: Resources and Final Goods, People's
Republic of China, 1950–85

39.0 per cent in 1940, to 31.2 per cent in 1950, to 27.5 per cent in 1960, to
26.6 per cent in 1970, to 26.2 per cent in 1980 and to 24.9 per cent in 1987
while the share attributed to producer goods increased accordingly (Kostin,
1989, p. 12). At the same time, about 33 per cent of the total Soviet industrial
production in the 1980s, chiefly producer goods and construction materials,
are economically useless outputs, or wastes (Uliukaev, 1989, p. 84; Arbatov,
1990, p. 72; Aganbegian, 1987). In the Soviet economy as a whole, capital
investment as a share of GNP grew in real terms from 24.2 per cent in 1960 to
28.7 per cent in 1970 and to 33.0 per cent in 1980, while, during the same
period, Western market economies invested about half as much (Offer, 1987,
pp. 19–788, 1806). This simply means that machines produce other machines
in order to produce other machines which extract additional resources in
order to produce more machines. Seliunin (1988, pp. 158–159) called this 'a
cannibalistic economy', 'the self-feeding and self-devouring industrialized
economy.' I recall an image from Moby Dick where a cut-up, wounded shark
devours, regurgitates, and again devours its own guts, spreading blood and
wastes around.

Figure 7.6 shows where this proliferation of resources over the production
cycle eventually leads. It presents Soviet estimates of how much energy it
takes and will take to produce energy over the period 1975–2035. In 1975,
energy inputs (including energy used to produce equipment for energy
extraction) constituted about 22 per cent of the energy output of natural gas.
This fraction grew to 28 per cent in 1980 and 32 per cent in 1985 and 1990,

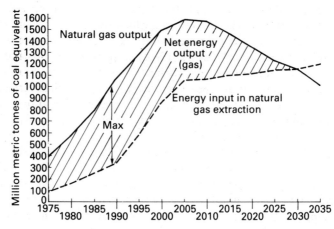

Note: Energy from 1 million metric tonnes of coal equivalent is equal to energy derived from 789 million cubic meters of natural gas.

Source: D Aksenov, 'Strategiia Chistoi Energii,' *Ekonomicheskaia Gazeta*, No. 16 (April 1989), p. 5.

FIGURE 7.6 Gross Output, Energy Input, and Net Output of Natural Gas Extraction, USSR, 1975–2035 (Reported and Officially Projected)

and it is projected to increase to 46 per cent in 1995, 58 per cent in 2000 and so on, until it reaches 100 per cent in 2030 and exceeds 100 per cent thereafter. Net energy output grew in absolute terms until 1989 and began to decline thereafter. Absolute declines of gross output are projected after 2005. Inputs have grown faster than output, at an increasing rate. This pattern applies to most economic activities. Eventually, the relationship becomes backward-bending, that is, inputs continue to grow while output declines.

The question of the cause of this pattern in socialist economies remains. I can offer a simple, quick and proximate explanation of the proliferation of the waste of resources over the production cycle. In the last few decades, at least, the prices of the supplies needed to produce most outputs have been cost-based. Enterprise profits are proportional to costs. If one does not believe that enterprise managers are loyal agents of the state but assumes instead that they are normal human beings who maximise profits for the sake of managerial bonuses, housing allocations for managers and workers, and other articles of wealth and power, a simple conclusion follows: in order to maximise profits, producers maximise inputs. It pays to maximise costs and waste over the production cycle since prices and, therefore, profits are based on them (see, e.g., Gorbachev, 1985, pp. 1–2; Valovoi, 1990, p. 3).

This is a proximate explanation. The readers who find it sufficient can skip the rest of this section and go directly to the concluding section which offers a global summary and future estimates of production under different scenarios.

Others may consider the new theory of the socialist economy proposed by Kornai (1979, 1980, 1982, 1986a, 1986b) from which I will draw heavily and which I will also modify. The pre-Kornai literature, from Soviet economists of the 1920s to Western textbooks of the 1980s, emphasises the demander-state in the absence of open competitive markets. The literature does not use this simple concept, though, but rather describes it via such familiar terms as central planning, the command economy, central management, and so forth. The demander-state means that the government determines the goods to be produced, their quantity and price.

But the new theory implies that the demander-state is itself only an outcome of the supplier-state. The supplier-state is really at the heart of the system in which the government maximises its power over individuals via economic means and also maximises its share of national income and its total revenues via suppressed wages. The supplier-state provides producer firms with inputs (resources, labour, and capital in terms of both money and producer goods) and households with consumer goods. In order to provide, the state needs to create producer firms and make them produce. The owner-state and the demander-state follow from this. Another implication is that the supplier-state which wants to maximise its supplier role must close access to its markets by others and set up agencies and/or large producer firms that are product monopolies. Indeed, in the Soviet Union in the mid 1980s, the entire industrial production was derived from 46,000 firms (USSR State Committee on Statistics, 1989, p. 330). Compare this with 1,401,000 industrial establishments with payrolls and 2,741,000 tax-paying industrial proprietorships and corporations in the United States (US Bureau of the Census, 1989, pp. 523, 517). In the Soviet Union, single corporations controlled by state agencies produce from 74 per cent to 94 per cent of the volume of particular outputs. The balance belongs to local monopolies (Kholodkov, 1989; Volkov and Matiukhin, 1989; Nikerov, 1990; Gurevich, 1990; Katsura, 1990).

Since the supplier-state is also the demander-state, these monopolistic producers are regulated state monopolies on which demand output quotas are imposed. In order to provide, the state has to maintain and expand production enterprises, and in order to assure production, the state has to maintain and expand the provision of inputs. Thus the state and its monopolistic firms are locked in a mutually dependent relationship of inputs and outputs. As with any large functioning body, the supplier-state becomes dependent on its own parts.

The five building blocks of Kornai's theory follow from this interdependence. These are, in turn, (a), state subsidisation of corporations (their soft budget constraint) (b), the continuous imposition by firms that sell on those that buy of their growing production costs (c), an insatiable demand by producers for inputs of money, labour, resources, and producer goods (d), perpetual shortages of all inputs and outputs combined with price inflation and (e), shortages of resources in the entire economy. Once producer firms

171

are provided with resources without the constraints of a budget, the state has to increase the output of resources and producer goods in order to supply its firms with inputs. Output maximisation becomes a central function of the supplier-state and the demander-state. The implication missed by Kornai is that the race between inputs and outputs becomes circular. The economy falls into a circular trap.

The tournament between the intra-dependent state and its regulated monopolistic firms also becomes circular. Inputs cannot be provided by independent, outside, competitive firms since they do not exist. The maximisation of outputs makes the supplier-state become more and more dependent on its own producer firms. But producer firms have their own vested interests. They are not loyal agents of the state, and they do not oblige with output maximisation. Instead, their interests are opposite to those of the state. The demander-state seeks more output at lower prices produced with fewer inputs while monopolistic firms seek to produce less output at higher prices using more inputs. In the words of Kornai (1986a, p. 55), this is the central issue over which the well-known phenomenon of 'plan bargaining' takes place. Ironically, the state, like any other consumer in a monopoly setting, has to succumb to the producer's power to charge almost any price and live with both shortages and high prices. Wassily W Leontief, during his recent trip to the Soviet Union, made a profound unpublished remark. He said that shortages exist not simply due to the excessive demand for, and use of, resources and other products (as Kornai's theory implies), but also because state-owned producers have a vested interest in shortages.

As do monopolies generally, monopolistic socialist firms maximise their rents through reducing output and raising prices, instead of maximising profits through an increased volume of output and price reductions (see Tullock, 1967; Krueger, 1974; Wenders, 1987). This alone leads to the low productivity of inputs, the failure to adopt advanced technology, and to a perpetually excessive use of resources. But the system absorbs inputs much beyond that. Unlike unregulated monopolies in many developing countries, where the government is not responsible for providing inputs and producing outputs, state-owned regulated monopolies cannot raise prices without the government's consent. They must bargain with the government, justifying price increases and reduced output.

From this there follows a missing central point of Kornai's theory. It is the lack of an explanation of why the firms do not economise their inputs. The theory did not explain why firms have an interest in the excessive use of resources, which goes much beyond the mere waste of free or subsidised goods. Consider that although enterprises do not have an effective budget constraint, they have a supply constraint. Not everything can be obtained for money. Why, then, do they not use inputs more efficiently?

The mutual dependence of the state and its firms and the resulting interdependence of output maximisation and input maximisation provide an

172

explanation. Like a poor and resisting secretary who receives less work from his or her boss than a good secretary, the regulated monopolistic firms are doing well by doing poorly. They raise costs, fail new technology, waste resources, hoard producer goods, and otherwise maximise inputs in order to both justify the cost-based price increases they request and sabotage output quotas imposed by the state. By maximising inputs, the regulated monopolistic firms get higher prices and higher profits while producing less. Enterprises show the state how many additional scarce inputs it will take to produce additional output at an even higher price – and the state stops applying pressure for additional outputs and pays the price at a mutually agreed level.

Input maximisation is thus the best profit-maximising strategy for regulated state monopolies. Cost-based prices and cost-proportional profits which generate input maximisation are in the interest of state monopolistic producers. This does not mean that the government is myopic, let alone blind, in allowing and even inviting these input maximising arrangements. Far from this, the government is fully aware that its producer firms will raise prices, maximise inputs and contract output, as a means to achieve these aims. Cost-based prices and cost-proportional profits are then in the interest of the government as much as they are in the interest of corporations. There are government monitoring devices which provide negotiating ground where input-output and input-price agreements are reached between the demander-state and producers. Kornai (1986a, p. VIII) pointed out that some socialist arrangements remind one of Western military industries. I relegate to Appendix 2 a more detailed and technical discussion of input maximisation.

Input maximisation at the enterprise level leads to the main paradox of the socialist economic system. The supplier-state strives for output maximisation but its own producer firms maximise profits via input maximisation. Since the state economy is simply a conglomeration of its producer firms, the entire system adopts input maximisation. The state actually maximises the production of inputs under the appearance of the maximisation of output. As long as economic growth continues and the government collects revenues via suppressed wages and residual enterprise profits (after subtracting management bonuses, housing and other direct allocations to enterprises and others), the government is content. It is when input maximisation eventually impedes economic growth and inputs exceed outputs that the government revolts against its own system.

The Socialist Economic System and Global Conflict

The survival of the socialist economic system depends on the proliferation and intensification of global conflict. Because regulated state monopolies pervert the state with the need for input maximisation, its survival becomes dependent on a continuously expanding flow of inputs. The state thus engages in a continuous expansion in the search for resources and cheap labour. Input maximisation would have invented claims on other nations if these claims were not a perennial part of human behaviour. The imposition of the socialist economic system on other nations brings about their withdrawal from the world market and links their resources and production to the Soviet economy.

At the same time, claims on one's own people (whose wages and consumption are suppressed for the sake of industrial input maximisation) are impossible to enforce without claims on the rest of the world and expansion in order to prove the validity of these claims. Only the expansion of claimant power and the proven commitment to destroy alternative economic systems makes the enforcement of domestic power credible. These are the two basic implications (one at the material level and the other at the political level) of the socialist economic system for global conflict.

Recent decades have provided evidence of the relationship between global claims and socialist input maximisation. As input maximisation intensified and inputs began to grow faster than output, Soviet leaders of the 1960s to the early 1980s became less selective in their global acquisitions than their revolutionary predecessors of the early 1930s and 1950s. Non-economic theories of conflict would have predicted an opposite trend. The concentration of Soviet efforts in the 1970s in the direction of Middle Eastern oil fits the economic explanation especially well. The often heard Western warning (especially after the invasion of Afghanistan) not to push the Soviet government against the wall came too late. It could not be helped: the Soviet economic system had long since pushed the state against the wall since inputs grow faster than output.

Figure 7.7 presents a scheme that shows how global conflict derives from the socialist economic system. The main objective of the power-maximising government is the dependence of the individual on the state. The socialist government becomes the owner of productive assets as well as the producer and provider of necessities. By default, the government becomes the employer. The government then derives economic rents in the form of suppressed wages as the main hidden tax on labour. The average tax rate via suppressed wages in the Soviet Union constitutes about 65 per cent (e.g., Koriagina, 1990, p. 20). Hidden sales taxes add another 10 percentage points. There are also explicit income taxes. Altogether, the total tax rate runs over 80 per cent. This rate is unprecedented outside socialist countries and perhaps in human history. The ability to claim and redistribute 80 per cent of national income continuously explains why the government socialised the economy. This also implies that the enforcement of claims of such a magnitude represents a political problem.

Thus Figure 7.7 begins with the functional triangle of the state which operates as the provider, the owner, and the producer. This combination leads to the interdependent input and output maximisation and to the

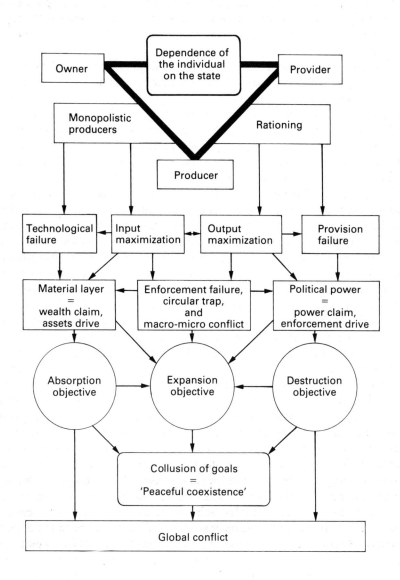

FIGURE 7.7 Derivation of Global Conflict from the Socialist Economic System

ensuing technological failure and low provision. The drive of the supplier and demander-state for various inputs is insatiable and ever-growing. The government of the low-productivity economy is in constant need of advanced technology which it hopes will induce monopolistic producers to increase their productivity. The wealth, resources, and assets of other countries emerge as potential and even necessary future inputs. This is shown on the left side of Figure 7.7. Input maximisation recognises no borders and no national property rights. Moreover, it generates the need to absorb the assets of other nations.

Two other links with the activation of global conflict can be derived from the socialist economic system. They are shown on the right side and in the centre of Figure 7.7. The bottom-heavy economy is a high-investment, low-productivity, low-provision economy. The real tax rate is very high and the real share of human consumption in the GNP is low. This has its political costs for the claimant government. If the domestic population is well informed about the difference in the standard of living in socialist and open market countries, the very preservation of the socialist system constitutes an opportunity cost (benefits foregone because the system is socialist) for Soviet citizens. Consequently, the very existence of Western open market economies constitutes an ongoing security threat for the socialist government.

Recently, in an official Soviet publication, a verbatim transcript of several meetings of the Soviet leadership which took place in the second half of the 1940s emerged (Simonov, 1988, pp. 59–61). This documentation shows the considerations of the Soviet leadership after it became aware that during and after the Second World War many Soviet people had obtained the relevant information about the opportunity costs of their economics system. According to this documentation, the Soviet government started both the Cold War and the domestic ideological crackdown in order to justify its existence in view of this unfavourable comparison.

Even if international comparisons are lacking, the shortcomings of the economic system are evident to the people. One can introduce here a concept of rational assessment. It is similar to the concept of rational expectations in modern macro-economics. People are capable of assessing what the standard of living should be at a given level of technological development (in technical terms, on a given production possibilities curve). People are fully aware that a country of spaceships and the highest output of oil and steel in the world could, under a different system, prevent children from dying of starvation and begging for bread in the streets (Voshchanov and Bushuev, 1990).

In a very serious sense, the socialist government has found itself, from the very beginning, in a situation in which it had to compete constantly for power with the spectre of capitalism. This created a continuous political claim on the future of Western open market economies, which I call a destruction objective. The socialist government cannot but strive to destroy competing economic systems in order to perpetuate its domestic claims and economic rents. This is shown schematically on the right of Figure 7.7.

The enforcement of domestic claims requires continual proofs of credibility. Like fiat money that is credible only as long as its purchasing power and universal acceptance is constantly proven (Kiyotaki and Wright, 1989) the fiat government needs to implement international claims in order to preserve domestic power. Constant expansion serves this purpose. The state creates, in concentric circles, an internal empire around the central Russian base, an external European and Asian empire around the internal Soviet empire, and an array of other acquisitions around the external empire. One can think of a wooden barrel where the outlying hoops help to hold the central hoop firm.

Finally, there is one more important link to both the material and political claims on other countries. It derives, paradoxically, from the conflict between the state and its managerial class. The circular trap of inputs and output and the degeneration of output maximisation in favour of input maximisation reflect the failure to enforce state goals. The managerial class of the monopolistic producer firms behaves like normal profit or rent maximisers rather than as a loyal agent of the state. The enforcement of state objectives often takes drastic forms, for example, the decades of terror against this very ruling class in all socialist countries. Global conflict serves as a political tool with which the state enforces output maximisation. The managerial class is assured that its constant sabotage and seeking of its own interests is not simply a seller's failure, it is high treason. The unfaithful agents of the state operate under pressure to produce. Their output may be stored or rot somewhere or be otherwise misused, but is, nevertheless, imperative for the struggle for the future of humankind. Since information is asymmetric, such an enforcement policy is rational. Thus, part of global conflict derives from a macro-micro conflict in the socialist economy between the state and its producer firms.

An interesting result follows from the conflict between the assets and power claims of the state, or between its absorption and destruction objectives. These two goals are complementary, yet they are not operationally compatible. The absorption goal has quantitative dimensions and is not necessarily an all-or-nothing game. The absorption objective can, for a period of time, settle for non-destructive pressure on Western economies. The subsidised flow of capital and technology may be sufficient. Conflicts and claims are not necessarily destructive. Appetites may grow, but not to the lethal end. Still, temporary exchanges between states cannot satisfy the absorption objective of the input maximising economy in the long run. Claims on assets may grow beyond any temporary gains from international exchange because the appetite for inputs is insatiable. However, the absorption objective may confine global conflict to non-lethal means for a long time.

At this juncture, expansion serves as a road of moderation. It allows the commitment to destroy Western market economies as an economic system to continue without destroying Western market countries. Expansion is flexible. It allows claims on assets on the periphery of the Western world while pursuing economic arrangements with the West which satisfy other input needs. The interrelatedness of the goals of destruction, absorption, and expansion underlies the peaceful coexistence of the Soviet Union and the West. Global conflict and peaceful coexistence between states are, in fact, two different names for the same phenomenon. An ironic conclusion is that the very coexistence of socialist and competitive market economies is the source of global conflict and that this conflict is a normal state of global affairs. This is, of course, as long as the socialist economic system lasts.

Soviet Dependence on Demographic Inputs and Soviet Economic Breakdown

Demographic forces sometimes play a pivotal role at the crucial junctions of history. I have mentioned earlier their role in the emergence of the Industrial Revolution in England (Schofield and Wrigley, 1986; Bernstam, 1987a). It is not an exaggeration, in my view, to attribute the breakdown of the socialist economic system in the Soviet Union and the ensuing start of the dissipation of global conflict to demographic forces.

The input-dependent socialist economy has evidently hit one of its main supply constraints; labour. Kornai (1979) prophetically pointed out that in the presence of a number of non-substitutable constraints, it is the most pressing constraint that is delimiting. Coming up against one such supply constraint is sufficient to cause the socialist economy to begin to decline.

Theoretically, the input-maximising economy is inherently doomed. The intrinsic dynamics of input-maximisation is such that, at some stage, inputs begin to grow faster than output. In order for the economy to be sustained, the supply of major inputs must then exceed the absorption of inputs by the economy. Examples are the large exogenous supply of capital due to domestic confiscation (e.g., the first wave of suppression of wages and rural incomes in the 1930s) or rising world prices of natural resources (the oil shock of the 1970s). However, the first instance was a one-time source and the second a happenstance.

A more permanent exogenous source of high growth inputs is the labour supply. It is exogenous for any given period because it derives from past trends of population growth and depends on the reserves, built up in the past of rural to urban migrants and non-working females to man urban industries. Since these reserves are exhaustible within several decades of economic development, one can conclude that, innately, the economies of input-maximising regulated state monopolies have only several decades to exist. The socialist economic system is a transient phenomenon by its very nature. A melodramatic writer could have called this the suicide of the Leviathan after the supply of drugs runs out.

Soviet economic development has been fundamentally different from that of open competitive market economies. A careful overview of evidence by Ofer (1987) found that:

> during the entire period [from the late 1920s through 1985], but more so with time, Soviet growth is generated by high rises in inputs and declining growth of overall input productivity. During the entire period 1928–85 inputs grew at 3.2 per cent [per year] and contributed 76 per cent of total GNP growth, while factor productivity grew 1.1 per cent a year, accounting for only 24 per cent of total growth. The relative contribution of inputs to growth grew to 80 per cent in the postwar period and became its sole component from 1970 on, when productivity completely stagnated or even retreated. The proportions of inputs and productivity are diametrically opposed to those of a normal modern economic growth pattern. . . . The main characteristic of labour inputs is that they grow over the entire period at a substantially higher rate than population growth. While the population increased at an annual rate of 1.3 per cent, the number of employed was growing 1.9 per cent annually (p. 1782). . . . Another result of these trends is an exceptionally high rate of participation in the labour force, much higher than in any other country (p. 1793). . . . All measures of growth, whether of GNP or of consumption, are lower [in the Soviet case] when they are measured per employed person [rather] than per capita (p. 1791).

One has to take into account that Soviet growth rates have been questioned recently by a number of Soviet and Western economists and adjusted downward by various degrees. Table 7.3 presents alternative and now widely-accepted estimates of Soviet economic growth and growth of capital by Grigorii I Khanin. I calculated the corresponding rates of growth of combined inputs, overall factor productivity, and contribution of inputs to economic growth. My results on the contribution of combined inputs to the growth of this input dependent economy are similar to Ofer's (79 per cent and 76 per cent respectively). Only once (in 1951–60) was this contribution lower. Inputs constituted the sole source of growth in 1976–85. Correspondingly, the growth of productivity was either zero or negative in this period.

Significantly, even a small contribution of productivity to growth in the past was indirectly dependent on labour inputs. The dependence of the socialist economic system on labour force flows can thus be discussed in terms of two major contributions to economic growth. One obvious dependence is on pure labour inputs. Another dependence is the match of labour and capital growth rates, when an increased labour force allows the introduction of new machines, the adoption of new technology, and an increase in overall productivity. As I discussed earlier, socialist management is not interested in adopting advanced technology and is often resistant to it, because it may reduce its production costs and thus its claims for economic rents from the state. New labour flows facilitate the installation by the state of

TABLE 7.3   Economic Growth, Inputs, and Productivity: USSR, 1929–1987 (average annual rates of growth in percent)

	1929–41	1942–50	1951–60	1961–70	1971–75	1976–80	1981–85	1929–87
Economic growth	3.2	1.6	7.2	4.1	3.2	1.0	0.6	3.3
Population	2.1	-0.8	1.7	1.2	0.9	0.8	0.9	1.0
Labor (manhours)	3.3	0.7	1.2	1.7	1.7	1.2	0.7	1.8
Capital	5.3	2.4	5.4	5.5	3.9	1.9	0.6	3.9
Land	1.6	-1.3	3.3	0.2	1.0	-0.1	-0.1	0.8
Combined inputs	4.1	1.3	3.0	3.2	2.6	1.5	0.6	2.6
(contribution to economic growth)	(1.0)	(0.81)	(0.42)	(0.78)	(0.81)	(1.0)	(1.0)	(0.79)
Factor productivity	-0.9	0.3	4.2	0.9	0.6	-0.5	0.0	0.7
Labor productivity	-0.1	0.9	6.0	2.4	1.5	-0.2	-0.1	1.5
Productivity of capital	-2.1	-0.8	1.8	-1.4	-0.7	-0.9	0.0	-0.6
Metal-intensity of production	1.7–2.0	1.1	-0.5	0.4	1.0	1.0	1.0	0.8–0.82

Sources: Economic growth, capital, and metal-intensity of production: G. Khanin, 'Ekonomicheskii Rost: Alternativnaia Otsenka,' Kommunist, No. 17 (November 1988), p. 85. Population: calculated from USSR Central Statistical Administration, Narodnoe Khoziaistvo SSSR, statistical yearbooks. Labor and land: Gur Ofer, 'Soviet Economic Growth: 1928–1985,' The Journal of Economic Literature, Vol. 25, No. 4 (December 1987), p. 1778.

Combined inputs are calculated using the following set of weights: 0.558 for man hours, 0.412 for capital, and 0.03 for land. Contribution of combined inputs to economic growth (in parentheses) refers to a given period and is calculated as the ratio of inputs to economic growth. Factor productivity is calculated as the difference between the rates of economic growth and growth of combined inputs. Labour and capital productivity are calculated as the differences between the rates of economic growth and growth of man hours and capital, respectively.

new plants where new equipment can be introduced without sabotage by an entrenched management. As Hanson (1981, p. 67) pointed out;

> the design of the Soviet system was aimed, in part, precisely at carrying through large investment projects, and at facilitating a process of technological change in which the construction of new plants played a dominant role.

New, more advanced producer goods were used by new labour, which was driven into new plants from the countryside and from home industry. This labour became more productive in new activities which, in turn, generated economic growth. At the same time, the installation by the state of new plants, equipment, and technology countered technological retardation in the older plants where the entrenched management stalled innovation. Labour force growth allowed for more specialisation and division of labour. This may have created increasing returns to the growing scale of the economy. Another important contribution to economic growth was the rising educational level of the growing labour force.

The induced transfer of labour to new industrial sites was a specific socialist policy. It was as important a part of the collectivisation of agriculture as the agricultural rearrangement itself. Tens of millions of peasants were driven to the cities and to penal labour institutions in the 1930s and 1940s. Over several decades, tens of millions of women were moved into the industrial labour force from family life and housekeeping. Almost unnoticed in the West, since the mid-1960s a very big campaign of rural resettlement drove another 45 million people to the cities and greatly increased the urban labour force (calculated from USSR State Committee on Statistics, 1988a, pp. 8, 110–111).

Figure 7.8 summarises the above discussion of the dependence of the socialist economic system on multiple demographic inputs. It underscores that past populaton growth is the ultimate exogenous factor and that the transfer of rural migrants to industrial areas, of female labour from the home economy to industry, and demographic growth are the three basic sources of systemic dependence.

The first two transfers of labour are clearly exhaustible for the supply runs out after having reached a certan point. Tables 7.4 and 7.5 show that this had happened in the 1970s and the 1980s. Table 7.4 shows that female participation in the labour force in the European Republics of the Soviet Union where most of Soviet industry is located was nearly 90 per cent in 1970. (Actually, the term 'European' here and thereafter is imprecise because the Russian Republic includes Siberia and transcends over Eurasia). Importantly, this was full-time year-round employment since part-time work for women virtually does not exist in the USSR. A female employment rate close to 90 per cent means that all non-pregnant and non-nursing women were already in the labour force in 1970.

Table 7.5 shows that in the Russian Republic the rural source of supply of

181

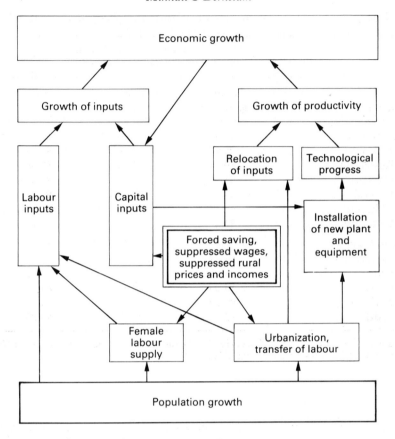

Figure 7.8 Demographic Inputs Dependence of Socialist Economic Growth

migrant labour for the cities and construction sites was at the point of drying up for age groups 15–35 by the late 1970s. The Russian Republic is representative of other industrial areas and is itself the largest industrial region of the Soviet Union where over 60 per cent of the Soviet GNP is produced. Non-European Soviet areas do not supply rural population transfers to European or other cities due to an array of Soviet economic policies discussed elsewhere (Bernstam, 1986, 1987c). Thus high past and present population growth in Central Asia and other Non-European areas provides no help for the Soviet economy.

Finally, the contribution of past population growth to the labour supply has been diminishing rapidly in the Russian and other industrial republics. Figure 7.9 compares birth rates, death rates and rates of population growth (the difference between them) in the Russian and Central Asian areas. One

Economic Systems

TABLE 7.4   Labour Force Participation Selected Republics of the USSR, 1970

Republics	Labour force participation rates in percent		
	Males aged 16–59	Females aged 16–54	Both sexes
European Republics	90.41	87.69	89.00
Latvia	95.15	94.19	94.67
Russia	89.84	87.79	88.80
Ukrainia	91.10	86.74	88.85
Estonia	94.63	94.98	94.80
Lithuania	95.80	86.82	91.26
Byelorussia	91.45	89.07	90.22
Asian Republics	86.32	75.76	83.41
Azerbaidjan	88.17	70.14	79.13
Kirghiz	88.99	80.77	84.80
Uzbek	89.36	80.92	85.11
Turkmen	90.19	78.67	84.56
Tadzhik	90.31	73.89	82.09

Source: A.A. Tkachenko, *Ekonomicheskie Posledstviia Sovremennykh Demograficheskikh Protsessov v SSSR* (Moscow: Statistika, 1978), p. 80.

TABLE 7.5   Rural Population by Age Groups as a Proportion of Total Population (in Percentages) The Russian Federated Republic, 1959–1987

Age group	1959	1970	1979	1987
15–19	45.7	32.0	29.1	26.1
20–24	42.1	25.2	25.3	23.3
25–29	43.6	29.4	23.9	19.1
30–34	42.1	31.8	21.5	21.6
30–35	44.2	36.2	26.7	20.4
TOTAL	46.0	38.0	30.0	26.0

Source: USSR State Committee on Statistics, *Naselenie SSSR. 1987. Statisticheskii Sbornik* (Moscow: Finansy i Statistika, 1988), pp. 48–51.

can observe an indication of a dramatic decline of labour force in the Russian Republic in the 1980s and 1990s. Compare population growth rates in the 1920s with the growth rates of the 1960s and 1970s. Persons born in the former high population growth period will exit the labour force in the 1980s

183

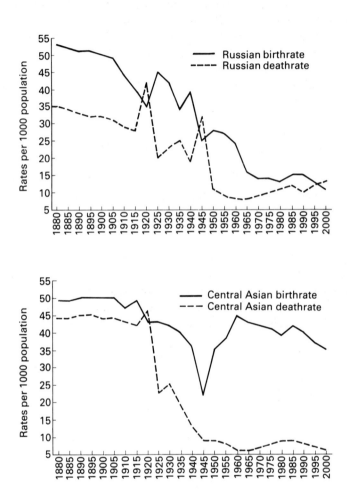

Sources: Estimated from various Soviet sources.

FIGURE 7.9 A: Russian Demographic Transition. B: Central Asian Demographic Transition

184

and 1990s while those born in the latter low growth period will enter the labour force in the 1980s and thereafter.

Figure 7.10 provides the actual trend in labour forces entrances, departure and net growth in the Soviet Union and in the Russian Republic from 1970 to 2000. The 1980s is the time of a major real crisis; a labour force squeeze in the entire Soviet Union and a dramatic shortage of labour in the crucial Russian Republic. Actually, 1985 is the worst year, the year when the crisis really hit. Is it a mere historical accident that this was the year when a qualitatively new leadership came to power in the Soviet Union and began an economic overhaul (not yet a reform)? I leave this question to the readers to ponder while studying Figure 7.10.

The twin demographic contribution of labour supply to economic growth, in terms of pure inputs of workers and of opportunities for technological application, had been exhausted and ended by the mid-1980s. Capital became the main available factor of production. But, due to its low technological content, the contribution of capital to economic growth, via increases in the overall productivity of the economy, had been moving to zero since the early 1970s. Even the growth of labour productivity was negative in 1976–85 (Table 7.3). Without new labour sources, either more technologically productive capital or larger amounts of it is needed for economic growth. The former strategy encounters the systemic constraint of managerial resistance, the latter is unfeasible due to the decline of economic growth from which additional capital should be derived. The Soviet economy has thus fallen into the growth-investment trap.

The system has evolved to the point where the state as the producer can no longer continue to be the provider, and the state as the provider cannot support all production needs. The point of exhaustion of last opportunities was reached in the mid-1980s when demography failed the economy.

Dismantling Socialism and Global Conflict

The second half of the 1980s provided a natural experiment in the reduction of global conflict through the attempts at economic reforms away from socialism. A similar natural experiment has been occurring in the People's Republic of China since 1976. They are living (or dying) proofs of the socialist origin of global conflict. When the government is willing to resign its role as a monopolistic economic producer, global conflict can dissipate on all counts.

The destruction objective is dissipated because the state no longer needs to justify the perpetuation of the socialist economic system by asserting its superiority over competitive markets. The expansion objective is dissipated as the need to contain the domestic population with concentric circles of acquisitions dissipates. The Soviet withdrawal from Afghanistan, the release of Eastern Europe, and the abdication of support for the socialist governments

185

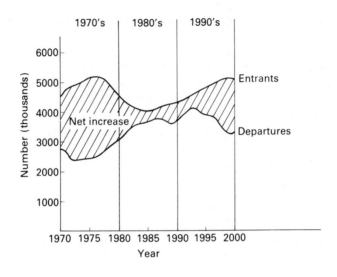

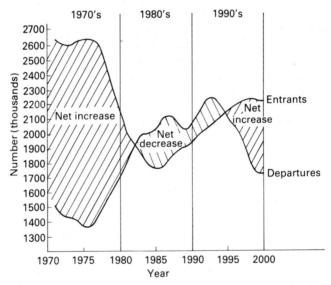

Source: Murray Feshbach, 'Population and Labor Force,' in Abram Bergson and Herbert S Levine, eds. *The Soviet Economy: Toward the Year 2000* (London: George Allen & Unwin, 1983), p. 97.

FIGURE 7.10 Entrants to and Departures from Population of Able-Bodied Ages, A: USSR, 1970 to 2000; B: The Russian Republic, 1970 to 2000

of Nicaragua and Cuba illustrate this point. Both the expansion and absorption objectives dissipate when the state abandons input maximisation by deregulating its monopolies, making it unnecessary to justify rising prices with rising costs.

The future of what remains of global conflict depends on the course of Soviet economic reform. Meanwhile, a series of new international conflicts may emerge as a result of inter-ethnic warfare inside the Soviet Union. The Soviet Union may turn into a Lebanon the size of Eurasia – a Lebanon with nuclear weapons. Whether this will happen also depends on the course of the economic transition from socialism to open competitive markets.

APPENDIX 1
BASIC DATA ON INPUT MAXIMISATION IN THE USSR

Compare some parts of the production cycle in the Soviet Union and the United States. The following data compare domestic output with total inputs which include exports and imports. In 1986, United States firms used 51.8 MMT of iron ore and produced 81.6 MMT of steel. Soviet enterprises used 214.0 MMT of iron ore and produced 160.6 MMT of steel. Although the comparative amounts of inputs of ferro-alloys are not available, the physical input/output ratios are clearly much higher in the Soviet Union. The most important difference here and in the data presented in Table 7.2 is the consumption of metals that is twice as high in an economy that is half as large as that of the United States. The USSR/US ratio of steel consumption per $1000 of GNP is about 4:1. These high Soviet input/output ratios and high use of resource-originated intermediary outputs relative to the United States occur throughout the production cycle from machines to grain to meat. In 1986, the Soviet Union produced 567,000 big tractors and 65,000 small tractors with power totalling 39.4 million kilowatts. Compare with 93,000 big tractors and 512,000 small tractors produced in the United States with 14.2 million kilowatts. There were 96,200 grain combines in the Soviet Union against 8,300 in the US. The Soviet Union used twice as much fertiliser and about 1.5 times the amount of pesticides as the United States. With all these inputs, the Soviet Union in 1986 produced 210.1 MMT of grain, one of its best harvests on record, and the United States produced 326.6 MMT. Adding imports and subtracting exports, the United States and the Soviet Union consumed almost the same amount of grain, about 235 MMT. Using the bulk of this grain as feed input, the Soviet Union produced 15.3 MMT of meat (carcass weight, adjusted for offal and lard), the United States produced 29.0 MMT, almost twice as much (US Bureau of the Census, 1989, pp. 643, 652, 654, 686, 740–741; USSR State Committee on Statistics, 1988b, pp. 123–124, 126, 170, 217, 603–604, 607, 744–645).

APPENDIX 2
A MODEL OF INPUT MAXIMISATION

Figure 7.A1 shows two combinations of quantities and prices on an inelastic demand curve DD. These two combinations reproduce Tullock's rent-seeking model (1967; see elaboration in Wenders, 1987). Once a product monopoly is obtained and the supply is inelastic in the absence of competitive markets, the demand also becomes inelastic. On an inelastic (vertically sloped) demand curve, it is more gainful for a monopolistic producer to sell the quantity Q_R at the price P_R than the quantity Q_C at the price P_C. The associated parallelograms drawn with broken and straight lines, respectively, show this.

If the monopoly is unregulated, there is no need to increase production costs. Higher prices can be charged and rents extracted subject to the demand curve and the highest profitable combination of prices and quantities, irrespective of costs. These unit costs are shown on the marginal costs curve MC. Even in the absence of competition and downward price pressures, it is profitable for producers to reduce marginal costs, although they do not have as strong incentives to do this as under competitive markets. But if the monopoly is state-owned and regulated and the tournament takes place between the government and the producer over the combination of prices and quantities, the game is different.

In order to reduce quantities to Q_R and raise prices to P_R, and to justify this most profitable combination, the regulated monopolistic firms have to increase and reshape their marginal costs curves. The government has to face the impossibility of additional production beyond the point Q_R unless the demand curve is moved outward, capacity is increased, supplies of input are increased, and prices even higher than P_R are paid. Since the demander-state is simultaneously the supplier-state, the given demand curve also signifies the supply constraints of inputs (not only money, but also labour, capacity, resources, and producer goods). Raising production costs under the supplier-state means demanding more inputs. The uplifting of the marginal costs curve from MC to MC' by monopolistic producers puts the government on the edge. The combination of P_R and Q_R has to be accepted. The above logic also suggests that the new marginal costs curve MC' has to be steeper than MC.

Alternatively, the government has to enforce lower marginal costs. This can be done either by terrorising enterprise management, by using forced labour and few producer goods, or by confiscating output at nominal prices and not providing inputs. The third option is most suitable for agriculture where people must produce for their own subsistence and where both subsistence output and inputs of seed and feed grains can be confiscated in lieu of saleable outputs. This option, however, cannot be repeated for long and does not provide for the necessary expansion of the supplier-state. The

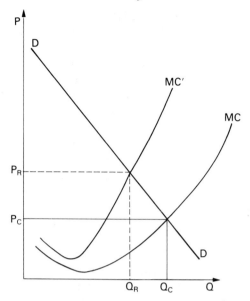

FIGURE 7.A1   Rent-Seeking and Input Maximisation under Unregulated and Regulated Monopolies

second option results in low productivity and the first option was rejected by the managerial class when it became more powerful. The uplifting of marginal costs curves then becomes the prevailing and winning game.

One needs to emphasise that under the supplier-state, raising production costs from MC to MC' principally means increasing physical inputs of resources and producer goods. These are the inputs whose maximisation is the most powerful weapon enterprises have to use against the supplier-state. Input maximisation is circular over the production cycle and is ever-growing. The supplier-state has to demand outputs which become the inputs that are being maximised. This game of output maximisation and input maximisation is repeated over and over, until the system can no longer sustain it.

References

A G Aganbegian, 'Otstupat Nekuda,' *Izvestiia* (Moscow), August 25, 1987, p. 2.

A Arbatov, 'Nezavisimost na Dushu Naseleniia,' *Kommunist*, No. 6 (1990), pp. 66–72.

W Brian Arthur, 'The Economics of Risks to Life,' *The American Economic Review*, Vol. 71, No. 1 (March 1981), pp. 54–64.

Gary S Becker, *The Economics of discrimination* (Chicago: University of Chicago Press, 1971).

Gary S Becker, 'Family Economics and Macro Behavior.' *The American Economic Review*, Vol. 78, No. 1 (March 1988), pp. 1–13.

Mikhail S Bernstam

Mikhail S Bernstam, 'The Demography of Soviet Ethnic Groups in World Perspective,' in *The Last Empire: Nationality and the Soviet Future* (Stanford, CA: Hoover Institution Press, 1986), pp. 314–368.

Mikhail S. Bernstam (1987a), Review on Population and Economy: Population and History from the Traditional to the Modern World, Roger S Schofield and E Anthony Wrigley, eds., *Contemporary Sociology*, Vol. 16, No. 6 (November 1987), pp. 832–833.

Mikhail S Bernstam (1987b), 'Competitive Human Markets, Interfamily Transfers, and Below-Replacement Fertility,' in Kingsley Davis, Mikhail S Bernstam, and Rita Ricardo-Campbell, eds., *Below-Replacement Fertility in Industrial Societies: Causes, Consequences, Policies* (New York: Cambridge University Press, 1987), pp. 111–136.

Mikhail S. Bernstam (1987c), 'Trends in the Soviet Population,' in Henry S Rowen and Charles Wolf, Jr., eds., *The Future of the Soviet Empire* (New York: St. Martin's Press, 1987), pp. 185–220, 335–342.

Ester Boserup, *Population and Technical Change: A Study of Long-Term Trends* (Chicago: The University of Chicago Press, 1981).

Jean Bourgeois-Pichat, 'The General Development of the Population of France since the Eighteenth Century,' in D V Glass and D E C Eversley, eds., *Population in History: Essays in Historical Demography* (London: Edward Arnold, 1965), pp. 474–506.

Reuven Brenner, *History – The Human Gamble* (Chicago: The University of Chicago Press, 1983).

James M Buchanan, *The Limits to Liberty* (Chicago: University of Chicago Press, 1975).

James M Buchanan, 'Rent Seeking and Profit Seeking,' in James M Buchanan, Robert D Tollison, and Gordon Tullock, eds., *Toward a Theory of the Rent-Seeking Society* (College Station: Texas A&M University Press, 1980).

Kingsley Davis, 'The Theory of Change and Response in Modern Demographic History,' *Population Index*, Vol. 29, No. 4 (October 1963), pp. 345–366.

Kingsley Davis, 'Population and Resources: Fact and Interpretation,' in Kingsley Davis and Mikhail S Bernstam, eds., *Resources, Environment, and Population: Present Knowledge, Future Options*, supplement to *Population and Development Review*, Vol. 16 (1990).

Mikhail S Gorbachev, 'O Sozyve Ocherednogo XXVII Sezda KPSS i Zadachakh po ego Podgotovke i Organizatsii,' *Pravda*, April 24, 1985, pp. 1–5.

V Gurevich, 'Tupiki Totalnogo Monopolizma,' *Ekonomika i Zhizn* (Moscow), No. 13 (1990), p. 5.

Philip Hanson, *Trade and Technology in Soviet-Western Relations* (New York: Columbia University Press, 1981).

Robert H Haveman, 'On Estimating Environmental Damage: A Survey of Recent Research in the United States,' in OECD, *Environmental Damage Costs*. (Paris: OECD, 1974), pp. 101–131.

Jack Hirshleifer, 'The Expanding Domain of Economics,' *The American Economic Review*, Vol. 75, No. 6 (December 1985), pp. 53–68.

A Illarionov, 'Paradoksy Statistiki,' *Argumenty i Fakty* (Moscow), No. 3 (1990), pp. 6–7.

Ellen Jones and Fred W Grupp, *Modernization, Value Change and Fertility in the Soviet*

190

Union (New York: Cambridge University Press, 1987).

M W Jones-Lee, *The Value of Life: An Economic Analysis* (Chicago: University of Chicago Press, 1976).

P M Katsura, 'Kak Poborot Monopolizm,' *Izvestiia*, March 3, 1990, p. 2.

Nathan Keyfitz, 'Population Appearances and Demographic Reality,' *Population and Development Review*, Vol. 6, No. 1 (March 1980), pp. 47–64.

John Maynard Keynes (1919), *The Economic Consequences of the Peace*, in *The Collected Writings of John Maynard Keynes*, Vol. 2 (London: Macmillan, 1971).

S Kheinman, 'O Problemakh Nauchno-Tekhnicheskoi Politiki,' *Voprosy Ekonomiki*, No. 3 (1989), pp. 65–74.

V Kholodkov, 'Diktat Proizvoditelia i Rynok,' *Ekonomicheskaia Gazeta* (Moscow), No. 22 (1989), p. 16.

N Kiyotaki and Randell Wright, 'On Money as a Medium of Exchange,' *Journal of Political Economy*, Vol. 97, No. 4 (August 1989), pp. 927–954.

T Koriagina, 'Moe, Tvoe, Nashe,' *Molodoi Kommunist*, No. 3 (1990), pp. 16–25.

Janos Kornai, 'Resource-Constrained Versus Demand-Constrained Systems,' *Econometrica*, Vol. 47, No. 4 (July 1979), pp. 801–819.

Janos Kornai, *Economics of Shortage*, Vols. 1–2 (Amsterdam: North-Holland, 1980).

Janos Kornai, *Growth, Shortage, and Efficiency* (Berkeley, CA: University of California Press, 1982).

Janos Kornai (1986a), 'The Hungarian Reform Process: Visions, Hopes, and Reality,' *Journal of Economic Literature*, Vol. 24, No. 4 (December 1986), pp. 1687–1737.

Janos Kornai (1986b), *Contradictions and Dilemmas: Studies on the Socialist Economy and Society* (Cambridge, MA: MIT Press, 1986).

L Kostin, 'Litsom k Cheloveku,' *Agitator*, No. 15 (1989), pp. 12–15.

Anne Krueger, 'The Political Economy of the Rent-Seeking Society,' *The American Economic Review*, Vol. 64, No. 3 (June 1974), pp. 291–303.

Ronald D Lee, 'Longrun Global Population Forecasts: A Critical Appraisal,' in Kingsley Davis and Mikhail S Bernstam, eds., *Resources, Environment, and Population: Present Knowledge, Future Options*, supplement to *Population and Development Review*, Vol. 16 (1990).

J Linnerooth, 'The Value of Human Life: A Review of the Models,' *Economic Inquiry*, Vol. 17, No. 1 (1979), pp. 52–74.

John M Marshall, 'Gambles and the Shadow Price of Death,' *The American Economic Review*, Vol. 74, No. 1 (March 1984), pp. 73–86.

Gur Ofer, 'Soviet Economic Growth: 1928–1985,' *The Journal of Economic Literature*, Vol. 25, No. 4 (December 1987), pp. 1767–1833.

Vilfredo Pareto, *Manual of Political Economy* (New York: A M Kelley, 1971).

William Petersen, *Malthus* (Cambridge, MA: Harvard University Press, 1979).

Sherwin Rosen, 'The Value of Changes in Life Expectancy,' *Journal of Risk and Uncertainty*, Vol. 1 (1988).

Paul A Samuelson, 'An Exact Consumption-Loan Model of Interest with or without the Social Contrivance of Money,' *The Journal of Political Economy*, Vol. 66, No. 6 (December 1958), pp. 467–482.

Roger S Schofield and E Anthony Wrigley, eds., *Population and Economy: Population and History from the Traditional to the Modern World* (Cambridge and New York: Cambridge University Press, 1986).

Theodore W Schultz, 'The Declining Economic Importance of Land,' *Economic*

Journal, Vol. 61, No. 4 (December 1951), pp. 725–740.

Vasilii I Seliunin, 'Glubokaia Reforma ili Revansh Biurokratii?' *Znamia*, No. 7 (1988), pp. 155–167.

Julian L Simon, *The Ultimate Resource* (Princeton: Princeton University Press, 1981).

Julian L Simon, *Theory of Population and Economic Growth* (Oxford: Basil Blackwell, 1986).

Julian L Simon, 'Lebensraum: Paradoxically, Population Growth May Eventually End Wars,' *Journal of Conflict Resolution*, Vol. 33, No. 1 (March 1989), pp. 164–180.

K M Simonov, 'Glazami Cheloveka Moego Pokoleniia: Mysli o I V Staline,' *Znamia*, No. 3 (1988), pp. 3–66.

Gordon Tullock, 'The Welfare Costs of Tariffs, Monopolies and Theft,' *Western Economic Journal*, Vol. 5, No. 2 (June 1967), pp. 224–232.

A Uliukaev, 'Novaia Istoriia Gammelnskogo Dudochnika,' *Kommunist*, No. 18 (1989), pp. 78–86.

United Nations, *Demographic Yearbook, 1949–50* (New York: United Nations, 1950).

US Bureau of the Census, *Statistical Abstract of the United States. 1989.* (Washington, DC: US Government Printing Office, 1989).

USSR State Committee on Statistics (1988a), *Naselenie SSSR. 1987. Statisticheskii Sbornik* (Moscow: Finansy i Statistika, 1988).

USSR State Committee on Statistics (1988b), *Narodnoe Khoziaistvo SSSR v 1987 Godu. Statisticheskii Ezhegodnik* (Moscow: Finansy i Statistika, 1988).

USSR State Committee on Statistics, *Narodnoe Khoziaistvo SSSR v 1988 Godu. Statisticheskii Ezhegodnik* (Moscow: Finansy i Statistika, 1989).

D Valovoi, 'Plata za Rastochitelstvo,' **Pravda**, March 2, 1990, p. 3.

N Volkov and G Matiukhin, 'Konkurentsiia i Monopolii,' *Pravda*, June 29, 1989, p. 4.

The World Bank, *World Development Report, 1988* (New York: Oxford University Press, 1988).

P Voshchanov and A Bushuev, 'Zdes Legko Obryvaetsia Detskaia Zhizn, *Komsomolskaia Pravda* (Moscow), April 25, 1990, p. 2.

Etienne van de Walle, *The Female Population of France in the Nineteenth Century: A Reconstruction of 82 Departments* (Princeton, NJ: Princeton University Press, 1974).

John T Wenders, 'On Perfect Rent Dissipation,' *The American Economic Review*, Vol. 77, No. 3 (June 1987), pp. 456–459.

J G Williamson, 'British Mortality and the Value of Life, 1781–1931,' *Population Studies*, Vol. 38, No. 1 (March 1984), pp. 157–172.

V V Zagladin, et al., 'Diplomatiia Glasnosti,' *Komsomolskaia Pravda* (Moscow), June 26, 1988, p. 1.

8

Demography and War: A Military Historian's Perspective

Brian Bond

Demographic considerations have been important throughout the history of warfare, but have seldom been examined by historians as a discrete theme, and even the exceptions, such as Quincy Wright, have been extremely tentative in their conclusions.[1]

The broad contentions in this chapter are that in the 18th century the rapid growth of the population in Europe made a significant contribution to military power and could even be rated as decisive in the era of French predominance between 1793 and 1815. However, the capacity of armed forces to exploit demographic advantages was still restricted in the Napoleonic era and was not to be realised to the full until the later 19th century; truly the climactic period for military manpower both in practical organisation of the forces and in strategic planning. In both world wars, the posession of superior manpower resources was still a valuable asset, but in operations was overshadowed by the enhanced power of weapons and technology. At the same time, war production made increasing demands on manpower – and womanpower. Lastly, though the Anglo-American democracies displayed remarkable determination in mobilising virtually the whole of their able-bodied adult populations in the Second World War, their governments proved more willing than in the First World War to accept that by no means every citizen can be made into a competent soldier. John Keegan suggests that this consideration will increasingly inhibit the democracies in their recruitment policies.[2]

Between 1700 and 1801 Europe's population rose from about 118 million to 187 million. In that century the population of England and Wales grew from around 5.8 million to 9.15 million; while between 1715 and 1789 France's population rose from 18 to 26 million. Armies became considerably larger in Eastern as well as Western Europe, but in the latter, particularly, a mounting intensity in warfare was apparent from the Seven Years War

(1756–63), rising to a crescendo in the years of the French Revolution and Napoleon. This may be seen in part as the outcome of pressures that population growth put on older social, economic and political institutions.[3]

However, despite the sweeping away of divine right monarchy and of many aristocratic privileges and institutions of the *ancien régime*, the organisation and equipment of European armed forces remained fundamentally conservative. Only when new industrial techniques began to affect naval and military weaponry and organisation in truly revolutionary ways in the early decades of the 19th century did the traditional military order begin to break up irretrievably.

More specifically, the military potential of an expanding population could not be anywhere near fully exploited until certain inhibiting factors had been overcome. One of the most important was the virtual impossibility of controlling the movements of an army of more than about 50,000 men. This was still, in Martin van Creveld's striking phrase 'the Stone Age of command'. Better methods of communication (in both senses) and accurate topographic maps had greatly reduced this obstacle to mass armies by the time of the French Revolution.[4]

The difficulties of supply constituted another very powerful constraint on 18th century European armies. Available transport simply could not concentrate enough food to support thousands of men and horses if they kept on the move for more than a few days. Thus the movement of armies was constricted by the condition of the roads and the location of magazines; if an inferior army was not completely defeated on the field of battle it could often make good its escape; large numbers could then be a positive handicap to the pursuer. Thirdly, the monarchies and ruling élites had a vested interest in keeping warfare limited: the exclusion of the great majority of the population from any but a passive tax-paying role in what were essentially dynastic conflicts imposed obvious restrictions on both the scale and intensity of warfare. Even so, John Keegan is probably correct in suggesting that historians have been overly impressed by the qualitative, tactical skills of 18th century commanders such as de Saxe and Frederick the Great. Tactical superiority and the general's genius could sometimes offset numerical inferiority, but not always. Thus, for example, Frederick the Great failed to divide the enemy's forces at Hochkirk and Kunersdorf and was beaten by superior numbers. The flaw in Frederick's thinking, was that he assumed large states were inherently inefficient – an error that would be repeated by some British exponents of mechanised warfare between the two world wars.[5]

Nevertheless, historians agree that it was the French Revolution which smashed the shackles which had restricted 18th century warfare, and in particular maximised the potential of military manpower through Carnot's introduction of the *levée en masse*. Between 1789 and 1796 the French standing army increased with astonishing speed from about 150,000 (already dwarfing the average army of the *ancien régime*) to 400,000. Needless to say, mere numbers without efficient weapons, organisation, staff work and command would have constituted a rabble, but, long before the appearance of the genius of Napolean, France had benefitted from a series of reforms and innovations to which the Revolution added the essential ingredients of nationalist fervour and ideological commitment to a crusading cause.

The significance of superior numbers, inspired by nationalist zeal and commanded by brilliant generals was seldom more conspicuously demonstrated than by the French defeat of Prussia in 1806. As one of the outstanding Prussian military reformers, Gneisenau, perceived:

> One cause above all has raised France to this pinnacle of greatness, the revolution awakened all her powers and gave to every individual a suitable field for his activity. What infinite aptitudes slumber undeveloped in the bosom of a nation![6]

His younger colleague, Clausewitz, while appreciating the crucial importance of the spirit pervading the French armies, also emphasised the decisive potential of numbers in an era when other factors were approximately equal. 'An impartial student of modern war', he wrote, 'must admit that superior numbers are becoming more decisive with every passing day. The principle of bringing the maximum possible strength to the decisive engagement must therefore rank higher than it did in the past'.[7] Post-1918 critics, such as Liddell Hart, were to find these opinions deplorable, but in the Napoleonic era they were simply objective statements of fact.

Liddell Hart was surely on firmer ground in his critical contention that, as Emperor, Napoleon relied increasingly on the waning asset of superior manpower resources while the military skills and finesse of earlier campaigns were allowed to decline. It must be noted though, that the upsurge in the French population continued for some twenty years from the start of the Revolution – providing a sufficient number of able-bodied young men to meet both civil and military demands for manpower. The demographic impact of conscription in France was ameliorated by the inclusion of annexed territories in the French 'nation' so that the population increased from about 25 million in 1789 to 44 million in 1810. Napoleon not only enrolled 1.3 million conscripts between 1800 and 1812, but in addition forced allies or subordinate, occupied states to contribute large contingents to the *Grande Armée*. Thus Italian, Spanish, Dutch and German contingents marched under French command with the remarkable consequence that only a minority of the forces which invaded Russia in 1812 were French-speaking. However, even with the supplement of these foreign troops, Napoleon's sources of military manpower were finite. From about 1812, conscription began to cause serious disruption in French civil society and by 1814, Napoleon was 'scraping the bottom of the barrel'. In the campaigns of 1813–14 and again in 1815 Napoleon was defeated by superior numbers as well as by improved allied generalship and co-operation.[8]

Brian Bond

William H MacNeill argues in *The Pursuit of Power* that the heavy imposition of the annual draft in France was one, unconscious, way of alleviating
social friction arising from rapid population growth. Furthermore he sees
France, Britain and Germany by diverse methods successfully avoiding the
worst effects of such demographic pressures in the first half of the 19th
century. Briefly, the French lowered their birthrate and harmonised population growth with expanding industrial and commercial activities. Britain
maintained a high birthrate throughout the 19th century but found a solution
in rapid industrialisation supplemented by emigration; there were as many as
10 million Britons among the 25 million persons who left Europe for overseas
settlement between 1750 and 1900. German development followed the same
course in the last quarter of the 19th century. Thus MacNeill contends that
by the middle of the 19th century the demographic pressures which had had
such profoundly disturbing social and political repercussions during the
French Revolution and the early stages of the industrial revolution were
under reasonable control in Western Europe. 'For the next ten decades,
liberal ideas of peace, prosperity, free trade and private property attained
greater plausibility than before or since'.[9]

From the military historian's standpoint, however, this optimistic viewpoint is hard to sustain. Demographic pressure as such, may have been
diminishing in Central and Western Europe by the middle of the 19th
century, but it was precisely at this time that the military potential of surplus
manpower was harnessed by intensely competitive nation states. Indeed, for
the military historian, the period is notable for the novel and even obsessive
concern, not simply with the size of standing armies and their reserves, but
also with the military implications of demographic trends.

A new military era was heralded by Prussia's victories in 1866 and 1870:

> The value of Prussia's short-service conscripts drawn from a complete cross
> section of her young men had not in 1866 completely convinced conservative
> defenders of long service professionals, but after 1870 there was no room for
> argument. True, Prussia's vital initial advantage derived from her superior
> mobilisation arrangements which enabled Moltke to cross the frontier in the
> first week of August with about 370,000 troops as against France's 240,000. But
> the deeper cause lay in Prussia's retention after 1815 of universal liability to
> three years military service followed by four years in the Landwehr. Contrary to
> orthodox military dogma, the mass Prussian armies of the 1860's proved to be a
> match for their opponents in marching and fighting and superior to them in
> education and motivation. The French belief in quality against quantity was
> proved to be mistaken. So too was subsequent faith in the untrained ardour of
> the people in arms. Henceforth the vital importance of short-service conscrip-
> tion, trained reserves and ability to mobilise the largest possible force in the
> shortest time was scarcely challenged as an ideal among the Continental
> Powers.[10]

Between 1871 and 1914 nearly every Continental European state, as well as

Japan, adopted some form of conscription following Prussia's successful example. The military repercussions of this renowned and extended emphasis on 'the nation in arms' were far reaching. The peacetime training and equipping of conscripts and reserves and their organisation took on enhanced importance, as did also staff work in general, and especially in the development of mobilisation plans co-ordinated with railway timetables. The belief grew up that superior numbers of trained soldiers and a superior mobilisation plan would be not merely important but decisive on the outbreak of the next great European war.

Beyond the strictly military sphere, demographic trends now became an important component of national security. 'The statistical future became important to policy, and introduced into it yet another "timetable" effect; planning had to take account of the likely availability of manpower resources twenty years ahead when the male infants of any given year would reach military age'.[11]

Between 1870 and 1900 Europe's population increased by almost 32 per cent or nearly 100 million people. Great Britain's population rose from 31 to 41 million; Germany's from 41 to 56 million; and European Russia's from 77 to 103 million. Only France was out of step, her rate of increase being scarcely more than half a million per decade – from 36 to 39 million. Within this overall trend, an important consideration was the number of males aged between about eighteen and forty. General staffs now anxiously studied demographic statistics since age categories can change more rapidly than populations as a whole.

Between 1870 and 1914 France was intermittently engaged in an arms race with Germany. Despite a growing concern with weapons innovation and technological development generally, the Franco-German arms race was predominantly viewed by both sides in terms of military manpower. This meant first and foremost the standing armies available at any moment of crisis, and secondly the numerous classes of reservists who would be recalled to service within six weeks or so of the order to mobilise. General staffs did not think much beyond this timescale nor, before 1914, did they truly grapple with the problems of economic mobilisation. In retrospect there is an air of unreality about this obsession with numbers *per se*, particularly as both parties tended to exaggerate the enemy's strength. France's smaller and almost stationary population put her at a severe disadvantage *vis à vis* Germany which she partly overcame by calling up a higher percentage of available young men: a remarkable 83 per cent against Germany's 53 per cent in 1911. The alliance with Russia from 1892 was also in part a deliberate move to offset numerical weakness since Russia was rich in manpower but desperately in need of financial backing for industrialisation.[12]

The development of 'nations in arms' among the major European Powers after 1870 was only made feasible by the prior existence of an excellent railway network. The perfection of railways for strategic purposes was the

197

overriding aim of general staffs in the era of the elder Moltke and Schlieffen. By 1914 the European railway network allowed armies to be moved at six times the speed at which Napoleon's had been, to deliver them much fresher at the railhead and thereafter to keep them supplied, provided they did not advance very far. Here lay the enticing vision of grand strategic movement concealing the trap of tactical immobility which resulted in the deadlock between mass armies in 1914–1918.

In addition to the famous civilian critic, Ivan Bloch, a few military leaders did at least dimly perceive that the obsession with numbers might be self-defeating. In 1883, for example, General von der Goltz calculated that the German armies then destined for the Western Front would occupy more than 200 square miles; there was scarcely enough room for them to deploy on the frontier, let alone manoeuvre.[13] In 1913 another authority calculated that along the likely zone of Franco-German confrontation there would be a ratio of five soldiers to each yard of front. For this reason, or because they thought larger armies harder to discipline and control, or even because they feared the social consequences of intensive conscription, some generals actually opposed the rigorous application of the draft. In Germany for example, conservative senior officers feared the dilution of the ranks with socialists and the swamping of the officer corps with undesirables from the middle class.[14]

Despite these reservations and forebodings by certain officers, it is fair to say that the full implications of military developments before 1914 were not thought through. The general staffs' attentions were narrowly focussed on mobilisation timetables and the mechanics of killing on the battlefield. Schlieffen expected (or hoped) that the railways would make possible a quick victory, while for Foch 'war was a matter of manpower and more manpower, with the initial battles undertaken by the barracks army and the victory ensured by the reserves of the nation in arms'. As Maurice Pearton acutely observes, faith in a military plan as a blueprint or formula which would inevitably produce the desired result had a stultifying effect. Reliance on fixed and unalterable timetables tended to exclude the very qualities which had traditionally offset the hazards of war – quickness of decision, adaptability and the power to improvise. 'They were all jettisoned in response to the timetable'.[15]

Soon after the outbreak of war in 1914, another serious flaw in military thinking became apparent. In their determination to put maximum numbers of troops into the field, for what were expected to be the decisive battles, the general staffs had spectacularly underestimated the equally acute needs of skilled labour for war production, not to mention the extra demands on food supplies for the vast armies as well as the civil population. Tsarist Russia, for example, mobilised about 37 per cent of the male working population, thus depriving industry of manpower and contributing to the army's shortage of rifles and boots. Similarly, France, by calling up nearly 3 million reservists in the first two weeks of August seriously dislocated the economy, the vital iron works being particularly badly affected. The British record was no better. To give just one example of obsolete thinking, ammunition expenditure, and hence reserves, were calculated on the basis of the South African War. It must be noted, however, that these enormous errors were soon assimilated, so that by 1918 analysts had widened their study of demographic trends to take in the entire economies of the belligerent states. In short, in 'total war' conditions virtually the whole economy had to be mobilised and centrally controlled, not merely men in certain age groups.[16]

In the crudest numerical terms it might be argued that, in the long run, the First World War was indeed decided by the 'big battalions'. Against the populations of the Central Powers (115 million with only an additional 15 million in the German overseas empire) Britain and France's combined populations were approximately 85 million but their combined empires totalled a further 448 million, and their Russian ally could draw on a further 164 million. According to Martin Gilbert the total number of Allied troops killed was 5,219,000 as against 3,415,000 for the Central Powers. Marwick gives different figures; namely 10 million men killed with a further 20 million maimed or seriously wounded.[17] Generalising very boldly in operational terms, Russia's vast military effort with correspondingly huge losses between 1914 and 1917 enabled Britain and France to hold the Western Front and then, when both had passed their peak in manpower terms, the United States' entry with her fresh troops and limitless potential more than offset Russia's collapse and defection. By August 1918, there were more than half a million American combat troops in France and by November there were over a million.[18] However, it must be noted that, with their expectations of a short war, neither the Entente nor the Central Powers had calculated on the United States' involvement when they went to war in 1914.

One can safely suggest however, that no general or statesman anticipated such huge losses when going to war or found much consolation afterwards in victory at such a cost. Britain and the Dominions suffered about 900,000 deaths, France nearly one and a half million and Russia nearly two million (excluding the civil war). These losses, and particularly the gruesome notion of victory through 'attrition' which had been adopted by the Germans at Verdun in 1916, created a widespread and lasting revulsion against pre-1914 military theories and against generals who were profligate with the lives of their troops.

While it would be an exaggeration to suggest that calculations of military manpower lost importance after 1918 – the victors' attempt under the terms of the Versailles Treaty to limit the German Army to 100,000 regulars – makes the point, nevertheless there was henceforth much more stress on the need to exploit science and technology to minimise casualties. France, though nominally a victor, displayed these concerns in an acute form in her army's reliance on artillery and the impregnable Maginot Line to rule out another Verdun. France too, throughout the inter-war years, evinced anxiety about her demographic inferiority to Germany, particularly as regards the 'lean years' resulting from the 'lost generation' of the years 1914–18, that is of the unborn males who would have been eligible for military service in the 1930's.

More generally, the new strategic theories evolved after the First World War placed heavy reliance on technology and science to revolutionise war by making operations mobile and decisive with a minimum loss of human life, whether military or civilian. This was especially true of the theory of strategic bombing which attracted so many adherents in the 1920's: aerial bombing of military targets or cities would doubtless be horrific but brief and decisive in its effects; indeed the very threat of bombing might prove an effective instrument of policy. Similarly in land warfare, it was argued by theorists such as Fuller and Liddell Hart that mechanisation would reduce the need for unprotected infantry and – in an ideal scenario – armoured forces might penetrate deeply into the enemy's rear and paralyse his command system with a minumum of bloodshed.

In many respects it can be argued against such theories that they were technically far ahead of their time; overestimated practical operational effects; or misunderstood their social and political ramifications. More fundamentally, perhaps, they erred in assuming that their techniques of war would enable quality to triumph over quantity, rather as European forces had generally succeeded in vanquishing superior numbers in colonial campaigns.

Whether the European war which began in 1939 was bound to become a 'total' global conflict may be disputed; Germany's series of victories characterised as *blitzkrieg* were essentially due to the *quality* of her armaments, operational strategy and leadership rather than to superior numbers of either troops or weapons. Indeed Hitler had notably failed to mobilise his manpower and economic resources in depth as quickly become apparent when Operation Barbarossa failed to defeat the Soviet Union in 1941. This dangerous gamble taken in June 1941, followed by Japan's attack on Pearl Harbor in the following December and Hitler's gratuitous declaration of war on the United States, converted 'the last European War' into the Second World War in which both quantity and quality were thrown into the scales against Germany and her European satellites, and her allies Italy and Japan.

In 1941, the Soviet Union lost troops, aircraft and weapons on a scale that would have doomed any other European state, but was saved by her vast territory and the armies she was able to transfer from Manchuria, secure in the knowledge that Japan did not intend to attack her. The Soviet Union eventually mobilised 22 million citizens compared with 17 million by Germany and 12 million by Britain, the Dominions and colonies.

Given her comparative military unpreparedness, even in 1941, the United States' contribution to the Allied war effort was prodigious. Over 15 million American men and women were mobilised for war. Overall industrial output was doubled, including the expansion of shipbuilding from one to 19 million tons a year. Aircraft production rose from less than 6,000 a year on the eve of war to more than 96,000. Its factories eventually employed 2 million workers who produced 275,000 aircraft. There were similarly huge and rapid surges in the American production of tanks, artillery, trucks and landing craft. With its homeland and population invulnerable to attack, the United States truly became the 'arsenal of democracy', unique among Second World War belligerents in entering the post-war world materially better equipped than at the start.[19]

The enhanced role of machines, science and industrial power in the two world wars had a very significant consequence for military manpower; namely that the administrative and supporting auxiliary forces ('the tail') tended to become larger and larger in relation to the front line combat forces ('the teeth'). This is not in the least a surprising development yet it is one which war leaders (such as Churchill) found hard to accept, and which poses difficult problems in assessing the overall manpower required to keep given forces in the field for a particular length of time.

Already, in the First World War, analysts noted that the supporting arms tended to grow to a much greater extent than in the fighting arms. This trend was underlined by the peculiar conditions on the Western Front: a 400 mile long siege operation, which demanded a vast expansion of supply, maintenance and medical services. Thus, for example, whereas the army as a whole expanded by a factor of 7.5 between 1914 and 1918, British infantry expanded by only 5.5. By contrast the Royal Army Ordnance Corps factor of increase was 16.2, and the Royal Army Service Corps was 22.5. The Labour Corps, which did not exist in 1914, by 1918 totalled nearly 400,000 men. Another important demographic consideration was that more than 40,000 women enlisted of whom about 10,000 served abroad.[20]

Experience in the First World War showed that what is now termed 'the divisional slice' was approximately 60,000 men; that is for an active division with an establishment of 15,500 combat troops an additional 34,500 supply and support troops were necessary. Churchill was reluctant to accept that this ratio still held good in the Second World War, but it was found that the saving on labourers from the First World War was offset by the increased need for maintenance services for the expanded armoured portion of the army. By 1945 the 'divisional slice' for the army as a whole had increased to 65,000; a total strength of just under 3 million was needed to keep in service the equivalent of 42 divisions.[21]

Dr F W Perry produces an interesting table to show that the British armed forces as a whole were slightly larger in June 1945 than in November 1918 (4,653,000 to 4,457,000) But nearly a million less were serving in the Army. This was mainly due to the near doubling of the Royal Navy (407,000 in 1918 as against 783,000 in 1945) and the fivefold growth of the RAF (291,000 in 1918 as against a maximum of 1,002,000 in June 1944). Dr Perry makes the important point that, in both World Wars, Britain attempted to maintain more divisions (and equivalent units) in service than could be supported by manpower in the vital age group 20–25. The peak in terms of manpower effort was reached in 1917 and 1944 respectively, and in both 1918 and 1945 units had to be combined or even disbanded. The situation was particularly grave at the beginning of 1944:

> The Army was preparing to return to the Continent in the knowledge that all of Britain's manpower was deployed and dependent on an assumed date for the end of the war.[22]

Perry's case study is a warning that political (and military) leaders can easily deceive themselves that the country is militarily stronger than it actually is. In both World Wars the British and Dominions' forces 'were all expanded to a greater extent than was justified by the manpower available and organisational contraction ensued piecemeal as the symptoms of this became apparent'.[23]

Military and civilian deaths in the Second World War, accompanied as they were by the wholesale expulsion or extermination of peoples and flight of millions more as refugees before the advancing armies, were demographically impressive.[24] Total Soviet losses are usually assessed at around 20 million – more than the dead of all the combatants in the First World War. Germany was the next highest sufferer (with the possible exception of the Chinese) with at least four and a half million dead, including about a million civilians. Total Japanese casualties were about two million. Britain, France and Italy all suffered fewer deaths than in the First World War, contrasting sharply with the United States who lost nearly six times as many. In Central and Eastern Europe, civilian deaths were particularly heavy since they included between 4 and 6 million Jews, at least another 4 million non-Jewish civilians and a million Yugoslav resisters. A conservative estimate of total war casualties would be 50 million.

William H MacNeill would certainly dispute this total because he believes that deaths in Eastern Europe alone may have reached 47 million. He sees this massive 'die-off' as a brutal but enduring solution to the problem of too many people living on too little land. He believes that this acute population pressure in East and Central Europe from about 1880 was an underlying cause of the military convulsions of the twentieth century. Mass emigration before 1914 and slaughter during the First World War alleviated the problem, but it took the Second World War to provide the 'solution' with much greater slaughter as well as massive flights and wholesale ethnic transfers. These experiences not only reduced the population severely but also led to the regulation of births to accord with economic circumstances and expectations. MacNeill concludes that this particular problem of population growth ceased to put any serious strain on European society after 1950.[25] As a military historian, I find it difficult to accommodate these demographic interpretations with the traditional political, balance of power approach, but they *do* seem plausible enough to demand more careful analysis than MacNeill provides in *The Pursuit of Power*.

The general conclusion from this impressionistic survey of modern warfare must be that demographic considerations – and more particularly the number of young men fit for military service – continue to be significant in conventional warfare but are unlikely to be decisive in themselves. Even in the period between 1870 and 1914, when contemporary experts thought primarily in terms of numbers, the outcome was inconclusive; indeed, it has been argued that it was precisely the huge numbers involved in 1914 that made a quick decision impossible. The resulting stalemate and bloodbath between 1914 and 1918 caused theorists to err in the opposite direction: in the delusion that technological innovation would permit weapons of superior quality to achieve a speedy victory without the need to involve large numbers of fighting men. The experience of the Second World War suggested that once Great Powers were involved who could not be physically overrun and conquered, the contest became one of both quantity and quality where the outcome could only be decided by a long period of attrition of both manpower and economic resources.

In modern warfare, the distinction between the home front and the military fronts has been increasingly blurred with the civil population seen as a more or less legitimate target since a large proportion of it would be involved in the war effort. This obviously complicates the calculation of the proportion of the population available for the armed services, and the analysis will become more difficult as the war supporting sector becomes more complex and as more women are recruited into the armed services.

We have noted also a tendency for the 'divisional slice' to grow larger, thus requiring more personnel to keep a fighting formation with a particular establishment in the field. In certain circumstances this may give an operational advantage to belligerents with less sophisticated weapons and a tougher culture, such as Japan in the Second World War, but by itself this is unlikely to be a decisive factor. To take just one consideration, the more sophisticated opponent (say, the United states) will tend to have much better medical facilities and will therefore save a much higher proportion of its sick and wounded.

Finally, after the heavy casualties of two world wars, and the numerous conventional conflicts since 1945, few governments today (though there are some exceptions, notably in the Middle East) are prepared to contemplate their available manpower of military age as a positive asset in fighting and winning wars. The prevalent attitude is rather of how to preserve internal security and external interests with the minimum risk or expenditure of life. Clearly there are a great variety of attitudes on this issue determined by such factors as political tradition and culture, international status, territorial ambitions against other states and strategic vulnerability. But, in general, the

Brian Bond

reluctance to associate demography with willingness to wage war may be considered as one of the hallmarks of a civilised state in the late 20th century.

References

1. Q Wright *A Study of War* (University of Chicago Press, 1951) Vol. 2, pp. 1118–1145.
2. J Keegan 'The Role of Manpower in Traditional Strategic Thought' in Gregory D Foster and Alan N Sabrosky (eds) *The Strategic Dimension of Military Manpower* (Ballinger Publishing, 1987, p. 49.
3. William H MacNeill *The Pursuit of Power* (Blackwell, 1983), pp. 145–146.
4. Ibid p. 148. M van Creveld *Command in War* (Harvard University Press, 1985).
5. MacNeill, p. 162. Keegan, p. 38.
6. Quoted by Keegan, p. 39.
7. P Paret and M E Howard (eds) *Carl von Clausewitz: On War* (Princeton University Press, 1976), p. 282.
8. MacNeill, p. 200. Keegan, p. 39.
9. MacNeill, pp. 200, 260.
10. Brian Bond *War and Society in Europe 1870–1970* (Fontana, 1984) Chapter 1.
11. Maurice Pearton *The Knowledgeable State* (Burnett Books, 1982), p. 101.
12. Ibid, pp. 102–104. Bond, pp. 52–54.
13. Bond, p. 47.
14. Bond, p. 64. Keegan, p. 44.
15. Pearton, pp. 132–133.
16. Pearton, pp. 158, 186. David French *British Economic and Strategic Planning, 1905–1915* (Allen & Unwin, 1982).
17. M Gilbert *Recent History Atlas* (Weidenfeld & Nicolson, 1967), p. 38. A Marwick *War and Social Change in the Twentieth Century* (Macmillan, 1974), p. 2.
18. Russell F Weigley *History of the United States Army* Batsford, 1968), p. 385.
19. P Calvocoressi and G Wint *Total War* (Allen Lane, Penguin Press, 1972), pp. 559–560.
20. F W Perry *The Commonwealth Armies: Manpower and Organisation in Two World Wars* (Manchester University Press, 1988), pp. 33–35.
21. Ibid, pp. 56, 74.
22. Ibid, p. 74.
23. Ibid, pp. 236–237.
24. Calvocoressi and Wint, pp. 551–553.
25. MacNeill, pp. 310–317.

9

Military Personnel Policies and Alliance Security

Simon Lunn

The momentous political changes in the last half of 1989 have transformed the security landscape in Europe. Many of the basic assumptions that have governed NATO's defence policy for the past 40 years have all but disappeared. For Alliance defence planners the world will now look a very different place. In recent years, defence planning had involved a never ending and thankless search for more and better capabilities from effectively declining defence expenditures. Under the demanding strategy of Flexible Response and faced with a numerically superior adversary, the demands of NATO's military authorities were rarely satisfied. SACEURs (Supreme Allied Commander, Europe), such as General Rogers, persistently warned of the ever-widening gap between the forces of NATO and those of the Warsaw Treaty Organisation. During the 1980s, another problem loomed large on the horizon to add to the force planners' litany of woe. Adverse demographic trends in a number of countries would produce in the 1990s a severe shortage of manpower available for service in the armed forces. Already outnumbered, the Alliance was to be even more disadvantaged. Defence planners concentrated their energies on the development of new policies that would counter these trends and ensure the future credibility of Alliance defence.

Now suddenly the picture has changed and the premises, the assumptions and the calculations which underlay these policies are no longer the same. In one sense, from the manpower perspective, life will be easier. A diminishing, if not disappearing, threat will make for smaller armed forces and hence fewer military personnel – 'demand' will be down. But despite this reduction in demand, 'supply' could still represent a problem. In the new circumstances it may prove difficult to recruit, motivate and retain military personnel and particularly to retain an effective and equitable draft. In the absence of the immediate military threat that has characterised East-West relations during the past 40 years, many will ask for what purpose they are being asked

205

to serve. What will be the rationale for armed forces? What roles and missions will they be asked to perform?

To a degree some of these questions were already being asked before the recent political upheaval. They will now be asked with renewed vigour and convincing answers will be needed if the existing problems of recruitment and retention are not to be exacerbated and if, in the longer term, armed forces are to retain their validity.

These new problems that will face defence planners in ensuring the availability of sufficient numbers of military personnel will be accompanied by rather more familiar ones – notably the allocation of scarce defence resources. An expenditure on defence continues to decline, competition between the various functional areas, for example, personnel versus procurement, will become even more acute. Hence the provision of the necessary resources to attract and retain the required number of personnel, even at lower levels of forces, will remain a problem.

As an issue, manpower will continue to preoccupy military planners, but in a manifestly different strategic environment. To assess the problem of providing military manpower in the 1990s and to see how armed forces are likely to evolve, it is necessary to look at the past – to identify the role that manpower has played in Alliance security: to understand the traditional problems NATO has faced in providing adequate numbers of military personnel, particularly the veritable patchwork of different national systems, and to see the role that NATO has played in co-ordinating and influencing national policies in this respect.

The personnel who comprise NATO's military forces have tended to be a neglected dimension of Alliance defence, overshadowed by the preoccupation with nuclear weapons and with the development and introduction of sophisticated new weapon systems. Yet they have been, and continue to be, significant to Alliance strategy and politics in several ways.

First, and in terms of Alliance strategy, NATO's inability to field adequate numbers of conventional forces in the face of what was perceived as overwhelming WTO (Warsaw Treaty Organisation) strength has been a major factor in the evolution of Alliance strategy, with its heavy reliance on nuclear weapons. Alliance efforts to raise the nuclear threshold have always involved initiatives to improve the numbers and quality of NATO's conventional forces.

Secondly, and at a less esoteric but more practical level, military personnel are important simply because the effectiveness of weapon systems depends to a large extent on the people who operate them. Furthermore, the motivation and morale of armed forces are probably the most important of the variables that would be critical in deciding the outcome of any conflict. Many observers have long believed that the quality of NATO's armed forces was a much neglected factor in standard assessments of the balance between NATO and the Warsaw Treaty Organisation.

Thirdly, at the crucial level of defence expenditure and the allocation of resources, the importance of personnel is reflected in the fact that NATO countries on average devote approximately 40 per cent of their defence budget to military pay and allowances, while only 16 per cent on average is directed to the procurement of defence equipment. Hence, in most Alliance countries, the provision, training and payment of service personnel is the single largest drain on defence resources.

Finally, there is an intra-Alliance dimension to this issue that is frequently overlooked – its significance to the politics of the burden-sharing debate. Solidarity and equity in the sharing of the collective defence effort are always said to be fundamental to the continuing credibility of Alliance defence – despite the fact that there is no satisfactory formula for measuring either the defence burden or the respective efforts that contribute towards meeting it. Nevertheless, it goes without saying that the quality of training and motivation of armed forces personnel are important elements in assessments of national defence efforts. A nation's military personnel and the degree to which it is able to motivate its citizenry to participate in the defence of their society is a factor which should be given due account in the reckoning of defence contributions. One of the most significant differences between the United States and many European nations is the involvement by the latter of a significant proportion of their population in defence through conscription. A recent Alliance study on burden-sharing stressed this discrepancy when it noted that:

> One member of the Alliance devotes more than six per cent of its GDP to defence and has active and reserve forces amounting to about two per cent of its population. Another makes available three per cent of GDP and can mobilize over seven per cent of its population. Which of the two constitutes the heavier burden is very much a matter of subjective perception.

In the past, this dimension has been an important element in responding to Congressional criticism of European defence efforts and to the consequential pressure for unilateral United States troop withdrawals. However, it remains to be seen whether, in the new environment, the burden-sharing issue will continue to be a factor of Alliance political life. Current political trends suggest that American troop levels will decline substantially in the relatively near future. A lower United States' contribution, a more cohesive Europe and a substantially diminished threat, may well silence the Congressional critics and lay the burden-sharing debate finally to rest.

Manpower, then, will continue to be an important determinant in Alliance security policy. Before assessing the individual ways that nations approach the problem of raising and sustaining their armed forces, it is appropriate to examine NATO's role in co-ordinating and influencing these national policies.

Simon Lunn

NATO's Role

With regard to the defence plans and contributions of the individual members of the Alliance, NATO performs a co-ordinating function through its Force Planning Process (FPP). The FPP is a two-yearly planning cycle in which the requirements of NATO's Military Authorities, established on the basis of political guidance and a military evaluation of the threat, are reconciled with the national force plans of the individual nations. This process involves a substantial amount of detailed consultation and finally a degree of compromise on both sides before each nation agrees to a set of objectives or Force Goals which it undertakes to fulfil. These Force Goals are directed at all areas of defence planning from levels and types of equipment to the training standards of the armed forces. Through this process, the views of NATO's Military Authorities on the requirements of Alliance security are brought to bear on, and finally reconciled with, national plans.

The objectives of the FPP are various. It tries to increase the NATO 'voice', or guiding hand, in national decision-making on defence, and sees that to the greatest degree possible Alliance considerations are taken into account in national decisions of any magnitude. In attempts to ensure that the collective resources of the Alliance are being spent in the most effective manner for the common defence. It allows NATO's authorities a comprehensive view of the numbers and the status of the national forces being made available to them. In general, it encourages the notion of collective responsibility and tries to ensure that, in their defence efforts, all countries are going in the same direction and at roughly the same pace.

However, it is important to note that NATO's ability to influence national plans is somewhat limited – the guiding hand has a distinctly light touch. As sovereign and independent nations, Alliance members bear sole responsibility for their defence policies. How much a nation spends on defence and the way it allocates this money is a question for each individual nation to decide. While NATO's Military Authorities can and do offer their advice on what forces they require, at the end of the day they have to work with the forces that nations provide for them. They can have little influence over the basic structure or composition of national defence budgets. This is particularly true of policies regarding armed forces personnel and the division of resources between personnel and other items of the defence budget, such as equipment. NATO recommendations via the Force Goals affect military personnel policy to the degree that they refer to manning levels and training standards. However, this aspect apart, a nation's military personnel policy is very much a function of national factors rather than NATO influence.

National Manpower Policies

The policies adopted by Alliance members towards the provision and upkeep of their armed forces personnel are, like the Alliance itself, diverse. The manner in which each nation has chosen to raise, train and equip its armed forces reflects the history, tradition and geostrategic location of that particular member. Military personnel policy within the Alliance is a mosaic that defies generalisation. While certain characteristics and problems are common to most countries, there are many particular and specific factors that make each individual country deserving of special attention. It is not possible here, nor indeed is it necessary, to provide a detailed assessment of the individual policies. What follows is a general description of some of the basic features and problems that characterise the various policies, including specific reference to individual systems to provide some indication of the magnitude of the diversity.

The basic differences within NATO are between volunteer and conscript forces. There are, of course, political and philosophical arguments concerning the merits of either. However, the more practical question, and more relevant to this chapter, is which system is more effective. It is traditionally claimed that volunteer forces are generally more professional and thus more capable than conscripts, but that conscript forces are generally less expensive and provide a larger pool of ready reserves. While, for the most part, these generalisations still hold true, there are certain exceptions which merit attention.

For example, several nations practising conscription pay their conscripts relatively well. Hence their expenditure on manpower is relatively high, although most would claim not as high as if they fielded the same level of armed forces paying volunteer wages. Only Turkey, as a conscript country, spends a significantly smaller percentage of its military budget on manpower than the volunteer countries. In addition, it can be argued that the administrative turbulence and high training costs of short-term conscripts in a technologically advanced military may offset the financial advantage of a lower pay base.

Just as generalisation about the relative costs of volunteers versus conscripts may often be misleading, similar characterisations of the quality of the forces under the two systems may be inappropriate. The quality of the soldier under either system is as much a function of the sociological base, the level of education and, for conscript systems, the method of selection, as other factors. In many functions, conscripts frequently fare as well as regulars, for example Dutch conscripts have performed consistently well against 'regular' crews in the annual NATO tank competitions. In brief, any generalisation about what makes a good soldier in an increasingly technological environment is likely to be questionable, the final proof can only be the battlefield – itself an increasingly remote possibility in Europe.

Britain, Canada and the United States have traditionally manned their armed forces in peacetime with volunteers, each with somewhat different terms of service, payment and eventual reserve commitments.

All other members of the Alliance, except Luxembourg, rely upon conscription and the mobilisation in wartime of large numbers of reserves. For example, in Germany, The Netherlands and Norway trained reserve forces constitute 60 per cent, 62 per cent and 81 per cent respectively of authorised wartime manning levels. Each system, however, differs in terms of method of conscription, length of service and reserve commitment, as the following examples demonstrate.

In Norway, the service obligation of the soldier is one year plus 24 years in the reserves. Over 90 per cent of the available pool are called up and the pay is modest. Norway places a heavy emphasis on reserves and the total defence concept and can augment the standing forces of 42,000 with 163,000 reservists and a further 80,000 for the Home Guard. Under its total defence concept, Norway effectively mobilises 8 per cent of its population.

By comparison with the 90 per cent in Norway, The Netherlands only drafts approximately 64 per cent of those eligible. To compensate for this unfair situation, conscripts are better paid than their contemporaries in Norway, though they are also required to serve a somewhat longer period in active duty. A highly significant role in the armed forces is played by what is known as the RIM mobilisation system. An active unit of battalion size is transferred to RIM reserve status after the normal 14 month period of active duty. During the next 18 months these units are subject to immediate recall. Within 72 hours or less the standing force of some 104,000 men can be reinforced by an additional reserve force of approximately 171,000. This is a system that is particularly suitable for a relatively small, densely-populated, cohesive society such as The Netherlands.

The Danish system works differently again. Only about 30 per cent of those registered for military service are inducted and it is government policy to compensate well those who have to serve. In fact, Danish conscripts receive the highest pay of any in NATO. Accordingly, of all Alliance members, Denmark spends the highest percentage of her defence budget on manpower. Yet again the Danish military establishment can expand from a force of 31,000 to over 100,000 upon mobilisation.

Belgium presents an interesting example of a country that attempted to move from a conscript to a volunteer army. In 1973 the Government initiated a 'professionalisation plan' for the armed forces. The original aim of the plan was to reduce gradually the service time of conscripts by increasing the number of volunteers serving in the armed forces. However, budgetary problems forced the Government to interrupt the plan in 1979. As a result, Belgium now has a very costly system in which career military personnel represent double the number of conscripts (61,000 to 30,000), hence the high proportion of resources Belgium is forced to allocate to manpower, around 45 per cent of its defence budget. However, in order to ease the situation, the volunteer force is being reduced and the number of conscripts increased through the extension of conscript service by two months. The Belgian armed forces can be augmented by a reserve component of approximately

140,000, but Belgium does not place the same emphasis on reserve and mobilisation requirements as the other three.

The geostrategic location of the Federal Republic has meant that the Bundeswehr has always occupied a central part in NATO strategy. Now with the arrival of German unity it is equally critical but for rather different reasons. In terms of its current structure the Bundeswehr comprises 495,000 active duty personnel of which regulars and short-term volunteers comprise 55 per cent and conscripts 45 per cent, and a heavy reliance on reserves with a total reserve of 1.1 million men in various categories. Approximately 50 per cent of the available pool of young men are exempt from service, including a relatively high proportion of conscientious objectors – in 1959 these amounted to 8.5 per cent, in 1989 close to 15 per cent.

The demographic trends are more serious in the Federal Republic than elsewhere and it was assessed that unless counter-measures were taken the government would be compelled to reduce the Bundeswehr to 200,000 in the mid 1990s. Accordingly, the Kohl government decided to: extend basic military service for conscripts from 15 to 18 months – subsequently abandoned; to reconsider the role of regular and temporary career officers in the manpower structure of the Bundeswehr; and to make extensive use of the reservist potential. Under these measures it was hoped to retain the overall strength of 495,000 but comprising: 456,000 active duty personnel; 24,000 standby readiness personnel; and 15,000 reserve duty training slots. In the 1990s, the active strength was expected to break down as follows: 206,000 conscripts as against 224,400 currently; and 250,000 professional and longer-term soldiers as against 266,000 currently.

The core of the Bundeswehr Plan was the Army's attempt to maintain its present force structure, particularly its 36 active brigades, and to fulfil its essential missions, that is readiness and availability in peacetime, quick reaction capability in time of crisis and high sustainability in wartime. In effect, it would have involved a reduction in the readiness of some of the active units by lowering the peacetime manning levels of some units, and placing greater reliance on reserves. By 1995, the active peacetime strength of the Field Army would have fallen to 318,000, that is 17,400 below today's levels.

These plans and calculations have now been put in question by the political changes in Eastern and Central Europe and the unification of Germany. The size and status of the armed forces of a united Germany is one of the critical elements in achieving a satisfactory settlement to the question of German membership of NATO. Hence, predictions on the future size and structure of German forces are difficult. However, in talks in July 1990 with Mr Gorbachev, Chancellor Kohl agreed a limit of 370,000 on the Bundeswehr, with no NATO-assigned forces on the territory of the former GDR.

These are random examples of the differences that exist between national systems. Finally, Turkey should be mentioned because it presents problems of an entirely different nature from that of its Allies. Among NATO countries, Turkey has the largest standing armed forces in Europe, a total of almost 570,000 men, a large proportion of whom are conscripts. Contrary to trends in other countries, it is difficult for the Turkish draft board to keep up with the nation's birth rate; in the past few years, there has been a conscription delay of two to three years. It is estimated that the number of 18–22 year olds will increase by 34 per cent between 1988 and 2010. In the absence of selective conscription, the Turkish armed forces will therefore continue to grow and, though paid minimal wages, this expanding force constitutes a considerable drain on scarce resources.

General Problems

The foregoing discussion should give some idea of the range of diversity concerning military personnel policies within the Alliance. While each nation has specific characteristics and problems that defy simple generalisation, there are several problems that to a lesser or greater degree they share in common, notably the questions of recruitment, retention and reserves.

While most nations experience difficulty in recruiting career-motivated personnel for the officer ranks, recruitment is a particularly serious problem for countries with volunteer systems, although as past experience for both the United Kingdom and the United States has shown, the problem of ensuring the level and quality of volunteers tends to be cyclical.

Likewise, most nations encounter difficulties in retaining both the officer and enlisted categories. The most serious officer retention problem is pilots. The United States, the United Kingdom and Norway all suffer from pilot shortages, with the Norwegians particularly concerned about helicopter pilots lured away by the offshore oil industry. There is an equally serious retention problem among enlisted men. Skilled enlisted technicians are requied for a wide assortment of sophisticated equipment and weaponry. Better pay and working conditions in the civilian economy are largely responsible for attrition among skilled personnel in the armed forces, many of whom gained their skills while on active duty.

One of the most serious areas of deficiency is in reserve forces. The three NATO countries with all volunteer forces have problems with their reserves and suffer shortfalls of varying degrees. For countries with conscripts the problems associated with reserves reflect different concerns and are of a lesser magnitude. For most of them the question is the size of the reserve force and the degree of efficiency to be obtained in terms of number of recalls, length of training, type of equipment, etc. The problem is that while all agree that reserves are a vital component of Allied strategy, resources allocated to reserves are inevitably at the expense of the standing forces. A NATO study in the late 1980s, undertaken on the initiative of Secretary of Defense Weinberger, examined the mobilisation potential of the pool of trained manpower that exists in a number of countries and is currently untapped. However, it concluded that the exploitation of this pool was not possible because no nation was willing to allocate funds for such a purpose.

Two other aspects of the military personnel policies of member nations merit attention. First, the existence of Trade Unions. Many European nations permit their military personnel to join Unions or form associations to bargain on matters affecting their living and working conditions. The precise effect of these unions in terms of higher costs, better recruitment and retention, and military readiness and effectiveness is debateable and beyond the scope of this paper. It is necessary here only to note their existence as a very real influence on the military personnel policy of several countries.

The second issue concerns the potential offered by a greater utilisation of women in the armed forces. Women serve in the armed forces of all member countries, except Italy. The actual percentages of women in uniform range from 1 per cent or less for Denmark, Norway and The Netherlands; 4 per cent for Belgium; and 5 per cent, 8 per cent and 8.2 per cent respectively for the United Kingdom, the United States and Canada. It is difficult to see how far countries will move towards greater integration of women into the military services. History suggests that the use of women in a military capacity has been, for whatever reasons, traditionally more a function of need than social or political philosophy.

Future Problems and Prospects

These are the problems that have confronted NATO planners during the 1980s. A mixture of specific and general problems exacerbated by the demographic trends suggested fewer available men to provide for the defence needs of the Alliance. How has this situation changed and how will the new strategic environment affect Alliance manpower policy in the future?

Alliance Strategy

The dramatic changes in the structure and nature of the forces in the former Warsaw Treaty Organisation (WTO) will allow NATO to reassess and readjust its defence requirements. The reductions in all post-communist states, the eventual withdrawal of all Soviet forces from Central and Eastern Europe, and the disappearance of the WTO as a functioning military alliance has meant the disappearance of the surprise attack potential – so long the nightmare of Alliance planners – and the effective creation of a buffer zone. Residual Soviet military power within the Soviet Union will remain a problem of which NATO will have to take account – but it will be of a different order and timeframe than in the past. In terms of the contingencies for which it must now prepare, NATO has gained Time and Space.

This radical restructuring of the strategic landscape will mean that the Alliance can reassess its strategic concepts of flexible response and forward defence and the forces required to implement them. While the Alliance will almost certainly hold to the notion of flexibility of response, efforts undoubtedly will be made to diminish the role and visibility of nuclear weapons within the strategy. In terms of forward defence, while the commitment to defend the territory and integrity of all Alliance members will remain, the operation and implementation of this principle will now be adjusted in the light of the political situation and the subsequently diminished threat.

The reassessment of NATO's strategic concept and the forces required to implement it will be conducted against the background of national reassessments. Expectations of the so-called peace dividend are high, perhaps unwisely so. However, most nations have put their defence budgets on hold and are currently reviewing their future defence needs. There can be little doubting their future direction – downwards. The only question is how far and how fast. In an ideal world, such national reassessments would await the collective redefinition of Alliance strategic needs. With luck, they will proceed in parallel: most likely, however, strategy will follow and have to accommodate national reductions.

With regard to manpower, a number of nations have already announced their interest in cutting military and civilian personnel. The American Secretary of Defense, Richard Cheney, recently announced plans to reduce United States' forces by 25 per cent over the next five years. Under this plan, 600,000 military and civilian jobs would be cut; the West German government has suggested the possibility of reductions to 400,000 by 1995, other German parties have gone further, the FDP proposing 350,000, the SDP 240,000. What these numbers mean in the context of an all-German army remains to be seen; without giving specific details, both The Netherlands and Belgium have indicated plans to reduce their active forces and the Belgian government has been examining contingencies for the withdrawal of their forces from Germany (27,000); likewise the United Kingdom has not yet indicated its future intentions but it is believed that its current defence review will involve substantial reductions in its forces in Germany; both Spain and Portugal have recently announced reductions in terms of the length of service for their conscripts. These are just the warning shots of what is to come.

Under this pressure from nations to reduce their forces, particularly stationed forces, Alliance commanders will have far fewer active forces available to them. There will be a greater dependence on cadre units and reserves and reinforcements – assuming the United States Congress is willing to pay the costs associated with this reinforcement (which includes the storage of equipment and the relevant sea and air-lift capabilities). Already there is discussion of reorganising the current NATO 'layer cake' arrangement of forces which is committed to defending as much as possible as far forward as possible. New concepts suggest a peacetime deployment of skeletal units involving a much greater reliance on warning time and mobilisation and greater defence in depth.

Multi-national forces have suddenly become a popular idea. They are attractive for a number of reasons. First, in a political sense it is argued that they would demonstrate Alliance, and particularly European, cohesion and involvement, and would be more acceptable to German public opinion. Secondly, they would appear to be the natural consequence, for some nations at least, of the inevitable reduction in the number and size of national units. However, as with all politically inspired military concepts, the practical details of such ideas will need to be studied carefully. It may make sense to move the existing multi-national Army Group command down to Corps level, but beyond that level of command the going gets rough. This is because the armed forces of each nation have a distinct national style and approach – with particular consequences for the all-important area of logistics – which makes integration at lower levels extremely difficult to achieve. Many argue that only by this form of integration will national differences be ironed out, but this may underestimate the scale of the problem and may involve a rather wasteful use of scarce resources.

Arms Control

The CFE (Conventional Forces in Europe) agreement will provide an important framework within which future security arrangements can evolve. In particular, it can play an important role in creating the necessary conditions of mutual reassurance – through codifying lower levels of forces, through increasing transparency and openness by means of thorough and intrusive verification, and hopefully by encouraging the reshaping of residual forces into postures that minimise their 'threatening' aspects. The CFE agreement will not in itself provide stability, but by establishing parity in key weapon systems it will make a contribution to a more stable Europe. But a stable situation depends on the location and orientation of military forces as well as the political context in which they are deployed. Arms control can help shape this environment.

However, in terms of sustaining force levels arms control, like strategy, may be left in the wake of unilateral reductions. While many nations indicated they would avoid radical action pending a CFE agreement, the agreement, when signed in November 1990, did not take NATO very far. Domestic pressures may seek to go beyond the existing CFE ceilings, which after all were conceptually developed in the good old days of pre-autumn 1989. The Alliance will certainly make every effort to harmonise national plans in order to sustain a coherent and collective defence, and through arms control attempt to impose a degree of order on a potentially anarchic process. However, it is likely that national expectations will drive the process further and faster than NATO's authorities would normally want.

In the near time, therefore, overall defence requirements will not change radically, numbers will go down, troops will go home, length of service for

215

conscripts will be reduced. But all this will take time. Like the destruction of equipment, the relocation or demobilisation of military forces pose a number of practical problems, both in terms of cost and social factors, and for host and hosted alike. Redundancy will be a particular problem. Some military men may find a new lease of life in the growth area of verification, but a large number will need to be absorbed in civilian life. On the other hand, attracting and retaining the right people, and for conscript nations justifying the principle of universal military service, will equally prove more and more difficult.

What of the longer term? For a number of reasons that need no articulation here, nations will continue to sustain armed forces, albeit for the most part in smaller numbers and in different configurations. However, the rationale for these forces, their size and shape, and the problems of motivation will vary from country to country. For example, Turkey's geostrategic location would appear to provide ample justification for the maintenance of substantial military potential, while the Benelux nations may find it more difficult in explaining the continuing need for military service. Likewise, nations with out-of-area aspirations, such as the United Kingdom and France, or non-NATO regional concerns, such as Italy, may find the case for military force easier to sustain. Similarly, the geographic isolation of a country like Norway could lend support to the notion of military service. While most nations will find some national rationale for the maintenance of armed forces, the collective Alliance need will become more and more difficult to sustain, particularly if and when the traditional threat finally disappears. Notions that NATO as a collective entity should turn its attention to out-of-area concerns or to functional areas such as combatting drug trafficking are unlikely to get very far. Likewise, talk of an all-European security force of 'blue helmets' for conflict resolution within the new CSCE (Conference for Security and Cooperation in Europe) framework would appear to be far away, even from today's rapidly developing environment.

However, focusing on the need for an external rationale for military forces ignores the fact that, for many, service in the armed forces has a purpose of its own. There is no need here to explore in detail the sociological reasons why people join the armed forces, except to say that the 'outward bound' or 'joy of flying' appeal may be sufficient to motivate men and women to join and serve. Clearly life in the armed forces has an appeal beyond simply preparing to fight and defeat a known enemy.

Finally, it is worth noting that the problems facing Alliance military personnel in adapting to the new strategic environment are fully shared by what used to be the other side – in fact personnel problems in the WTO countries are even more acute. All non-Soviet Warsaw Treaty countries are in the process of reducing and restructuring their forces, albeit in slightly different ways, but in almost all cases causing substantial redundancies, particularly among the officer corps, which in most of these countries has been closely associated with the old Communist Parties. For example, in East Germany it has already been decided that East German officers have no part in a future Bundeswehr because of their previous Party connections. In the Soviet Union the military appears to be undergoing something of a crisis of confidence as their popularity wanes and the consequences of the 'strategic retreat' or 'loss of empire' becomes apparent. It would be wrong to over-exaggerate the implications of these developments for the overall standing of the Soviet military. However, there is absolutely no doubt that unilateral reductions and withdrawals are causing great hardship, particularly to the officer corps, as they return to the Soviet Union to no homes and no jobs. Moreover, it is also clear that the principle of universal military service is now being openly challenged.

One thing then is clear, the ending of the Cold War has very considerable consequences for the military professionals and soldiers in all European countries. The adjustment of the military to the co-operative spirit of the 1990s would suggest itself as an ideal area for all European co-operation.

10
Warsaw Pact Cohesion and the Crisis of 1989–90: Demographic Trends and Ethnic Conflict
Teresa Rakowska-Harmstone

The political and military disintegration of the Warsaw Pact in 1989–90 illustrates a point that a cohesion of a multi-national military alliance or a multi-ethnic army depends as much on the relative strength and position of the members, as on their mutual perceptions. The strength and the perceptions are shaped by 'objective' factors, such as size and resources of the partners, and by 'subjective' developments such as the history of their past relations and the impact of their domestic and foreign policies, that build on the first and shape the latter. Multi-national/multi-ethnic constructs run by a hegemonial partner, where adherence of lesser members is involuntary and internal conflict and particular aspirations are kept in check only by the exercise of force, are prone to fall apart when the dominant power is perceived to have weakened, both by its leaders and by its satellites. Such weakness may be the outcome of a decline in the objective attributes of power attendant on demographic change and/or policy failures, especially if accompanied by a perception, on the part of the hegemonial power of a need for a change, and a reluctance to continue to rely on the use of force.

All of these factors were at work in the rise and fall of the Warsaw Pact, and in the developments in the Soviet Union that led to the current crisis in Soviet domestic and bloc politics. The cohesion of the alliance no longer exists, and the Soviet political system is disintegrating rapidly, as both are undergoing a process of accelerated transformation. But it is still important to assess factors and policies which led to the formation of both and contributed to their original strengths and weaknesses. The military establishments of the Warsaw Pact member states remain. The Soviet Armed Forces (SAF), the Pact's largest and most crucial component, is now undergoing a crisis of its own. The armies of the Non-Soviet Warsaw Pact (NSWP) members are also searching for a new role. All continue to be influenced by the legacies of the past and the impact of their differential characteristics and origins.

The Soviet Union's population[1] and resources have outweighed by far the combined populations and resources of its East European partners,[2] and the 5 million strong Soviet Armed Forces (SAF) have dwarfed the 1 million plus total of East European armies[3] with corresponding differentials in economic strength. The alliance was imposed on the region by the Soviet Union in the wake of its military victory over Nazi Germany, and the resulting division of Europe into a Soviet and a Western sphere of influence. But communist governments established through the region under Soviet tutelage failed to develop legitimacy, not the least because social costs of 'building socialism' proved to be infinitely greater than the benefits: Marxist-Leninist systems failed to provide their societies with the most basic social, economic and political needs.

The Soviet Union came into being as the result of the 1917 Russian Revolution, but it has inherited the Imperial ethnic mix. One half of the Soviet population consists of ethnic Russians, who had retained their hegemonial role, while the other half combines a multitude of large and small national groups. The mix has made for an endemic ethnic conflict, with significant spill-over effects in the armed forces. Differential demographic trends in the 1960s, 1970s, and 1980s served to aggravate ethnic hostilities further and contributed significantly to the challenge posed to Moscow's political leadership by rising ethnic nationalisms, which filled the vacuum left by the bankruptcy of the ruling ideology. The crisis was further aggravated by the economy finally grinding to a standstill, despite tinkering with reforms, and by ecological disasters brought about by years of misplaced priorities and careless management of resources.

The perception of a crisis by the new (1985) Soviet leader Mikhail Gorbachev, led to a commitment to reforms that shook the very foundations of the system and released forces of change at home and in the bloc which proved impossible to stop. Perestroika, combined with glasnost' and a general reluctance to use force, led to a collapse of communist governments in and Soviet political withdrawal from Eastern-Central Europe. Political changes in the Soviet Union eroded the power of the Communist Party and the centralised government to the point when, at best, the future promises a loose confederation of major republics. In the process national frustrations of the main actors in the drama combined with fears of demographic and ecological change. The interplay between these factors, and their military implications are the subject of this chapter.

Background

The non-Russians were absorbed by the Russian Empire partly by conquest, partly via economic and political expansion. Their desire for independence

Teresa Rakowska-Harmstone

and/or autonomy contributed to Tsarism's fall in 1917, and resulted in an effort in 1917–18 by the nations of the periphery to break-away. Ukraine, Belorussia, the three republics of Transcaucasus, the Central Asian Khanates and Russian Turkestan were all reconquered by the Red Army by 1921, but the resentment at being returned under the rule of Moscow remained. It was kept alive by the upheavals caused by centrally determined policies of collectivisation, industrialisation and cultural Sovietisation, which destroyed traditional élites and purged 'bourgeois nationalists' among minority communists. Paradoxically, new policies also brought forth new communist-educated minority élites, which became spokesmen for the new nationalism. New resentments enhanced the old Russophobia. The Russians staffed most of the central political and economic apparatus and its provincial agencies, and new Soviet norms and value systems were inevitably rooted in the dominant Russian culture. Many Russians, however, were not happy with their culture's vulgarisation by Marxism-Leninism, and increasingly perceived themselves as being used and abused in the interest of 'younger brothers' at home and abroad, as they shouldered the imperial burden.

The Baltic states, Poland and Finland, were successful in establishing independent statehood in the inter-war period, but came back into the Soviet sphere of influence in 1944–45. Lithuania, Latvia and Estonia were incorporated outright. Poland's new imposed communist government transformed the country into a Soviet satellite, and Finland's independence was made hostage to Soviet acceptance of its policies, thus giving a name, 'Finlandisation,' to a new type of limited sovereignty. Other countries of Eastern Central Europe which, like Poland, found themselves occupied by Soviet troops, were also forced to accept communist régimes. These proceeded to 'build socialism' on the Soviet model. The direct Soviet hegemony in the region established by Stalin was eventually made more palatable by the institutionalisation of an international regional system of formally sovereign states.[4]

Nonetheless most of the East Europeans remained politically and culturally Western-oriented. All but two (Czechoslovakia and Bulgaria), have strong historical anti-Russian traditions, and most of their peoples resisted communist transformations and Soviet tutelage. All efforts at open resistance – the East Berlin riots in 1953, the Hungarian Revolution of 1956, the 1968 attempt in Czechoslovakia to establish 'socialism with a human face', and the 1956, 1970, 1976, and 1980–81 events in Poland – were terminated by force. It is not surprising, therefore, that popular attitudes in the NSWP states were mostly anti-Soviet and anti-Russian, and communist régimes' acceptance at home was directly related to the degree of their divergence from and resistance to Moscow.

Systemic characteristics of communist régimes: the monopoly of power enjoyed by the ruling parties ('the leading role of the party'), the centralised control ('democratic centralism'), and the command planning system of economic management with its emphasis on the priority of heavy industry –

all determined the character of decisions which, directly and indirectly, shaped the military establishment. Apart from low priority assigned to the consumer sector, two major sets of decisions appear to have had long-range negative effects on attitudes and quality of military manpower: the management of the ethnic factor in multi-ethnic systems, and the management of the resources and the environment. The first, which contributed to an increase in ethnic conflict in the society at large and in the military, has been the subject of in-depth research by this author and many others.[5] The second, has become visible only recently, and remains largely unexplored. It has had, nevertheless, far-reaching effects on the health and attitudes of the populations affected, and will have an important long-range impact on future demographic trends.

Under Stalin, Soviet ethnic politics were largely determined by the requirements of an 'ethnic security map', namely the perceptions, by the ruling élite, (predominantly Russian since the purges), of how politically dependable a minority was.[6] These perceptions survived through the Brezhnev period, while ethnic conflict escalated because of an increase in the minorities' national self-assertion. The Russians' ethnic fears stimulated a revival of Russian nationalism, and coincided with the élite's determination to preserve the system and their leading role in it. The determination extended to the Soviet bloc, where East European nationalism has posed a constant threat to Soviet interests.

In the Soviet Armed Forces (SAF), and notwithstanding the formally federal character of the Soviet state, security requirements precluded an establishment of territorial military units that would reflect ethnic character of a given national republic or ethnic minority area.[7] National military formations, promoted by minority communist leaders, were, in fact, tried in 1924 in addition to, and as a part of, the core regular army. But they were gradually phased out and finally abolished in 1938. They were revived in the Second World War because of the need to mobilise the minorities for the defence of the country. But, regardless of its high motivational value, ethnic autonomy in the forces was decisively rejected in the post-war period in favour of an integrated national (Soviet) army.[8]

Thus, all Soviet citizens have been subject to universal military service on the basis of individual recruitment, and have served in ethnically mixed units. The actual distribution of ethnic manpower in the service has conformed to the centre's perceptions of recruits' reliability and their capability to function adequately. Minority soldiers have not been allowed to serve in their national areas. The 'safe' and well-educated (primarily Russian and Russified) elements have predominated in combat and élite units, 'unreliables' have customarily been used in non-combat roles. The forces' 'internationalist' character has always been emphasised officially but except for its multi-ethnic soldiers, the SAF has remained an essentially Russian army. The language of command is exclusively Russian, ethnic Russians dominate the professional cadre, and Imperial Russian traditions have survived in military ethos, in approaches to doctrine and technology and in training methods.[9]

Within military structures of the Warsaw Pact the SAF projects an image of a national Russian army and Soviet soldiers are popularly perceived as 'the Russians.' On the Soviet side, Moscow's perception of an 'ethnic security map' within the alliance was reflected (until 1990) in the operational integration of East European contingents into the SAF. This was achieved by the Soviet control of the C3 structures (command, control, communications and intelligence), by the fragmentation of East European military contingents within the Soviet force structure, and by the use, under Soviet control, of Soviet models for political socialisation, military training and exercises, the latter based exclusively on coalition warfare. All NSWP forces used Soviet-type equipment, with a substantial share of their economies diverted to its production. Senior East European military officers were trained in Soviet staff schools, and all key command and staff positions in the WP were held by Soviet general officers. Soviet (officially WP) liaison missions were attached to all NSWP military headquarters, its members deployed in all service branches and territorial commands.

All these and other measures were designed to neutralise particular anti-Soviet nationalisms, and to pre-empt East European capabilities for independent military action, inclusive of a capability to defend their own national territory.[10] But, by highlighting the perception of Soviet hegemony, these mechanisms fed East European national resentments among the military rank and file, and even among the senior cadre, despite their personal interest in the preservation of the system.

Motivated by political rather than economic stimuli, Soviet-type economic policies emphasised accelerated industrialisation and development of heavy industries at the expense of agriculture and the consumer sector. Human and natural resources were grossly mismanaged in the process, totally disregarding environmental concerns and health and safety standards. The results are the heavy industrial and agricultural (fertilisers and pesticides) pollution of air, land, and water resources and, in the case of the Chernobyl disaster, the nuclear contamination of millions of people in the Ukraine and Belorussia, with the fall-out extending into Europe. The destruction of the environment combined with shortages of housing, poor nutrition and inadequate health services, caused a decline in the general standard of public health that was without precedent in a developed and industrialised country. In consequence, there was a rapid growth in the incidence of infectious and chemically-induced diseases and an increase in mortality rates not only amongst infants but particularly amongst young men. In the case of the latter, the effects of wide-spread alcohol and drug abuse took a heavy toll. Small wonder that the whole situation led to a general decline in life expectancy.

The impact on the populations, and consequently on military manpower, has been physical as well as psychological. Military sources in the Soviet Union and Eastern Europe have complained of the poor physical condition and health of incoming recruits, many of whom are deemed physically unfit for the service. There are complaints of epidemics in military garrisons. In the long run, poor health and high mortality rates are bound to affect rates of growth of all the populations in the region. Psychologically, the perception of a biological threat enhances ethnic and political resentments and contributes to the growth of nationalism. Soviet minorities blame the Russians; the Russians blame the system and past leaders who were not Russian – Stalin, after all, was a Georgian. East Europeans blame the Russians *and* the system; not infrequently one hears a bitter joke that under socialism Eastern Europe was able finally to achieve a level of development comparable to that of the Third World!

Bloc-wide economic crisis, growing social and national frustrations, recurrent popular upheavals, and a conviction on the part of the new Soviet leadership that a reform was both imperative and inevitable, and that a use of force to maintain the status quo in Eastern Europe did more harm than good, all converged to make the changes in 1989–90 possible. The call for reforms emanating from Moscow, was resisted by the conservative leaders of the GDR, Czechoslovakia and Romania (with good reason, in view of subsequent events), but was accepted with alacrity by the reform communists of Poland and Hungary. An agreement between the Communist Party and re-emergent Solidarity in Poland in the spring of 1989 to share power, led to parliamentary elections there in June, which cost the communists all the seats but those specifically reserved for them, and resulted in the formation of the first ever government in Eastern Europe since 1949, dominated by the erstwhile opposition.

The milestone was passed when the Solidarity-led government was officially recognised by the Soviet Union on 24 August 1989, Gorbachev having rejected the demands of the bloc's conservatives for an armed intervention. This meant that the Brezhnev doctrine was dead, a message that quickly spread to the rest of the bloc. Popular upheavals which followed (led and/or aided and abetted in most cases by communist reformers), swept the ruling Communist Parties out of power: first in Hungary (September), then in the GDR (October), Czechoslovakia and Bulgaria (November) and finally and violently in Romania (December). Within the next few months, all these countries had reclaimed their sovereignty, spelling an end to Soviet domination of East-Central Europe, and an end to the Warsaw Pact as the instrument of Soviety policy. The military implications of the change will be discussed below.

In the Soviet Union also the combination of glasnost', perestroika and democratisation brought the national conflict to the surface. Fuelled by social and economic frustrations and East European examples, expressions of ethnic discontent accelerated in proportion to the perceived erosion of power at the centre. In 1988–90 ethnic demands and ethnic unrest proceeded on an accelerated but differential timetable, and were expressed in several ways. Inter-ethnic violence, reflecting traditional hatreds and/or a conflict between the indigenous and the immigrant groups, erupted primarily in the southern republics. The resentment of the Russian immigrants in non-Russian areas, combined with the reality of the many years of heavy-handed controls from Moscow, turned into an open Russophobia. All the republics voiced the demands for greater autonomy, and some – first and foremost the three Baltic republics – pressed for outright independence. The degree of intensity and articulateness of these demands has been contingent on the stage of development of a particular national consciousness, an existence (or an absence) of national popular fronts, and the success the nationalist elements have had in contesting the federal and local elections held under perestroika.

Moscow's response has included selected use of force. Regular troops were used in some cases. Overall, the dynamics of the ethnic situation have had a profound effect on the SAF, supplying one of the main components of the crisis that had affected the forces since the intervention of Afghanistan, and under the impact of perestroika, the military cuts, and the 'loss' of Eastern Europe.

THE USSR ETHNIC POLITICS, DEMOGRAPHIC TRENDS AND THEIR MILITARY IMPLICATIONS

The Ethnic Mix

The Soviet ethnic mix is uneven. Over 100 groups were enumerated in the last (1989) census, but almost 80 per cent of them counted for less than four per cent of the Soviet population. Ethnic Russians, on the other hand, constituted one half of the total, and there were 21 other major ethnic groups of at least 1 million people each. By location, and in terms of ethno-cultural identity, the population in 1989 was divided into two main clusters: the Slavs (70 per cent of the population total) and the Muslims (19 per cent), in addition to three small but important subgroups: the Christian Georgians and Armenians of Transcaucasus (3 per cent)[11], the Balts (2 per cent), and the dispersed Jews and Germans (1.2 per cent) (See Table 10.1).

There are sharp contrasts in culture and in economic development between the developed Christian northwest (Slavs and Balts), and the still largely traditional Muslim southeast. Religion has been an important determinant of national identity: Orthodox Christianity for the Russians, eastern Ukrainians and Belorussians, Moldavians, Georgians and Armenians, Catholicism for the Lithuanians, western Belorussians and Poles who are Roman Catholics and western Ukrainians who are Uniates, i.e. Catholics of the Eastern rite. Latvians and Estonians are Lutherans and see themselves as a part of the

Warsaw Pact Cohesion

TABLE 10.1   USSR. Major National Groups. Weight in Population Total

National Group	Numbers (000s) 1979	1989	% Change 1979–1989	Share of USSR Population 1979	1989	% Change 1979–1989
(S) *Russians*	137,397	145,071	5.6	52.4	50.8	(1.6)
(S) *Ukrainians*	42,347	44,136	4.2	16.6	15.8	(.8)
(M) *Uzbecks*	12,456	16,686	34.0	4.8	5.9	1.1
(S) *Belorussians*	9,463	10,030	6.0	3.6	3.5	(.1)
(M) *Kazakhs*	6,556	8,138	24.1	2.5	2.0	.4
(M) *Azerbaidzhanis*	5,477	6,791	24.0	2.1	2.4	.3
(M) Tatars	6,185	6,646	7.4	2.4	2.3	(.1)
(C) *Armenians*	6,151	4,627	11.5	1.6	1.6	0
(M) *Tadzhiks*	2,898	4,217	45.5	1.1	1.5	.4
(C) *Georgians*	3,571	3,983	11.6	1.4	1.4	0
Moldavians	2,968	3,355	13.0	1.1	1.2	.1
(B) *Lithuanians*	2,851	3,068	7.6	1.1	1.1	0
(M) *Turkmen*	2,028	2,718	34.0	.8	1.0	.2
(M) *Kirgiz*	1,906	2,531	32.8	.7	.9	.2
Germans	1,936	2,036	5.1	.7	.7	0
Chuvash	1,751	1,839	5.0	.7	.7	0
(B) *Latvians*	1,439	1,459	1.4	.5	.5	0
(M) Bashkirs	1,371	1,449	5.7	.5	.5	0
Jews	1,811	1,449	(20.0)	.7	.5	(.2)
Mordvins	1,192	1,154	(3.2)	.5	.4	(.1)
(S) Poles	1,151	1,126	(2.2)	.4	.4	0
(B) *Estonians*	1,020	1,027	0.7	.4	.4	0

Notes:
1. The USSR population total in 1979 was 262 million, and in 1989 – 285.7 million, a 9 per cent increase.
2. Moslem groups enumerated in the 1989 census other than Moslem union republic nations, numbered 5.6 million (2 per cent of the population total).
3. Union republic nations are underlined. Tatars, Chuvashi, Mordvins and Bashkirs all had autonomous republics within the RSFSR. Jews, Germans and Poles had no autonomous status and were dispersed.
4. Ethnic designations: S – Slavs; M – Muslims; C – Caucasian Christians; B – Balts.

Adapted from Ann Sheehy 'Ethnic Muslims Account for Half of Soviet Population Increase,' *Report on the USSR* (RFE/RL Munich) 19 January 1990.

Scandinavian world. Islam is such an important determinant of the identity of the Soviet Turkic and Iranian peoples that they are collectively known as the Muslims.

Russian language is the lingua franca of the Soviet Union but it has been used also as the vehicle for the transmission of Russian culture to non-Russians. Soviet policy over the years has been to maintain the forms of

225

national/ethnic cultures of the minorities (including the preservation and development of indigenous languages), providing that the substance of their cultural expression conformed to obligatory 'socialist' ideas, and provided that non-Russians learn Russian, the functional language of the new Soviet state. This has been an uphill struggle. Central authorities have ceaselessly complained that the minorities' cultural expression was tainted with 'bourgeois nationalist' and reactionary views. Moreover, proportionately fewer non-Russians were apparently fluent in Russian in the 1970s and 1980s than they were in the immediate post-Second World War period.

In the absence of opinion surveys, language statistics are the best tool available to measure a national group's integration into the dominant value system, assuming that such a system can be accessed only through the medium of the Russian language. Linguistic assimilation of a non-Russian into the Russian language implies attitudinal integration, i.e. an assimilation into the dominant value system; bilingualism on the other hand, i.e. the knowledge of Russian as a second language, is synonymous with functional integration and implies, at least outwardly, a conformity to prevalent norms. But a failure to learn Russian indicates an inability or unwillingness to integrate and a continued adherence to an individual's original culture.

While the measure is necessarily crude and allows for exceptions, linguistic assimilation has often been assumed to mean cultural assimilation by Soviet ethnographers. It has proved useful for an assessment of political reliability in military service, given the Russian character of the SAF. A recruit who does not speak Russian is undesirable in the service both because he is non-functional, and because he is assumed to be potentially unreliable. But a non-Russian recruit who speaks Russian as his first language is assumed to identify with the Russian ethos and military traditions which permeate Soviet military establishment and is thus eligible for élite units; a recruit who can communicate in Russian is, at the least, functional, and fills the needs in-between.[12]

Using the 1979 language statistics to assess the level of integration of Soviet national groups, 59 per cent could be considered integrated in attitudinal terms. In addition to the Russians this figure included the 15 million of Russified non-Russians (an approximate one sixth of their total). Of the remaining non-Russians over 60 million (one half of their total), were bilingual, but 45 million (over one third of their total), declared themselves to be unable to speak Russian – a rather poor showing for the 60 years of intensive effort at socialisation. A closer look at the statistics revealed an even higher level of alienation (up to 70 per cent of group total), among Muslims of Central Asia, Georgians and, unexpectedly, the Estonians. (See Table 10.2).

The information on linguistic assimilation into Russian and on non-speakers of Russian was not yet available for 1989, but other data from that year did not indicate much of a change. Assimilation into Russian is a likely outcome when the indicators both for the adherence to one's own language

TABLE 10.2 USSR. Union Republic Nations. Attitudinal and Functional Integration 1979–89 (linguistic indicators; in percentage of group total)

Union Republic Nation	Adherence to own language		Attitudinal integration (Russian as native language)	Functional integration (bilingual in Russian)		Non-integrated (do not speak Russian)
	1979	1989	1979	1979	1989	1979
Ukrainians	82.8	81.1	17.1	49.8	56.2	33.1
Belorussians	74.2	70.9	25.4	57.0	54.7	17.6
Moldavians	93.2	91.6	6.0	47.4	53.8	46.6
Lithuanians	97.9	97.7	1.7	52.1	37.9	46.2
Latvians	95.0	94.8	4.8	56.7	64.4	38.5
Estonians	95.3	95.5	4.5	24.2	33.8	71.3
Georgians	98.3	98.2	1.7	26.7	33.1	71.6
Armenians	90.7	91.6	8.4	38.6	47.1	53.0
Azerbaidzhani	97.8	97.6	1.8	29.5	34.4	68.7
Uzbeks	98.5	98.3	.6	49.3	23.8	50.1
Kazakhs	97.5	97.0	2.0	52.3	60.4	45.7
Tadzhiks	97.8	97.7	.8	29.6	27.7	69.6
Turkmen	98.7	98.5	1.0	25.4	27.8	73.6
Kirgiz	97.9	97.8	.5	29.4	35.2	70.1

Note:
In 1979 the total number of non-Russians was 124.7 millions, of whom an estimated 18 million declared Russian as their native language, 61.5 million declared themselves bilingual in Russian, and 45 million (more than one third), did not speak Russian at all. In 1989 the total number of non-Russians was 140.6 millions, but except for the data on adherence to the original language and on bilingualism, no further breakdown was available.

Sources: Adapted from *Naselenie SSSR po dannym perepisi naseleniia 1979 goda*, (Moscow, Politizdat, 1980), and Ann Sheehy 'Russian Share of Soviet Population Down to 50.8 Per cent.' *Report on the USSR*, (RFE/RL Munich), Vol. 1, No. 42, 20 October, 1989.

and for bilingualism decline. This seemed to be the case only for the Belorussians, among whom the level of assimilation was already high. The decline in Uzbeks' bilingualism was a correction of inflated figures included in the 1979 census at the insistence of the then first secretary of the Uzbek party; that in Lithuanians' bilingualism was probably an outcome of extreme nationalist agitation in the republic at the time of the census. An increase for the Estonians probably corrected the nationalist bias of the 1979 figures, widely interpreted as showing the Estonian resentment of the influx of Russian immigrants. Overall, percentage increases in bilingualism were modest (in the 5 to 10 per cent range), and were probably reflected in a corresponding decline in the share of non-Russians who did not speak Russian. (See Table 10.2). In absolute figures their numbers probably stayed the same, or increased, especially for the groups with high growth rates.

Teresa Rakowska-Harmstone

Demographic Trends

This background is necessary to assess the military significance of current Soviet demographic trends. The growth of the Soviet population showed a substantial birth deficit in the 1917–1953 period because of two world wars and a sequence of man-made disasters attendant on the 'building of socialism.' Rates of growth picked up in the 1950s (an annual increase of 1.8 per cent), but began to decline thereafter: from 1.3 per cent annual increase in the 1960s to 0.9 per cent in the 1970s, and 0.8 per cent in 1980–81. Two factors caused the reduced growth: a decline in fertility (expected in view of the country's modernisation), and an unexpected increase in mortality rates.[13]

Overall, the Soviet birth rate started to rise again, however, in the 1980s, while mortality rates began to decline[14], although the decline was not likely to continue in view of the exponentially growing impact of the ecological crisis. In the nine years since the 1979 census, the population of the Soviet Union increased from 262 million to 286 million (a 9 per cent change). Most recent projections indicated a population total of 354 million in the year 2200, an increase by almost one fourth in the 1988–2200 period, and thus a rate of growth at a level well above replacement.[15] This figure could hardly be a cause for jubilation among Soviet military planners however, because, when growth rates projections are disaggregated for Soviet national groups, it is clear that while some of them were doubling their numbers every thirty years or so, others were on the verge of non-reproduction.

First indicators of change came in comparing the results of the three population censuses (1959, 1970 and 1979). While the fertility rates declined for the Soviet Union as a whole, there were marked variations among major national groups, reflecting their different rates of modernisation and differential exposure to disease and pollution, as well as cultural differences. The rates fell most steeply in the northwest, while there was little or no decline in the southeast. The change marked a sharp loss of demographic dynamism by the Slavs (Russians in particular), while at the same time there was a Muslim population explosion.

The differentials continued into the 1980s. The results of the 1989 census confirmed that the birth rates of the titular groups of the three Slavic republics, and the three Baltic republics were barely adequate for a simple replacement of their populations. Thus the Soviet Union's population growth accrued solely because of the high rates of growth of the southern groups, most of them Muslims. In the nine years between the two censuses, the indigenous populations of the four Central Asian republics (Uzbeks, Kirgiz, Turkmen and Tadzhiks) grew by between 33 and 45 per cent, that of the two other Muslim republics (Kazakhs and Azerbaidzhani), by 24 per cent, and that of the other two Transcaucasian republics (Armenians and Georgians), and Moldavia, by 11 to 13 per cent. The rate of growth of the Slavs and the

Lithuanians, on the other hand, hovered at between 5 and 8 per cent, and that of Estonia and Latvia, around 1 per cent, below the All-Union average (See Table 10.1). As Ann Sheehy correctly notes, the increase in the number of Tadzhiks may well have been inflated by the newly awakened national consciousness of the Tadzhiks living in Uzbekistan, who heretofore registered as Uzbeks,[16] but their fertility rates were still phenomenal.

The new census also yielded interesting information on smaller national groups, reflecting both greater official willingness to enumerate ethnic groups below union republic status (the Gorbachev régime has expressed special concern for minorities in union republics), and a general increase in national self-consciousness of all Soviet peoples. These groups, most of which are located in the RSFSR (the Russian republic), have had a tendency to assimilate into the dominant Russian group. But in the 1979–89 inter-censal period, two new trends were noted: first, a marked increase in the numbers of some of them, probably as much the function of newly awakened nationhood and the official willingness to record it, as that of natural growth and, second, the decline in numbers of the groups which have had high predisposition towards assimilation, such as the Mordvins, the Finns and the Karelians.[17]

The last census also revealed changes in internal migration patterns. In the 1979–89 period, high rates of in-migration into border republics continued only in the case of the Baltic states and the Ukraine, but ceased into southern republics, where, in most cases, there was a net out-migration instead. Since high inter-regional mobility has been characteristic of only the three major Slav nations, the shift clearly reflects the perception, on their part, among Russians in particular, of being unwelcome, and fleeing from violence or a threat of violence. So far the resentment shown by the Baltic populations has not stopped the Slavs from coming into the Soviet 'West', where standards of living are higher than anywhere else in the country. But even there, the rates of in-migration dropped after 1989 and there was some net out-migration. Compensating for the outflow from the south, there was an increase in the number of immigrants into the RSFSR, amounting to almost 2 million people in all.[18]

The ethnic violence of 1989–90 generated many internal refugees, the relocation of whom was a major problem in the country where residence in major cities requires a special permit, and where shortages of housing are so severe that a wait for a living space extends into years, families live in one room sharing a bathroom and a kitchen with others, and newlyweds move into the parents' one room. By mid-1990, there were about a million internal displaced persons in the Soviet Union, refugees from Azerbaidzhan and Armenia and from various hot spots in Central Asia. In Moscow alone, there were 40,000 refugees without residence permits and without prospects for permanent settlement.[19]

A comparison of the last few Soviet censuses shows that a substantial change was taking place in the national composition of the Soviet population,

Teresa Rakowska-Harmstone

a change that was of major concern to the central leadership, not least because of its military implications. Already, there was a shift in the relative weight in the population of the two major clusters. The combined share of the three major Slav groups dropped from 76 to 70 per cent of the total between 1959 and 1989, (a two per cent drop in the last intercensal period), while that of the Muslims increased from 12 to 19.2 per cent. The Muslim groups, taken together, grew at a rate five times faster than the non-Muslims, and accounted for 50 per cent of the total increase in the last 10 years,[20] despite the fact that their rate of growth has slowed down somewhat in comparison with the preceding (1970–79) period, probably partly by choice and partly because of the health factors (see below). Future projections indicated a continuation of the changing balance between the two groups. One analyst concluded that by the year 2050 all the Slavic populations combined will cease to be a majority, and that by the year 2080 the share of the seven major Muslim groups will equal the weight of the Russians, each accounting for 41 per cent of the Soviet population.[21]

Ecology and Health

The destruction of the environment was not openly discussed in the Soviet Union prior to the nuclear disaster at Chernobyl in the Ukraine in 1986, and even then the Soviet government was slow to admit the problem. By 1990, however, there was an open concern and discussion of the ecological crisis. According to the information released by the Soviet Academy of Sciences, 20 per cent of Soviet citizens lived in 'ecological disaster zones', and 35 to 40 per cent more were exposed to 'ecologically unfavourable conditions;' the sum total of those critically exposed numbered some 175 million people.

The Soviet economy was dominated by smokestack industries, grossly inefficient in the use of raw materials, releasing untreated industrial waste into the environment. Some 60 million tons of pollutants were pumped into the air annually, and atmospheric pollution was described as 'critical' in 68 industrial centres, where permissible levels of pollutants in the air were exceeded hundreds of times. Agricultural regions were also affected because of massive use of chemical fertilisers to boost yields, which poisoned soils and leached into the water. In Azerbaidzhan, for example, 40 kgs of pesticides were used per hectare for vegetable growing, and 180 kgs per hectare in vineyards. Preoccupation with cotton monoculture in Central Asia, has both diverted river flow into irrigation (thus drying out the Aral Sea) and poisoned land and water because of the massive use of fertilisers.[22]

An emergency plan, adopted by the Soviet government in March 1990, called for a ban on all discharges of untreated waste by the year 2000 and an adoption of broad measures to ameliorate water supply and a better utilisation of resources. The costs of environmental controls are very high and the implementation of these measures depended on a turn-up in the Soviet economy which did not seem imminent. These measures were declared to be inadequate by a high official, who also said that 'in two or three years our country will face an ecological catastrophe.' Incredibly, he noted also that in 1989 the use of agricultural pesticides skyrocketed 400 percent.[23]

The degree to which the health of Soviet citizens was affected by environmental hazards was made clear from disease and mortality statistics, which began to be published in the 1980s. The impact of unhealthy environment was magnified by poor nutrition and unsanitary living conditions, poor quality of doctors' training and inadequate health services. When disaggregated for particular republics, these figures reflected differences in living conditions between the northwest and the southeast, as well as the economic specialisation (hence the type of pollution) of particular regions. Average life expectancy in the Soviet Union (69.5) compared unfavourably with that in the West, as did the indicators for men's and women's life expectancy, 64.8 and 73.6 respectively. Predictably the indicators were below average for the less developed republics of Central Asia and Moldavia; in the cotton growing Muslim republics of Uzbekistan and Tadzhikistan, the male life expectancy was above and the female life expectancy below comparable indicators for the Soviet Union as a whole.[24]

The average Soviet infant mortality rate in 1988, 25 per 1,000 live births, was almost double the indicators for Greece and Portugal, Western Europe's poorest countries. But the rates were staggeringly higher still in Central Asia, reflecting both the poverty there and the poisoning of the environment. (See Table 10.3). In the Karakalpak Autonomous Republic, located in Uzbekistan adjacent to the dying Aral Sea, infant mortality rates were the highest in the country, registering at 60.1 per 1,000 live births; in one Karakalpak region the figure reached 111 per 1,000.[25]

The disease statistics revealed high incidence of infectious diseases which have long been rare or extinct in North America, such as diphtheria, typhoid and hepatitis. Overall, the type of diseases most prevalent in certain regions reflected the type of pollution related to the regions' economic specialisations and their poverty levels. Infectious diseases, such as intestinal infections, typhoid, hepatitis and tuberculosis occurred at levels much higher than national averages in the less developed and predominantly agricultural southern republics, while acute respiratory infections and cancer were more prevalent in the industrialized West. It should be added that the statistics reflected only the registered numbers, with overall totals probably much higher. (See Table 10.4).

The tie between infectious diseases and poverty was illustrated by official reports that two thirds of registered acute intestinal infections, and 85 per cent of the meningitis-type infections affected children of up to 15 years of age, and were the result largely of poor sanitation. In the early part of 1988 there was no public water supply in 23 cities with more than 200,000 people and 606 urban settlements (15 per cent of the settlements' total), and no

231

TABLE 10.3   USSR. Infant mortality Rates. By Republics
(0 to one year old/per 1,000 live births)

	1970	1988
USSR	24.7	24.7
RSFSR	23.0	18.9
Ukraine	17.2	14.2
Belorussia	18.8	13.1
Moldavia	23.3	23.0
Lithuania	19.4	11.5
Latvia	17.9	11.0
Estonia	17.8	12.4
Georgia	25.3	21.9
Armenia	25.3	25.3
Azerbaidzhan	34.8	27.0
Kazakhstan	25.9	29.2
Uzbekistan	31.0	43.3
Kirgizia	45.4	36.8
Tadzhikistan	45.9	48.9
Turkmenia	46.1	53.3

Source: *Narodnoe Khoziaistvo SSSR v 1988* g. (Moscow: 1989), p. 29.

central sewage system in 310 cities with over 4 million inhabitants and 1930 settlements (48 per cent of total). Mortality from tuberculosis was said to be from two to 10 times higher than in the developed western countries, and incidence of cancer in the Baltic republics and in the Ukraine was from 5 to 11 per cent higher than the Soviet average. The share of the people found to be in late (and thus incurable) stages of the disease constituted about one fifth of the known sick in the country, and was highest in Central Asia (in the Uzbek, Turkmen and Kirgiz republics) and in Estonia, where it reached almost one third of the total of cancer cases. On the hopeful side, alcoholism-related diseases declined by 8 per cent overall between 1986 and 1988, and syphilis and gonorrhoea infections from 26 to 9 per cent respectively, but there were increases in individual republics. Drug addiction also increased in the period by one and a half times.[26]

Impact on National Attitudes

Demographic changes and perceptions of their aftermath, and biological threat posed by the ecological disaster have had a major impact on popular attitudes, reinforcing national and political opposition. As the heretofore taboo subjects came to be discussed and past policies criticised, it became

TABLE 10.4   USSR. Incidence of Diseases, 1987

Disease	Proportion of population		
Intestinal infections	/ 10,000	602	(1)
Typhoid and paratyphoid	/ 10,000	4.5	(2)
Viral hepatitis	/ 10,000	305	(3)
Flu and acute respiratory infections	/ 10,000	210	(4)
Meningitis infections	/ 10,000	5.4	(5)
Tuberculosis	/100,000	43.7	(6)
Cancer – general indicators	/100,000	233.9	(7)
Cancer – standardized indicators	/100,000	192.5	(8)
Mental diseases	/100,000	396.2	(9)
related to alcoholism		180.7	(10)
related to drug addiction		8.6	(11)
Venereal diseases – syphilis	/100,000	5.6	(12)
Venereal diseases – gonorrhoea	/100,000	86.3	(13)

Following republics had indicators above the USSR average:
 (1) RSFSR, Uzbekistan, Kirgizia, Turkmenia and Tadzhikistan (2x);
 (2) Kazakhstan, Kirgizia (3x), Uzbekistan (4x), Turkmenia (10x), and Tadzhikistan (12x);
 (3) Kazakhstan, Turkmenia (2x), Kirgizia (3x), Tadzhikistan (4x) and Uzbekistan (4x);
 (4) RSFSR, Ukraine, Belorussia;
 (5) RSFSR, Belorussia, Kirgizia and Moldavia (2x);
 (6) Moldavia, Azerbaidzhan, Uzbekistan, Tadzhikistan, Turkmenia, Kirgizia, and Kazakhstan (2x);
 (7) RSFSR, Ukraine, Belorussia, Lithuania, Latvia and Estonia;
 (8) RSFSR, Belorussia, Lithuania, Latvia and Estonia;
 (9) RSFSR, Ukraine, Lithuania, Latvia, Moldavia;
 (10) RSFSR, Belorussia, Moldavia, Lithuania, Latvia, Kazakhstan;
 (11) Ukraine, Kazakhstan, Kirgizia, Turkmenia (over 3x);
 (12) Ukraine, Moldavia, Latvia, Georgia (5x), Armenia, Uzbekistan, Kirgizia, Tadzhikistan, Turkmenia (2x);
 (13) RSFSR, Belorussia, Moldavia, Lithuania, Estonia, Georgia, Kazakhstan.

Source: *Sbornik Statisticheskikh Materialov*, (Moscow: 1988), pp. 216–226.

even clearer to the Soviet populace that the origins of the crisis were political and that the fault lay with the régime. In the circumstances, the desire for economic improvement and political democratisation, the mushrooming 'green' movement, and the national demands for greater autonomy and even sovereignty were all joined together. All Soviet national groups were affected, Russians and non-Russians. Expressions of ethnic nationalism became more widespread and the threshold of ethnic conflict escalated. The Russians, facing a future of shrinking numbers and a decline in their political status, gradually ceased to identify with the central government and acquired new interest in their own national political future. The non-Russians began to articulate their national demands more boldly and more insistently, reflecting new freedoms, new confidence, and new fears. A brief survey of the attitudes of each group will illustrate the point.[27]

The Slavs

The Russians

In view of their numbers, their historical position, and their actual leading role the Russians are the core group and their attitudes are of crucial importance. For years, they have taken for granted their hegemonial role, but under Brezhnev they already became aware of the tide of non-Russian nationalism and became uneasy over their position in non-Russian republics. A perception of a threat to their political status was augmented by a perception of a threat to the Russian culture and cultural values and, last but not least, to their biological survival in view of the demographic and health indicators of the 1970s and 1980s. These new perceptions have affected a very broad spectrum of Russian public opinion, from dissidents to high level state and party officials.

In the non-Russian mind the Russians were the Russifiers who ruled by force and were responsible for all the problems. But for most Russians their self-image has been that of the noble people of unique spiritual worth who tried to lead in the building of a new and better society at great sacrifice to themselves, selflessly helping out lesser 'brothers' but reaping only ingratitude in return. Many feel themselves to be victims of a régime based in 'alien' Marxist-Leninist ideology, which used and exploited them, exposed them to biological hazards, and attempted to destroy and subvert the very essence of Russian culture and spiritual values. Their view, as described by the late Hugh Seton-Watson, was that

> Though . . . the regime gladly exploited Russian military pride, and treated non-Russians in a manner that recalled Russification under the Tsars, all that they had to offer was a castrated Russian national culture . . . Thus to thinking Russian patriots the Russian nation was the victim of the régime, no less and perhaps even more than the non-Russian nations.[28]

Initially two main currents were visible in revived Russian nationalism. The first, represented by the quote above, were the Revivalists (*Vozrozhdenniki*), who saw culture and religion as key markers of Russian identity and rejected Marxism as an 'alien' and destructive creed, a view reminiscent of the 19th century's Slavophiles. Solzhenitsyn is the best known spokesman for this view. The other current, described as 'national Bolshevism' or 'statism', saw the Soviet state as a continuation of Imperial Russia. Its adherents were to be found in the armed forces, the KGB and the Komsomol (communist youth organisation), reputedly under a tacit patronage of some members of the Politbureau.

At least two official publications expressed a Russian nationalist viewpoint in the 1970s and 1980s, the *Molodaia Gvardia* (an organ of the Central Committee of the Komsomol) and *Nash Sovremennik* (an organ of the Writers' Union of the RSFSR).[29] With the onset of *glasnost'*, the extreme right of Russian nationalist spectrum formed a new organization, *Pamiat'*, which became known for its virulent anti-Semitic and racist views. A minority, mostly among intellectuals, felt that nothing but autocracy and slavery had ever resulted from the Russian heritage, and that only Western-style democracy could reform Russia, thus repeating the views of 19th century Westernizers.

In the late 1980s and in 1990 the Russian national spectrum differentiated further and broadened its constituency, beginning with a revival of the Russian Orthodox Church, which celebrated a millennium – a one thousandth anniversary of Russia's baptism – in 1988. Russian patriotic groups mushroomed, devoted to the preservation of the Russian culture and its monuments, and looking to Orthodoxy and back to Tsarist times for inspiration. Thus they opposed and distrusted Gorbachev's reforms, as yet another effort at Westernisation. Most important among them was the Russian Federation's (RSFSR) Writers' Union. The predominantly Russian blue collar workers organised around a radical populist movement to defend their interests, which had been undercut by the reforms: the United Front of the Workers of Russia. But the support for *perestroika* was also widespread, and many Russian intellectuals turned to Russian liberal traditions, as the proper base for the implementation of Western-type reforms, a view best represented by the literary magazine *Novyi Mir*. The 'national bolshevik' wing grew weaker, on the other hand, as the power of the central Party and government apparatus eroded and the republics asserted themselves. Although widely different, the various Russian viewpoints began to converge around the need to revive a Russian national state. By the end of 1988, as Bill Keller astutely observed, Russian patriots began to cultivate three crucial constituencies: the military, blue collar workers, and stranded party bureaucrats in search of a new power base.[30] So far the most promising alliance proved to be that between Russian nationalism and frustrated *apparatchiki*. Most popular among the latter has been Boris Yeltsin, who left the Party to devote himself to the presidency of the RSFSR.

Taking a leaf out of the Balts' book, who were the first to proclaim independence, Yeltsin steered the legislature of the Russian republic in June 12, 1990, into a declaration of its sovereign status (albeit still within the Union), thus radically changing the rules of the game and the country's future. The RSFSR now claims control over its resources and financial institutions, proceeds with economic reform at a pace faster than that of Gorbachev, considers its laws superior to that of the Soviet Union, and pioneers direct contacts with other republics and with foreign countries. Yeltsin promised, for example, to sign treaties with the Baltic republics recognising their sovereignty. Pointedly, however, he did not endorse their independence.[31] According to Yeltsin, the republics have all the residuary powers and the central government has only the power delegated to it by republics.

At one stroke, the RSFSR's bid for sovereignty deprived Gorbachev's central government of its power base in the plans for a 'new federal union.' The Russian republic comprises 76 per cent of the Soviet Territory and 51 per cent of Soviet population, the bulk of Soviet Union's resources and of its economic and administrative infrastructure. It may well be able to control the Soviet legislative process, with three fifths of the 2,744 members of the Congress of Peoples' Deputies elected from the RSFSR. If the Russians actually give up their imperial ambitions, at least for the time being, a break-up of a centralized Soviet state cannot be avoided.

At the same time the Russian republic may well expect a replay of the current nationalist explosion within its own borders. 18.2 (1989) per cent of the RSFSR's population is non-Russian and some among them, such as the Tatars (who constitute 3.6 per cent of the total) and the Yakuts (who number only 382 thousand people but whose autonomous republic comprises most of the Soviet gold and diamonds, and many other resources), have a strong sense of separate national identitry and have already articulated far-reaching autonomous demands. By late August, both the Karelian and Yakutian autonomous republics had declared their sovereignty in relation to the RSFSR as well as the Soviet Union (*NYT* 13 and 15 August 1990). Sixteen out of the 20 autonomous republics, 5 out of 8 autonomous provinces and 10 out of 10 autonomous districts in the Soviet Union – each of which is the national territory of a minority – were located in the RSFSR.

Ukrainians and Belorussians

The Ukrainians and Belorussians, the two other major Slav groups (the rapidly assimilating Poles are the third) were also negatively affected by the demographic decline, and now suffer from ecological damage. More important, both are victims of the Chernobyl disaster of April 1986, which proved to be perhaps the most important recent catalyst of nationalist feelings there. The radiation hazards were admitted only slowly and grudgingly by the Soviet government. According to a deputy from Chernobyl, Alla Yaro-shinskaya, at least 4 million people more should be evacuated from the region. Describing the effects as 'worse than Hiroshima,' she said that people in both republics still live on contaminated soil, the produce is still grown there and processed and distributed country-wide, the children are sick, animal mutants abound, and radioactive silt is carried by the Dnieper river to the Black Sea.[32]

After the RSFSR, the Ukraine is the most important republic in the union, with one-fifth of the total Soviet industrial potential. Ukrainians are still the second largest population in the country. Belorussians, now fourth, lost their third place to the Uzbeks in 1970. Ukrainians and Belorussians both have been vulnerable to Russification, especially those living outside their home territory. (See Table 10.2). Next to the Russians, they are the preferred manpower for military service and the only non-Russians who are prominent in the officer cadre.

Indicators of nationalism and assimilation were different in both republics for eastern and western regions. Western Ukraine and Belorussia were parts of Poland in the inter-war period, and local élites there developed a strong sense of ethnic nationalism. This was especially true for the Ukrainians. Incorporated into the Soviet Union in 1944, the Ukrainian armed nationalist resistance in the western region was finally crushed only in the early 1950s and, to this day, the military authorities see Western Ukrainians as politically unreliable. The nationalist 'infection' spread also to Eastern Ukraine, despite high levels of assimilation there and heavy Russian in-migration. Many Ukrainian 'bourgeois nationalists' were purged in the post-war period throughout the republic in recurrent waves of repression. In the eyes of Moscow, even official Ukrainian élites were infected. Petro Shelest, First Secretary of the Ukrainian Party and many lesser officials were purged for 'nationalist deviations' in 1972.

Open expressions of nationalism and nationalist demands nevertheless emerged in the Ukraine again since the onset of *glasnost'*. The Ukrainian Popular Movement for Perestroika, *Rukh* for short, was organised on the eve of the March 1990 elections to the local soviets (legislative assemblies). It won one-third of the seats in the Ukrainian Supreme Soviet, virtually sweeping western Ukraine and making significant inroads also in the East.[33] Since March *Rukh* has come to dominate the deliberations of the legislature and was instrumental in the Ukraine's declaration of its sovereignty (within the Union), following the lead of the RSFSR, 16 July, 1990.[34]

Much weaker than their brethren to the south, Western Belorussian nationalists were wiped out after the incorporation. The republic as a whole lacked visible signs of nationalism until current reforms, but signs of nationalist revival, particularly on the cultural front, emerged in the late 1980s, and made up for lost time in 1990. The Popular Front of Belorussia, the Ecological Union (a result of Chernobyl), and The Society for the Belorussian Language were formed prior to the March 1990 elections. These organisations were able to elect a number of deputies to the legislature despite harassment by the Party and under the impact of events elsewhere their viewpoint came to dominate the Belorussian legislature. On 27 July, 1990 the

Belorussian Supreme Soviet unanimously passed a declaration of sovereignty very much on the same pattern as the other two Slav republics.[35]

Moldavia

The Moldavian republic was created after the Second World War largely out of the territories ceded by Romania. The Moldavians, who are the majority in the republic (64 per cent of the total), are in fact Romanians and speak the Romanian language. This is another republic where integration indicators are low, but there were few open manifestations of nationalism there prior to Gorbachev's era. The dormant nationalism came to life in 1989, when the newly formed Moldavian Popular Front demanded greater autonomy and the use of Moldavian (Romanian), as the state language. The November 1989 riots in support of these demands in Kishinev (the republic's capital), were suppressed by Soviet troops. But the Front emerged as the dominant force in the Moldavian Supreme Soviet after the March 1990 elections. On 31 May the Soviet formally recognised the sovereignty of Lithuania, so far the only soviet republic to do so, and on 23 June it passed the declaration of its own sovereignty. The Moldavians have their own minority problems, however. Their Ukranian and Russian populations are substantial, and a relatively small Turkic group, the Gagauz, organised its own national front, and, in fact, declared its own republic.[36]

The Baltic Republics

The Lithuanians, Latvians and Estonians never accepted the enforced incorporation of their states into the Soviet Union, and thus consider all the relevant legal instruments invalid, beginning with the secret protocols of the Ribbentrop-Molotov Pact of August 1939 which consigned them to the Soviet sphere of influence in the division of spoils between Nazi Germany and the Soviet Union, and ending with the USSR Constitution. Separatism has always been characteristic of ethnic nationalism in the three Baltic republics and separatist demands were openly articulated there since the 1960s. The mass base of Baltic national movement was expressed in open petitions to the authorities and to international organizations signed by thousands, and in mass demonstrations, despite severe repressions.

In the 1970s and 1980s the Balts' nationalism was further stimulated by a perception of an immediate threat to their national survival, biologically, culturally, and politically. The Estonians and the Latvians were particularly worried, because they are numerically small and barely reproduce themselves, and have been inundated by a steady stream of Russians and other immigrants. All three republics resisted development of new industries on their territory, first because of the pollution, second because of the influx of immigrants. In all three nationalism has run in tandem with the demands for civil and human rights. In Lithuania, armed resistance to Soviet occupation ended only in the early 1950s; Catholicism has been an integral part of Lithuanian nationalism, and demands for religious freedom always accompanied the demands for the restoration of independence.

Gorbachev's reforms were welcomed in the Baltic republics: *glasnost'* opened up new opportunities for national expression, and popular national fronts were formed in all three. At the same time, the 'official' Balts took advantage of *perestroika*, asking Moscow for extensive autonomy in its implementation. The National Fronts in Latvia and Estonia, and *Sajudis* in Lithuania, came to dominate political life in their respective republics in 1989–90, and to control their newly elected legislatures, despite Moscow's efforts to organise immigrants into pro-Union popular fronts. The three movements consult in order to coordinate policies, and have pioneered contacts with other emerging national fronts, such as those in the Ukraine, Moldavia and Transcaucasus. They sponsored the talks in Riga (1 February, 1990) between the Armenian and Azerbaidzhani national fronts then fighting over Nagorno-Karabakh (see below). Baltic mediation led to a temporary truce.

Lithuania was the first to declare total independence (11 March 1990), and proceeded with the implementation of legislation. The saga of its struggle with Moscow, including the imposition of an economic embargo by the Centre, and a threat of the use of military force, are too well-known to be repeated here. The Latvian and Estonian legislatures also passed declarations of independence, but with minor variations providing for delays more palatable to Gorbachev: Estonia declared its *intention* to become independent on 30 March (but proceeded to implement legislation anyway); Latvia declared independence on 4 May but agreed to *a transition period*. All three denied the legality of the incorporation, and thus an existence of any sphere of state activities outside the control of their national governments. On 12 May the three republics established a Baltic Council (a throwback to the Baltic Unity Pact of 1934).

Although paying lip-service to the right to secede, guaranteed to union republics by the USSR Constitution, Gorbachev has been totally hostile to the efforts of the Balts to leave the Soviet Union, stressing interdependence of Soviet republics and proposing to re-establish common ties, if on a more decentralised basis. Although talking of economic independence of the republics, and the 'broadest possible' opportunities to develop their national identity, he has always argued explicitly from Leninist positions, which meant the safeguarding of the supremacy of the Centre.[37] The turning point seems to have come only after the RSFSR declaration of independence. Negotiations with the three Baltic presidents were resumed on the very day (12 Jun) and the blockade of Lithuania was lifted shortly (2 July). Although conciliatory moves were also made by the Balts to facilitate the negotiations, they did not retreat from their original position of total independence.[38] But

239

Teresa Rakowska-Harmstone

there is little doubt that Gorbachev will make every effort possible to prevent the three republics from cutting off their ties with the Soviet Union.

Transcaucasus

In the Caucasus, the edge of the ethnic conflict has been turned inward more than against the Russians, and it has run along the traditional Christian-Muslim religious cleavage. The cleavage exists within and between the three Transcaucasian republics as much as it does between the diverse ethnic populations of North Caucasus. The Armenians, who have tended to play a role of 'surrogate Russians' and to dominate urban centres in the Caucasus (the three republics have relatively few immigrant Russians), are universally disliked in the area, and each of the three republics has had minority problems.

The dominant conflict has been that between the Armenians and the Azerbaidzhani (Azeri Turks), not only for historical, cultural and economic reasons, but because of the conflict over national enclaves, as seen in the currently (1988–90) explosive case of the Nagorno-Karabakh Autonomous Province (NKAO), an Armenian enclave in Azerbaidzhan. The other possible bone of contention is the Nakhichevan Autonomous Republic, populated by Azeri Turks, located within the Armenian SSR (on the border with Iran) but administratively a part of Azerbaidzhan. The Georgians in Azerbaidzhan complain of national oppression, but are themselves accused by their national minorities, the Abkhazians in particular, of pursuing policies of assimilation.

Both the Georgians and the Armenians are fiercely devoted to their ancient language and culture (centred in each case on the respective Orthodox Church), but Armenians integrate readily in functional terms, while Georgians rank with Muslims in their failure to integrate. Mozt Azeri are Shia Muslims, (more Azeris live across the border in Iran than in the Soviet Union) while all other large Soviet Muslim groups are Sunni. Historically, Azeri Turks were modernised earlier, and were less isolated than other Soviet Muslims. Thus their nationalism directed primarily against the Armenians but now turning more against the Russians has a fierce edge. All three major nations of Transcaucasus have maintained fertility rates above the reproduction level, but not as high as among Muslims of Central Asia. Their national demands and, most recently, environmental grievances, have been articulated openly and with growing intensity.

The Azeri-Armenian feud erupted into an open violence over NKAO in February 1988, and was followed by a massacre of Armenians in Sumgait (Azerbaidzhan), which required an entry by Soviet troops. The NKAO problem has yet to be resolved, with the political battle waged between the Armenian National Movement and the Azerbaidzhani Popular Front, both sides fielding armed units engaged in mutual slaughter. Moscow has been caught in between, and has used internal security and regular troops several times to stop the clashes. After Sumgait, the Soviet military deployed troops in Armenia (September 1988), occupied Yerevan and Baku (Armenian and Azerbaidzhani capitals, respectively) for several days in November 1988 to stop riots. Troops were deployed in NKAO in August 1989, and established martial law in Azerbaidzhan in January 1990, ostensibly to stop the killing of Armenians and other immigrants, but in Azeri eyes to prevent the republic from declaring independence.[39] Every time Soviet troops intervene, nationalist fervour goes up a notch and so does the Russophobia; any casualties immediately become national martyrs.

Since mid-1990, Soviet troops have remained in Azerbaidzhan, but clashes between the two republics continue. Both nationalist movements started organising functional nuclei of national armies operating illegally but Soviet occupation prevented the development of such units in Azerbaidzhan. The Armenian units, on the other hand, reached thousands with thousands more ready in the wings. Nationalist units include many veterans of the Afghan war, ranking officers among them. They are well armed with weapons stolen, won or bought illegally from the SAF or carried across international frontiers. A Moscow decree of 25 July 1990, ordering all illegal armed units to surrender within two weeks or face the security and regular forces, was not obeyed in Transcaucasus. As a way out of the dilemma, Armenia legalised its units as a national militia, the first republic to create a *de facto* national army. By the end of August 1990, the Azerbaidzhan legislature had proclaimed the republic's sovereignty and the Armenian legislature had passed a declaration of independence.

In Georgia, a week of ethnic unrest in Tbilisi, the capital, in April 1989, followed hunger strikes by nationalists demanding independence. A repression by special Soviet riot troops with clubs and shovels and with a use of toxic gas, resulted in a number of casualties, and caused a political crisis which gave new impetus to Georgian nationalism. But Georgia's movement is fragmented into many quarreling factions. Nonetheless in March 1990 the Georgian Supreme Soviet requested Moscow to start negotiations on Georgia's independence and in June it appealed to the RSFSR Supreme Soviet to abrogate a 1921 treaty under which Georgia lost its sovereignty; following in the Baltic footsteps Georgian nationalists denounced the 1921 incorporation as illegal.[40] The Georgian national movement also has to face internal ethnic unrest, because non-Georgian minorities agitate for their national rights. Violent nationalist riots in the Abkhazian autonomous republic in July 1990 were put down by the police and regular Soviet troops, and there was unrest among the Ossetins.

The Muslims of Central Asia and Kazakhstan

The attitudes of the rapidly growing Muslim group[41] are obviously of crucial importance for military as well as economic and political reasons. Their

Teresa Rakowska-Harmstone

demographic explosion has been accompanied by a remarkable upsurge of national self-assertion. Under Brezhnev, local political élites established better representation in Moscow and, at the price of supporting his policies, were able to carve out a substantial power position for themselves at home. Through the 1960s, 1970s and early 1980s their self-confidence escalated, aided also by a perception of Central Asia's foreign policy importance vis-à-vis the Third World in general and the Middle East in particular. Soviet Muslims' exposure to the Islamic world across the border made a quantum leap during the ill-fated Soviet adventure in Afghanistan.

National cultures managed to flourish even within the socialist straitjacket. Based in Islam, they developed separately since 1924 when the region was subdivided into separate republics. Their educational systems succeeded in producing substantial indigenous élites, the characteristic of which has been a preference for humanities and social sciences (taught primarily in local languages), rather than for science and technical/economic specialties (taught mostly in Russian). The result was that, while the cultural and political infrastructure in the republics came to be dominated by the native elements, economic management and technical specialties remained in the hands of immigrants, mostly Russians. Under Soviet rule, the economy of Central Asia was converted to cotton monoculture, with industry in a subsidiary role. The three main cotton-growing republics were Uzbekistan, Tadzhikistan and Turkmenia. Oil and gas extraction was an important industry in Turkmenia (as in Azerbaidzhan) with agriculture and industry of equal importance in Kazakhstan. Muslims dominated agricultural labour, while immigrant skilled workers were employed in the cities and at industrial sites.

The bulk of the rapidly growing Muslim population remained in the countryside in cotton-growing collectives and refused to emigrate to the cities (or out of the republic), forming an enormous pool of unskilled and uneducated labour, plagued by massive unemployment and underemployment, and grinding poverty. In 1987, in Uzbekistan, there were 1 million unemployed among the 7 million people of employment age in the rural areas; in Tadzhikistan every tenth young person was not working, and there were 130,000 young people who neither worked nor went to school.[42] An explosive potential of unemployed youth, living in extreme poverty and seething with resentment against 'outsiders', is not difficult to imagine.

Islam has determined the cultural characteristics of the area, and a post-war religious revival included a reappearance of illegal Sufi brotherhoods (especially in Azerbaidzhan, but also in Central Asia). In a modern setting, Islam has also become an integral part of the new nationhood of the Uzbeks, the Tadzhiks, and all others, a marker that separated their Muslim 'we' from the Russian 'they'. Self-segregation has been a dominant characteristics of relations with immigrants. It has been strikingly illustrated by such culture-determined indicators as the Muslims' unwillingness not only to emigrate but also to urbanize, their high retention of their native languages and low bilingualism in Russian; their low participation in the socialist sector of the economy, but heavy involvement in the subsidiary or secondary (black and grey) economy and a near monopoly of collective farm labour, and their many children and extended traditional families.

The resentment of 'Russians' (i.e. European) immigrants, also extended to other Muslims, such as the Crimean Tatars and the Meskhetian Turks, both deported to Central Asia by Stalin, who were not indigenous to the area, and being better educated gained economic avantages over the locals. The indigenous Muslim community itself was far from homogeneous, having been historically divided between the nomads and the settlers, the Iranians and the Turks, and the warring Khanates. These differences, submerged earlier, surfaced as the Central Power began to recede from the region.

Except for *glasnost'* which gave them a new forum for the airing of grievances, Muslims have been hit hard by Gorbachev's new policies. Their hard-won Brezhnev-blessed autonomy was undercut by the purges resulting from the anti-corruption campaign and by the new policy of parachuting central cadres into Central Asia announced at the 27th CPSU Congress. This brought a new influx of Russian functionaries. Uzbekistan has gone through three purges of the local officials who flourished under the many years of rule by the late first secretary Sharaf Rashidov. In Kazakhstan, the replacement, by a Russian, of an old Brezhnev crony, the Kazakh First Secretary and CPSU Politbureau member, Dinmukhammed Kunaev, caused nationalist riots in the capital of Alma-Ata in December 1986, the first such riots in the region in Gorbachev's era.

An Uzbek-speaking colleague has summed up a list of grievances heard on a visit to Uzbekistan in the spring of 1988 which are now openly voiced in the republic.[43] They come under several major headings. The Uzbeks are worried about the Russification of their culture and resent the scorn they detect in the Russians' attitude towards them, and the falsification of the history of Uzbek-Russian relations, which makes them appear totally backward until the Russians came to help. For this the Uzbeks are supposed to be eternally grateful, even though most Russians who come are 'scum' bent only on enriching themselves. The Uzbeks resent the fact that all the decisions affecting them have been made in Moscow and that they cannot communicate with foreign countries except through Moscow. The new influx of functionaries sent from Moscow 'to watch over us' and the hypocrisy of the anti-Rashidov campaign are also subjects for resentment.

But the Uzbeks' major grievance centres on being forced to cultivate cotton to the exclusion of other crops (such as food crops) under pressure always for better and bigger yields. This they see as the main source of their economic and environmental problems: the ecological disaster of the disappearance of the Aral Sea with its tragic consequences on climate, health and the economy, the pollution of water caused by the seepage of defoliants from badly constructed irrigation canals, as well as back-breaking labour in the fields which makes Uzbek women old at 30, and forces children to pick cotton instead of going to school. They also point out that the need to meet the ever-growing cotton targets has forced their leaders to falsify statistics and engage in corrupt practices which in any case, did not differ in any way from those followed in other republics. But only Uzbeks (and other Central Asians) were made into public scapegoats. Finally, they accused the Russians of trying to stop their women having many children, by forcing contraceptives on the women, and trying to induce the men to leave the republic; a long list of grievances, which is confirmed by other sources.

1989 has seen outbreaks of ethnic violence in Central Asia, as well as the emergence in Uzbekistan of a national front movement, *Birlik*, agitating for greater autonomy. In June 1989, riots started in Fergana valley of Uzbekistan against the Meskhetians, who were accused of appropriating jobs which should have been given to the Uzbeks. Soviet troops intervened, and 16,000 Meskhetians were airlifted out. Some reports claimed that the violence appeared to have been well organised by local Uzbek élites. Also in June 1989, there were riots in Novy Uzen in West Kazakhstan, by unemployed young people against foreign workers, which eventually spread to five other cities along the Caspian Sea. Soviet troops were used there also.[44] The trigger in these riots appears to have been the poverty and unemployment of local youths, and their resentment of 'outsiders', who appeared to be economically better off; once the riots started, however, nationalist overtones were visible, some of them anti-Russian.

Massive riots also broke out in the capital of Tadzhikistan, Dushanbe, in the spring of 1990, against an alleged resettlement there of the Armenian refugees from Baku. The mob made several demands which combined political, economic and environmental concerns, and Tadzhik party and government leaders resigned (but were reinstated) after the SAF commandos were called in to restore order. Finally, in June and July 1990, fighting broke out between the Kirgiz (indigenous nomads) and Uzbeks, (immigrant settlers) in the Kirgiz province of Osh, when the Uzbeks discovered that the Kirgiz were given housing plots: the fighting spread to Uzbekistan's Andizhan. Casualties exceeded 100 killed and many wounded, and the troops were called in again.[45]

In mid-1990 Uzbekistan became the first Central Asian republic to declare sovereignty. Spurred by *Birlik*, a declaration was adopted June 20, 1990, by the Uzbek Supreme Soviet, claiming authority over domestic and foreign policy and, following the example of RSFSR and other republics, declaring Uzbek laws supreme over Soviet laws. By late August 1990, Turkmenia and Tadzhikistan followed with their own declarations of sovereignty and the legislatures of Kirgizia and Kazakhstan were preparing similar moves.

The Military Implications; From the 1960s to the 1980s

Attitudes

It is an open secret that the successive young cohorts of Soviet conscripts have dreaded the military service, but most of them (except for national dissidents and conscientious objectors), have complied with the inevitable. But in the 1970s and 1980s, more and more official complaints began to appear, of young men's 'corruption,' 'pacifism,' and avoidance of the draft. An estimated 20 per cent of each annual two million strong cohort eluded conscription in the 1970s, either because of 'papa's influence,' or using bribery, false medical certification, or even self-mutilation. In 1982, a drastic reduction in educational deferments captured a substantial number of the prefered recruits: the young Russian students; but efforts at draft evasion multiplied in the 1980s, because of the war in Afghanistan (the deferments were restored at the war's end).

Thanks to *glasnost'* the problem began to be discussed openly in the late 1980s. An irate 1988 article in a military paper castigated young mens' unwillingness to serve, (quoting some as saying that the service was comparable to a term in 'concentration camp'), and letters on the subject from ex-servicemen began appearing in the press. Fictionalised accounts of life in the armed forces began to appear, such as a novel of military life published in the journal *Yunost'* (Youth) in 1987, castigated by military press but reviewed favourably in *Literaturnaia Gazeta*.[46] The picture which emerged was not a pretty one, and it was denounced repeatedly by military spokesmen as 'unfair.' A unique feature of army life which came into the open in the discussion was the brutal hazing of new recruits by the 'oldsters' (second year men), a time-honoured method of maintaining 'discipline' in the barracks in which the officers did not interfere.[47]

The conscripts' trauma of being exposed to (by all accounts) the extreme brutality and primitive conditions of the Soviet military environment, has served to focus on and to escalate ethnic perceptions and stereotypes, and an existence of ethnic conflict in the ranks was a matter of common knowledge. Until the late 1980s, however, official Soviet sources referred to its presence in the ranks only indirectly, and even afterwards the issue was addressed in guarded terms. The truth was that ethnic soldiers in the ranks sought co-nationals, or individuals from the same locality or cultural group in order to band together in informal sub-groups for mutual protection and support. Such groups were formed primarily to minimise the effects of the inevitable hazing by defending the victims and punishing offenders; but they also served to express ethnic views and antagonisms.

Ethnic stereotypes were thus reinforced in the Service, and not only among conscripts. They were shared and abused by the professional cadre. The Muslims, for example, were never allowed to forget that they were inferior to the Europeans. The Balts, on the other hand, who are the most 'European'

245

among Soviet groups, were customarily called 'fascists', and accused of political disloyalty. They were persecuted because of their alleged collaboration with the Germans in the 'Great Patriotic War'.

Main ethnic cleavages in the ranks were between the Russians and all others, and between the 'Europeans' and the Muslims. Traditional ethnic antagonisms, such as the Armenian-Turkic feud, and others, were also magnified there. Ethnic fights erupted even in the predominantly Russian élite units, because of the presence there of Russified minorities, such as the Tatars, for example, whose ethnic feelings were ruffled in the hot-house atmosphere of the Service. A major study based on emigré evidence came to the conclusion that the ethnic conflict, the hazing, and the hierarchy of social privilege in the service were major depressants of military morale.[48] It was known also that the conflict occasionally erupted in physical violence. Under combat conditions in Afghanistan fights between Soviet soldiers of different nationalities, and the 'fragging' of officers were quite frequent in the Soviet expeditionary corps.[49]

There was little evidence of ethnic conflict within the officer ranks, although it could appear if non-Russian recruitment increased. There was evidence, however, that the cadre shared strong Russian nationalist sentiments. This was reflected in their unwillingness to see a dilution of the Russian character of the forces, and influenced their treatment of the servicemen. Ethnic preferences were frequently followed by officers in making assignments or recommending promotions. The military press acknowledged this in reverse: i.e. expressing the official 'internationalist' line, it criticized the many deviations from it found in the Service.

Demographic Constraints

The power governing the distribution of conscript military manpower, is determined by the General Staff, and has been implemented by local military commissariats. Ethnic considerations were applied within the context of two basic general rules: First, that all military units must be ethnically mixed, and second, that conscript soldiers cannot be stationed in their own national territory. The latter rule seems to have been applied more rigidly to minority soldiers than to the Russians, and did not seem to apply to officers. Key variables in determining preferable status for assignments have been technical and intellectual capabilities, physical health and stamina, the knowledge of the Russian language and political reliability. All of these favoured urban Russian youth and Russified integrated urban elements, and discriminated against rural non-integrated minorities; the non-Russians who were integrated functionally occupied the middle ground. Information available indicates that political reliability was an important criterion. Jews, the three Baltic nations, Crimean Tatars and Western Ukrainians were the minorities whose political loyalty was *ipso facto* suspect, and they were treated accordingly.

The outcome, (known from an occasional item in official sources and from emigrés and defectors), resulted in the following ethnic distribution of military manpower: the KGB troops, and the élite and special mission combat units were staffed almost exclusively (90 per cent of the total) by Russians and other Slavic groups; the ratio of the choice elements was somewhat lower in regular combat formations (80 per cent of the total). The Muslims, on the other hand, constituted an approximate one half of non-combat troops (the construction and railroad batallions known popularly as *stroibaty*), with the other half composed of about 20 per cent Slavs and 30 per cent of all others. The criteria for an assignment to *stroibaty* were: lack of education and technical know-how, inability to communicate in the Russian language, political unreliability and a criminal record. *Stroibaty* were used for economic work (such as construction and harvesting). They were a replacement, under Brezhnev, of Stalin's GULAG slaves, and became an essential element in the fulfilment of economic plans; the soldiers' pay was a fraction of that being paid to civilian workers. Muslims were also assigned in large numbers to MVD troops, primarily prison guards, where their ignorance of Russian and cultural alienation were an asset rather than a liability in the guarding of dissidents.[50]

An indirect admission of differences in ethnic composition of particular units was made by General Yazov, Soviet minister of defence, in an 1989 article. He said that 'in military districts there were soldiers of 90 to 95 nationalities, in divisional units – 40 to 50 nationalities, and in regimental units and in the Fleet – up to 30 nationalities.' He also admitted that more than 125,000 draftees were unable to speak Russian in 1988, which was 12 times the number of the recruits unable to speak Russian among the 1968 draft cohort.[51]

The predominantly Russian ethnic composition of the officer cadre has been governed not only by a long standing tradition, political preference, and social and educational background, but also by the fact that a choice of a professional military career by a non-Russian implies a decision to Russify. Members of minorities with strong attachment to their national culture and traditions were generally not interested. While no official ethnic breakdown of the officer corps was available, Western estimates based on an analysis of names agreed that approximately 90 per cent of senior Soviet officers were ethnic Slavs (80 per cent of them Russians). For junior officers, an analysis of a sample of more than 10,000 names for 1976–78, showed that only 7.5 per cent of the total were non-Slavs. Among them only three per cent were Muslims.[52]

An exact ethnic composition of the SAF General Staff was unexpectedly revealed in a 1989 interview with a deputy chief of General Staff, Colonel General Kleimenov. Predictably, the Slavs constituted 98 per cent of the total

(Russians, 85 per cent, Ukrainians 10 per cent and Belorussians 3 per cent); the remaining 2 per cent included Armenians, Tatars, Mordvins, Chuvash and others. General Kleimenov emphasized that the choice of staff officers was based entirely on merit, and required 15 to 20 years of outstanding military service and a tour in one of the military academies, and frequently also a tour in the General Staff Voroshilov Academy.[53]

Manpower problems

The military manpower situation was deeply affected by demographic and environmental change and by related ethnic attitudes. A summary based on Soviet military sources of the 1970s and 1980s singled out several key problems:

▶ Demographic trends significantly reduced the supply of the preferred recruits, while the numbers of non-integrated young men increased exponentially. Already there was a shortage of Russian youths – traditionally the backbone of the armed forces and the core of the professional cadre – while more and more conscripts were of inferior quality: they came from rural areas, they were culturally alienated, they spoke little or no Russian and they had few technical skills. They resented being drafted, could not function in military service and their political loyalty was doubtful. Colloquially this became known as the 'Muslim problem.'

The 'Muslim Problem' was seen to combine two related aspects, the 'language problem,' and the 'patriotism problem'. The proposed remedy for the first one was to force the non-integrated young men to learn Russian, and to motivate them to apply to officers' schools. The remedy for the second was to improve the quality of political education in the alienated areas, a standard approach; but the content was to promote greater 'internationalisation' of the military service, including the creation of a special military ethos for the 'Muslims', building on their exploits in the 'Great Patriotic War.' Both remedies were tried in the late Brezhnev period continuing under his successors, Gorbachev included. But neither has worked, largely because of the resistance by the interested parties. The Muslims and other alienated groups did not want to integrate and had little interest in military service. The officer cadre resisted the attempts to 'internationalise' the service on patriotic and professional grounds.

Thus the problem remained and loomed ever larger, in view of the demographic estimates, which envisaged a much higher proportion of the Muslims in the draft cohorts than in the population at large, because of the differential age structure. Already, in the late 1980s, their share in annual cohorts approached 40 per cent of the total. This meant a drastic reassessment of the deployment of the Soviet Armed

Forces in general. This was a bridge that was yet to be crossed, but much thought was beginning to be devoted to the subject.

►There has been an overall decline in health standards of the recruits, a catastrophic increase in alcoholism, and a doubling of mortality rates among young men of military age. Moreover, all these factors seemed to have affected the preferred manpower more than the non-integrated groups, thus compounding the problem above.

►The shortage of competent, functional and integrated manpower has pitted the needs of the military against the needs of the civilian economy, resulting in shortfalls for both.

►At the same time, the changing needs of military service required high levels of technical competence, initiative and reliability, because of the growing complexity of the weapons systems and the changing requirements of potential battlefield conditions.

►The level of ethnic conflict in the SAF escalated, reflecting its emergence in civilian life.[54]

1989–90: SAF in Crisis[55]

By the end of the 1980s the problems discussed above were looming ever larger because of the impact of past and current policies, all of which converged by 1990, creating a veritable crisis situation. The withdrawal from Afghanistan had significant consequences for military morale and social prestige, and under *glasnost'* the SAF became a favourite scapegoat of the reformist press. Gorbachev's *perestroika* confronted the military with substantial cuts and a deterioration in their living conditions, while the 'new thinking' in foreign policy led to changes in the strategic balance in Europe that alarmed them, and required changes in structure and training. At home, the erosion of central Party and government power and the democratisation of the political system led, on the one hand, to the republics' claims of sovereignty, with far-reaching military consequences, and, on the other, to the politicisation of the professional cadre and an emergence of divergent views within the SAF on the subject of the future shape and role of the armed forces.

Two sacred and cherished military myths were shattered in the aftermath of the Afghan adventure: one was that the Soviet Armed Forces were invincible, the other, that Soviet soldiers, officers and equipment were the best in the world. The shock was the more acute because of the generations nurtured on the myths of the 'Great Patriotic War.' In the ranks, the morale sunk to the bottom, because their pride in the might of the Soviet Union, the one psychological compensation for all the miseries of the Service, was suddenly gone. One of the outcomes was the emergence into the open of the ethnic conflict as the key variable in the hazing that became ever more brutal, especially when directed against draftees from separatist national groups.

Another was a breakdown in military discipline that was reflected in the intensification of other types of criminal behaviour such as stealing and bribery.

For the general public, the trauma of losing the myth of the Soviet might was also intense. It led to mushrooming of draft resistance, not only among the young people of the minorities infected with nationalism, but also among the Russian core; military service no longer had the prestige or the benefits, and the certainty of its role was lost. Mothers were demonstrating against the mobilisation of Russian youths needed to replace unreliable 'ethnics' in the units earmarked for intervention in Transcaucasus. A military journal reported that between April and October 1989, 1,527 draftees failed to report for draft in the district military commissariats of the city of Moscow, and a further 300 refused to be drafted and were sought by the authorities.[56] General Yazov complained of draft evasion in the national republics and revealed that 65,500 young men evaded the draft in the call-up of the autumn of 1989.[57] The dimensions of draft evasion were apparently much greater in the call-up of the spring of 1990.

Another aspect of public disillusionment with the military was the appalling treatment at the grass roots of the veterans of the Afghan war, the so-called *Afgantsy*, and their families. The situation of the legions of disabled veterans was particularly bad: prostheses, medical equipment and proper medical and psychological care were mostly not available, and large numbers of veterans had no jobs, no housing and no food. The problem was bitterly and frequently denounced in the military press. But the problems persisted, largely because local authorities had insufficient resources to take care of the general populace, let alone of the veterans with special needs. In the civilian press, on the other hand, there was an open season on the military. General incompetence revealed in the Afghan operations, and the various scandals, having to do with thefts of military property – from weapons and gasoline to food and supplies – were regularly denounced. One of the most common themes was the criticism of hazing practices, now openly discussed and called '*dedovshchina*'. Hazing was also broadly denounced in the military press as 'non-regulation behaviour' but there the readers were advised that it was disappearing, which did not seem to be the case in reality.

Perestroika hit the military hard. There was a need to cut costs and to streamline, professionalise and improve the performance in order to correct problems discovered in Afghanistan; there was a need to reorganise, and to change and improve training methods, in order to accommodate the shift in the military doctrine from an 'offensive-defensive' to a 'defensive-defensive' posture. Sweeping changes were carried out in the personnel at the command level in 1988–89, and a cut of half a million men, of whom 150,000 were members of the professional cadre (100,000 officers and 50,000 warrant officers) was announced in December 1988, and began to be implemented in 1989–90. Under pressure from the new governments of the NSWP members, and East-West negotiations, withdrawals were announced from Eastern Europe and preparations begun to carry them out. This meant uprooting many of the élite formations which were faced with the cuts and dismal prospects for re-location.

The cadre, already demoralised by the loss of prestige, low pay, bad food, lack of health care and abysmal housing conditions (on the evidence of the military press a substantial proportion of serving officers and their families either lacked adequate housing or were given no housing at all), was now faced with the uncertainties of potential discharge and transfer to civilian life. The criteria for discharge were by no means clear, and there was no assurance that adequate benefits would be available at separation; it was clear, on the other hand, that the home areas of retired servicemen had neither jobs nor housing for them and their families. General dissatisfaction may be gauged by the fact that a trade union 'Shield' was organised in October 1989, as a Union for the Protection of Servicemen, Draftees and Their Families. But according to its spokesman, the Ministry of Defence did not approve of its activities. In consequence, its scope for action was very limited.[58] The uncertainty made some officers look for jobs elsewhere, and resignations by younger officers, previously rare, became fairly common.

The situation was further complicated by the pressure placed on the military facilities as the withdrawals from Eastern Europe started. Inevitably, housing was the major problem. The withdrawals, even though planned on a very extended timetable, brought home to the military the new realities of the changing Soviet strategic position. In the minds of many officers, in stark terms the change meant crossing out all the gains won by the Soviet Armed Forces at a tremendous price in the 'Great Patriotic War': Eastern Europe was 'lost' and Germany was just about to be re-unified. Certainly this point of view was articulated with a great deal of bitterness by the military participants at the 28th Congress of the CPSU. There was evidence also of second thoughts about military retrenchment among the SAF high command, precisely because of what they saw as a deteriorating Soviet strategic position.[59]

On the domestic front, the key problem for military leaders was, undoubtedly, the erosion of power of the Central Government, and thus their inability to enforce the draft and to counteract the republics' challenges in the military sphere. The Russian Republic's declaration of sovereignty included a claim to control its military affairs, but Boris Yeltsin's perception of a future union envisaged the delegation of this control to the Centre[60]. However, all the other republics' claims envisaged national management of military affairs. This was reflected in the demands to have their young men serve in their national territory, and in the protection of deserters and draft evaders. Organisations sheltering them were established in the Baltic and Transcaucasian republics and in the Ukraine. Some republics went further, introducing legislation which denied the legality of compulsory Soviet military service (the Balts, invoked international conventions which exempt young men from serving in an 'army of occupation'), introduced alternative service, or declared the right to set up their own armies, now or in the future. Transcausus national movements set up their own well armed national units, and a similar trend seemed to emerge in Central Asia.[61]

The Estonian legislature, for example, first declared compulsory service in the SAF to be illegal (30 March, 1990); then it abolished compulsory military service (12 April), but later established a Home Guard, swearing in male and female volunteers (20 May).[62] Lithuania, which was the first to refuse to comply with the draft and to challenge the legality of Soviet military service, was also the first to take legal steps to establish its own army. On 17 July 1990 the Lithuanian legislature enacted a law under which 'all 19 year-olds would be conscripted to serve as border guards, internal security troops, paramilitary firefighters and security guards', with alternative service available for conscientious objectors, and volunteers allowed to join the SAF. The law also envisages that 'national security detachments' will be set up which will form a nucleus of a future Lithuanian army.[63]

Ukraine's *Rukh* has insisted from the beginning that Ukrainian young men should serve in their own republic, and that movement also patronised new paramilitary nationalist youth organisations which sprang up and are popularly seen as nuclei of a future Ukrainian army. In the western Ukraine there is a Union of Independent Ukrainian Youth modelled on the forces of the Ukrainian independence movement of the Second World War; in the east (Kharkov), there is an organisation named 'Falcon.' The Ukrainian declaration of sovereignty of 16 July included the right to establish separate military forces and to control troops stationed in Ukrainian territory. A follow-up declaration on 30 July called for a return of all Ukrainian draftees currently in the SAF by the end of 1990, and demanded that all Ukrainian soldiers should be removed from units currently engaged in internal suppression in the various Soviet 'hot spots'.[64]

In the Transcaucasus, the Georgian authorities have repeatedly demanded that their draftees should serve only at home, and have protected draft evaders. As noted earlier, the Armenian and Azerbaidzhani nationalist movements actually organised their own units which had engaged in actual combat, and the Centre's effort to force their dissolution did not promise much of a success. In Armenia, however, where a nationalist leader took over the presidency in early August, some of the units were legalised as a national militia, thus establishing the first *de facto* national army. Demands that the local boys should not be shipped out of their republics have also been made by the Central Asians, and draft evasion has been widespread there.

It was not difficult to see that, if current trends continued, the SAF would find itself without a manpower base, and that it was important to re-think both its future role and its future structure, although the final shape of future Soviet military forces, and in fact their very existence, obviously would depend on a political resolution of the conflict between Moscow and the republics. The problem was very much in the forefront of military thinking, but there was no agreement, and a heated debate in the military and civilian press, and in public fora, revealed radically different conceptions.

The discussion of re-structuring pitted the advocates of the existing central All-Union army against those who would prefer national armies, or a combination of a cadre army and national militias, as under the 1924 model; and the defenders of a multinational 'internationalist' draft army were hard put to reject arguments for a volunteer professional army. In terms of the armed forces' social role, strong voices were heard in support of an army designed solely for external defence, as against those who favoured an additional internal defence role in support of the political *status quo*, and an economic role; there was a debate also whether or not the Communist Party should retain its controlling influence within the forces, i.e. whether the current system of the Military Political Administration (MPA, a department of the CPSU Central Committee and at the same time an administration within the USSR Ministry of Defence) should be retained.[65]

The real innovation of the Gorbachev era was that, unlike in the past, the SAF did not speak with one voice but with many voices. There was a clear division between the views of the high command and that of the middle and lower level officers. As the late Andrei Sakharov was heard to observe, the generals were concerned more over the cuts and disarmament, and the failure of the discipline in the country, while the views of middle and lower officers reflected the unrest within the ranks and general social concerns; but there was a variety of views within each group.[66]

As of mid-1990 the official line expressed by President Gorbachev, and the top military leaders, unequivocally supported the *status quo*. There were no concessions on the ethnic front, except a tacit agreement to allow a proportion of draftees to serve in their national areas, especially in the republics where most fuss was made, such as the Baltics, and Georgia. There were no concessions on the principle of a central draft-based army – a volunteer force was dismissed as 'hirelings', and an argument was made that it would be too costly.[67] There were no concessions in the army's internal role: its use for the suppression of domestic disorders was justified, still, in class terms, and its use for economic tasks continued to be considered essential. In practice the armed forces were used to intervene in internal disorders, but only in the southern republics and almost exclusively in cases of inter-ethnic conflict. Although a none too subtle threat of force was employed against the Baltic republics, Lithuania in particular, force has not been used, so far, against a national republic united in its demand to break away.

Also, there were no concessions on the continued Party control over the Armed Forces. President Gorbachev was consistently on record opposing the abolition of the MPA – at the May Day 1990 speech, in a speech to the Supreme Soviet in June, and finally at the 28th Congress of the CPSU in July. The Congress in fact voted down a proposal from the floor suggesting an abolition of Party organisations in the Army and the security police.[68] Gorbachev's adviser, Professor Shakhnazarov was quoted as saying that the retention of Party cells in the military at the present time was essential for the country's stability: 'their role is moral patriotic education in the spirit of dedication to the country and the Party. If all these functions are taken away from the Army, it will be very dangerous,' [69] a disingenuous statement in the light of what is known about the poor performance and lack of effectiveness of the military political education system, and in the light of the progressive loss of power by the CPSU, but reflecting, perhaps, a fear of military disintegration.

A radically different view was expressed by a colonel writing in the *Moscow News:* 'knowing the mood of the majority of the officer corps, I can say that they are for expelling all Party organisations from the army.' [70] The first officer to express this kind of sentiment openly in 1989 was another colonel, a deputy to the USSR Congress of People's Deputies elected in preference to an officially sponsored general, who said that the MPA has become obsolete and should be phased out.[71]

On the subject of the nationalist challenge and the eroding draft base, there was much interest among middle and junior officers in the 1924 mixed system of a core army combined with territorial militias. But overall, a strong sentiment existed in favour of a smaller but qualitatively better, volunteer, professional army. In the minds of many officers, such an army would be free of current military pathologies; it would regain its professionalism and its prestige in society, and it would best fulfill its primary task of defending the country from an external threat. An unspoken but strong undercurrent represented in this view was that it would exclude all the unfit and the unwilling, which would help to preserve the historical military traditions and ethos of the SAF.

Advocates of a professional army were generally also critical of the use of the Regular Army for internal suppression which, they felt, was an improper task for the Army and destructive of its proper role, and should be done by the police and the militia.[72] They were critical also of the use of military construction units for economic work. The construction units tend to include 'a large portion of young persons with physical and moral defects and with criminal records,' as one spokesman for this view put it, adding that 'even the naked eye can see . . . that the involvement of the Army in carrying out plan quotas for the economic department . . . is being turned for them into a permanent source of unskilled and cheap manpower, and posed a rhetorical question: 'What sort of a military specialist is this who is professionally involved, for instance, in raising cabbages or as a house painter?' [73]

To sum up, the Soviet military establishment was still outwardly a formidable one in mid-1990. But the evidence of social rejection and internal turmoil indicated that military morale was at rock bottom, and that the Forces' internal cohesion and potential effectiveness were, at best, badly shaken up. There were thus many questions which needed to be asked. Some of them were:

▶How long will it be possible for the Soviet political and military leadership to maintain the SAF in its present organisational and social form?

▶How effectively will the SAF perform in case of an emergency, especially a large scale domestic emergency?

▶What kind of an army will the Soviet Union have in the year 2000 and, indeed, is there going to be a Soviet Army?

The Soviet military future depends on the Soviet political future and on the shape of a new 'Treaty of the Union', promised by Mr Gorbachev for December 1990. The blueprint projected in mid-1990 by the Soviet leader was very different from that suggested by those national republics which are crucial to the maintenance of the union, namely, the RSFSR and the other two Slav republics. The latest information available indicates that Mr Gorbachev envisaged a scenario under which the republics would voluntarily cede powers to the union in eight areas: defence, border control, and security (meaning the maintenance of the SAF and the KGB), human rights, high technology, energy, money supply, and movement of goods and people.[74] Mr Yeltsin, on the other hand, saw the Soviet future as 'a community of sovereign states on the basis of a confederation,' with 'two or three things delegated to the Centre, including defence and internal security;[75] If the two leaders can agree, the SAF is likely to re-acquire its Russian heritage openly.

Other republics, nonetheless, have been rather specific on the subject of their own national military formations, and these included the Ukraine, and, as a statement of principle, Belorussia. The three Baltic republics, which were on record as agreeing to sign treaties with the union, insisted, nevertheless, on doing this from a position of total and complete independence, such as that now enjoyed by the East Europeans. The Transcaucasian republics, Georgia in particular, were also edging in the direction of independence. In general, popular demands appeared to be building up faster than they could be articulated by their nationalist spokesmen in newly elected legislatures. Moscow, on the other hand, was lagging far behind in its willingness to recognise the latter, let alone to accommodate them. This made for an explosive situation in which the armed forces may come to play an important role. The dynamics of the political as well as the military situation depended on the success – or failure – of the economic reform.

Teresa Rakowska-Harmstone

EASTERN EUROPEAN FORCES AND THE WARSAW PACT
1989–90

Changes in the Warsaw Pact

The primary mission of the Warsaw Pact, articulated many times over the years of the Alliance's existence, has been the 'defence of the gains of socialism on the internal and external front.' In plain language, it meant that its purpose was to defend the Marxist-Leninist régimes in Eastern Europe from their internal enemies, and to defend the Soviet hegemonial role in the region against NATO, the external enemy. Gorbachev's decision not to prop up the bankrupt Polish Party by force, and the domino-like effect the decision has had on the collapse of other Marxist-Leninist régimes in the region, deprived the Alliance of its political and military *raison d'être*.

The backbone of the Pact's decision-making was political consultation between the ruling Communist Parties, which collapsed when the East European parties lost power, leaving the CPSU without its satellites. The Pact's Political Consultative Committee, designed specifically for such consultations (although rarely used as such because Soviet leaders preferred to rely instead on bilateral contacts), was rendered obsolete. Ideological unity, and the common goal of 'building' and 'defending socialism,' were also lost. What was left were the Pact's formal structure for consultation between the governments, and its military structure. The latter no longer conformed to the new East European governments' perceptions of their national interests, and were also becoming inconsistent with the new balance in East-West relations. This meant that far-reaching changes were needed in the Pact's political and military organisation, and that its future was problematical.[76]

The changing situation was recognised in Moscow, but it was nevertheless crucial for the Soviet leaders to maintain the organisation as long as possible, in order to salvage a degree of influence in the region, and to provide an umbrella for keeping at least some Soviet troops there, out of the 500,000 deployed in 1989. (See Table 10.5). The official version was that the organisation would be transformed from a military-political into a political-military regional alliance, reflecting the national interests of the members. Soviet sources stressed that the WP was necessary to maintain stability, and hinted that the East Europeans, who were poor and weak, still needed 'to count on the might and support of the Soviet Union in dealing with the rich countries of the West.[77] Accordingly, Soviet representatives fought a rear guard defensive action against the demands by new East European governments, which threatened the very existence of the organisation and sought the removal of Soviet military presence from their soil. These were stated bluntly.

Czechoslovakia and Hungary openly declared that their membership of the Pact was the result of an invasion and demanded Soviet troops' withdrawal as soon as possible. The East German participation was caught in the East-West negotiations over the future of Germany. Only the Polish Government, still

256

TABLE 10.5   NSWP Forces Totals; Soviet Forces in Eastern Europe, 1988–90 (000s; prior to cuts and withdrawals)

	National forces		Soviet forces
	Nos.	Length of service	
Bulgaria	117.5	2 years	none
Czechoslovakia	199.7	2 years	70
GDR	173.1	18 months	380
Hungary	91	18 months	65
Poland	412	2 years	40
Romania	171	16 months	none

Source: *The Military Balance 1989–1990*, IISS, (London: Brassey's, 1990) pp. 38–40, 45–51.

under the presidency of the ubiquitous General Jaruzelski, and concerned over possible claims by a united German state to the German territories incorporated by Poland in 1945, was willing to stay in the Pact for the time being, and to allow Soviet troops to remain in Poland. But Solidarity's leader, Lech Walesa, demanded their withdrawal on behalf of the opposition. Bulgaria and Romania, with no Soviet troops voiced no special demands. Their new governments were still dominated by (reform) communists. Romania, at any rate, had maintained only a token membership in the Pact under Ceausescu, and its new leaders were preoccupied with problems of internal stability.

On the future of Germany, President Gorbachev found little support among his erstwhile allies for his insistence that a new Germany cannot join NATO. At a meeting of the Warsaw Pact in March 1990 all the NSWP members expressed themselves in favour of such a membership despite Soviet objections.[78] But it took the Soviet Union another four months before it also accepted the inevitable (but not before negotiating a generous payoff), under the proddings of West Germany's Chancellor Kohl.[79] Soviet leaders also had to agree gradually to withdraw the troops. Under pressure from the new governments of Hungary and Czechoslovakia and popular pressures building up behind these demands, treaties of withdrawal were signed with Czechoslovakia in February and with Hungary in March 1990, providing for the evacuation of all Soviet troops from both countries by the first of July 1991.[80] As noted earlier, the Polish Government did not request a withdrawal of the Soviet garrison, although the Soviet Union announced that it was willing to do so if asked. The only condition was that sufficient troops should remain to provide logistical support for Soviet troops in East Germany as long as they stayed there. This was accepted by the Poles.[81]

The question of Soviet troops in the GDR was more complicated. The 1989 unilateral cuts in the SAF strength were already reflected in some reductions in the Group of Soviet Forces in Germany (GSFG). These were halted, however, because of the difficulties of re-locating the units withdrawn within the Soviet Union. Moreover, the size of the Soviet contingent in the GDR was very large (see Table 10.5), and its future depended on the general East-West negotiations. The final outcome was that the Soviet Union agreed to withdraw its troops from Germany over the transition period of three to four years. But the agreement came at considerable cost to the Germans. Chancellor Kohl agreed to help pay both for the troops' maintenance while still on the German soil, and for their withdrawals. In the meantime, the popular mood of the East German population changed, displaying growing hostility towards Soviet soldiers, while the Soviet troops themselves were reluctant to leave in view of the difficulties at home.[82] As German unification proceeds, and East Germany becomes more and more integrated into the Federal Republic, the continuing presence of a large Soviet garrison there will undoubtedly be a major irritant, and may well become untenable.

By mid-1990, the initial open or implicit rejection of the Warsaw Pact by the NSWP members gave way to a consensus that the Pact should remain as a regional consultative political organisation until such time as new all-European security arrangements are established. The initiative apparently came from Czechoslovakia, Poland and the new East German Government. Jiri Dienstbier, the Czechoslovak foreign minister, described the new arrangement, (to which the Soviet Union agreed at the WP meeting in Moscow 7–8 June), as the conversion of the organisation 'from a military alliance under Soviet control to a political grouping fully respecting the sovereignty of its seven member nations.' This would mean that all NSWP armies will be effectively under national control and that the PCC will be converted into a genuine decision-making body of the Alliance. Dienstbier added also that the retention of the WP was very important to avoid isolating the Soviet Union and thus giving it a 'Versailles complex.' A new commission was set up to effect the transition.[83]

The consensus view was expressed by Poland's new (non-communist) defence minister: 'The Warsaw Pact guarantees European security, and Poland will remain a member until there is a new collective European security arrangement.'[84] Hungary was the only one of the NSWP countries which did not fully subscribe to the consensus. Its newly elected parliament instructed Hungarian defence minister, Lajos Fur, to negotiate Hungary's withdrawal from the Warsaw Pact by the end of 1991; Hungary also repeatedly expressed a wish to join NATO and, in July, to join the European Community.[85]

Although nothing was said of the change in the WP strategic military arrangements, it was clear that the deployment of troops in the Soviet Western and Southwestern Strategic Military Directions and its subordinate theatres of which NSWP forces were a part,[86] was no longer viable. It was to be expected also that the various integration mechanisms, such as joint manoeuvres, training of the NSWP senior cadre in Soviet military academies, co-ordinated military-political education, and the like would be discontinued (or in some cases greatly reduced), and that the unequal bilateral treaties with the Soviet Union would be re-negotiated. It was to be expected also that NSWP countries would cease to act as proxies in the training of personnel of, and supplying advisers and military equipment to, Soviet client states in the Third World.

Changes in NSWP Armies

The process of the 1989–90 political transformations affected all the NSWP armies. The most complete change took place in the East German Army (NVA), the one NSWP army that had been totally integrated into the Group of Soviet Forces in Germany (GSFG) and which now faced both an identity crisis and a certainty of dissolution. Reports indicated that, as its strength went down (from 170,000 to 100,000 in March 1990), the morale among officers and men disintegrated, soldiers refused to perform military tasks and were going absent without leave. Many officers and men offered their services to the *Bundeswehr*. In the words of Egon Bahr, one of West Germany's leading politicians, 'the NVA cannot be used for war any more.' [87] As plans for German unification developed, and the screening of the NVA's career cadre for Communist Party/security ties commenced, it became clear that only some will be acceptable to the *Bundeswehr*. So far 60,000 have taken a new oath in order to qualify. Some may be employed in a new East German territorial army, although only some 15 to 20 thousand of the ex-NVA personnel were envisaged in a proposed 50,000 total. Some may join the Federal Border guards. But many will obviously find themselves in the ranks of the unemployed.[88]

No other East European army has faced such drastic changes, but all were in a process of a three-way transformation: they were undergoing re-nationalisation, depoliticisation and reorganisation, the process required to make them into genuine national armies, after the many years of acting as the swords of their ruling Communist Parties, and serving as Soviet auxiliaries.

Renationalization took place first and foremost in the form of military doctrines' changed definition of the armed forces mission. The defence of the national state and national borders against an external threat replaced the former obligatory WP formula of 'defending socialism on the internal and the external fronts'.[89] It has been reflected too in the restoration of national symbolism and a corresponding rejection of the Soviet one. Red stars are being replaced by national coats of arms, and the Polish eagle has reacquired its crown. The two adjectives, 'socialist' and 'peoples', which had dominated the military and political lexicon of NSWP states until 1989, became very unfashionable, and have been dropped in favour of traditional national imagery.

De-politicization has been reflected in the removal of Party cells from the armed forces and in the abolition of the Soviet-type MPA system which heretofore had served a double purpose of political control and socialisation, and was orchestrated for the NSWP armies by the Soviet MPA. In some countries, the formation of Party cells in the military was forbidden by decree; in others the cells collapsed of their own accord as the mother parties collapsed.[90]

Reorganization was still in the early stages. It was reflected in the proposed cuts in the strength of the forces, and reductions in the length of service of the drafted manpower and in provisions for alternative service for conscientious objectors. There was also a trend towards an increased reliance on volunteers, maximising the share of the professional element in the Armed Forces, especially in the Air Force and the Navy.[91] The share of the cadre in NSWP armies was always higher than in the SAF, reflecting the concern over draftees' reliability: now it is being directed towards elimination of the unwilling and unfit elements, and towards greater professionalisation of smaller armies, enhancing thereby their military capabilities. The one problem all the armies faced in the latter task was the economic cost it entailed in conditions of economic crisis which affected the region as a whole.

The overall aim was to adapt the national armies to the performance of their new mission of national defence, and their withdrawal from the integrative framework provided for under the WP Joint Command. The WP commission established in June to effect the transition will undoubtedly concern itself with the dismantling of joint military arrangements, and the respective governments will proceed with the drafting of new treaties governing the relations between the NSWP states and the Soviet Union.

Nationalism, and health and ecological factors were as important in an assessment of future military capabilities of NSWP post-communist states as they were in the Soviet Union. The intensity of national feelings in Eastern Europe was a major factor in the region's emancipation from under the Soviet tutelage, and national identity and interests became even more important as the East European states resumed their independent existence. With democratisation and reintroduction of political pluralism, the parties which appeared to have gained the strongest popular base were the nationalist-centre parties, rather than left-of-centre liberal parties. In foreign relations, old regional quarrels and nationalist stereotypes, claims and counter-claims begun to re-emerge, promising a great deal of instability for the region. Moreover, although none had a range of internal ethnic problems comparable

260

to that of the Soviet Union, some countries were divided along ethnic lines, and some had minorities many of which straddled borders. These minorities were by no means left out when it came to newly articulated self-assertion. The Slovaks in Czechoslovakia made many new demands for greater equality with the Czechs, and the Hungarians in Romania agitated for greater autonomy, and were, in fact, responsible for triggering the violence which led to the fall of President Ceausescu. Other Romanian minorities, mistreated in the past, felt increasingly insecure. The minorities in Poland, very small in comparison with their size in the inter-war period, were none-the-less important, both in view of outside developments and because of the revival of nationalism in domestic politics. Similarly, the Germans gained prominence, because of their potential demands for the restoration of the German territory by the new Germany. So too did Western Soviet minorities in Poland and Poles across the border in Soviet Western republics, in the light of the latter's self-assertion. Even the Jews, no longer present in significant numbers, were still a convenient scapegoat for supernationalists.

In Bulgaria, the Turkish minority resisted efforts at assimilation and was the object of popular derision and official persecution. The Hungarians, on the other hand, were beginning again to articulate old demands for reunification with the Hungarians cut off from the mother country as the result of the settlements after two world wars. This placed them on a potential collision course not only with Romania but with Czechoslovakia and Yugoslavia.

The destruction of the environment affected the East Europeans as much as it did the Soviets and for the same reasons, more so perhaps because of the East European states' smaller size and resources. The worst pollution, by all accounts, was in the belt extending from Leipzig in the GDR across northern Bohemia in Czechoslovakia into the Polish Silesian basin to Cracow, the most industrialised parts of Eastern Europe. According to a study made by the Polish Academy of Sciences, a third of Poland's 38 million people live in 'areas of ecological disaster,' the worst of which is the coal/steel belt of Silesia and Cracow where life expectancy is four years below that in the rest of Poland. According to the Czechoslovak Academy of Sciences, one half of Czechoslovakia's drinking water does not meet the standards of safety, and mortality rates in northern Bohemia are 12 per cent higher than in the rest of the country. In the GDR, cancer and lung diseases deaths were found to be 15 to 25 per cent higher in Leipzig than in Berlin.

The forests of the Silesian belt are almost all dead from acid rain. Eighty-four per cent of all Polish forests are under a threat of destruction, 74 per cent in the GDR and some 60 per cent in Czechoslovakia, as compared to 50 per cent in Bulgaria and 25 per cent in Hungary.[92] The regions' rivers, the Elbe, Oder, Neisse and Vistula, polluted by raw sewage and untreated industrial waste, are open sewers, and carry the pollution into the Baltic Sea, 25 per cent of which was already dead by 1990. The Danube was somewhat less affected but still absorbed pollutants across its length, and discharged them into the Black Sea already poisoned by effluents from Soviet rivers. Radiation was a potential danger. The impact of Chernobyl awakened fears in Eastern Europe of a similar disaster: in the last 20 years the Soviet Union built 23 nuclear plants in Eastern Europe (5 in the GDR, 8 in Czechoslovakia, 4 in Hungary and 6 in Bulgaria). According to East European experts, the equipment was unsafe but the Soviets withheld all information relating to nuclear safety, thus there was a danger of nuclear accidents.[93]

No East European disease statistics are included here, but information available indicates that poverty levels and chemical poisoning of the environment are as lethal for the health of the population of Eastern Europe as they are for the peoples of the Soviet Union. On the whole, demographic indicators for the NSWP countries were comparable to those in the Soviet Western republics of similar levels of development. With the exception of Poland, the East European populations are in decline (Hungary, especially, showed negative growth), and their infant mortality rates are higher, and their life expectancy lower, than in the West. (See Table 10.6).

All these factors have affected the quality of their military manpower. The falling national growth rates are reflected in the estimates, for the year 2000, of the size of cohorts of 18 year-old males. There was a significant decline, in comparison with 1989, for Hungary, Romania and Bulgaria, although small increases were noted for Czechoslovakia and the GDR, and a substantial one for Poland. (See Table 10.6). An overall decline in health standards is reflected in the health and physical stamina of young men of military age. East European sources have voiced complaints, similar to those noted in the Soviet press, that among the current draft cohorts many young men were of smaller stature than previous averages, were in poor health and were, in fact, unfit for military service. Many of the unfit, not surprisingly, come from the heavy pollution belt identified above.

The decline in the quality of the current draft cohorts may not necessarily affect the quality of East European forces in view of their new reliance on smaller armies with a higher share of volunteers. But it is bound to affect the size and the quality of the pool of military manpower available to them in the future.

PROSPECTS

The review referred to above shows that one can no longer refer to the cohesion of the Warsaw Pact. Whatever future the organisation still has, it will not be as a military alliance. But regional co-operation consistent with national interests of individual states is not excluded. The NSWP countries show a clear preference for ties with Western Europe (returning to the interwar pattern of relations), over those with the Soviet Union. But, in the

TABLE 10.6   NSWP Countries; Demographic Indicators

	Bulgaria	**CSR**	**GDR**	**Hungary**	**Poland**	**Romania**
Population (000s)†						
1970	8,490	14,334	17,058	10,337	32,526	20,250
1987	8,970	15,573	16,641	10,613	37,664	22,925
est. 1995	9,392	16,155	16,998	10,661	39,600	24,690
Birth rates/1,000‡						
1970	16.3	15.9	13.9	14.7	16.6	21.1
1987	12.9	13.8	13.6	11.8	16.1	15.8★
Death rates/1,000‡						
1970	9.1	11.6	14.1	11.6	8.1	9.5
1987	12.0	11.5	12.9	13.4	10.1	10.9★
Rates of natural increase/1,000‡						
1970	7.2	4.3	−0.2	3.1	8.5	11.6
1987	0.9	2.3	0.7	−1.6	6.0	4.9★
Infant mortality rates (0 to 1/1,000 live births)‡						
1970	27.3	22.1	18.5	35.9	33.4	49.4
1987	15.0	13.1	8.5	17.4	17.4	25.6★
Life expectancy‡★★						
General	71.2	–	72.4	69.	71.0	69.8
Males	68.2	67.5	69.5	65.3	66.9	67.0
Females	74.4	75.0	75.5	73.2	76.3	72.6
Number of males each year reaching age 18 (000s)§						
1989	66	112	117	75	271	195
est. 2000	62	122	119	67	352	174
% change 89–00	−6	+9	+2	−11	+30	−11

★   in 1985
★★   varying years: Bulgaria, 1984–85; Hungary and GDR, 1906, Czechoslovakia (CSR), 1987; Poland, 1985–85; Romania, 1982–84.

Sources:
†   *European Marketing Data and Statistics* (London: Euromonitor Publications Ltd., 1990), p. 135.
‡   *Statisticheskii Iezhegodnik Stran Chlenov SEV* (Moscow: 1988), pp. 16,19,20.
§   *The Military Balance 1989–1990*, IISS (London, Brassey's, 1990), p. 239.

Teresa Rakowska-Harmstone

current international context of reshaping European alliances, they recognise that it is safer to have the Soviet Union within a regional alliance than to leave it outside, not only for their own interests but in the interests of a new European security arrangement, which is to include the United States as well. There may still be significant benefits, moreover, for individual countries in maintaining Soviet ties, for political and economic reasons.

Under President Gorbachev, the Soviet Union also has an abiding interest to keep a foot in the European door, even if it is no longer able to maintain control of Eastern Europe. But political transformations in the Soviet Union are far from complete, and it remains to be seen whether the successor states – should such states emerge – will have similar interests.

In the aftermath of the 1989–90 changes in Eastern Europe, some pluses and minuses may be singled out from the point of view of regional military collaboration. On the credit side, there are the 40 years of cohabitation in the common Soviet military home, which made for uniformity of training, equipment, and administrative habits, and a general reciprocal familiarity. At the same time, the reassertion of national sovereignty gave a significant boost to the military morale of individual armies, which was strengthened further by a new sense that they now fulfill their proper military missions. The proposed reorganisation and professionalisation should also contribute to greater effectiveness in common undertakings.

But the reassertion of national sovereignty carries with it also the negative consequences of reviving old national claims and antagonisms, breeding conflicts and political instability, and reaching outside the immediate region to traditional partnerships. One such return has been the interest of Czechoslovakia and Hungary in resuming the old Habsburg connections with Austria, Italy and Yugoslavia. The economic crisis which has affected all the NSWP states, and negative trends in their health and demographic indicators, also have to be placed on the debit side.

Notes

1. 286 million in 1989, 289 million in 1990.
2. 112.8 million in 1988 and 113.2 million in 1990. The figures combined the populations of Bulgaria, Czechoslovakia, East Germany, Hungary, Poland and Romania. Albania and Yugoslavia were not members of the Warsaw Pact in the 80s. Yugoslavia was never a member. Albania was one of the founding members, but it ceased to participate in 1961 and officially quit the Pact in 1966. Thus neither Yugoslavia nor Albania are considered here.
3. *The Military Balance 1988–89*, IISS, (London: Brassey's, 1990), p. 32.
4. Referred to as the WTO-CMEA (Warsaw Treaty Organization – Council for Mutual Economic Assistance) regional system. The CMEA, established in 1949, includes all members of the WP in addition to non-regional actors of identical or sympathetic political orientation. The WP was established in 1955 for 30 years. It was renewed in 1985, for the same period.

Warsaw Pact Cohesion

5. See the three volume study by T. Rakowska-Harmstone, C.D. Jones et al. *Warsaw Pact, The Question of Cohesion*. Phase II. (Ottawa: Department of National Defence, ORAE, February 1984-March 1986), on which much of this paper is based. Hereafter cited as *WP.11*.

6. The concept, adapted here, originated with Cynthia Enloe in *Ethnic Soldiers: State Security in a Divided Society* (Middlesex: Penguin Books, 1980).

7. First federal constitution of the Soviet Union was adopted in 1924. New federal constitutions were adopted in 1936 (Stalin) and 1977 (Brezhnev) and far-reaching changes were introduced by Gorbachev. In the 1980s there were 16 union republics, (SSR's) the largest of which was the Russian republic (RSFSR), which extended from ethnic Russian areas west of the Urals to the Pacific, 20 autonomous republics (ASSR's), 16 of them in RSFSR, two in Georgia and one each in Uzbekistan and Azerbaidzhan, and 18 autonomous provinces/districts, 15 in RSFSR, one in Georgia, one in Tadzhikstan and one, the recently become famous Nagorno-Karabakh Autonomous Province, in Azerbaidzhan. Largest national groups dwelling in border areas have union republic status; these range from over 40 million Ukrainians to one million Estonians. Large internally located national groups have autonomous republic status; ethnicity of smaller groups is recognized by autonomous province (oblast) or district (okrug) status.

8. See WP II, Vo I. 1, *The Greater Socialist Army: Integration and Reliability*, ORAE Extra-Mural Paper No. 29, February 1984. Chapter 5 by Christopher Jones.

9. See WP II. Vol. 3 *Union of Soviet Socialist Republics; Bulgaria, Czechoslovakia and Hungary; Bibliography*, ORAE Extra-Mural Paper No. 39, March 1986, 'USSR,' by Teresa Rakowska-Harmstone.

10. The initially controversial thesis of operational integration of East European military establishments into the SAF was first advanced by C D Jones (*Soviet Influence in Eastern Europe: Political Autonomy and the Warsaw Pact*. Praeger, 1981), and T Rakowska-Harmstone and C D Jones et al. (*WP.II, Vol. I op.cit.*) It has been developed also by other analysts such as J Simon, *Warsaw Pact Forces; Problems of Command and Control*, Westview, 1984 J Yurechko 'Command and Control for Coalitional Warfare: the Soviet Approach'. *Signal*, December 1985, and Michael Sadykiewicz *The Warsaw Pact Command Structure in Peace and War*, R-3558-RC and *Organizing for Coalition Warfare: The Role of East European Warsaw Pact Forces in Soviet Military Planning*, R-3559-RC, (Santa Monica, CA.: RAND Corporation, 1988) and confirmed by a Polish staff officer who defected in 1981, Col. R J Kuklinski, *Kultura* No. 4,/475 (Paris: 1987.) English translation in *Orbis*, vol. 32, no. 1, (winter 1988).

11. The third important group of Transcaucasus, the Azerbaidzhani (Azeri Turks), are Muslim.

12. This is a much abbreviated version of an argument presented in *WP II, Vol. 3 Union of Soviet Socialist Republics, Bulgaria, Czechoslovakia and Hungary*, ORAE Extra-Mural Paper No. 39, March 1986, pp. 85–91. The concepts of attitudinal and functional integration were developed to measure reliability in military service. The use of language statistics for the purpose of measuring integration is based on three assumptions: that Soviet norms and value system approximate to Russian norms and value system (an oversimplification that is nevertheless valid in the military setting); that the linguistic assimilation approximates to ethnic assimilation (the assumption is customarily made by Soviet ethnographers); and

Teresa Rakowska-Harmstone

that bilingualism indicates a willingness to conform and to function within the prevalent norms and value system.

13. Based on Murray Feshbach, 'The Soviet Union: Population Trends and Dilemmas, *Population Bulletin* 37 (August 1982).
14. A Vishnevski, 'Led tronulsia?' (Is the ice moving?), *Kommunist*, No. 6, 1988.
15. John Saunders, 'Population Change in Europe', paper for the Conference on Demographic Change and Western Society, London, 21–22 July, 1988. Table I.
16. Ann Sheehy, 'Russian Share of Soviet Population Down to 50.8 Per cent,' *Report on the USSR*, Vol. 1, No. 42, 1989, 20 October, 1989.
17. Ann Sheehy, 'Ethnic Muslims Account for Half of Soviet Population Increase,' *Ibid.* Vol. 2, No. 3, 19 January, 1990.
18. Ann Sheeny, '1989 Census Data on Internal Migration in the USSR,' *Ibid.* Vol. 1, No. 45, 10 November, 1989.
19. Jeri Laber, (Executive Director of the Helsinki Watch), 'Refugees in the Soviet Union,' *The New York Times*, 24 June 1990.
20. Ann Sheehy, 'Ethnic Muslims . . .' *op. cit.*
21. Mikhail Bernstam in R Conquest, ed. *The Last Empire Nationality and the Soviet Future.* (Stanford, Ca.: Hoover Institution Press, 1986).
22. 'The poisoned giant wakes up,' *The Economist*, (London), 4 November, 1989, pp 23–26.
23. Vladimir Andreev, the Soviet Union's deputy chief prosecutor, interviewed by *Izvestiia*, 7 August, 1990. Andreev interview repeated much of the information *ibid.*
24. *Narodnoe Khoziaistvo SSSR v 1988 g*, (Moscow: 1989), p. 31.
25. *The New York Times*, 14 August 1989, (Esther B. Fein)
26. *Sbornik Statisticheskikh Materialov*, (Moscow: 1988), pp. 216–225.
27. The review here for the early 1980s is based on an extensive analysis of the attitudes of each national group in *WP II, V. 3, op.cit.* pp. 91–141.
28. Hugh Seton-Watson, 'A Culture Castrated' *Times Literary Supplement*, 1 June, 1984.
29. See John B Dunlop, *The Faces of Contemporary Russian Nationalism*, (Princeton, Princeton University Press, 1984). Mikhail Agurski *Ideologiia natsional – bol'shevizma*, (Paris, YMCA-Press, 1980: Aleksander Yanov, *The Russian New Right: Right Wing Ideologies in the Contemporary USSR* (Berkeley: Institute of International Studies, 1978), Roman Szporluk, 'History and Russian Nationalism' *Survey* 24 (Summer 1979).
30. Bill Keller, 'Russian Nationalists; Yearning for an Iron Hand,', *The New York Times Magazine*, 28 January, 1990.
31. *The New York Times*, 28 July, 1990, (Francis X. Clines). The distinction, currently made by nationalist movements in the Soviet Union, bears noticing. 'Sovereignty' does not exclude a continued membership in the federation. 'Independence' means total separation and independent statehood.
32. Quoted by Jeri Laber in 'Refugees . .' *op. cit.*, Kiev, Ukraine's capital, and Gomel in Belorussia are located in the irradiated zone, but authorities keep the information quiet for fear of generating panic.
33. *The New York Times*, 26 March, 1990, (Bill Keller).
34. *Ibid.* 17 July, 1990, (Francis X Clines)
35. *The Ottawa Citizen*, 28 July, 1990.

36. *The New York Times*, passim.
37. The very core of Leninist nationality policy has been the control by the Centre of the substance of policy (via the top to bottom hierarchy of the CPSU), whatever forms of national statehood were allowed to the republics. Gorbachev's reforms have in fact destroyed the mechanisms on which the Party's leading role depended, but the other basic Leninist principle, that of 'democratic centralism' still presumably operates within the governmental structure. As late as the RSFSR declaration to go national, and despite the fact that Gorbachev's conception of the 'new union' has yet to be clearly articulated, it was obvious that he still envisaged the supremacy of the Centre and regarded claims to independence as unacceptable.
38. Unless otherwise specified the recent information in this section is based on *The New York Times*, passim.
39. See an interesting analysis of the case for the KGB orchestration of the nationalist upheaval by Bill Keller in *The New York Times*, 18 and 19 February, 1990.
40. Based in the information from *The New York Times*, passim.
41. The discussion primarily covers the main Turkic-Iranian union republic nations: Uzbeks, Turkmen, Kirgiz and Tadzhiks of Central Asia and Kazakhs of Kazakhstan. General points apply to Azeris, who are geographically located across the Caspian Sea from the Turkmen.
42. From *Sel'skaia Zhizn* as reported by *The New York Times*, 29 March, 1987 (Felicity Barringer), and a report of the Plenum of the Tadzhik Communist Party and Tadzhik Komsomol, *Pravda*, 26 September, 1989.
43. William Fierman, 'Uzbek Writers on Culture and Economic Issues', an unpublished paper, June 8, 1988.
44. *The New York Times*, 14, 20, 21 and 25 June 1989, (Esther Fein).
45. *Ibid*, passim (Craig Whitney and Esther Fein).
46. *Krasnaia Zvezda*, 9 April 1988.
47. In forcing East European armies to imitate the Soviet model in everything, the practice of hazing was transplanted there and caused a great deal of additional resentment.
48. Richard A. Gabriel, 'The Morale of the Soviet Army: Some Implications for Combat Effectiveness,' *Military Review*, October 1978. Other information in this section is based on *WP. II. V. 3*, pp. 228–243.
49. See Alexander Alexiev, *Inside the Soviet Army in Afghanistan*, R-3627-A (Santa Monica CA: RAND CORPORATION, May 1988).
50. *WP II. V. 3*, pp. 171–184.
51. Gen. D Yazov, 'Armiia druzhby i bratstva narodov,' *Krasnaia Zvezda*, 22 September, 1989.
52. Allen Hetmanek, Bruce Thompson and Richard Trout, *Ethnic Composition of the Soviet Officer Corps*, (U); Directorate for Intelligence Research, US Defense Intelligence Agency, September 1979.
53. 'Ofitser General'nogo Shtaba,' an interview with a deputy chief of the General Staff of the Soviet Armed Forces, Col. Gen. A Kleimenov, *Krasnaia Zvezda*, 29 October, 1989.
54. *WP II. V. 3*, pp. 141–156. For a more recent treatment of the subject covered in this and two preceding sections see this author's 'Nationalities and the Soviet Military,' pp. 72–94 in Lubomyr Hajda and Mark Beissinger, eds., *The*

Teresa Rakowska-Harmstone

Nationalities Factor in Soviet Politics and Society, The John M Olin Critical Issues Series, (Boulder, San Francisco & Oxford: Westview Press, 1990).

55. For a more extensive treatment of the subject see this author's 'The Soviet Armed Forces; The Challenge of Reform and the Ethnic Factor,' pp. 156–186 in Uri Ra'anan, ed. *The Soviet Empire and the Challenge of National and Democratic Movements*, (Boston, MA.: Heath Lexington, 1990).

56. *Kommunist Vooruzhennykh Sil*, No. 19, October 1989.

57. *Krasnaia Zvezda*, 12 March, 1990.

58. *Trud*, 28 October, 1989.

59. See Stephen Foye, 'Rumblings in the Soviet Armed Forces,' *Report on the USSR*, Vol. 2, No. 11, 16 March, 1990.

60. *The New York Times*, 31 May 1990, (Celestine Bohlen)

61. *Ibid.* passim. The Tadzhik legislature decided, after a heated debate, that they could not afford national military units.

62. *Ibid.* 13 April (Esther Fein) and 21 May, 1990.

63. *Ibid.* 19 July, 1990 (Bill Keller)

64. *Ibid.* 26 March (Bill Keller), 17 July (Francis X Clines), and 13 July 1990.

65. See the debate, for example, in *Kommunist Voooruzhennykh Sil*, Nos. 18 (September) and 19 (October), 1989.

66. *Polityka*, (Warsaw) No. 47, 25 November, 1989. An interview with Andrei Sakharov by J Malczyk and S Popowski.

67. Some softening on the subject of a volunteer army was noted in interviews with both General Yazov and General Moiseyev (SAF Chief of General Staff) in February 1990. See Robert Arnett & Mary FitzGerald 'Is the Soviet Military Leadership Yielding on an All-Volunteer Army?' *Report on the USSR*, Vol. 2 No. 13, March 30, 1990. Also, Mikhail Tsypkin, 'Will the Soviet Navy Become a Volunteer Force?', *Ibid.* 2 February 1990. In a surprising announcement in late August, President Gorbachev promised a military reorganisation for January 1991, hinting that it might include national militias and a volunteer regular army. *The New York Times*, 18 August 1990 (Bill Keller).

68. *The New York Times*, 13 June (Bill Keller) and 21 June (Francis X Clines)

69. Ibid. 6 July, 1990 (Bill Keller)

70. *Ibid.*

71. See Stephen Foye, 'Role of the Political Organs in the Armed Forces Questioned,' *Report on the USSR*, Vol 1, No. ? 11 August, 1989.

72. See Stephen Foye, 'Domestic Role of Soviet Armed Forces Debated,' *Ibid.* Vol. 2, No. 3, 19 January, 1990.

73. Col. O Belkov, in *Kommunist Vooruzhennykh Sil*. No. 19, October 1989, in JPRS-UMA-90–003, 24 January 1990. pp. 9–10.

74. *The New York Times*, 25 July, 1990 (Bill Keller). The very fact that Gorbachev was speaking in terms of the republics ceding powers to the Centre was in itself a concession, further evidence of his skill in step-by-step withdrawal in the face of the overwhelming odds.

75. *Ibid.* 2 August, 1990 (Celestine Bohlen).

76. For a detailed discussion of the WP original integrative mechanisms see *WP II*, *V. 1*, op.cit. For a discussion of the WP in the Gorbachev era, see Teresa Rakowska-Harmstone, *Warsaw Pact Political and Military Integration: A Political Analysis*, (Stanford, CA.: Hoover Institution, 1990).

77. Sergei Karaganov, 'WTO – Where to and How?,' *Moscow News*, No. 40, 8–15 October 1989, in JPRS-UMA-89–06, 9 November 1989. p. 21.
78. *The New York Times*, 18 March, 1990. (Celestine Bohlen)
79. *Ibid.* 17 July, 1990 (Serge Schmemann)
80. *Ibix.* 27 February and 11 March, 1990.
81. *Ibid.* 12 and 15 February, 1990.
82. *Ibid.* 17 and 31 July, 1990.
83. *Ibid.* 13 June, 1990.
84. Admiral Kolodziejczyk in an interview with 'Zolnierz Rzeczpospolitej,' quoted by *Echo* (Toronto, No. 139, July 19–25, 1990 p. 8.
85. *The New York Times*, 27 June and 18 July, 1990.
86. See The Military Balance, 1989–1990, *op.cit.* pp. 37–42.
87. *The New York Times*, 9 and 11 March, 1990.
88. *Ibid.* 23 July, 1990.
89. It is interesting to note that in the on-going debate in the Soviet military press, on the subject of using the armed forces for internal suppression, referred to earlier, an advocate of such a role specifically used the example of the imposition of martial law in Poland in December 1981 as an illustration of a correct exercise by an army of its internal defence function ('we feel that it is an invalid thesis of the anti-social forces that the introduction of martial law in Poland was an action against the people.') The Czechoslovak Army, on the other hand, was castigated for its failure to act against 'the counterrevolutionary coup' in 1968. Col. P Skorodenko in *Kommunist Vooruzhennykh Sil.* No. 19, October 1989, quoted in JPRS-UMA-90–003, 24 January 1990, pp. 12–13.
90. See Rakowska-Harmstone, Warsaw Pact: Political and Military Integration, *op.cit.*
91. See Douglas Clarke, 'Conscription, East and West,' *Report on the USSR.*, 10 November, 1989.
92. *The New York Times*, 19 March and 8 April, 1990, and Andrzej Milczanowski, 'The Health Crisis in Poland,' in *The Public Health Crisis in Communist Systems*, Institute for the Study of Conflict, Ideology and Policy Publication Series No. 4, (Boston: Boston University, June 1990.
93. *The New York Times*, 7 May and 24 June, 1990.

11

Demographic Change, Political Priorities and Western Security

Yves Boyer

Demographic change is altering the traditional patterns on which Western security has been established since the end of the Second World War.

Three sets of problems with an impact on security requirements for the West can be identified:

First, there will be a growing awareness of the existing discrepancies between zones of increasing economic prosperity with slow growing or even declining populations and zones of deepending under-development with strong demographic pressures. The present disequilibrium will be adversely affected by the structure of the age pyramid. In areas such as Africa, Asia and Latin America, the ratio between young people (under the age of 15) and older people (over 65 years old) is 9.5 to 1 whereas in areas such as Europe (excluding the Soviet Union), the ratio is 1.6 to 1[1].

A second set of factors with strong implications for the West's security derives from the internal evolution of demographic trends. It is concerned with immigration as well as with the more socio-cultural aspects of demographic behaviour such as the marriage role, and the share of children born out of marriage, etc. Such factors can modify attitudes towards defence.

A third problem arises from the growing shortage of manpower available for the military. Are there means to compensate this decrease? How can new weapons, particularly with the development of High-Tech systems, compensate for the lack of human resources? Will the West be saved from these questions in the end by the break-up of the Warsaw Pact?

Tensions Arising from Demographic Disparities

Historically, there seems to be a link between demographic growth and assertiveness in international affairs. In Germany, under Bismarck, the fertility rate was leading to a fivefold increase of the population in a century.

270

Demographic Change

Such an evolution was associated with vitality and expansionist policies which were translated into three wars in less than one hundred years.

In other words, demographic vitality has, among other results, the potential development of what, Gaston Bouthoul, a French sociologist described as aggressive impulses within a population where the percentage of young men is particularly high[2]

If one looks at the demographic evolution, the area covered by the NATO-Warsaw Pact is not a zone of turbulence. According to IISS estimates, between 1979 and 1999 both alliances will register a decrease in the number of their populations aged between 17 and 30 years old. NATO resources (including the United States) will fall from 130 million to 114 million, while, at the same time, the countries that have been members of the Warsaw Pact will lose around 9 million people, falling from 89.5 million to 85 million[3].

TABLE 11.1   Population in NATO and Warsaw Pact 1987 (in millions)

NATO			WARSAW PACT		
Norway	=	4.2	E. Germany	=	16.7
Denmark	=	5.1	Poland	=	37.8
W. Germany	=	61	Hungary	=	10.6
Netherlands	=	14.6	Czechoslovakia	=	15.6
Belgium	=	9.9	Romania	=	22.9
Luxembourg	=	0.4	Bulgaria	=	9
United Kingdom	=	56.8			
France	=	55.6			
Spain	=	39			
Portugal	=	10.3			
Italy	=	57.4			
Greece	=	10			
Turkey	=	51.4			
Iceland	=	0.25			
W. Europe/NATO	=	375.6	E. Europe/WP	=	112.6
USA	=	243.8	USSR	=	284
Canada	=	25.9			
TOTAL	=	645.3	TOTAL	=	396.6
USA	=	37.8 per cent of total	USSR	=	71 per cent of total

Generally speaking, the whole of Europe will suffer from the same decreasing fertility trends with the exception of areas of Muslim influence (such as the Muslim Republics of the Soviet Union: Azerbaidzhan, Kazakhstan, Uzbekistan, Turkmenistan, Tadzhikistan, and Kirgizia) or Catholic influence (such as Poland and Ireland).

271

Yves Boyer

The Effects of Urbanisation

In each NATO country about a quarter of the population live in the five most-populated cities against 1:15 in the Soviet Union[4].

The urban concentration of the Western population is a factor which could have a profound impact in time of international crisis or war. New York City itself, for example, has a population of around 20 million people (in 1980), almost equivalent to the population of the ten most important cities in the Soviet Union. This phenomenon is the same in Western Europe, with a particular concentration of population within the triangle Rotterdam-Paris-Stuttgart.

NATO guidelines rule out any evacuation of urban populations in time of crisis or war. However, large urban concentrations may be very difficult to supply and one must assume that security forces would be called upon to play a fundamental role in maintaining law and order. This task may come in addition to preventing sabotage, by terrorists or special forces, of, for example, electricity and water supplies, all of which are vital to the functioning of big cities.

North-South Mediterranean

Population growth south of the Mediterranean counterbalances that of the EEC. Egypt and Turkey alone have as many births per annum (1.8 million each) as the twelve countries of the EEC.

If we compare the three countries of North Africa (Morocco, Algeria, Tunisia) with Spain, France and Italy, the population ratio in 1950 was 1 to 3 in favour of the North (53 million against 150 million). By 2015, the ratio will be 3 to 4 (112 million in the South, 153 million in the North).

By that date, there will be 3.1 million births each year in the Maghreb countries against 1.6 million in the North, whereas, in 1985, the number of young people (under the age of 15) was 32 million in the three European countries bordering the Mediterranean against 24 million in the South. By 2015, this age group will be 70 per cent larger in the Maghreb (43 million) than in the North (25 million). Not only will the population rates of the Mediterranean show a significant drop in the youngest age groups but, at the same time, the area will become far 'older' (26 million people aged 65 or more) than the Maghreb (4 million).

This demographic vitality of the Maghreb may affect political stability in the Western Mediterranean and create a new dimension in the way West Europeans may envisage their security requirements.

These requirements will vary according to the management of economic and internal political tensions erupting in the Maghreb as a result of the demographic increase. Co-operation needs to be developed by the EEC in order to facilitate economic and industrial development in the Southern

Demographic Change

TABLE 11.2   USSR – Number of Inhabitants in the Ten Most Populated Cities

1950	10 cities with more than 500,000 inhabitants – Moscow and Leningrad each had over 1 million people
1960	The ten most-populated cities had more than 1 million people each, their total amounting to 12.6 million people
1984	The total population of the ten most-populated cities reached 24 million people.

TABLE 11.3   Percentages of Urban Population[5]

	1950	1985	2025
North America	63.9	74.1	77.3
Europe	56.3	71.6	79.5
USSR	39.3	65.6	74.1

TABLE 11.4   Population Growth in the EEC and North Africa (in millions)

Year	E.E.C.	N. Africa	Ratio
1960	279.9	51.8	5.4
1985	321.6	123	2.6
2000	323.8	175.6	1.8
2025	306.4	260.8	1.2

TABLE 11.5   Population Growth in France and the Maghreb (in millions)

	1960	1985	1990	2025
France	45	54	55	57
Maghreb	27	52	61	126

273

Mediterranean. The Lomé Conventions provide a good example of what can be done. This will require in the future a much more active diplomacy with countries such as Algeria which in the year 2020 will have roughly the same population (49 million) as some leading West European States.[6]

If, however, there is a failure of this policy, one can fear a growing influence and role of movements such as Muslim fundamentalism. Consequently, tensions may erupt and one should already think of measures to limit the spread of certain kinds of weapons in that area.

Agreements between Western countries such as the Missile Technology Control Régime of 1987, to avoid the spread of ballistic missiles with ranges above 300 kilometres and capable of delivering a nuclear warhead, prefigures the policies one should have with those countries in the future.

The Caribbean Basin, Central America, North America

Similar problems will arise on the southern borders of the United States. The population of the Caribbean Basin and Central America amounted to 60 per cent of the US population (137 million) in 1985. In 2010, the two populations will be equal. In the long run, however, the trends play in favour of the south. The net demographic increase (3.8 million) in the Caribbean Basin and Central America is already two and a half times greater than that in the United States. In 2015, it will be multiplied by seven.

TABLE 11.6 Population Growth in the United States and Mexico (in millions)

	1960	1987	2020	GNP 1987–$bn (World Bank)
USA	181	243.8	297	3998
Mexico	37	81.9	138	170

There can be no doubt that these demographic changes, coupled with the question of Hispanic immigration will polarise attention in Washington. This may lead to a redeployment of American forces or at least a reallocation of reserves for military contingencies in the Southern Command (SOUTH-COM) where 10,000 US military personnel are already stationed in 19 countries, the majority being based in Panama. There is no doubt that, in the long term, the security interests of the United States in that zone will compete with the current emphasis put by Washington on the European theatre.

Demographic Evolutions, Internal Changes and Security

The demographic crisis in the northern hemisphere is already having serious effects on security issues. A very important one relates to the function and role of national defence in societies which are increasingly affected by radical transformations. The collective memory of nations starts altering when a large number of people have left or will leave rural areas for big cities. Internal migration contributes to the erosion of the past as a cement of national identity. If collective memory tends to vanish, what reasons, values or motives could encourage people to pay or to give up part of their time for defence?

This trend is particularly apparent in Europen societies and tends to be aggravated by two factors. The first is the partial dislocation of the traditional system based on family values. Between 1972 and 1985, the number of marriages in France diminished by one third, from 417,000 to 273,000, while, at the same time, divorces multiplied by three (120,000 in 1985).

This leads to a growing atomisation of modern societies where the transmission of a common heritage is becoming increasingly difficult and affects national attitudes towards defence.

TABLE 11.7   Birth Structure of French Society[7]

Among 182 children born in 1985:
22 had a mother of foreign origin
36 had unmarried parents
44 will probably see their parents divorce
80 will be educated in a traditional way

This growing fragmentation and fragility of Western societies is also accentuated by the problems stemming from foreign immigration which tends to modify the population structure.

Within its former borders, the Federal Republic of Germany (FRG) counted 340,000 foreigners in 1939 (0.9 per cent of the population), in 1961 they had more than doubled to 686,000 (1 per cent). By 1985, they had reached 4 million (7 per cent). Not only has immigration considerably increased, but its structure has been modified.

In 1975, 60 per cent of Turkish immigrants arriving in the FRG were children. Ten years earlier they had represented only 5 per cent of the total[8]. This phenomenon is not specific to the FRG: in 1980, there were 6.3 million active foreigners working in the EEC, mostly from the Southern Mediterranean. A lot of them wish to remain in the country in which they

275

work and ask for citizenship. The case is much the same in France where, on average, there are 120,000 new French citizens of foreign origin every year. This immigration from the Southern Mediterranean is not without problems. First, because it is difficult really to control the migration flux (each year 25 million people arrive in or leave France), in spite of the prospect of the harmonisation of immigration policies among EEC countries under the aegis of informal meetings of Interior and Justice Ministers (Groupe Trevi). Second, because, rightly or wrongly, this is creating a feeling of uneasiness among certain segments of the European population which already has political implications. In France, this explained the rise of the National Front of Jean-Marie Le Pen who gained more votes than the French Communist Party during the May 1988 Presidential elections[9].

In addition to those attitudes and reactions, internal modifications of the demography in the West affects security issues in different ways:

The ageing of the population and the relative desertification of vast zones will increase costs for the maintenance of collective equipments (railways, roads) or those related to health and retirement benefits. In France, even as long ago as 1984, for each 100 FF spent on family or maternity care, 300 FF was being spent on the aged[10]. These costs will undoubtedly increase. The burden they will impose on national budgets will have to compete with the defence expenditure at a time when the pressure on that expenditure must remain significant because of the increasing sophistication of equipment and the higher cost of personnel, due to a significant rise in qualifications. For example, the United States Navy needs more and more nuclear submarine specialists while in Norway and Denmark, there are fewer pilots available than planes!

Clandestine immigration is unlikely to be checked and will increase the risks of seeing vast depressed areas developing in the periphery of big cities, encouraging violence and marginalisation, as witnessed since the early 1980s (riots in Brixton in the United Kingdom and in Les Minguettes near Lyons in France for example). Control of such depressed areas will request huge investments in security forces and necessitate changes in the ethnic recruitment of police forces. Particular care will have to be taken to avoid the creation of 'ghettos', becoming 'fish-ponds' in which hostile countries or terrorist groups can recruit agents.

The phenomenon of immigration or of populations of different ethnic origins living together is not specific to Western Europe. The Soviet Union is also confronted with the demographic increase of its citizens of Muslim origin. In the year 2000, the number of people living in the Muslim republics will double from 30 million to 60 million. This development is particularly striking since, with the exception of the RSFSR, only four republics have a population which includes more than 25 per cent of Russians. In the other republics, the average is 7 per cent whilst in Armenia, the proportion is the weakest, with a percentage of only 2.3 per cent.

Demographic Decline and Prospects for the Armed Forces

With the exception of Turkey, which registers roughly the same number of births as the FRG, Italy, Holland and Belgium put together, NATO as a whole will suffer a sharp decrease in the number of young men available for the military forces.

Collectively, the 16 nations of NATO will register a 12.4 per cent decrease in the number of draft-age males (18–22 years old) by the year 2000.

What are the possible remedies to correct the effects of declining human resources available for defence? One is to find new methods of recruitment and new structures for the Armed Forces. These are discussed by Simon Lunn in Chapter 9.

Another means of offsetting the decline in Western demographic resources is through the intensive use of new technologies. This offers many opportunities but also many challenges. Technology is undoubtedly a 'Force Multiplier': military objectives may be reached with greater efficiency with fewer men and less material. Consequently, longer-range acquisition of targets and intelligence, communication between sensors, commanders and weapons, data fusion capabilities to consolidate intelligence, sophisticated platforms with stand-off smart weapons and ammunition will represent an increasing component of Western armed forces and will enhance their capabilities.

However, if one looks at NATO forces, one sees that the combat slice is but a small part of overall manpower resources, which are dominated by support forces. There is no evidence that new technologies could significantly alter this ratio. Indexes show the contrary: already in the United States Air Force 28 per cent of the enlisted personnel are used for maintenance duties. To identify the technologies which will be both usable and affordable is a great challenge. It is perhaps fortunate that it has to be met in political circumstances far more favourable to the West than could have been hoped for four years ago.

Notes

1. *Populations et Sociétés* – Edited by the Institut National d'Études Démographiques – Septembre 1987, n° 216
2. Gaston Bouthoul, *Avoir la Paix* – (Editions Grasset), 253 p.; Gaston Bouthoul, René Carrère, *Le défi de la guerre* 1740–1974 – (PUF 1976)
3. Jean-Claude Chesnais, Les déséquilibres démographiques et leurs implications en matière de défense – *Stratégique*, 3ème trimestre 1984, FEDN

Yves Boyer

4. *The Military Balance* 1983–1984 – The International Institute for Strategic Studies.
5. From: World Population Projections As Assessed in 1984 – *Population Studies* no 98, New York, 1986
6. *Population et Sociétés*, op.cit.
7. From Defense no 42 – AAIHEDN October 1986, *Le facteur démographique*, Général Bertaux
8. Michèle Tribalat, *Revue population*, May-June 1986
9. This uneasiness is largely taken into account by intellectuals worried by the clash of different cultures. See for example: Jean Raspail, *Le Camp des Saints*; Alfred Sauvy, *L'Europe Submergée*
10. Philippe Bourcier de Carbon, Les déséquilibres démographiques, *Défense* no 45 – AAIHEDN, October 1987.

12

Population and Geopolitics

Pierre Lacoste

The study of matters connected with peace and war, conflict, strategy, international policy, international crises, military affairs and so on inevitably involves consideration of the demographic factor. There is ample evidence in history to show that broad changes occurred in the world situation under the pressure of demographic expansion: for example, barbarians assailed the Roman Empire for centuries and their invasions from the North East were one of the main reasons for the fall of Rome. Several other historical features are related to demography: in Europe, up to the beginning of the 19th century, French power was derived from a large population – the Napoleonic wars could never have occurred had the French not been so numerous. The British, Dutch and other colonial expansions had evident demographic origins. The rise and prosperity of the United States were mainly due to the great migratory movements across the Atlantic from very poor and over-populated European countries such as Ireland, Poland and Sweden.

For years, military power has been directly related to numbers of men under arms; up to and including the First World War, military strength relied mainly upon the individual combatant carrying his own weapons: sword, shield, pike, spear and so on. It is even partly true today: the Red Army in the 'Great Patriotic War' relied upon mass. The concern during the Cold War over Soviet military superiority derived from their superiority in the number of active and reserve divisions in their order of battle.

However, demographic superiority is not always decisive: with a population of 4.5 million people, Israel has fought successfully for 40 years against a far greater number of Arabs – enemies who surround her on every side, possess powerful modern weapons and enjoy the necessary wealth from petrodollars to enable them to wage modern warfare.

Looking ahead into the future, the demographic factor is also an evident matter of concern for all those who observe the very rapid growth of populations in some parts of the world when, simultaneously, other countries are engaged in an actual decline. For example, high and low pressures are

279

developing very rapidly between the southern and northern shores of the Mediterranean; threatening clouds are appearing on the horizon: economic and social disasters, disturbing phenomena such as fanaticism, terrorism, outbreaks of violence, possible slaughters, civil wars, local or regional conflicts are about to burst out as a consequence of unbalanced demographic situations.

We know that many other social and human factors have to be taken into account, in order to explain, control or prevent conflicts. Demography itself is just one branch of the social sciences, the study of populations. Specifically it concerns the knowledge of total population numbers, breakdown by age groups, birth and death rates, reproduction trends, migrations and expansions. Other branches of these sciences include sociology, studies of cultures, civilisations, religions, political science, education, ethnic groups, languages, law and history. Moreover, over and above the social factors, individual psychology has an important part to play in the study of conflicts; we know, for example, to what extent the leadership of bright individuals was decisive in many historical circumstances. Or, on the contrary, how the personal weaknesses of other statesmen brought their countries to disaster.

Lastly, geopolitical and geostrategic situations depend also upon many other factors: such as economic buoyancy, military power, technological advance, geography, and transportation. It is not necessary to enumerate all the other related aspects to demonstrate how complex those matters are.

These introductory sentences stress the necessity of a methodology to keep a sense of relativity and to determine what is exactly the role of the demographic factors among others. Several approaches are available. Mine is just one of them. I believe it can help to clarify the debate.

*   *   *

My methodology is founded upon three complementary approaches.

The first aspect is 'polemology', that is to say the historical, sociological and theoretical analysis of past conflicts.
The second is strategy, namely the rational conjunction of action and decision-making processes in a conflict situation.
The third is prospective, which is a method of looking ahead into the future, taking into account the time frames of long periods and delineating the relations between the past, the present and the future.

Polemology

The word 'polemology' was created by Gaston Bouthoul, with the intention of studying wars and major conflict situations as social objects; he analysed them from both the historical and sociological points of view, with the help of other social sciences and disciplines. The result of several years of research offers an interesting overview of hundreds of past and present conflicts, with the description of their main features, their effects and origins, through a specific typology (see references in Note 2 to Chapter 11).

Several analytical methods help to determine the main factors of conflict study; risks, vulnerabilities, tensions and other important aspects of organised political violence. A current work was devoted to the study of conflicts involving minorities in different areas of the world; other studies are focused on the problem of refugees. Terrorism is another matter of concern.

All types of armed conflict, from insurrection to general war, have evident and inevitable demographic consequences. Heavy losses on the battlefield take their toll of one specific group – the young men of military age, thereby altering the normal pattern of the population. There are many historical examples. In the recent past, just as the First World War had a particularly terrible effect upon French and British youth, so did the Second World War devastate the populations of Germany, Russia and Japan. Over the last decades, we have seen new trends emerging. More and more do the victims of conflict appear to be civilians. Aerial bombardment has killed thousands upon thousands of men and women, not only young adults but vast numbers of children also. Indeed, urban populations appear to have become more vulnerable than the fighting men. Massacres, death camps and mass deportations of whole populations have had terrible demographic consequences.

When polemology deals with the effects of war, the results of the studies are clear. But this is not always so when it tries to discern the origins and causes of conflict. In the demographic field, for many years one of the main contentions has been that wars were often due to an excess of population; that the thrust of outnumbered countries, as well as the unbalanced situation between overcrowded and underpopulated areas, was one of the main reasons for military conflicts. It is true to say that Hitler's claim for 'vital space' (*Lebensraum*) was one of the most popular keywords of Nazi propaganda, but historians know very well that there were many other reasons for Hitler's aggression. Polemologists have a more subtle approach today to the demographic causes of conflicts; although they are conscious of the interactions of that specific factor, amongst others. They observe that each particular situation deserves to be studied in itself, and that on a few occasions only, was demography a decisive cause at the very roots of a conflict. Besides, their studies allow other related aspects of demography (like refugees, immigrants or minorities) to take their place in the spectrum of regional, cultural and historical investigations.

Here lie the benefits of the methodological approach from the polemological point of view.

To undertake a strategic approach, it is useful to recall that strategy is subordinated to political choice: the goals and aims that the strategist is expected to reach have to be defined by a political project.

According to one of its most useful definitions, strategy is the art of combining all the elements (assets as well as vulnerabilities), in order to achieve political goals through specific related objectives. That is to say that strategy is mainly devoted to the choice of the best possible ways and means, according to the best possible knowledge and intelligence of all elements of the situation.

In that prospect, the demographic factor appears to be for the strategist one element among others. Sometimes it can be a decisive one: during the Second World War, the very large Soviet population combined with the depth of the Russian territory was certainly one major reason for Hitler's defeat on the Eastern front. More recently Iran's strategy in its war with Iraq was based on the numerical superiority of the Iranian population, but the failures of their early offensives proved this strategy to be a wrong one. Today, due to the performance of modern weapons, the demographic advantage is no longer a key to military success. On the contrary, one of the most striking and characteristic evolutions of modern demography, that is the gathering of population in huge urban centres, has developed new forms of vulnerability. The deterrent effect of nuclear strategic forces is based on the absolute impossibility for any military system to protect large cities effectively against the attacks of modern weapons of mass-destruction; 'mutually-assured vulnerability' remains the best of all arguments for a prudent behaviour of the superpowers in the conduct and control of political crises.

It is not possible to draw general conclusions about the influence of the demographic factor in strategic situations. Every problem is a single one, every conflict has its own characteristics. However, the rules and methods of strategic evaluation do offer an excellent way to discriminate its relative effects. Some strategic factors, like geographical, economic and military elements of power can be evaluated objectively. Demography too is an objective one, with quantitative observable factors.

Other factors are more subjective: ideologies, religions, cultures, propaganda, the individual psychology of charismatic leaders and fanaticism, deserve a more subtle analysis. The combination of such factors with demographic situations could either provoke war-mongering effects or peaceful ones. The convergence of destabilising elements could germinate the seeds of war; for example, the dynamic aspects of a large population added to other disturbing factors would multiply the possibilities of conflict. But on the contrary, adverse elements sometimes contribute happily to create restraining effects, limiting aggression and compelling leaders to follow a more prudent course. The fear of the terrible demographic consequences of the use of atomic weapons is certainly one of those stabilising factors.

The Prospective Approach

The third methodological approach is prospective.

Geopolitical or geostrategic surveys are more or less designed to scan the world's future. To prevent wars, and hence achieve one of their most

Population and Geopolitics

commendable goals, statesmen need a clear overview of the future. The prospective methodology is able to help them in the preparation of policies as well as in the conduct of strategies.

A first step of the methodology tries to discriminate, amongst all possible components of future situations, which of them will remain unchanged in any circumstances: those immovable elements, such as geographical features, or main infrastructures, belong to the world of today as well as of tomorrow.

A second step should be to study the lessons of the past and to scrutinise the trends of the present, in order to find out which amongst them are likely to become long-run tendencies. Such topics as the characteristics of civilisations, languages, religions and cultural habits, allow us to catch a glimpse of what might be the prevailing situation tomorrow. Demography is another example in the same category: one perfectly knows the figures of today's babies, and that they certainly will become young adults within 20 years; the extrapolation of demographic trends (with the necessary caution of upper and lower hypotheses), also provides us with a good knowledge of future world populations, even if no one really knows whether or not the reproduction rates will remain the same.

Finally, we must recognise that many other events are unpredictable. This is why futurology will remain a very controversial discipline, but this reality constitutes no grounds for us to refrain from thinking about it.

It does indeed seem quite difficult to build up plans about war and peace, world crises or periods of relative stability. We know, however, that with the help of history, social sciences and polemology, we can establish which are the main stabilising and destabilising factors. Prospective methods, with the integration of past-present-future surveys are introducing new tools for systemic and inter-related approaches. For example, in the field of demographic science, such studies show that several specific regions seem to be more dangerous than others; high and low demographic areas, migratory movements, cyclical uproars, catastrophic evolutions are more or less predictable. Today, three main lines of demographic instability are visible in the Caribbean, in the Mediterranean and in the Indonesian regions. Risks and vulnerabilities deserve close attention, in conjunction with other ideological, political, economic and social factors in those areas. The prospective attitude is certainly useful to control the evolution of such dangerous situations.

⋆　　⋆　　⋆

To conclude, I am conscious I was not able really to answer the difficult question of the importance of demography among other geopolitical and geostrategic factors. As I said in the beginning, demography is but one of the social sciences, one of the many aspects of human society. Complexity is the main word; like modern natural scientists, who today are fully aware of the necessity to be prudent and humble when dealing with the deep knowledge of

283

Pierre Lacoste

nature – for the more we learn, the more we know we are ignorant – strategists and political scientists must adopt a prudent attitude. But when acting with the new tools of modern methods, they are able to design more subtle approaches and to help the decision makers in the conduct of international affairs.

Conclusion

Lawrence Freedman

The first drafts of these chapters were presented before the major changes in the international situation which gathered pace in 1989 and has now taken us through the collapse of communism in Europe, the unification of Germany and a war in the Gulf.

Where possible the papers have been updated to take account of these changes and in a number of cases were substantially rewritten. However many of the issues that have been addressed in these pages are long-term in character and are only marginally affected by the twists and turns of international affairs, even when these are momentous in nature.

One of the underlying themes of the collection is the difficulty of formulating the relationship between population change and security questions. There clearly is some relationship and at some points it is profound but because the demographic factor is only one factor among many in the security calculations of states, one cannot readily generalise about its influence. As John Saunders notes in his Introduction, population trends do not by themselves cause conflict that brings about events that affect national security.

In methodological terms it is interesting to note the differences between the perspectives of the two scholarly communities. The demographer, more than any other social scientist, is able to offer confident projections based on the composition of the existing population and well established trends with regard to its fertility and life-expectancy. Much of the fascination of the subject stems from the extent to which changes in social conditions and expectations influence these trends, which then feed back on to the state of society.

The demographers are able to warn of emerging problems – of a differential fertility rate between two communities living in close proximity which could become explosive if the faster growing community starts to be seen as a threat to the well-being of its neighbours, or of imminent shortages in the workforce posing a choice between greater immigration, possibly accompanied by social tensions, and the acceptance of lower growth and the economically active accepting the burden of an expanding number of dependants. When military strength was measured in terms of a mobilisable population, then a declining birthrate suggested military decline and vulnerability to more fertile enemies.

Whether these projections turned into reality would depend on the impact of other variables, such as crop failures and epidemics, or the numerous individual adjustments to changing circumstances, such as more people (in particular women) becoming or remaining economically active or new technologies and working practices altering the demands for labour. As the Lees note in their chapter, 'Neither the young nor the old are physically or mentally the same as they were in Bismarck's day'. Attracting and maintaining manpower for the armed services still remains a headache for military planners in the West, as Simon Lunn demonstrates. But raw numbers now count for far less than before, although the corollary of this is that equipment is more sophisticated and this raises the level of technical competence required in the services. Yet with all these qualifications, the size and composition of a state's population is still relevant to its internal cohesion and international standing and a failure to pay attention to developing trends can cause a government problems in its labour market, provision of services and political management.

Few governments have a good record in anticipating problems unlikely to emerge until after the next election (or coup). Democratic politics allows short-term preoccupations to drive out the long-term. This can also be a feature of strategic studies. While the demographer can draw attention to emerging problems for well into the next century the strategist tends to have a much more immediate perspective. It is only as the differential birth rates or the waves of immigration or the population declines are actually causing difficulties that proper note is taken of developments for which a degree of early warning was available.

So demography helps to shape the strategist's world even though the strategist may pay insufficient attention to population trends until they actually generate crises. Equally strategy also helps to shape the demographer's world.

The impact of strategic developments on demographic trends has been particularly marked over the past two years. Major events that impinge directly on the lives of tens of millions of ordinary people can induce radical shifts in patterns of behaviour. Fears of economic collapse or violence or simply the removal of a barrier to the promise of a better life lead people to move homes. A breakdown in political and economic order can lead to people succumbing to disease or different rates of fertility.

It was not surprising to discover that one of the most marked indicators of the turmoil through which East Germany has been passing since its unification with the West in October 1990 has been a precipitate drop in the birthrate. It is a natural response to a period of great economic and social uncertainty. It provides a warning of how even the demographer's projections can be overturned by an unexpected political upheaval. The various projections by Ward Kingkade indicate how the differential make-up of the Soviet Union depends on various assumptions concerning fertility rates, which will in turn depend on the economic and political conditions of the country – including the extent to which it survives as a unified state. At some point an awareness of trends – such as the greater fertility of the Asian as opposed to the European parts of the Soviet Union – can begin to have an important influence on political behaviour. Kingkade concludes that the continuing attempt to subordinate local interests to the priorities of the national economy now must contend with the 'non-European native élites' in the Soviet Union 'sensing the potential impact inherent in their increasing numbers'.

The general crisis in the old socialist system, discussed in Mikhail Bernstam's chapter, which suffered because it paid 'to maximise costs and waste over the production cycle', thereby generating labour shortages, undermined its capacity and then its will to compete politically with the capitalist world.

As he hints and Teresa Rakowska-Harmstone comprehensively demonstrates, the consequence of the collapse of socialism has been to throw into relief simmering ethnic and national conflicts which are being fully reflected in the armies of Eastern Europe as well as the Soviet Union.

For most of the time most of the people are marginal to everyday political life within and between countries. But at times of great change they push themselves to the fore and play their role in history-making. In the most extreme form this appears as insurrection, but it can appear as mass migrations or inter-communal violence.

It is symptomatic of the political upheavals of recent years that demographic questions have been raised with great frequency. The collapse of the hard-line communist states was the result of the people of East Germany suddenly finding themselves with an opportunity to get to West Germany, a country to which they were entitled to automatic citizenship. With the haemorrhage of its population, the communist régime panicked and ended up by legalising the outflow in the hope that the immediate urge to leave would be reduced once it was known that the option would be there in the future. But the urge was too strong. Not even the promise of a reformed non-communist East German state was sufficient to stem the flow. In the end the only solution was rapid unification, even though the result was the precipitate collapse of the East German economic and social structure before West Germany was able to construct anything to put in its place.

Now the post-communist disorder in the East is leading politicians in Germany and other Central European states to be fearful of a wave of immigration as desperate people seek to escape the deprivations of their mismanaged societies and seek access to the wealth of the West. For years the

West demanded of the Communist Bloc that it permit the free movement of people; now that free movement is underway, the West is having second thoughts.

It could be said that some of the most troublesome conflict areas come at those points where relatively poor societies with rapidly expanding populations meet the relatively rich with their static or declining populations. For the latter this creates fears, easily fanned by populist politicians, of a comfortable way of life being overwhelmed by mass immigration. For some years this has been an issue in Southern Europe as a result of immigration from North Africa. This concern is reflected in the chapters by our two French contributors, Yves Boyer and Admiral Pierre Lacoste. It is now an issue in Northern and Central Europe as a result of pressure from the former communist bloc. One of the factors keeping Turkey out of the European Community is the anxiety among the existing members that Turkey's high birthrate would lead it to export its surplus population throughout the Community.

Immigration is one of those issues with which politicians tend to cope badly. The economic consequences can be extremely valuable, especially if it fills shortages in the labour market and introduces people with drive and enterprise. However the social consequences, especially when the cultural differences are marked, can be traumatic and the immediate strain on social services can breed resentments. The inclination therefore is to keep immigration down to a minimum. One consequence of this is to add to the pressures faced in the originating societies of the aspiring immigrants, for emigration can act as a safety valve and even a source of income as remittances are sent home by migrant workers. From this perspective the attitude of the West is selfish and uncaring.

The lurid imagery of conflict between the rich North and the poor South, bursting with excess population, is overstated if only because the South is not a coherent political grouping and is incapable of organizing itself as such. The prospect therefore is not of a global 'class struggle' – perhaps taking over from the Cold War – but of a series of localised and painful encounters. The decline in the number of people within prime military age in Western Europe as against those in countries of the former Warsaw Pact forecast by John Long may not seem to matter so much now that the Pact has disbanded, but it could become relevant again if the division between non-communist and communist Europe turns into one between the rich and poor.

In these encounters, does the advantage lie with the populous South or the technically-advanced West? Where Western countries have been most embarrassed is in guerrilla conflicts where it is not so much sheer numbers but insensitivity to local conditions that has worked against them. This was especially true during the anti-colonial wars of the 1950s and 1960s. The evidence of more regular conflict is that numbers alone do not make the difference. In 1991, the Gulf War provided a particularly striking example of this. Saddam Hussein boasted that he would win because his forces could take thousands of casualties on one day (as they had done during the war with Iran) while this would be intolerable in the United States.

It was not that long ago that Western countries did take such casualties. The searing memories of mass slaughter during the First World War and the Nazi holocaust in the Second provide one explanation of widespread distaste for the institution of warfare which is seen to be in every sense regressive. Nonetheless, there is no reason to doubt that Western countries would accept a high level of casualties if the state itself was at risk in total war but they are more reluctant to accept casualties in the pursuit of more limited objectives overseas, especially when, as in Vietnam, the conflicts appear inconclusive and morally ambiguous.

At any rate, if Saddam's strategy was to turn the Gulf War into one in which the West suffered high casualties in a futile conflict, he miscalculated, for the West's technical superiority was used to devastating effect. The ratio at the end was of one Allied casualty for over 1000 Iraqi.

Whether in the new political conditions Western countries will ever again worry about mass armies is an interesting question. They may feel that the receding risk of total war and the possibility of intervening in limited conflicts with relatively small but professional and well-equipped forces obviates the need for such armies. This may be too premature a conclusion to draw from the Gulf experience, for a more intelligent opponent could have caused the Allies many more difficulties and they were fighting in conditions which flattered their sophistication, including the advantage of months of preparation and intelligence gathering. Nonetheless, as Brian Bond observes, there appears to be a secular trend reducing the significance of purely demographic factors in the conduct of war. If it is concluded that mass armies are becoming obsolete in the West then that will have important conse-quences for such matters as conscription which may become unnecessary, although in the past it has been seen to be of importance in forging a sense of shared citizenship.

Mass armies came to the fore during the Napoleonic age and grew in significance as modern means of transport made it possible to send reserves of young men to the front. If they are now of declining significance in the Western world then that is because these societies have developed to a point where they can compensate for numerical inferiority. On the statistical evidence of this book that may be just as well.

Index

Index

293

Index

demographic trends   228–30
demography and economic
   break-down   178–85
ecology and environment   219, 222,
   228–31, 236–7, 261–2
Chernobyl   236–7
economy   167–92
energy resources, use of   165–74
ethnic diversity/conflict   2, 56, 68–9,
   164, 187, 218–21, 224–7, 229,
   234–49
labour, transfer of   181
labour force participation
   rates   69–72, 179, 181, 185–6
life expectancy   84–5, 222, 231
maternity incentives   62–3
migration   4, 66
   forced   154
mortality rates   58–60, 66, 84–5,
   222, 228, 231–2
nationality groups (smaller than
   Union republics)   86, 224–5,
   229, 236–8, 243, 246
   of 1 million or more   225
population
   age composition   70–1
   growth rates   2, 22–3, 37, 56–127,
      197, 219, 224–5, 227–8, 230,
      240, 252, 271
   Central Asian   57, 60–1, 64, 228
   European   56–8, 60–2, 70, 197,
      224–5, 228, 240, 252
   Muslim peoples   17, 57–8, 60–1,
      64, 224–5, 228, 240–9, 276
   (see also Republics, Union for
      individual Muslim republics)
   non-European   57, 69, 224–5, 228,
      230
   non-Russian   227
   Slav   228, 230
public health   59, 222–3, 230–3, 236
refugee problem   229
Republics, Soviet

see under Republics, Union and
   Republics, Autonomous
Russian as principal language   68,
   73, 225–7, 247–8
and First and Second World
   Wars   199–200, 202, 221

Walesa, Lech   257
Wars
   Afghanistan   17, 174, 185, 224,
      241–2, 245–6, 249–50
   Arab-Israeli   13
   Boer   199
   Falklands   13, 164
   Franco-Prussian   30, 196
   Gulf   288–9
   Iran-Iraq   14, 17, 164, 282
   Napoleonic   152
   Seven Years War   193–4
   First World War   16, 30, 198–203
   Second World War   151, 200–3, 221
Warsaw Pact   22, 129, 147, 213,
   218–69
   armies of   218–22, 224, 226, 240–1,
      244–69
   changes in   256–69
   demographic indicators   263
   demographic trends   219, 228–30
   environmental destruction   261–2
   ethnic conflict/problems   2, 56, 68–9,
      164, 187, 218–21, 224–7, 229,
      234–49
   military manpower resources   11,
      145–6, 205–6, 219, 271
   military personnel policies   216–17
   population growth rates   144–5, 271
Weinberger, C.   212
World population growth rates   37, 157
   and income redistribution   3–4

Yeltsin, Boris   235–6, 251, 255
Yugoslavia, population growth
   rates   22–3
   and Second World War   202

295